Sustai
Transitions to Sustainability in the Surfing World

Edited by
Gregory Borne
Jess Ponting

Paperback edition published in the United Kingdom in 2020 pssrg.com United Kingdom.

ISBN 978-1-52726-094-8

© 2020 pssrg.com

© 2020 Gregory Borne, Jess Ponting, Wayne 'Rabbit' Bartholomew, Doug Palladini, Fernando Aguerre, Bob McKnight, Jeff Wilson, Derek Sabori, Rob Machado, Jessica Toth, John Dahl, Cris Dahl, Todd Woody, Shaun Tomson, Scott Laderman, Tetsuhiko Endo, Cori Schumacher, Mark Marovich, Pierce Kavanaugh, Kevin Lovett, Chad Nelsen, Jim Moriarity, Nev Hyman, Easkey Britton, Peter Robinson, Andrew Coleman, Kevin Whilden, Michael Stewart, Emi Koch, Sean Brody, Andrew C. Abel, Danny O'Brien, Serge Dedina, Eduardo Najera, Zach Plopper, Cesar Garcia, Malcolm Findlay, Michelle Blauw, Tony Butt, Emma Whittlesea, Sam Bleakley, Ben Freeston, Glenn Hening, Chris Hines, Hugo Tagholm, Brad Farmer and Fred Hemmings. The rights of the authors of this work have been asserted by them in accordance with the Copyright, Designs and Patents Act 1988.

A CIP catalogue record of this book is available from the British Library

Cover photograph: Grant Davis

All rights reserved. No part of this publication may be reproduced, stored in a retrieval system or transmitted in any form or by any means electronic, mechanical, photocopying, recording, or otherwise, without the prior written permission of pssrg.com. Any person who carries out any unauthorised act in relation to this publication may be liable to criminal prosecution and civil claims for damages.

Printed and bound by Amazon

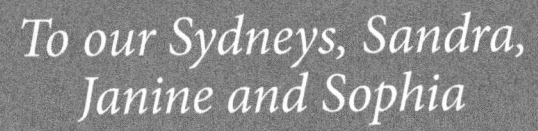

To our Sydneys, Sandra, Janine and Sophia

Contents

Chapter One: Sustainable Stoke – Introduction   1 – 1
Gregory Borne & Jess Ponting
The Making and Breaking of a Surfer's Paradise   1.1 – 8
Wayne 'Rabbit' Bartholomew
Surfing and Sustainable Development   1.2 – 18
Gregory Borne

Chapter Two: Umbrella   2- 30
Smart Business: Linking Environmental Health to
  Corporate Wellbeing   2.1 -32
Doug Palladini
Surfing, Sustainability, and the Pursuit of Happiness   2.2 – 36
Fernando Aguerre

Chapter Three: Industry   3 -48
Quiksilver and Sustainability: The View from the Top   3.1- 50
Bob McKnight
'If Not Us, Then Who?'   3.2 – 54
Jeff Wilson
Transitions to Sustainability   3.3 – 60
Derek Sabori
Sustainability in the Surf Industry   3.4 -64
Rob Machado & Jessica Toth
It's Time to Bring the Image of the Surfer into the 21st Century   3.5 -74
Todd Woody

Chapter Four: Critique   4 – 78
Pro Surfing and the Art of Inspiration   4.1 -80
Shaun Tomson
Beyond Green: Sustainability, Freedom and   4.2 -84
  Labour of the Surf Industry
Scott Ladderman

Crimes Committed in the Spirit of Play	4.3 – 88
Tetsuhiko Endo	
Shifting Surfing Towards Environmental Justice	4.4 -94
Cori Schumacher	
Shared Stoke: 'Only a Surfer Knows the Feeling'	4.5 -98
Mark Marovich	
Exploring Sustainability in the Surf Industry through Film: *Manufacturing Stoke*	4.6 – 100
Pierce Kavanaugh	
Chapter Five: NGO Response	5-108
Surfonomics: Using Economic Valuation to Protect Surfing	5.1-110
Chad Nelson	
Protecting the Waves We Love So Much	5.2- 116
Jim Moriarty	
Sustainable Transitions: From Firewire to NevHouse	5.3 -118
Nev Hyman	
Just Add Surf: The Power of Surfing as a Medium to Challenge and Transform Gender Inequalities	5.4-124
Easkey Britton	
Museum of British Surfing, The Long View: Charting Britain's Surfing History	5.5 -134
Peter Robinson & Andrew Coleman	
Transforming Surf Culture Towards Sustainability: *A Deep Blue Life*	5.6 -136
Kevin Whilden & Michael Stewart	
Chapter Six: Case Studies	6- 148
Grommets of the New Age	6.1 -150
Emi Koch	
Sustainable Stoke: Liberia	6.2 -154
Sean Brody	
Negotiating Communities: Sustainable Cultural Surf Tourism	6.3- 162
Andy Able & Danny O'Brien	
Surfing and Coastal Ecosystem Conservation in Baja California, Mexico	6.4 -174
Serge Dedina et al.	
Embedding Surf Stoke in Academia	6.5 -180
Malcolm Findlay	

Chapter Seven: New Knowledge and Solutions	7 -196
The Audacity of Stoke: Surfing the Ivory Tower	7.1 -198
Jess Ponting	
Surf Craft: Essential for the Future of the Surfing Industry?	7.2- 208
Michelle Blauw	
Surf Travel: The Elephant in the Room	7.3 -210
Tony Butt	
Greening Events: The Case of Boardmasters Surf and Music Festival, UK	7.4 -224
Emma Whittlesea	
Making Cultural Pearls out of Political Grit	7.5 -230
Sam Bleakley	
The World Wide Web	7.6 -234
Ben Freeston	
Chapter Eight: Call to Political Power	8 -238
Stoke in a Sea of Uncertainty	8.1 – 240
Kevin Lovett	
The Future of Surfing is Not Disposable	8.2 -252
Glenn Hening	
Surfing Can Change The World	8.3 -260
Chris Hines	
Waves, Environment, Community: Surfing, Sustainability & Surfers Against Sewage	8.4 – 272
Hugo Tagholm	
Managing the Surfing World in the 21st Century	8.5 – 276
Brad Farmer	
Surfing Sustainability	8.6 -288
Fred Hemmings	
Epilogue: The Next Set	294
Surf Wax Genealogy	295
John & Cris Dahl	
Ebb & Flow	298
Gregory Borne & Jess Ponting	

About the Editors	302
About the Authors	304
References & Notes	320
Bibliography	330

Stoke

...excited, pleased, happy, thrilled. "Stoke" is an English adaptation of the 17th-century Dutch word stok, *used to describe the rearrangement of logs in a fireplace in order to bring up the flames. California surfers began using the word in the early or mid-'50s, and it never went out of fashion.*

– *Encyclopedia of Surfing*

Sustainable Stoke
Introduction

Gregory Borne
Jess Ponting

Sustainable Stoke is intended to create a formal start to the conversation on sustainability and the surfing world. We came up with the idea when we were dripping wet, midway along the dusty fifth trail at San Onofre State Park the day after the 10th Annual Surfing Arts Science and Issues Conference, in February 2012. The conference, *Surfing's New Aloha: The Growing Trend of Giving Back*, had highlighted the sustainability efforts of a range of different stakeholders in surfing including Vice Presidents for Sustainability in publically listed surfing companies, academics, Surfrider's founder, non-profit start ups and surfing legends. Pro surfer and environmental activist Dave Rastovich even skyped in from a teepee in his backyard in Byron Bay. It seemed clear that the surfing world was at a tipping point and that sustainability was an inevitable, if distant, destination for the broader surfing world and its residents. What was missing was a central point of discussion, a forum, a discursive snapshot of what the best minds in surfing were thinking about sustainability – and the surfing world's transition to it. After two hours of overhead and uncrowded surfing amongst the stunning beauty of the San Onofre bluffs, punctuated by exploding ordinance from Camp Pendleton to the south and framed by the twin globes of the nuclear power station to the north (leaking), the contested nature of a 'Surfing Nirvana' in a globalized and rapidly developing world had never been more stark.

Sustainable Stoke showcases some of surfing's best minds and most powerful players. Our approach was not to give explicit direction to the contributors of the book, but rather to establish the broad context of sustainability in the surfing world as we understand it. We wrote the following statement:

Sustainability in the surfing world involves more than just the greening of surf industry supply chains and supporting environmental initiatives. Social and cultural issues like the preservation of surfing history, building an understanding of etiquette into surf school curricula, supporting youth development and education, the social-cultural impacts of surf tourism in destination communities, and the leveraging of surf contests to support local, social and cultural initiatives are equally as important. Additionally, economic issues such as the creation of sustainable livelihoods related to surfing, creating economic growth centres around surf breaks, the value of surf tourism, complimentary services and backward linkages into other economic sectors are important. These issues encompass environmental, social-cultural and economic concerns from the micro level of individual behaviour and choices, to the macro level of corporate governance and political decision-making.

With the context of the book framed, some preliminary questions were used to inspire contributors' thinking on the topic: *What is the single greatest challenge to the sustainability of surfing? What are the transitions to sustainability in your area of expertise? Are there any transitions you are particularly passionate about? What is your personal view of these transitions?* Beyond these questions we gave no additional guidance other than direct feedback. The idea was to allow a discourse to develop around the questions themselves in a non-prescriptive manner. Authors were afforded the space to explore sustainability and transitions from their own perspectives. Contributions came in a range of formats, from provocative hard hitting 'thought pieces', to broader essays and even primary data-driven pieces and case studies that demonstrate the coalface of the surfing world transitioning to sustainability. Each shines a unique and personal light on a particular aspect of sustainability and surfing. Combined, they form a whole greater than the sum of the individual parts that, for the first time, provides a multi-stakeholder discourse on the state of surfing's transition to sustainability.

The principle goal in publishing this range of contributions is to fuse this debate across sectors. Not only are solutions suggested to some of the big questions of sustainability in surfing but, even more important, lines of communication have been opened and a common language developed for the disparate members of the surfing world to communicate constructively about sustainability. As the editors, we saw the content and themes of the various contributions start to suggest patterns and relationships to each other. We were able to begin to map relationships between themes, stakeholder groups and author positions. The picture came into focus gradually. A number of important themes emerged, some of which have synergies with other industries and sectors and some that are very specific to surfing. It is important to explain the structure of the chapters to provide a conceptual 'map' through the complex and evolving landscape of the often contradictory visions the authors presented us with.

First, Rabbit sets the scene. Greg then discusses the overall idea of sustainable development, which provides the context. What follows is a high-level surf industry perspective of where sustainability is in the surfing world and what the opportunities and roadblocks are. We then present critiques of the surf industry's performance to date from a range of stakeholder positions. The positions of Non Governmental Organisations (NGO) and Surfing Development Organizations (SDO) are outlined in their responses to the challenges of sustainability. There are case studies of these principles in practice, alongside advances in some specific elements of sustainability in the surfing world. The finalé is a political call to action from some of surfing's most senior statesmen.

The opening contribution of the book comes from the 1978 World Surfing Champion, former Association of Surfing Professionals President, Gold Coast local, Wayne 'Rabbit' Bartholomew. Rabbit's contribution is a personal history of the Gold Coast, with his insight into the significant human interventions in natural systems that have taken place there, and surfers' responses to protecting the resulting world-class surf they created. Chapter One continues with co-editor and Devon surfer, Greg Borne. He complements Rabbit's piece by exploring the history of sustainable development as a concept and its status as an ambiguous, contested concept. He explores the rapid rise of sustainable development within the surfing world in the last three years and some of the events that have acted as a catalyst in this transition.

Chapter Two contains contributions from the presidents of the peak surf industry and sporting organisations. Doug Palladini is the Vice President and General Manager for the Americas at Vans and President of the Surf Industry Manufacturers Association (SIMA), which represents the interests of 150 brands. Fernando Aguerre is the founder of Reef and the President of the International Surfing Association (the main body for 96 member nation surfing associations). He is a fierce advocate for spreading the 'gospel of stoke' through surfing, as far and wide as possible. Both contributors reflect on sustainability within the brands they directly influence, but also comment from their positions of influence driving and guiding the sport and industry of surfing on a global level.

Chapter Three investigates the corporate culture of two of surfing's most famous brands more deeply and looks at how sustainability is factored into operations through the contributions of Bob McKnight, former CEO and current Executive Chairman of the Board at Quiksilver, and Derek Sabori,

Senior Director of Sustainability at Volcom. Jeff Wilson, former head of Quiksilver's global sustainability initiatives, shares his experiences attempting to 'green' the company's supply chain and reflects on the process of the broader issues facing sustainability in the surf industry. Southern Californian pro surfer Rob Machado conducts a brief study of the sustainability claims and performance of a number of brands that he rides for and appreciates. Finally, noted journalist Todd Woody comments on the mainstream media's attention span for surfing issues and the multifaceted nature of sustainability in surfing. This chapter does not present a homogenous industry perspective: some of the contributors have diverse and conflicting views of how sustainability should, or could, be integrated into industry operations and functions. Others scrutinise industry claims of sustainability.

In Chapter Four, the contributors expand the critique of the industry and examine some underlying assumptions often made about sustainability and the surfing industry. Shaun Tomson, 1977 World Surfing Champion and founder of two successful surf brands, questions the direction of the industry in the 21st century and points to significant 'mission drift'. Other authors in this section go even further to provide a critique that not only includes surfing but also details how the global capitalist systems interface with surfing culture. This includes the cultures of the places that surfing has an impact in all its guises – from tourism to manufacturing.

Scott Laderman questions the ethics of the corporate supply chain whilst journalist Tetsuhiko Endo shines a post-colonial light on the globalisation of surf culture and the vanishing frontier of international surf tourism. Then, three times World Women's Longboarding Champion, Cori Schumacher, highlights issues of environmental injustice. The Greener Blue's Marc Marovich questions the wisdom of exclusivity in surfing identities when surfers are positioned to drive positive change. Pierce Kavanaugh, independent film maker and San Diego Surf Film Festival Founder, relates his disappointment with the industry's weak sustainability performance on one hand, and, on the other, joy that the surf industry is not the beating heart of surf culture. This chapter contains an incisive critique, not only of surfing, but also where the industry's perspective fits into broader social and environmental patterns.

In response to this, Chapter Five presents the positions of individuals from a range of leading surfing NGOs, SDOs and companies that are leading the way in social and environmental innovation. Surfrider Foundation CEO Chad Nelson explains the notion of 'Surfonomics' which has been used successfully to demonstrate the economic value of surfing amenity. Former CEO Jim Moriarty calls for surfers to assume responsibility for the sustainability of the surfing resource. Nev Hyman founder of Firewire Surfboards explains how technological innovations and investment in research and development has made Firewire one of the most successful surfboard companies in the world, and how his drive for sustainability has led to the innovative NevHouse initiative. Easkey Britton, Irish big wave surfer and women's surfing champion, articulates the transformative power of surfing when harnessed for positive change. Peter Robinson and Andrew Coleman explain how the British Surfing Museum both conserves surfing heritage and helps to promote sustainability in its community. And finally Sustainable Surf, winners of *Surfer* magazine's 2014 Agents for Change award discuss how they have successfully catalysed the surfing industry towards sustainability.

Chapter Six develops the broader arguments seen in Chapter Five in a series of case studies of surfer-driven organisations putting principles into practice. These range from in-depth discussions on the evolution and implementation of well known surf NGOs, to those from young NGO founders Sean Brody and Emi Koch who emphasise the importance of surfing on a local and national level where surfing has empowered and changed the lives of local communities. Academic Danny O'Brien and President of the Papua New Guinea Surfing Association, Andrew Abel, describe the development of surfing and surf tourism in Papua New Guinea and argue this has been a catalyst for nation building. Serge Dedina and his co-authors then outline surfing and coastal ecosystem conservation in Baja California, Mexico. Finally, Malcolm Findlay discusses the rise and fall of the first academic programme specially focused on Surfing, The BSc (Hons) Surf Science and Technology at Plymouth University.

Chapter Seven goes beyond established programmes and organisations to highlight the active development of new best practices in specific areas of sustainability in the surfing world. This includes co-editor Jess Ponting outlining a number of initiatives stemming from the world's first Center for Surf Research, which itself was a response to the identification of problems with the sustainability of surf tourism. Michelle Blauw then explores the important role of surf craft and the need to maintain and promote the skills this involves for future generations. In addition, Tony Butt makes a critical comparison in discussing what surfers believe their relationship to nature is, and what it actually is, in the context of carbon footprints and climate change and Emma Whittlesea presents the first data ever collected on the greening of a surfing event. Sam Bleakley, writer and British and European longboarding champion, weaves a personal and prosaic narrative highlighting multiple sustainability dimensions in the Maldives. Concluding this chapter Ben Freeston, founder of Magicseaweed, provides invaluable insights into the role of surf forecasting and what this means for community and sustainability.

Chapter Eight specifically covers political action and power. Can surfing, as a political force both within the political system and outside it, effect a transition to sustainability on multiple scales? This chapter presents the thoughts of some seminal figures that have promoted change through surfing. Earlier discussions culminate in this section that now suggests how we drive forward, from a political standpoint, to sustainability on a local and international level. Kevin Lovett was one of three Australians to discover the perfect surf at Lagundri Bay on the Indonesian Island of Nias in 1975. Kevin watched the Bay become a 'surf slum' and he is an outspoken proponent of sustainable surf tourism management and protected areas.

Glenn Hening, disproved the conventional wisdom of the time that the term 'surfer organisation' was an oxymoron, by founding the world's largest and most successful surfer NGO. Similarly, in the UK Chris Hines co-founded Surfers Against Sewage (SAS), which lobbied until national legislation lead to measurable improvements in water quality around the UK. For the first time, surfers were given a sense of identity and purpose. Current director of SAS Hugo Tagholm discusses recent initiatives and the importance of actively engaging with government. In Australia Brad Farmer founded Surfrider Australaisa and later National Surfing Reserves that led to the creation of World Surf Reserves. World Surfing Champion of 1968, co-founder of the first professional world tour and professional surfing organization and former Hawaiian senator, Fred Hemmings, highlights the need for surfers to have a seat at the table of political power to ensure the sustainability of the surfing resource. The book's final section looks to the future. The epilogue sees a contribution from John and Cris Dahl as well as some last words from us.

Sustainable Stoke has brought together some of the most influential figures in surfing to explore what the future holds. It is by no means complete; this is the beginning of just one conversation and there are many conversations to be had and multiple voices to be heard.

1.1

The Making and Breaking of a Surfer's Paradise

Wayne 'Rabbit' Bartholomew

As a born-and-bred Gold Coaster, I have witnessed the place morph from a sleepy coastal strip of sun, sand, surf and fishing to Australia's tourist capital. There has always been a fine balance between maintaining the natural assets, whose charm and vitality were the catalyst for growth, and the development of the glitter strip into a highrise collosus, Australia's answer to Miami, or even Waikiki. From a surfing perspective, the real Surfers Paradise was the perfectly foiled sand bottom point breaks that adorned the southern end of the Gold Coast, incorporating Snapper Rocks, Rainbow Bay, Greenmount, Kirra, Currumbin and Burleigh Heads. On their day, with the right combination of swell and accompanying conditions, a myriad of fine beachbreaks could be found from Duranbah to The Spit, and beyond to South Stradbroke Island.

Surfing has been around for decades. The father of modern surfing, Hawaii's Duke Kahanamoku, graced the shores of Greenmount Beach in 1915. It is well known that Duke had given a famous demonstration of surfing at Sydney's Freshwater Beach, however it is less known that after a swimming demonstration at Chandler Pool in Brisbane, Duke visited the southern Gold Coast. At that time of year the winds would have been offshore and I for one am pretty sure that if Duke saw nice peelers wrapping down the point he would have had to sample a few Goldy point waves.

Nowhere on earth have there been more modifications and man-made interventions than on the Gold Coast. For the most part, we have been quite lucky, for example, the bookends of the Goldy, Duranbah and South Straddie, were not surfing beaches before man's intervention. Then there was the Kirra Groyne, which worked, then suffered adversity when modified, but I will return to mentioning those beaches down the track. Raised in the twin towns of Coolangatta/Tweed Heads, the beach was already the rage well before I threw myself over the ledge. All roads led to the surf when the California-inspired surf craze hit in the 1960s, surfing exploded. I went down to Kirra Point with my father to watch the 1964 Queensland Junior Champion, Billy Stafford Jnr., surfing before school. During the longboard era, there was a strong surfing community along the Gold Coast, surfing the famous points of Snapper, Rainbow Bay, Greenmount, Kirra, Currumbin, Burleigh and all the lesser known beaches in between.

The chain reaction began with the lengthening of the rock retainer wall at the mouth of Tweed River. Deemed a dangerous entrance, due to both its narrow bar and exposure to the south-east swells, the walls were extended in 1962, deflecting the natural south-to-north littoral drift of sand. This, in turn, starved the southern Gold Coast points of their lifeblood, sand. The impact wasn't felt until Cyclone Dinah in 1967, which ravaged the Gold Coast and eroded beaches. In the tourism capital, Surfers Paradise, old car bodies were heaped upon each other as a buffer against the raging ocean, while the surf clubs along the coastal strip were all hanging ten into the abyss.

The problem was that the Tweed River entrance was in New South Wales, whereas Southern Queensland beaches bore the brunt. Something had to be done so, in 1972, the Gold Coast City Council constructed a groyne at the end of Kirra point. The surfers of my generation, including Michael Peterson, Peter Townend and Wayne Deane, were mortified at the thought of this, but back in '72 surfers were not only far from being organised activists, but also were at the very bottom of Australian society. Kirra was a perfect barrel, I still maintain that in '72 Kirra turned on like never before; we were riding 6 foot waves that threw out 20 feet and enjoying 15-second barrel rides, which were arguably the longest on offer on the earth.

For two years, Kirra was deep water, but fortunately Burleigh, Currumbin and Snapper were going off. The result of the original Tweed River wall extensions also created Duranbah, which was transformed from a no-man's-land of raging rip current to a world-class beachbreak, a fortunate slice of luck that would be repeated when the northern Seaway walls were extended in the '80s. This, combined with a sand-pumping regime, created world-class beachbreaks at South Straddie. By a stroke of good fortune, the Big Groyne extended Kirra Point. It created a perfect angle for the predominant east and south easterly swells to hit the natural bank. Tucked in Coolangatta Bay, by the time the swell lines reached Kirra, they were ruler-edged and with the bank groomed to perfection. The likes of Michael Peterson, Peter Townend, Wayne Deane and myself, to mention a few, were able to ride deeper and longer, and the bonus was that not only could Kirra hold a bigger swell, but also there was a groyne to jump off to reach the line-up too.

Between the southern points of Snapper, Rainbow, Greenmount and Kirra and their northern neighbours, Currumbin and Burleigh, the Gold Coast was blessed with decades of great surf during the '70s, '80s and into the '90s. The great weather, warm water and excellent surf attracted lots of new surfers. Whether it was people migrating north, parents introducing their kids to surfing or kids just finding it themselves, all roads seemed to lead to the surf. An industry built up around it, surf shops thrived, surfboard factories sprang up, surf wear and accessory factories were either born or relocated to the Gold Coast, and it became a surf destination and industry hub.

Professional surfing events have been part of the landscape since the famous Stubbies Classic events of the '70s, through the Billabong Pro era and onto the present, Quiksilver Pro era. Surf schools popped up, surfing excellence programmes were incorporated into school sport and in excess of 70,000 recreational surfers call the Gold Coast home. Sustainability was always going to be a huge issue with regard to surf amenity. At government and council level there was no correlation between the vast economic impact surfing had on the Gold Coast and the economy at large.

By the mid '90s, the build up of sand on the Tweed Bar, created by the diversion of the natural northern drift following the wall extensions, was depriving the southern points of their lifeblood, SAND. It was an arduous route for the sand to get from D/Bah to Snapper, and there were periods of up to two years when not a skerrick of sand reached Snapper. It seemed cruel, the locals watched the sand slowly crawl from D/Bah to Froggy Beach, then make its way into Snapper, build a perfect bank, then see a big swell wash it away overnight, knowing that the next surf at Snapper may not be for another 18 months.

The only saving grace for the town, and I state this because the Chamber of Commerce had yet to realise the equation: Surf + Sand = Success, was that Kirra was going off. When word spread that a Marina was being proposed for Kirra, we formed KEPT (Kirra Environmental Protection Trust) and I organised a pro event. My theory was that Kirra would speak for itself, and in '92 we had perfect barrels for the inaugural event, win US$5,000 in prize money. On the back of this, I convinced Billabong founder Gordon Merchant to raise the prize money and make it a Two Star World Qualifying Series event on the ASP World Tour.

Kirra spoke again, and the perfect barrels enticed Kelly Slater, Rob Machado and Sunny Garcia, the world's leading surfers, to attend the event in '94. Perfect

6-8 foot Kirra greeted them, and after this, Gordon upgraded the event to a World Championship Tour. The following year, Shane Beschen scored three perfect tens in one heat, a record that has stood the test of time, and Kirra had spoken so loudly that not only was any talk of a marina extinguished, but people flocked from within Australia and around the world to experience – even behold – the magic of Kirra. But the Groyne was shortened by 30 metres and we experienced 18 years of barren Kirra. The irony was that we had been to several years of meetings pounding out parameters for the upcoming Tweed River Entrance Sand Bypass Project (TRESBP). As concerned members of Snapper Rocks Surfriders Club, Bruce Lee and myself attended the very first public meeting announcing plans for TRESBP, kicking up such a stink that they invited us to not only contribute submissions on behalf of the club, but also to sit on the Advisory Committee. I have been the Queensland Community Representative on the AC since 1992.

The primary purpose of the sand bypass was to make the Tweed River entrance a safer passage for commercial and recreational boats. It was not about surfing at all, it was about navigability, a deed between NSW and Queensland. The sand would be scooped up as it travelled along Letitia Spit, which stretches out to the south on the opposite side of the river to Duranbah, and pumped via underground pipes to outlets across the border in Queensland. Seeing the opportunity to use the sand to groom the southern points, I introduced the term 'wave quality' into the equation for Queensland.

The architects of the system accepted this, scouring the world for an expert on wave quality. A Hawaiian, Kimo out of Scripps Institute for Oceanography in San Diego was appointed and I took him on a tour and provided observations on optimum sand contours for the classic sandbanks. Kimo completed his survey and sent his findings and recommendations to the project managers. A tender process was completed and TRESBS came to fruition in 2000. Permanent outlets were established at East Snapper Rocks (Froggies Beach) and Kirra, while Duranbah would be nourished on a need-to basis with moveable pipes.

A major pumping programme began to pump sand to Snapper and the place was transformed into one of the most consistent waves in Oz. The problems began when the 30 years of sand, built up on the Tweed bar, was dredged and dumped in Coolangatta Bay. This made the bay too shallow, resulting in cloudbreaks when the swell reached six feet and all the sand buried Kirra Point and the various reefs around Kirra, with disastrous effects. Closer to shore though, it was a different story as the sand fed Snapper, then connected Rainbow, Greenmount and Coolangatta Beach.

Superbank sprang into life and for several years the loss of Kirra was masked by Superbank that delivered a fabulous kilometer-long barrel, and wave after perfect wave. More and more people were relocating to the Gold Coast, the lure of Superbank attracted surfers from all over the world. I was appointed CEO/President of ASP International in '99, I relocated Head Office to a slick location overlooking Superbank. ASP introduced Event Licences in 2000, then Qucksilver swooped on the Gold Coast Licence and domiciled the event at Snapper, resulting in over a decade of consistently good quality waves at the head of the Superbank.

The Gold Coast has grown up. Long gone are the Tolkien-like days of empty point waves and pit stops at the Healthy Bee for smoothies between surfs. It is now the sixth largest city in Australia. The growth is not all about the waves, the secret is the weather. The climate offers over 300 perfect days a year, we have a six to eight week winter, the water temperature barely drops below 20 and the crime rate, until recently, has been very low. Approximately 30,000 people migrate north to the 'Goldy' every year, and a good proportion of their children find the surf very appealing.

The added notoriety of Superbank with its ridiculously long barrels, 12-day swells, a season that stetches from Christmas to late August, not to mention having a reputation for providing a day-care service for future world champions, made for a heady mix of dreams and expectation. Damon Harvey linking a 2.2 km super ride from Snapper to Kirra, combined with Kelly Slater commenting that Superbank was better then Kirra, created a magnetic 'tsunami' that resulted in thousands of surfers doing almost anything to get to the Goldy.

Several universities sprung up on the Gold Coast – and between Griffith, Bond and Southern Cross a host of teenagers chose the Goldy as their desired destination to garner academic qualifications. Running parallel to this were a plethora of language courses, which appealed to young Brazilian, Japanese and European students – they also wanted to ride the famous Superbank. A fair number of this demographic were reasonably proficient at surfing; combined with the tens of thousands of second and third generation surfers emanating from the annual influx and the homegrowns, the surfing population exploded.

During the '80s and '90s the locals still ruled – while accepting that surfing numbers exploded during traditional holiday periods, visiting surfers still had to exude a semblance of respect. The caveat here is that Aussies in general are very hospitable hosts; but the place was overwhelmed by sheer volume of numbers and we were overrun in the stampede.

The Gold Coast, both by way of attrition and as a science experiment, is ground zero, a kind of snapshot of the future many iconic surf breaks will face as numbers swell to the point of unsustainability. As a test tube experiment, like observing the behaviour of too many rats in a cage, it makes for an interesting thesis on human process. Take Burleigh as an example. Easily one of the finest waves on the planet, a growing Brazilian contingency set up camp there about 10 years ago. While the Snapper/Superbank was being overwhelmed, the Burleigh boys dug in. When a few surf zone skirmishes brought it to a head, a few hard heads rallied the troops and the Burleigh boys moved the trouble makers on, in all probability down to Coolangatta.

I intend this piece to be a cautionary tale. There are only a finite number of iconic surf spots worldwide – where you can actually live, work and raise a family. That is the definition of a sustainable surf break, the rest is but a dream only to be achieved if you leave the world as you know it, relocate to an exotic location, settle in the indigenous village and embrace a subsistence lifestyle – all the while living within a paddle of an unbelievably perfect wave and just 'go native'. I am a great believer in the vision that, for all the adolescents embracing the surfing lifestyle, today is still the good old days. It is remarkable how they adapt to the crowds, but I guess it is my generation that carry the scars, that mourn the passing of a time when free and easy surfing at uncrowded point/reef/beach breaks was not only taken for granted but was also almost a birthright. Without foresight, without realistic demographic mapping and sustainable planning, the surfing dream will be stretched to breaking point.

I introduced the phrase 'wave quality' to the TRESBP Project as I am convinced that surfers, with some level-headed leadership, backed by watertight statistics, can make a difference. We had so many rallies to bring Kirra back, highlighted by three major public meetings, but I came to realise that the reason the politicians, the councils and state and federal governments were paying lip service to all these highly emotive outpourings of raw, anecdotal testimonials was because they only react to events that either result in collateral damage or have the potential to be an election issue. I began to realise that the equation for being taken seriously lay between the synergy of coastal engineers and economic impact studies. The engineers were the 'go to' folk for local councils and state governments; their recommendations, in tandem with environmental sustainability, were major factors in moulding coastal management policy. When coastal engineer, Neil Lazarow, drew relevant economic impacts for individual beaches, this in turn instigated a deeper, far reaching EIS for the contribution that surfing, in all its forms, made to the Gold Coast economy. The significance of this was not lost on our collective effort to not only bury the last vestiges of the 'surfing stigmata', but also to bring the Gold Coast into the reality of the values of contemporary society.

It has long been a frustration for me that the Gold Coast doesn't know which side its bread is buttered. The stigma of the '60s and '70s was somehow still lingering, leading to major mistakes in forward-thinking policy making. I maintain that the true barometer on society is mothers: they are protective, most see the world for what it really is. When I was young, mothers were wary of surfing and fathers were downright against it as not many surfed pre '60s, but mothers were the first to back you if they could see true passion.

Today, mothers drive their children to the beach. They encourage them to surf, for no other reason than they understand what surfing offers for life. It is a youth pursuit, allows fantastic social interaction, generates a feeling of well being and belonging, is amazingly healthy, eliminates youth boredom, encourages camaraderie and respect, and instils, or at least is embryonic, in the formative process of development as an individual in a chaotic world. Mothers worldwide 'get' this and that has made a big difference. Now we need to catch up with reality!

The potential threats to various surf spots have made it necessary to put a value on each surf location, and the Gold Coast as a whole. For example, a proposed shipping terminal at the northern end of the Gold Coast placed South Straddie on the endangered list. It was revealed that surfing at South Straddie pumped about AUS$26 million into the economy. That's just one beach, albeit a world-class surf break. Surfing in all its forms, mostly recreational surfing but also the surf industry, pro surfing, surf tourism, surf schools, club surfing etc, contributes a staggering AUS$3.5 billion into the Gold Coast economy annually. This is a pretty significant amount, making surf second only to the tourism industry. Surfing dwarfs the combined contribution to the economy of rugby, AFL, rugby league and soccer, plus cricket and motor sport. Any interest group that pumped over three billion dollars into any city's economy would be pandered to. AUS$100 million stadiums are built but the general rule of thumb is that surfing gets nothing, even less if diminishing surf amenity with the loss of a couple of key surf spots is included.

This is also due to laws that don't recognise the surf, or even the beach, as a recreational amenity, or even a public amenity. Governments have never recognised anywhere beyond the high tide mark as public space. Surveys indicate that natural assets, such as the beach and surf zone, are the most attractive elements of the Gold Coast, so perhaps it is time to review legislation in this area. When surfers speak among themselves, the mention of surf amenity is clearly understood, yet these two words don't seem to mean anything at government or city council level.

There are some very positive signs, perhaps years of lobbying and education by groups such as Surfrider Foundation, Kirra Point Inc., and National Surfing Reserves have finally yielded results. The Governor of Queensland bestowed National Surfing Reserve status on the Gold Coast Points, which offers some protection, even if it is only symbolic. KPI has had a big breakthrough with the Gold Coast Mayor, Tom Tate, aspiring to return Kirra to its former glory by putting the lost 30m of rocks back on the Big Groyne at Kirra, and an overarching council has been formed to represent all future challenges and threats to our surf breaks. The key to all this is future planning, strategically setting in place measures that will ensure the sustainability of our most treasured assets. There are only a finite number of surf breaks, the points are already beyond capacity, and still people come. Younger and younger age groups are being introduced to surfing, or are finding it themselves. All roads lead to the surf on the Gold Coast and the kids surf in quality surf nearly year-round. The challenge, though, is to not only stem the tide of diminishing surf amenity but to enhance surf amenity.

The key to the future is in wave parks and artificial reefs because there is only one Burleigh, one Kirra, one Snapper. I have watched the evolving technologies closely in these areas and I think the Gold Coast is a prime location, even if it's just based on accommodating the tens of thousands of future surfers that will be wave-hunting in future decades. I have had the good fortune to consult and be a test pilot for the Webber Wave Pool and I firmly believe that the eight years of research and development that Greg Webber has invested in this technology will create something that mimics the best qualities of some of the best waves in the world. There are other technologies and there is little doubt that wave parks are a lot closer to reality then we imagine.

Places like the Gold Coast are so reliant on sand. Following major erosion, the place is under threat, having lost its lifeblood. The Council pumps tens of millions of dollars into beach nourishment programmes, aimed at recovering lost sand, but it is a short-term fix because the next major storm is somewhere out there beyond the horizon. I like to think of surfers infiltrating every aspect of society, and having surfers as part of beach protection departments within councils will open the door to working on strategies that will not only provide long-term solutions to protecting the beaches, but will also incorporate a surf quality outcome, such as an artificial reef, or a hybrid wing attached to a control point designed primarily as a buffer.

I will be the first to put my hand up as having a conflict of interest, if and when I sit on an Advisory Committee, created by any future overarching beach and surf strategy group. I firmly believe that there is a place for Wave Pools and Artificial Surf Reefs. Further to that, I see them as the only future option when dealing with the surf amenity issue. I am all ears as to alternative measures, however permits and licenses and other restrictive actions are simply not viable. Firstly they would be impossible to police, one can never stop a desperate and determined surfer, and two, the resources required would make it prohibitive. Sadly we cannot rely on common courtesy or any surfers code, not with so many mouths to feed on the Goldy. The City Council has already identified certain 'Control Points', specific areas of vulnerability to long term erosion and irreversible storm surge damage. Future buffer structures will be established at these locations and there is no reason why quality surf breaks cannot be incorporated into the outcome. I don't think we have five years to twiddle our thumbs, the tipping point of unsustainability of surf breaks will head us off at the pass if we don't plan ahead. We need more surf amenity, it must happen to avoid catastrophic overcrowding and the resultant negative social outcomes.

Why not factor waves into future planning? To be able to devise strategies that protect the sand and create a fun surf spot for a minimum increase in spend is sound forward thinking. The economic impact of having a local surf spot is proven: there are a lot of mouths to feed and surfing is far from being the fringe interest group it once was. By making these important social benefits part of election campaigns is pretty smart. With about 100,000 recreational surfers in the electorate, it would pay to listen to this collective voice.

A lot can be learned from the Gold Coast experiment, from both past mistakes and happy slices of unplanned good fortune. Surfers need to step up, they are generally the great silent majority who grumble among themselves but step back from agitating politicians and council departments. The time has come to be a united voice, to stand up for our surf amenity, wave quality and the sustainable future of what we love to do. It is important to be organised, having clear policy and solid leadership. Every surf destination has its own set of challenges. The end result justifies the effort. If we ensure the wave riding experience for future generations, we will perpetuate the dream of the surfing lifestyle.

Rabbit in his heyday at Rocky Point, Hawaii by Dick Hoole, 1957 (Courtesy of Wayne 'Rabbit' Bartholomew and the WSL)

1.2

Surfing and Sustainable Development

Gregory Borne

Rabbit very eloquently writes about so many pertinent issues that relate to sustainable development and sustainability, done with the focus firmly on the Gold Coast, covering the environment, society and the economy, all the while emphasising the interaction between them. As you read through the contributions you will see how many of these issues are relevant to different parts of world and in different contexts. Moreover, you will be able to build your own mosaic of how it fits together and what it means to you. But before you take this deep dive into sustainability within surfing, I want to just step back for a moment and explore sustainable development as a concept: its history, its perspectives and where it is going in the future. Whilst many diverse actors contribute to the evolution of sustainable developement, you will forgive me if there seems to be an emphasis of the role of the United Nations in this story. This is partly because it has and does have a central role in the rise of sustainable development and partly from my own personal experiences and interests.

The idea of a sustainable development and sustainability[1] is here to stay and there has never been a more important time to explore the multiple interpretations of the concept. Whist sustainable development and sustainability are not necessarily synonymous, the term sustainability as we understand it in the context of this book has its origins in the concept of sustainable development. What follows is an exploration of the concept of sustainable development, which is the central theme of *Sustainable Stoke*. Firstly, I will provide a brief timeline for the concept that will explore some of the main publications and events that have contributed to making sustainable development. Secondly, I will introduce the concept of sustainable development, emphasising it as a contested and ambiguous concept meaning many different things to different groups and organisations. Thirdly, there will be a discussion on emerging perspectives on sustainability and, finally, I will discuss what a transition could actually mean.

Sustainable development is a response to the increasingly detrimental impact that we are having on the environment. At all levels of our biosphere, land, sea and air, there is increasing evidence of pollution, acidification of the oceans, loss of fisheries and habitats, deforestation, desertification and rises in CO_2 levels contributing to climate change. Many of us recognise that our current developmental pathway is unsustainable. As a concept, sustainable development can be charted through a number of key publications, although there are other factors and key events that have contributed to the evolution of sustainable development over the last fifty years.

It is largely held that Rachel Carson's book *Silent Spring* (1962)[2] represents the emergence of what we understand as environmentalism today. It brought together research on toxicology, ecology and epidiology to suggest that agricultural pesticides were building to catastrophic levels. Later on in 1968, Paul Ehrlich's *The Population Bomb*[3] warned that a rapid increase in population size would have a negative effect on the natural environment because we would exceed the carrying capacity of the planet. That is quite simply the ability of the planet to support the human race.

In 1972, The Club of Rome published their controversial *Limits to Growth*[4] report which painted a very dire picture for the future of the planet if it continued along its present course of development. The cumulative effect of increased awareness of environmental degradation prompted the United Nations Conference on the Human Environment (UNCHE) at Stockholm, also in 1972. It was in the wake of the UNCHE that the United Nations Environment Programme (UNEP) was created and it was at this point that sustainable development, as a concept, began to gain currency in political and social dialogue.

The often quoted definition of sustainable development was coined in the *Report of the World Commission for Environment and Development: Our Common Future* (WCED) in 1987. This is more commonly known as the Brundtland Report, named after the chair of the commission Gro Harlem Brundtland, the then Prime Minister of Norway. It suggests that sustainable development is:

'Development that meets the needs of present populations without compromising the ability of future generations to meet their own needs'[5].

This emphasises the need for intergenerational equity and considers what legacy we leave our children and grandchildren. Perhaps the most well-known conference was the United Nations Conference on Environment and Development, held in Rio, in 1992. This was more popularly known as the Earth Summit and was the largest environmental conference ever held, with more than 30,000 people and over 100 heads of state in attendance. Whilst the success of this event is disputed, there were a number of important outcomes. These include the Convention on Biological Diversity, the Framework Convention on Climate Change, Principles for Forest Management[6], the Rio Declaration on Environment and Development and *Agenda 21* (see page 27).

In 2002, the World Summit on Sustainable development (WSSD) was held in Johannesburg. The Johannesburg Declaration on Sustainable Development[7] added weight to a global commitment to many multiple issues that come under the umbrella of sustainable development and addressed in *Agenda 21*. Directly following the WSSD was the 57th United Nations General Assembly and I was fortunate enough to be stationed at UN headquarters in New York as a member of the United Nations Environment Programme. This was my first taste of international politics in the flesh, and the experience altered my perception of the world and how it is run in a very profound way. And whilst the United Nations has been criticised for being little more than a talking shop, it serves an invaluable role for humanity. For me the UN is an arena of ideologies and values, a forum for discussion and negotiation and not necessarily a place of operations. And what was clear during my time there was that sustainable development was a central concept.

In 2012, the United Nations staged the Summit on Sustainable Development (UNSSD) or Rio +20. An important outcome of the UNSSD was to begin the process of designing the Sustainable Development Goals, which will replace the Millennium Development Goals in 2015. Although these are not yet published, there have been calls to ensure that the world's oceans are represented with a specific sustainable development goal[8]. What issues these goals should cover are discussed in the journal *Nature*[9] but, whatever the final incarnation may look like what is certain is that the term is here to stay. Interestingly, the image that accompanied the aforementioned article in *Nature* is an adaptation of Japanese artist Hokusai's *The Great Wave of Kanagawa*. This is an interesting choice for *Nature* to begin an article on the Sustainable Development Goals, and particularly pertinent for this book on three counts. Firstly, it's a wave, of course. Secondly, the iconography of this wave is presented to illustrate unsustainable development. And thirdly, *The Great Wave of Kanagawa*, was the inspiration behind the now globally recognised Quiksilver logo. I could not have planned

(*Source: Griggs et al 2012* [10])

a more apt image to make the connection between surfing and sustainable development.

Nature's version shows the huge wave, bearing down on a flimsy life boat, driving it towards a rocky shore line. The four figures stand at the helm, their life rings have been thrown asunder. Within this context, the wave is the impending destruction that humanity faces if it proceeds along its current developmental pathways, the boat is humanity attempting to safely navigate its way to calmer waters and, in this metaphor, a sustainable future. But navigating this tiny boat in stormy seas is no simple affair, especially so in this depiction as the only rudder that can steer this boat is broken in two and thrown into the ocean. This is representative of many debates on how, and if, humanity can steer itself into a sustainable future.

Some argue that it is too late and that we are beyond the tipping point, exponential population growth, rampant resource depletion combined with no real political will or scientific know-how to avoid a global catastrophe. Others argue that technology will come to the rescue and that we will inevitably respond to the problems we have created through, for example, clean renewable energy sources, advancements in material technologies or the ability to recycle and reuse existing materials. This is sometimes referred to as a weak form of sustainable development as it does not suggest a wholesale reorganisation of our social and political systems. Yet others argue that a strong form of sustainable

21

development is necessary that involves a radical reordering of the current systems of production and consumption upon which we all depend because technology alone is not going to be enough[11].

With all of the above in mind what is really essential is that we understand how sustainable development and, by association, sustainability is being used in multiple sectors and at multiple levels. Even though the idea of the wave is selling a dream the world over, and indeed as much as the article in *Nature* is selling us its representation of sustainable development, we need to be critical and we need to understand what the concept means in any given context.

You don't have to look very hard to find criticisms of sustainable development, so to illustrate this lets look again at the Brundtland definition, 'Meeting the needs of current generations without compromising the ability of future generations to meet their own needs'. Meeting the needs of present and future populations is a hugely subjective idea; what is a necessity for one group is unlikely to be a necessity to another. And who is responsible for deciding what those needs are and how those needs are met? How can we accurately gauge what the needs for future generations might be with so many variables interfering with our ability to model and forecast possible future scenarios? From the outset, sustainable development, encompasses a number of challenges.

As a concept, it has been described as an oxymoron, that no development by its very nature can be sustainable. Sustainability means so many different things to different people that ultimately it is ineffective as a concept to drive policy, implement programmes, create legislation and generally promote solutions. Perhaps the most serious accusation levelled against sustainable development is that it is a term that does nothing more than legitimises existing modes or production and consumption. This has often been termed 'greenwashing', where sustainable development is used to make whoever is using it appear to be doing the right thing. And, in different contexts, all of these criticisms are seen to be true. So why then then do we have a term like sustainable development at all? And why has it now become one of the dominant concepts of the 21st century?

There are two principle reasons for this. Firstly, the idea of constructive ambiguity. The concept is so vague that it *can* mean all things to all people and as such provides a focal point for different groups and ideologies to come together, learn, share and understand. Secondly, whatever your opinion of sustainable development, there is little doubt that the pathway that humanity is currently on is quite simply unsustainable. As a result, the idea continues to grow and embed itself in all facets of life, so we need to understand what it means in

Venn Diagram Explanation

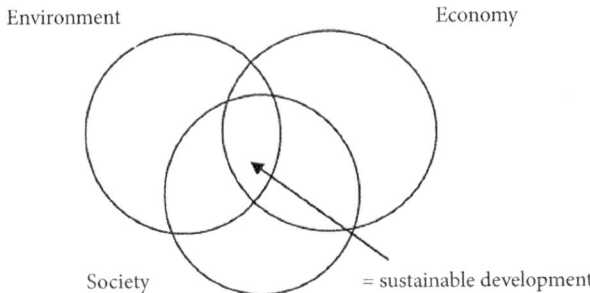

Russian Doll Explanation

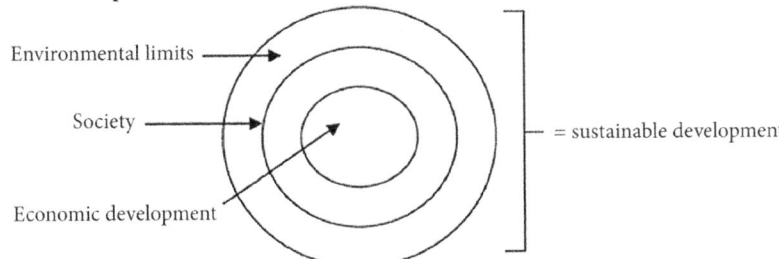

different contexts and I have attempted to do this, from the United Nations to local government and through to the 2012 Olympic Games[12].

Here the spotlight is turned on the surfing world as a collective yet highly diverse community of interest. This is in part a response to the broader transitions that are happening throughout the world in different sectors and different organisations, but it is also a response to the recognition that the perception of surfing as an innately sustainable pursuit has come to an end. Many contributors allude to this within this book and present different ways of understanding sustainability and I will not elaborate on this here. What I will do is discuss how sustainable development has created a new way of looking at the world. The starting point for this is the relationship between the three dimensions of human interaction with the environment, namely, society, environment and economy. This has been variously presented, and the Venn diagram and the Russian doll (above) are the simplest and clearest representations of this.

The Venn diagram model shows us that sustainable development exists at the intersection between the environment, economy and society. In the past two decades however there has been a move to explore sustainable development

```
                Institutional imperative - Strengthen participation
                        justice        democracy
                           burden sharing
                                                    Social imperative -
                                                    Safeguard cohesion
Enviromental imperative -
Limited throughput                care    access
               eco-efficiency

                Ecomonic imperative - Improve competitiveness
```

(*Source: Scottish Executive* [13])

from a more sophisticated perspective. The Russian doll model suggests that all economic activity should lead to social progress and that both social and environmental concerns must be considered within environmental limits. With this in mind both the Venn diagram and the Russian doll models remains simplistic and tell us very little about the complexity inherent within sustainable development. The three dimensional model (above) attempts to elaborate on the previous models including more dimensions and issues such as justice, democracy and access. And whilst these visualisations of sustainable development are useful and start us off on the journey to a better understanding of the interaction between humanity and our environment, they remain limited. They are limited because, as we explore ways of achieving a sustainable future, it is recognised that the problems faced by the world today, and the risks that come with them, are themselves complex, uncertain and non-linear, crossing disciplinary boundaries, sectors and nations. Climate change is an example of this and whilst there is an increasing consensus that humanity is significantly altering our climate, the direct cause and effects are still unclear.

With this in mind, sustainable development, as a way of viewing the world, must be able to mirror the complexity of humanity's interaction with the environment if it is to be in any way effective. To this end, an entire paradigm shift has emerged around sustainability that has impacted on how we create and use knowledge within society. This has been very aptly termed sustainability science[14] and is defined as "an emerging field of research dealing with the interactions between natural and social systems and with how those interactions affect the challenge of sustainability"[15].

Sustainability science emphasises notions of reflexivity, complexity, uncertainty and systems theory[16] and the idea of a system is particularly pertinent here. Systems theory is an interdisciplinary field of science that studies the nature of complex systems in society, nature and technology. At its core, it provides a framework for analysing a group of interrelated components that influence each other, whether these are a sector, city, organism or an entire society. The advantage of this approach is twofold. It is a useful theoretical approach for understanding the complex issues that relate to achieving a sustainable development, but it also emphasises practical solutions at ground level and provides a number of methods for doing so. This can include developing models and/or scenarios, using focus groups, and interviews. It emphasises participation and the inclusion of multiple stakeholders and multiple forms of knowledge, knowledge that can range from the scientific to the local. And this is exactly what this book achieves. This book is a result of this approach, with multiple perspectives and multiple sectors coming together building a picture of what a transition to sustainability might mean.

What becomes apparent is that what constitutes a transition is as tricky to tie down as is sustainability itself. I understand a transition as a fundamental change in structure, culture and practice. Structure can include physical infrastructure, economic infrastructure or institutions. Culture refers to the collective set of values, norms and perspectives and paradigm in terms of defining problems and solutions. And practice refers to the ensemble of production routines, behaviour, ways of handling and implementating at the individual level. In reality these three areas cannot be separated but provide a very useful way of understanding extremely complex processes. Sometimes these transitions are obvious, but often they are subtle, gaining momentum slowly until they reach a tipping point. I believe the tipping point within surfing had been reached for a number of reasons. All of the contributors in this book allude to this in different ways either through positive reinforcement or critical analysis. For me, a number of indicators have presented themselves over the past three years.

Firstly, the mediums for the serious exchange of ideas, thought and commentary within the surfing world have significantly evolved and/or grown up. The creation of the website, The Greener Blue[17], with a specific focus on surfing and sustainability is a good example of this, as is The Inertia[18]. Secondly, a very visible change is the increasing effectiveness of non-profit organisations that specifically focus on sustainability. Sustainable Surf with its programmes related to market transformation within the surfing industry is an example of change towards a more sustainable model of doing business. Their Waste to Waves programme has been successful not only from a recycling perspective but also in moving the debates around recycling and pollution in surfing into the mainstream media. Recently, they have implanted a number of programmes which they discuss later in the book

Thirdly, the establishment of the world's first Center for Surf Research at San Diego State University. This has provided a focal point for industry, non-profit organizations, and academia to come together and discuss the specific and unique dynamics of the surfing world. The conference in February 2012, organised by the Center and the Groundswell Society, Surfing's New Aloha: The Growing Trend of Giving Back, drew on a range of people related to the surfing world all trying to make a difference and understand the future of many different aspects of sustainability and surfing. Some of the speakers and panellists from that conference discuss their views on sustainability in the coming chapters.

As with the Rio conference, this book represents a process that begins to articulate the problem in a comprehensive fashion that, in turn, facilitates discussions of the solutions galvanising and catalysing the transition towards sustainability. *Sustainable Stoke* and all those contributing to it represent another significant part of this transition so far, helping sheer that tiny boat to calmer waters. The difference for us as surfers is that we are untied by and utilise the waves for positive change. But don't take my word for it, keep reading.

Agenda 21
A non-legally binding programme of action for sustainable development. Adopted at the UN conference on Environment and Development, it is a document that is comprised of forty chapters and is intended to guide the actions of governments, aid agencies, local government and other actors on environment and development issues.

Elements	Issues
Social and economic dimensions to development	Poverty, production and consumption, health, human settlement, integrated decision-making
Conservation and management of natural Resources	Atmosphere, oceans and seas, land, forests, mountains, biological diversity, ecosystems, biotechnology, fresh water resources, toxic chemicals, hazardous radioactive and solid waste
Strengthening role of major groups	Youth, women, indigenous people, NGOs, local authorities, trade unions, businesses, scientific and technical communities, farmers
Means of implementation	Finance, technology transfer, information, public awareness, capacity building, education, legal instruments, institutional frameworks

The table outlines the four broad areas of *Agenda 21*. It is argued that *Agenda 21* is the most significant and influential non-binding instrument in the environmental field. Essentially, it establishes a framework, or 'package' of long term goals. For some commentators it is nothing less than the most comprehensive document negotiated between governments on the interaction between economic, social and environmental trends at every level of human activity. It has, however, been criticised for promoting a vision of sustainable development that does nothing more than perpetuate the enlightenment goals of progress, through economic growth and industrialisation at all costs. But, despite the criticisms, *Agenda 21* is a pivotal document that deals with a diverse range of sustainable development issues. Since the publication of *Agenda 21*, however, there has been a substantial movement in the way that sustainable development is perceived. This is best represented by examining the role of the World Summit on sustainable development in this process.

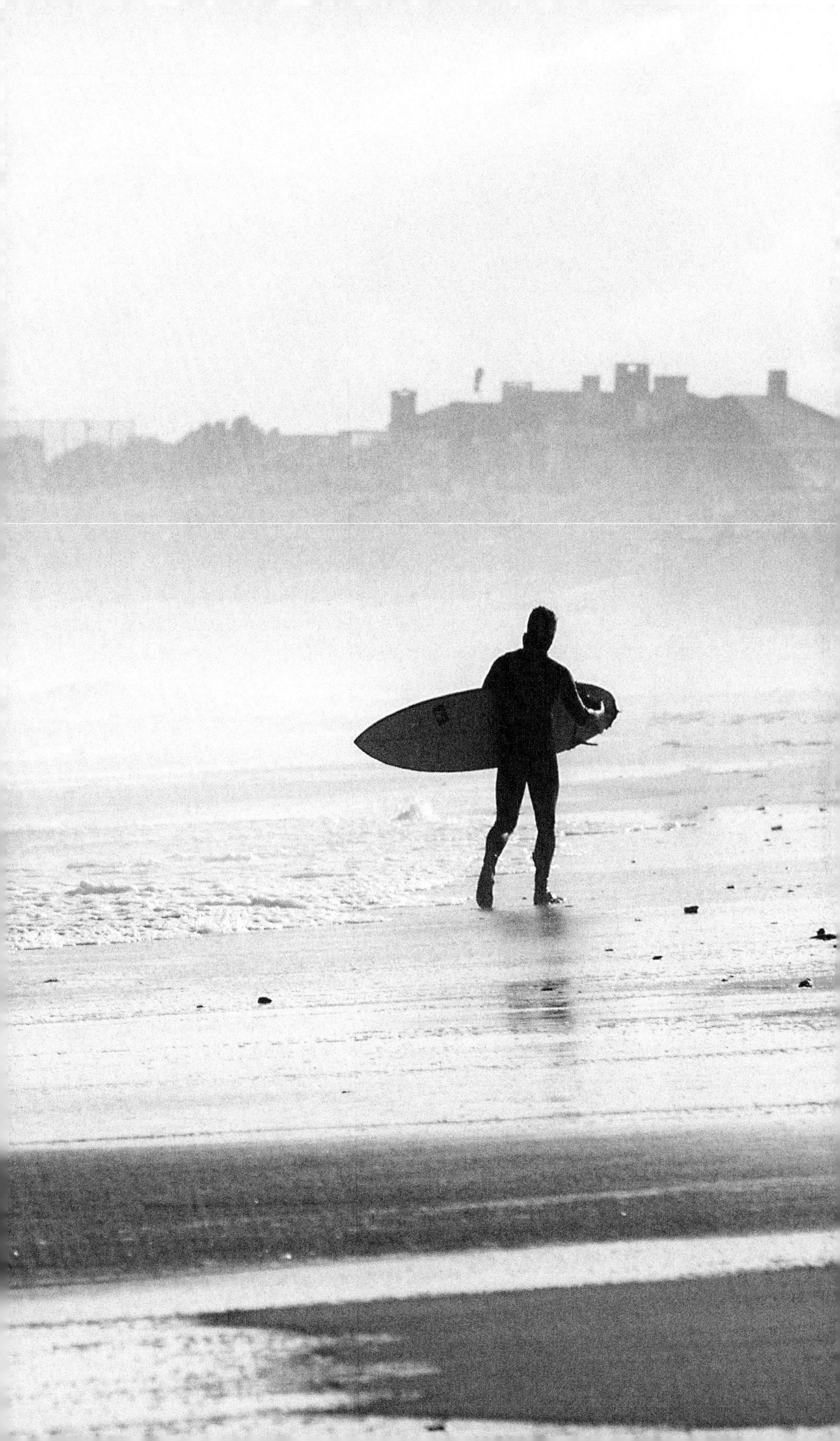

Chapter Two
Umbrella

The previous chapter set the scene, the context and the rationale for this book. Chapter Two now begins to explore what sustainability may mean in surfing and it begins to do so at what we are describing as the umbrella level. Two pieces constitute this chapter from two of the most prominent and influential men in surfing today. Each discusses the role of sustainability and surfing not only from their unique roles as leading figures in specific surfing industry brands but also from a broader, collective industry perspective.

Doug Palladini, President of the Surf Industry Manufacturers Association (SIMA) and the Vice President and General Manager for the Americas, Vans, explores sustainability both from a SIMA perspective and that of Vans. From the latter's perspective, Doug highlights that supporting grass roots organisations, as well as educating SIMA's constituent members, are the principle way in which the organisation promotes sustainability. The role of education is emphasised again when it comes to achieving sustainability through consumer knowledge. Doug emphasises the importance of embedding sustainability within all aspects of the industry's operations as well as the need for experimentation and innovation in achieving sustainability. As Director of SIMA Humanitarian Fund and President of the International Surfing Association, Fernando, our second contributor to this chapter, is able to explore the broader contours of the surfing industry. As is the case with Doug, he also operates from an informed industry perspective as the founder of Reef. Fernando gets straight to the heart of sustainability by identifying the term as contested and ambiguous, arguing that it means many different things depending on the context. He goes on to examine how sometimes sustainability is achieved unintentionally using the example of recycled cardboard boxes for packaging. Fernando's role as the president of the ISA is to bring surfing to the Olympics; the notion of 'legacy' plays a central role in what sustainability will mean. Together, Doug and Fernando raise many interrelated issues that range from personal commitment to achieving sustainability to the areas that need improving within and beyond the surfing world.

2.1

Smart Business: Linking Environmental Health to Corporate Wellbeing

Doug Palladini

The Surf Industry Manufacturers Association (SIMA) is for all intents and purposes the trade organisation for the business of surfing: it promotes and fosters the growth of the surf industry. That's going to be very difficult to do if beaches are closed and it's not possible to surf in the sea. There is a direct correlation between the health of the beaches and the ocean and the health of our industry. We live and die by the health of the ocean, the health of the beaches around it and the health of the entire coastal environment. We don't have an industry without it. So, SIMA's job is to ensure that we remain committed to keeping beaches clean and keeping oceans uncontaminated and open for surfing. A big part of our mission at SIMA, is to give back to the environment that supports our industry. The two main ways we do this are: by supporting grass roots environmental organisations, and by educating our constituents.

Our members contribute through an annual fundraiser, The Waterman's Ball, to an environmental fund that has given hundreds of thousands of dollars each year, for the last 15 years, to dozens of groups that are fighting to keep the beaches and oceans clean. That's a really important part of what we do. Coastalwatch, Surfrider Foundation, those that protect the streams that flow into the ocean, are the ones doing great work on the ground. Our job is to support their efforts, to give them a platform and share their message with the 150 brands that SIMA represents and to ensure our members understand what they do and to make sure they have the resources they need to be successful in their activities. SIMA also takes on the role of educating brands on sustainable initiatives through our big industry gatherings. For example, we organise industry seminars known as a 'boot camps', and once a year we dedicate one of these to sustainable practice in our industry. We also run an annual 'Surf Summit' in Cabo San Lucas that includes sustainability education – we had the honour of Robert Kennedy as a guest speaker. He is a leader in the environmental movement and that was a standout example of what we do to enlighten and inspire our industry. We bring in the best minds to talk to our industry, to enlighten and educate about sustainable practice in manufacturing processes and, as a result, we've seen a dramatic change. All the inks, all the glues, all the fabrics are now being influenced by science in terms of sustainability. We still have a long way to go, but significant changes for the better have been made.

When it comes to the consumers and the kids who buy our brands, that's an ongoing process of education as well. My feeling is that the average American teenager thinks that sustainability is something that all brands should practice but it's something that should be built in. It's not something that they should have to pay extra for. It's not something that they should have to have marketed to them or pushed down their throat. They just expect us to build that into what we do. They appreciate it, but it's not like their seeking it out, demanding it, paying extra for it. They're looking to the brands to really lead them and incorporate sustainability into everything that we do. This has been an interesting process at Vans. Last year we hired a Director of Sustainability. The company that owns Vans, VF Corp, is committed to sustainability and has built a large infrastructure to make sure that we're building best practice into our manufacturing around the world. We're one of the biggest supply chains of any apparel company in the world and we've really had to start at the systemic level to build best practice.

From Vans' perspective, we're going to build sustainability into everything we do. I don't think you're going to see us select something small to put a green leaf on or make the logo green. We'll let people who want to know about it know about it, but we're not going to use it as a marketing focus. We're already well underway and we're assessing every single thing that we do, from the most basic vulcanised rubber to the canvases we use, everything in our apparel and accessories. Around the world, we are working on our factories and our offices and how we can make them sustainable. I don't think we'll be the brand that shouts it the loudest, but we will make a difference.

The biggest barrier to building sustainability into surfing today is education. There are still many people out there that think they can't do it because it's cost prohibitive, because their market won't appreciate it, that they can't do it because it doesn't fit with what their brand stands for, that there's an infrastructural cost that they can't absorb. The companies that have taken the time to fully understand what sustainability means to their business are the ones that have adopted it. I think we'll eventually reach a tipping point and you'll see it move quickly across the board. We need to get beyond 'greenwashing' and the hot air that gets blown around and figure out in a considered way how to build sustainability into our businesses. Our industry needs to come to understand that sustainability is not about charity, it's not about altruism, and it's not about philanthropy. It's about smart business. The impact of beach culture and how pervasive it is outside our specific industry will disappear if people can't look at the beach as something they aspire to and look forward to.

I see a lot of experimentation in the surf industry around sustainable practice and environmental responsibility. I also see a lot of experimentation in how the brands want to communicate their role in these. I think the experimentation is good and the brands will find their own path for absorbing sustainable practice into their companies. You might see false starts and trial and error – that's OK, that's healthy. These are brands trying to find their way. I don't think any of the brands in the surfing world want to be 'me too'. I think that's why you see the brands trying to carve out their own place. They're trying to find their own spot. Volcom and Sol Tech for example: they're trying to find their own path and reflect on who they are as a brand. I think that kind of innovation and experimentation is healthy. Ultimately, however, it must be embedded into the bigger business practices. If you're saying "I'm going to choose these few cool little products and make them sustainable, but I'm not going to touch t-shirts and boardshorts", when 90% of your business is T-shirts and boardshorts, it's not going to be meaningful in the long term. We welcome the little products and innovations but, long term, we hope it's applied to the biggest parts of business in the surf industry.

When it comes to professional surfing and the Association of Surfing Professionals (ASP), there's a pretty significant transformation happening. The ASP has been purchased by a new group and the governing body is going to become more of a professional sport organisation in future. I think this will mean a lot more cohesion around the world for professional surfing and hopefully the ability to speak with one voice everywhere we go. Surfing is not an onsite stick-and-ball type of thing with 50,000 people coming to every event. A lot of the best waves in the world are in reef passes that are on little islands and it's hard for fans to go there and see this. What we have instead is a virtual audience. Every time we run the Vans Triple Crown of Surfing we have 10 million webcast streams. What an audience! The audience is there but it's there only in a virtual sense. The opportunity to bring all the production together around those events, and bring some non-endemic brands in to create a more singular and global voice for surfing, is a tremendous opportunity for surfing as a whole. Surfing hasn't had the credit it deserves as a professional sport. The professional athletes who are among the best in the world aren't given the credit they deserve. I think the new face of ASP can help bring that level of cohesion to the sport of surfing.

The future of the surf industry is very, very bright. We have many young talented people who are passionate about our culture – the culture of the ocean. The culture of the beach is pervasive. You see it in TV commercials, in the advertising industry because of the powerful effect on people when they think about the ocean and beach culture – it makes them think about a life worth living. It makes them happy. We have a strong platform to build on, but what could potentially destroy it is losing focus on clean beaches and oceans that are open for everybody to enjoy. If we lose that we lose everything. As long as we keep our focus on providing beautiful coastlines and amazing waves all over the world, the surf industry will have a bright future.

2.2

Surfing, Sustainability, and the Pursuit of Happiness

Fernando Aguerre

Sustainability; the biggest challenge is that we first have to agree on what it is. Words are only concepts that represent meanings. The meaning of sustainability changes from culture to culture and it also has a lot to do with the industry or sector in which you work. For some, it may be the ability to preserve things the way they were when you found them. This is hard to achieve because most things are changed by interactions with human beings. For example, I read an interview with Yvon Chouinard recently and he drew a hard line on sustainability saying: "I don't believe sustainability exists, as human beings, we are not sustainable". In my opinion, the biggest challenge to sustainability is that we all need to agree on the need to stop, or severely slow down, the growth of the human population. This very desirable goal has not found the support needed amongst governments and religions, which are the biggest influencers in human behaviour around the world. As Chouirnad said, we are not sustainable, and the higher the population the less sustainable we become.

The sustainability of the sport of surfing itself depends on what you are talking about. If you're talking about people who feel like locals in Palos Verdes, sustainability might be not allowing even one more surfer in Palos Verdes. If you're talking about the tourism office in San Diego or Hawaii, sustainability for them is simply more people. The consequences don't matter as they can always build more hotels and expand the airport. Sustainability requires a lot of discussion before we can agree on what it is and how we will measure it. People that have access to resources will tend to support limits on the access of others to those resources in the name of sustainability. The people who do not have access will not support any restrictions. For example, the sustainability of a bar in Pacific Beach might be 100 patrons as per the fire department permit. For the guys that are outside in the line, the limit appears stupid because they want to get in for a cold beer. For the guys already in the bar that restriction is just fine, they don't mind, they're happy. Any topic we discuss, anywhere, will have two opposing forces and that is a key challenge to defining, measuring and achieving sustainability.

The Pursuit of Happiness and the Exploding Surfer Population

When I came to California in 1984, in La Jolla people only really surfed at the 'surf spots' like Windansea, Big Rock, Hospitals, and Horseshoe. Twenty guys out at those breaks is fine, thirty guys is somewhat fine, forty guys and you might get a wave. Fifty guys or more, you don't get waves. People become impatient, some people might even get angry or even violent. My way to deal with this situation was simple: every time the number of surfers was above what is sustainable for a fun surfing experience I would wait half an hour and 10%, 20% or 30% of the people would come in because they weren't getting any waves. Then the place would be sustainable again and it could take more people, and I will jump in the water.

Between the late '60s early '70s, until the late '80s early '90s, there were no longboards, no hybrids – basically everybody was shortboarding. Shortboards require a certain quality of wave to have fun. You can't really have fun on a one foot wave on a shortboard. In the early '90s, longboards made a comeback as lightweight longboards and this allowed people that weren't in good shape to surf. At some surf spots they weren't welcome because some longboarders weren't particularly well educated in wave sharing or in taking turns in the take-off areas. Some longboards went into the hands of wave hogs who tended to be older guys who saw their longboards as tools for world (water) domination. As a result, they were rejected by the shortboarders and tensions built up between the two groups.

As locals grew up and got older, instead of riding a 6'2" they moved up to a 7'0", a 7'6", 8'0" hybrids, then eggs, then the funboards and fishes which perform like longboards but they are shortboards. These are all boards that you can surf in lousy waves. Beachbreaks that were previously considered lousy waves that nobody wanted to surf became fun places to surf. The equipment change raised the level of what is sustainable in terms of how many people could surf in an area on a particular day, and which places were fun to surf. Additionally, at the shortboard level, around 15 years ago and increasingly in the last decade, shortboarders took to the air, manoeuvres that don't require a quality point break. So the waves are no longer just a place to go gliding and go from top to bottom, they are now also used as a ramp. To perform the greatest air reverse you don't really need a great point break, a hollow wave that closes out after two manoeuvres is a great ramp for flying. So, in those previously unsurfed lousy closeout waves, you now have beginners that never really had a place to surf because the 'surf spots' were all controlled by locals and if you're a beginner you don't get waves. And, on top of that, in any line up you have longboards, fun boards, fishes, younger kids, particularly the aircrew, that don't really need the point breaks and reefs. It's like the famous analogy where you take a jar and fill it with rocks – the jar appears full. Take sand and put it in the jar and shake, and the sand settles into the spaces between the rocks – the jar appears full. When you pour in water, it finds the spaces between the sand. The reality is that by having different equipment we have been able to raise the carrying capacity of the breaks.

One of the biggest problems I have with all the surfboard manufacturers and most surf retailing is that the promotion of the sport did not come along with any real promotion or education of etiquette in the water. Where do you paddle if you're paddling out and a wave comes? You don't go to the shoulder, despite your instinct to scratch for the shoulder to avoid getting hit by the lip, you go to the foam to keep out of the way of the riding surfer. All these things need to be taught, and I think for sure that would make the water a more enjoyable place. If you look at American shores, you would think we're crowded; there are ten times more surfers than 20 or 30 years ago. But for the most part, people don't drop in on each other, its not considered a cool thing to do. In terms of surfing, America has evolved a lot. Certain places around the world are not like that at all. Surfing there becomes very quickly unsustainable for the happiness and peacefulness of the surfers.

Hawaii is really rough because there are just too many people and the surf is so good for so little time. Pipeline is probably not sustainable any day of the year. It's not enjoyable unless you're Kelly or one of the top guys, or a very good local Hawaiian. Otherwise you're not really surfing, you're not taking off where you want to take off, you take off wherever they let you. In some Latin American countries, for example, surfing has been promoted so effectively in urban areas that most surf spots have become crowded. The difference between these places and the United States is that, in Latin America, there is less respect in the water and there are no drop-in rules enforced in many surf spots. It's like car traffic:

when you go to Latin America or Asia or Africa you realise that people drive at any speed because there are street signs but no cops. I'm not advocating cops in the water at all, but when we promote the sport around the world, we must also promote the rules of engagement and how we can make surfing enjoyable on a sustainable basis for the largest amount of people. This means respecting each other while looking for waves.

In my 2013 SIMA Waterman of the Year acceptance speech, I cite one of the articles of the Declaration of Independence – the unalienable right to the pursuit of happiness. When we go surfing we are pursuing happiness. We are there to relax, to disconnect from the tensions of civilization. If you go to some places, say to Tourmaline in San Diego, for the most part it is about wave sharing. It's like Waikiki, if you go to Canoes or Queens there's not really any priority, its just about people surfing together. In these places wave sharing is not only possible, it's desirable. In other places it's not only impossible, its risky. Wave sharing at Big Rock in San Diego, would be super-dangerous, at PB Point it would not be OK, at Tourmaline it is absolutely fine. I think these are things that we need to explore if we want to have sustainable surfing. We need to ensure the stoke and happiness of people in the water. If we reach a level where we're not happy when we're surfing, we're in a bad place. I was a surf pioneer in some areas of many countries, and I've seen them go from nobody surfing, to places where the locals became so nasty that you can't enjoy surfing there. The locals can't even enjoy surfing there – nobody does.

Sustainability and Manufacturing: Reflections on the Development of Reef
At the beginnings of Reef, I don't think that any one of us thought specifically about sustainability, it came as a result of seeking economically driven efficiencies. For example, I was a surf industry pioneer in using recycled cardboard boxes. But, honestly, I wasn't thinking about the environment. As a business guy, I was thinking that I could get overprints much cheaper than regular brand new boxes. I was shipping Reef sandals in reused boxes that had 'Washington Apples' on the outside. People would ask me why I was doing this, I said these boxes are cheaper and you're just going to throw them away when the sandals reach you. In the first year of reusing boxes, our box costs dropped from US$400,000 to US$250,000 and at the same time we shipped 30-40% more stock than the year before. We effectively cut our expenses in half. For the first 10 years of Reef, Reef sandals came in all sorts of different boxes – we were very Latin American in our approach to sustainability. It was coming from a place of economics for

us, but at the same time we were saving trees. We did that all the way until the company grew so big that, for logistical reasons, we needed standard boxes for a standard conveyor belt so the boxes could be taped by a machine. By then I was a committed environmentalist, so I was doubly bummed out that we were not reusing boxes and we were also spending more on boxes.

The footwear industry is one of the dirtiest industries that exists; it was a lot of chemicals and a lot of dyes. When you make the soles of sandals you get a lot of leftovers. In the process of looking at those piles of waste rubber, we discovered that we could recycle it by bringing it back into the mixer. New sheets could not be made of 100% recycled materials, but we were able to recycle all our offcuts and cut our rubber expenses by 10 or 15%. It was great for the environment and it cut our costs. Sustainability is not just the right thing to do for the environment but it's also the right thing to do for financial reasons. You could do well *and* do good at the same time. It's beautiful when it happens! Every time you leave from the house and all your lights are off, you're doing a service for the world, but also for your own utility expenses. We've all had to reassess the ways in which we relate to the resources around us.

Yvon Chouinard is a leader for sustainability and at one point he decided that he would make all T-shirts from organic cotton, regardless of the cost. If people didn't buy them because of the higher price, then his way of thinking was that he wouldn't sell T-shirts. That's the benefit of being a private owner of a company. With public owners, the board of directors is going to call you and say, "You can't do that mister, we need to sell more T-shirts". However, now that companies such as Walmart are starting to recycle and sell organic cotton shirts, it's clear that we're not alone when we try to make things better. There is a big shift towards sustainability even with some of these big publically owned companies, but it doesn't happens by an Act of God. It's a result of public pressure. A good example from the hospitality business is in hotels around the world you have the choice to reuse your towel. Due to public pressure, the hotels realised that it was good for the earth and also good for business. This is what I call 'do good and do well'. You can have both.

Sustainability, the ISA, and the Pursuit of Happiness

My goal and the ISA's goal are to promote the sport of surfing around the world. Half of what we do is in Western countries, in Europe and North America, and also in Japan and Australia – the rich countries of the world. But we're also promoting the sport in countries that are anything but rich, in Latin America,

Asia, and now in Africa. We promote the use of waves as a resource for pursuing happiness with the locals. It can also ultimately help to establish and drive a new tourism industry. The most important thing is that we bring the sport to new people along with the knowledge of how to use it as a tool for happiness. Otherwise a surf spot that is empty today, in 10 years will be all brawls and fights in the water because we never established a right of way in the water and how it works.

If you give a six year old a knife you have to be very careful to teach him how the knife is used, how sharp it is, not to touch the sharp edge with your finger. In that way the knife is used for good and not for playing with his siblings and maybe killing one of them. If that happens, the knife is not guilty; the person that provides the knife without instructions or education is to blame. At the end of the day, everything good that happens in life has to do with somebody helping somebody else. Whenever something bad happens is because of the opposite. With that in mind, the ISA has a strong sense of stewardship for the sport. All stakeholders in the sport, it doesn't matter who we are, have an obligation to be stewards of the sport. Not just to deliver surf goods to be consumed, but also to deliver the culture, the good parts of it: why we do it, how we do it, and how it can continue to be a great experience rather than deteriorate to the point that it becomes negative. I know what the sport has done for me, I've seen the happiness it brings people all over the world and I want to continue to share that in a personal way, but also as the leader of the ISA.

The Olympic movement has its own definition of sustainability. It includes 'legacy'. It used to be that there was often no use for the massive capital projects like stadiums, highways or railway stations once the games were over. There was no legacy. The International Olympic Committee (IOC) is very big on legacy and they want proposals from potential host cities to demonstrate not just that they can stage the Olympic Games, but also what the investment is going to do for the country over a long period of time. So sustainability is not only about what happens at the Games, but also what happens after the Games.

In the case of Olympic Surfing, in some places we could have surfing on naturally produced waves, but, for the most part the quality of the waves that we now require at world championship and Olympic level would make that impossible. In the beginning, surfing was done on 100-pound wooden boards and it was all about what you did on the board. Now it's all about what you do with the board and that requires the quality of the waves to be much better. Other sports have also evolved in terms of the quality of courts and fields as well as equipment like bicycles, javelin and bows for archery. As a result, I think surfing in the Olympics will require man-made waves and that these constructions will create their own legacy.

Surf park technologies are unrecognisable from 20 years ago when water was lifted and dropped to create a tsunami kind of wave. Foil technologies, like Wavegarden, are very energy efficient. Maybe this is because they need to make the waves cheaper so people actually want to build them as a business, but the end result is that they are less taxing on the environment. Once you have a body of water with a reliable perfect wave, that becomes an incredible training ground, not just for Olympic competitors, but for people learning to surf. There will always be purists who will say, "No way, if you want to surf, come to the ocean". That's all fine but if you're living in the industrialised world, only wealthy people live by the ocean. It means for example that there are almost no African American surfers because most African Americans don't live by the ocean. I think if we have a man-made wave in Atlanta, there is a chance that a 'Tiger Woods of surfing' will emerge in the next five or ten years. This falls neatly under the Olympic goals of using sport to integrate culturally and economically diverse groups.

My number one role at the ISA is not to bring surfing to the Olympics but to promote the sport so that people who don't know how much fun it is can enjoy it. I was talking to the Minister for Sport for Ecuador about two months ago about having swimming lessons, not in the pool but in the sea so people can body surf and swim in the sea without fear. Many Ecuadorians live by the sea but they're scared of it. They perceive it as a deadly place where people drown. I think that bringing surfing to the masses will be an amazing chance to share happiness with people who have the waves, but don't have the means because they don't know how to body surf. Jacques Cousteau said that you need to know something to love it and to defend it. The more people that know the ocean, the more defenders and soldiers of the ocean we will have. It might sound selfish because I'm a surfer, but the day we screw up the ocean we screw up ourselves as a species. As surfers, we literally submerge ourselves in the ocean; we are completely exposed to the ocean. If the ocean is sick we get sick, we are the guinea pigs of us. The more human beings become friends with the ocean, the better it will be for our planet and for mankind. And that is a good reason to work hard as a volunteer as the President of ISA.

Personal Intensity, Sustainability, Philanthropy and Philosophy
I put energy and passion into everything I do. You can be lukewarm in your approach to life, or you can be intense: I'm intense. I want to be a force of goodness in the surfing world, and I want everybody to know that they can also be a force of good. I want everybody to help. I want everybody to be affected. I want everybody to be pissed off at the way things are in many areas. I've been lucky and have been able to be effective in many different ways. I helped Blake, the founder of Tom's Shoes, whom I met shortly after he started his wonderful company. I helped him with ideas because I came from Reef. I was basically advising him for free. I'm not claiming responsibility for his success, but I was there offering help to a guy who for me, was figuring out a different way of doing business.

I was raised in a house with a very right wing dad. My father came from a wealthy family, one of the founding families of Argentina. They took the land from the Indians and sent in the settlers. Not the most honourable thing to do, but it was the way things were done 150 years ago all over the world. On my mother's side, my great grandfather was an anarchist who came to Argentina from Italy, trying to build a world where equality and equal opportunities weren't just nice words, but a reality. Hence, I am a practical idealist who is always trying to do the right thing for the greatest number of people – always – whatever it is. Sometimes this is done through environmental causes, sometimes through humanitarian causes. Sometimes it's going and sitting with the President of Nicaragua and talking about surfing and how to develop tourism in a country like Nicaragua, while warning him about building 10 storey buildings by the ocean.

As human beings, we all have the right and the opportunity to add our grain of sand, which might be the size of a house, in the size of a grain of sand, to the effort to build a better sand dune for everybody. I approach everything with hope, but hope is never my plan. Hope is my fuel my plans are very practical. At 16, I was organising parties for the students association in Argentina, so I know how to throw nice parties. If you can have a good party and people are excited, then people will give money to good causes. So everything I do, I try to do it so it's fun for everybody, me included. The problem with a lot of NGOs is that they are boring. People like to be excited. The UCSD Cancer Luau recently named me Honorary Chair, I was the second Honorary Chair in 20 years. I opened my house to all these people that surf, so everyone was very appreciative of my collection of surfboards and they could see the surfing culture of the world in my home. When I was asked to give a speech, I talked about happiness. I said the best antidote for cancer is the way you live your life: what you eat, how you sleep, who you sleep with, the thoughts you have, the feelings in your heart. It goes back to the pursuit of happiness and the founding fathers in the USA Declaration of Independence. I can't be happy if I'm only accumulating wealth. Happiness is when you discover good ways of giving it back. It must use the tools I have due to my material success to reach out to people. That's why I can sleep six to seven hours a night very happily.

I started riding waves when I was three and standing up on surfboards when I was 11. I'm 55, so I have been surfing for 44 years. I have taught countless friends and family to surf and many others that I don't know as a consequence of what I do and have been doing for decades. For example, in the '70s, I led a fight to lift the ban on surfing by the military dictatorship in Argentina and a year later I got surfing legalised. In one year, Argentina's surfing population went from 200 to 5000 people. The common thread between all surfers is that it's great to surf, but each surfer knows that surfing alone is not enjoyable. We need other human beings whether it's a friend or a family member or just a kid you met that day in the lineup. It's great to get waves, but we must also give some waves. I ride longboards now and when I go out, I don't go out to hog the point. Normally I paddle halfway out and get a couple of insiders and then go all the way out and wait for a set. I don't take a wave before all the guys who were out before me, have all caught a wave or have had the chance to paddle for a wave, or unless they say "Just go". This is an attitude that we can all have and polish. As animals we are selfish, we eat all we can eat until we can't eat anymore. Being human means that if we have enough food we might want to share it with someone that doesn't have enough. That's what makes us different from most other animals and to me, that is the beauty of how we can all work together for a sustainable surfing future and a better surfing future.

Fernando (left) and Doug (right) at the 24th annual SIMA Waterman's Ball in 2013 where Fernando received the Waterman of the Year award.
(Courtesy of ISA and Shawn Parkin)

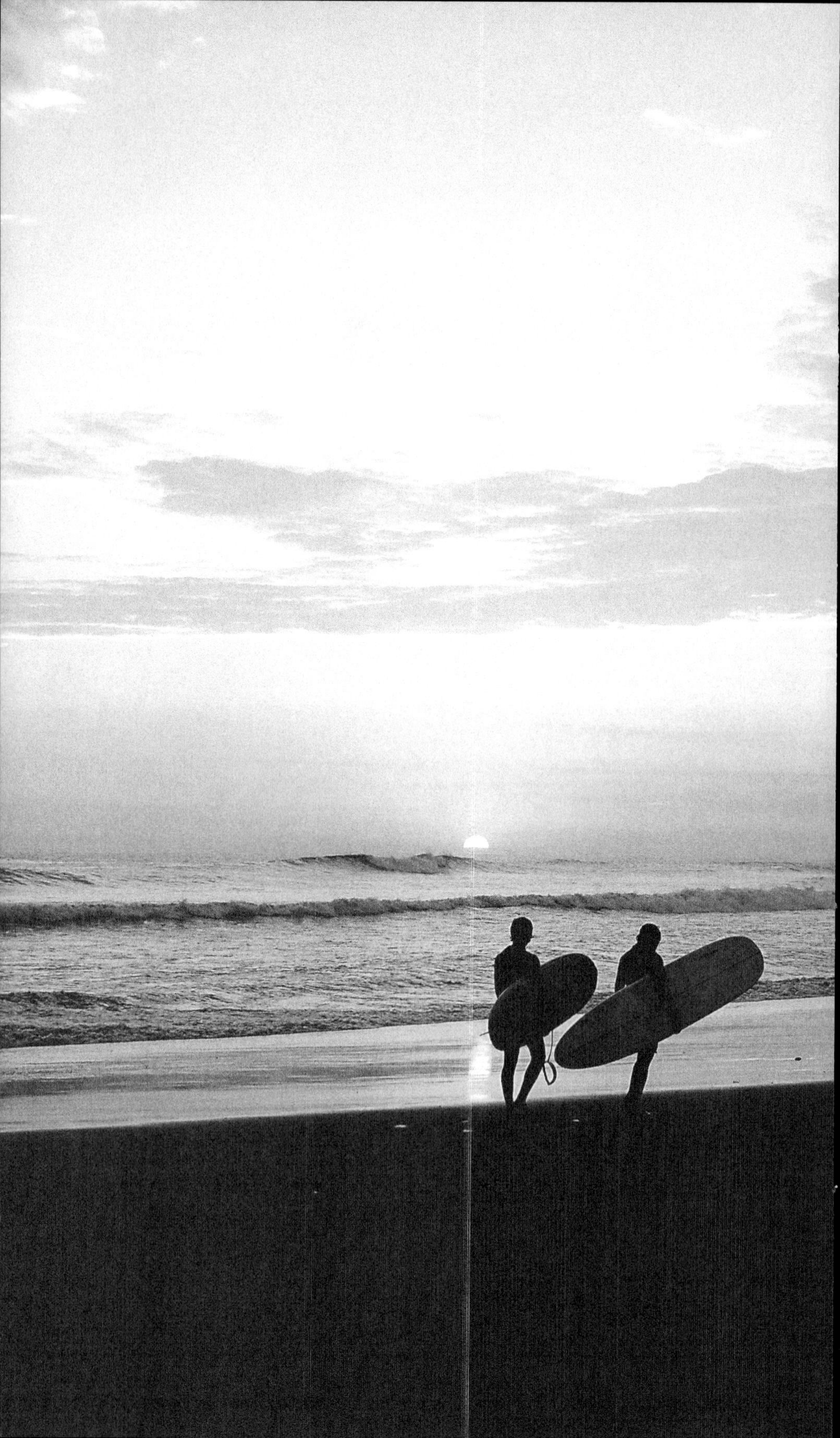

Chapter Three
Industry

Chapter Two gave a macro level analysis of the surf industry's interpretation of sustainability allowing Chapter Three to drill down into the operationalization of sustainability at the corporate level from a CEO/Executive Chairman position, to Vice Presidents of sustainability and philanthropic foundations, and a pro-surfer with strong industry ties and a strong environmental consciousness. Contributors in this chapter discuss the various models in which sustainability should be integrated into the governance structures of multi-national corporations and beyond.

The architecture of the surfing industry is complex and evolving as we speak. For example, Quiksilver has appointed a new CEO, Andy Mooney, with backgrounds in Nike and Disney, corporations that have a track record in sustainability and bring a different dynamic to the surfing world. Mooney contracted the focus of the business' philanthropic foundation and decentralized oversight of sustainability initiatives. The broader landscape of the corporate world, where non-surfing corporates are now entering the surfing space, has profound implications for the future of surfing. For example, in 2012, ZoSea Media Group bought out the ASP World Tour and, by utilizing an executive team of non-surfing sports media specialists from mainstream arenas like the NFL, Fox Sports, and ESPN, they are radically changing the nature of how the world tour will be run and broadcast.

Their hope is to bring non-endemic brands and industries into professional surfing and encourage massive growth in professional surfing viewership. This raises questions about how sustainability of surfing will be impacted by these changes and how it can and should be incorporated into the daily operations of surfing corporations. This year, the ASP has officially morphed into the World Surf League, "overseeing the key product areas of the elite men's and women's World Championship Tours, the Qualifying Series (QS), the Big Wave Tour, the Big Wave Awards, the World Longboard Championships and the World Junior Championships". Our contributors are able to provide very unique insights into what sustainability is in the industry and how it could be integrated and implemented. It goes without saying that Bob McKnight's insight as the former CEO and current Executive Chairman of Quiksilver provides, for the first time and at the highest level, a unique perspective on what responsibilities the surfing industry has in terms of sustainability.

Jeff Wilson offers a different perspective on sustainability governance and how it should be reflected in corporate organizational structures. On one hand, an argument is made that sustainability has devolved to the operational components of the organisation where embedded expertise can achieve the greatest benefits through best practices and efficiency. An alternative perspective suggests that simply embedding sustainability at the component levels is not enough and a higher, umbrella regulatory sustainability layer needs to be implemented.

Derek Sabori charts his journey with Volcom from working for the company for free to becoming Senior Director of Sustainability over a period of 17 years. Derek explores the challenges of building a sustainability department in a large multifaceted organisation, the leadership challenges, and the need for a collaborative approach as well as 'the grilled cheese model' for achieving this. This idea of providing heat from the top and the bottom to achieve sustainability is something that resonates strongly throughout this book and is an important insight into how transitions may occur.

Following on from Derek, Rob Machado and Jessica Toth's contribution presents a viewpoint that covers multiple areas. Machado himself sits at a nexus of complementary and competing viewpoints. He is one of the world's most famous surfers and, as such, a celebrity with huge power and impact. He is also part of the industry structure and thereby perpetuates an industry ethos. However, he is also a committed environmentalist with his own philanthropic organization, the Rob Machado Foundation. Rob and Jessica offer a benchmark of the industry progress on sustainability so far by presenting industry insights and new knowledge. They offer a balanced commentary and recognise the power of celebrity in influencing behaviour and the capacity for positive change. Indeed these issues are raised in the final contribution of this chapter from environmental journalist, Todd Woody.

Todd's contribution begins to explode the stereotype of the surfer and the need for the mainstream media to more effectively represent the cross section of the population that actually surf. Todd highlights the relationship between mainstream and surfing media and how this feeds into every aspect of surfing life and culture. Todd emphasises that breaking through these stereotypes represents overcoming a significant barrier and achieving a transition to sustainability.

3.1

Quiksilver and Sustainability: The View From the Top

Bob McKnight

Sustainability wasn't even on the radar for us when we started Quiksilver in the US in 1976 – we just wanted to build good board shorts. We built them out of 100% cotton, but sustainability wasn't really an issue, our thing was just building really good shorts for surfing, looking after our accounts, marketing our shorts well, and trying to survive financially.

Our sustainability initiatives started when Jeff Wilson came to work for us. Jeff is an old high school friend of mine, he'd come out of a stint in the travel world with Delta Airlines and we wanted to form an in-house travel agency. Jeff's first job was to develop our travel department, encompassing all the corporate travel, hotels, car rentals, pick ups, drop offs, the whole thing. Through this work, we figured we could save 20%, which we did, so it worked. Then the second job was to establish Outdoor Adventure Travel. Families wanted to book customised adventure trips. Surf camps and boat trips were starting to happen. Now there are camps from Nicaragua to China and all through Indonesia – it's all happening. Jeff spotted early that there is a market of older surfers, with disposable income and family/kids who want to get away from cold water and crowds. These exotic escape surf trips are fantastic and in demand.

Jeff's degree in environmental practices meant he was trying to educate us at the same time that Yvon Chouinard's ideas were coming out: the earth has a problem, so all of us should band together and do the best we can to save the planet in individual ways. Jeff had always talked in those terms, but we didn't pay much attention because we were trying to run our business. Soon it became apparent globally, so we began to align ourselves with saving the planet to see what we could do. My sister started the Quiksilver Foundation, geared towards raising money for grants in science, education, kids, the ocean, the environment, and other organisations with aligned environmental and humanitarian missions. It was all grounded in those five or six areas.

Over the past 10 years we've given away millions of dollars and product. My sister left after five years, so we had to re-align the structure. We put Jeff in charge of travel and sustainability (seeing as he has a passion for it, which included the Foundation). He was the ears and eyes on best practices for product development, sourcing, freight, warehouses (packaging, hangers and boxes), and our facilities (with light bulbs, recycling and all that stuff). Ryan Ashton ran the Foundation because that became a full-time job with screening applications, grant requests, writing cheques, and running the fundraising side (the golf tournament and other events we do to raise money). The foundation's budget is about US$2-2.5 million a year. It's successful and it's respected.

Quiksilver Travel saved us a lot of money on corporate travel. Outdoor Adventure Travel was great, although it began to change. Many people contact island camps or rental condos directly. They find cheap tickets online and bypass the surf travel companies. We eventually shut down Quiksilver Travel. The surf travel business has grown in terms of volume but, from a surf travel agency perspective, it is receeding quickly because of the trend towards organising your own adventure surf travel online. It's a struggle for a lot of these companies now. When people go direct, they feel like they are saving money and they enjoy the personal planning. Maybe they are, maybe they're not, but they feel like they are saving money because they are bypassing the filter that gets a cut. Quiksilver Outdoor Adventure Travel was a brand exercise, to an extent, so hopefully people would have a good time.

Sustainability is going well. We got the facilities under control and started adapting better practices, globally. A member of staff in Europe and in Australia reported to Jeff. We are all trying to operate within best practice on product design – for instance we're using crushed plastic bottles, leading to hundreds of thousands of boardshorts. Now all our designers think about sustainability, from materials to hang tags, hangers, packaging and shipping: it's all considered. Our sourcing agency is programmed to thinking through how we can do a better job. We're part of Quest, which is the factory system that has a policing agency attached to it to ensure Quiksilver is in compliance and that best practice for the environment is factored into the running of the factories. Mervin Manufacturing completely changed how they make snowboards to be completely free of environmental problems; there's no dust or fibreglass and they invented an entirely organic surfboard.

Our CEO is Andy Mooney. With him, we've spent a lot of time reviewing the company, thinking about what's great about it and what's wrong with it.

We know what we need to fix, what we can fix now, what we can fix later. The main thing is that we have too many moving parts. For a hundred days we went round the world and Andy checked in to every part of the company, met with every manager, deciding what he thinks is right, what he thinks is wrong. The theme of our mantra now is 'focus'. We have too many brands, too many SKUs (clothing styles) and too many projects. Everything is in triplicate because we have centres of design and operations in Europe, the US, and Australia.

Since 2006, the company has struggled with profitability, so we need to turn Quiksilver around. Now we have five or six people watching over sustainability and green issues, rather than one. We hire people who understand that sustainability is important and care about it. These are modern people who get it and they do all they can, when they can, to watch over all things environmental. We have confronted the fact that there are certain areas in the business where you can't avoid having a negative environmental impact. We make wetsuits, surfboards, eye wear, plastic sandals, etc. We try our best, but these products are what consumers want. We're a public company, for profit. I can't afford to give away 1% for the planet right now, I have to keep the 1% in the company so that we sustain and survive. Our current approach to sustainability is really a philosophy that filters down through the organisation to make sure we are all speaking the same language and applying ourselves. We are doing everything we can to be good corporate citizens.

Where we consume the most is in the packaging: the plastics, the cardboard and the movement of product. Those are the big-ticket items for us and technology comes into play in this area. There are new hangers and packaging, our vendors know that we want best practice in supplies. For example, there are freight ships now that use natural gas and wind for their energy. We're receptive to these new technologies, we're as on top of it as we can be. To be clear though, we're not spending our capital and buying machines ourselves, our job is to challenge suppliers to discover what is available to help us be greener.

Some years ago, surf industry manufacturers started using organic cotton and crushed bottles and organic denim. These products were more expensive and the consumer didn't buy them. If our organic denim jeans were priced at US$90 and a standard denim pair was US$60, the consumer would go buy the US$60 pair. Why? They either didn't care as much about saving the planet as we thought or the recession means they can't afford it, or they don't see the value in paying US$90 versus US$60. Everybody rushed to the table thinking that this was really important to the consumer. It might have been important in the mind of the consumer, but it didn't translate to their spending. We all had to take a step backwards, apply best environmental practices to less of the line and make sure we covered ourselves. Now we are slowly but surely raising the consciousness of the consumer so they will buy these things, because they know it's better for the environment. Changing weather patterns may build a sense of urgency. At the same time we're starting to see some relief from the suppliers who are reducing some costs, so it's finding its own financial level and therefore true wholesale and retail values.

As fast as we want to get to it, there's a lot to learn about what is going on out there. We can't sacrifice our whole business on a conscience. We have also learned not to get on a soapbox to brag about the things we do, because someone will always say, "So Mr McKnight, you have some hangars out there that are made of plastic. You make sunglasses and surfboards". Then we're guilty and defensive; we prefer to admit that we're guilty, but know that we will try our best.

The transition to sustainability is happening, but at a pace appropriate for the market. More and more younger consumers have heard about it and they want to make a difference. Sustainability will increasingly become a greater part of consumerism. By that I mean our consumerism: surf, skate, snow, 14-20 year old consumers. I think that manufacturers will have to continue to do the best they can, from design to merchandising, to freight, to sourcing, to warehousing, to shipping to accounts, inside Quicksilver buildings. We also need to reach out and support other groups that share the same mission. In 1990, urban runoff was closing beaches, we realised that even beaches aren't safe. Depleting ozone increased the risk of skin cancer. Further negative publicity made people think, "To hell with the beach, we're out of here". If we don't have oceans and safe beaches, we don't have an industry anymore.

3.2

Transitions to Sustainability: 'If Not Us, Then Who?'

Jeff Wilson

We live, breathe and sometimes die in the water and on the mountains for lifestyle passions we love. The fact is there is no one better than us to lead the work of Sustainable Development. Let's start at a pretty elevated level, taking a look at the macro dynamics as I see them. Although the surf industry has started driving sustainability into its operating language and behavior, there has been little demonstration of ongoing, long term progress towards that. Certainly some great work has been done in various areas by certain companies with energy, waste, water, product and philanthropy. But as an industry on the whole, with a consolidated effort, framework and overarching mantra producing measureable results across the spectrum of company operations, it has been lacking. And I'm not trying to single out the industry as slacking. There are many industries exactly the same or even lagging. But the issue here is transitioning our industry to one of sustainability leadership.

When I led the global sustainability initiatives for Quiksilver, Roxy and DC Shoes, I was surprised by this lack of commitment to lead. For an industry so dependent on a healthy climate, mountains and oceans, I did not expect the obstacles I encountered, none more so than the attempt with Roian Atwood at Sole Technology and Derek Sabori at Volcom to form an industry collaborative we ended up calling 'The Sustainability Collective'.

We worked for over a year on a value proposition, organisation structure, budget and funding and we received positive feedback from almost everyone in the space. But as we neared implementation, there was no movement to step up with resources to make it happen. In contrast, the Outdoor Industry, through the Outdoor Industry Association Sustainability Working Group (OIA SWG), committed to this work in 2007 and has been actively involved with many work streams to deliver information, education, tools and resources to the hundreds of brands that are members of the OIA. Last year, the OIA joined the Sustainable Apparel Coalition and the two groups are working together to co-develop sustainability initiatives for clothing, footwear and equipment retailers, brands and suppliers representing close to 50% of the global production. Both are exceptional examples of segments of our industry not only leading on their own but collaborating for the benefit of everyone. Why is this not happening in the surf industry? There's no single reason, it's complex and complicated. There's no one in any of our stakeholder groups that would advocate for environmental or social harm. We all want social, environmental, and economic wealth and well-being – but it gets complicated.

Right now (and I think since the downturn) the industry has been whipsawed by economic dynamics that it was not fully prepared for. The competitive dynamics of maufacturing have changed and now include more mainstream markets with very large players leaving the surf industry with a cost disadvantage in the marketplace. Similarly the retail distribution landscape has changed with much larger, big box style players serving much more price sensitive customers. In a way, it's a sort of race to the bottom. It is hard for a Quiksilver tee to sell at US$22 retail when one can be had at Target for half that.

So what does all that really mean? This is treacherous territory, but I think the 'elephant in the room' is capitalism. Now let me state very clearly, I am a big advocate for and supporter of capitalism. I think it's proven over the last 30 years, in particular, to be the theory, concept, philosophy, ideology, economic system, whatever you want to call it, that elicits the very best of humanity: free will, creativity, innovation, independence, drive, motivation, aspiration, and economic well-being. These are not small attributes. However, as we've known for centuries, it is hardly a perfect system. Certainly, part of the role of government has evolved to address the liabilities and shortcomings of capitalism. We've all come to know and love/hate this role, but it is undeniably needed.

As we look to address the growing environmental pitfalls of capitalism, from a sustainable development perspective, where are the gaps? Again, complicated, but I think the fundamental gap is in the economic concept known as 'externalities', in this case, negative externalities. Capitalism has evolved thus far that the basic natural capital that our biosphere is composed of – air, land, water – are viewed largely as commons, pretty much free for the taking. This has been known for centuries, dating back to European shared pasturelands the destruction of which from overgrazing is know as 'The Tragedy of the Commons'. In the last 100 years of massive economic development and industrialization, capitalism did not evolve to factor in the external costs of our now entrenched model of 'take, make, use, waste' production and consumption. So the reality we are grappling with is 1) transforming capitalism to view these externalities as costs that need to be priced into the economics and 2) somehow figure out a way to price them and account for them financially. Carbon is a perfect example and it's very evident how challenging that has been on both of these.

That is an incredibly simplified discussion of the topic, but I believe it is at the heart of limiting progress towards sustainable development in a more mainstream way, and for the surf industry, again being whipsawed by more basic fundamentals of economics, an even bigger challenge to embrace. Nonetheless, some progress is being made. We read more and more about capitalism 2.0. Work has been done to establish an alternative legal designation of incorporation called the 'B-Corporation', where governance is legally protected to pursue not only financial wealth to shareholders but also economic, social health and wellbeing. We hear about the notion of 'shared values' in corporations. There are efforts being undertaken to attempt valuations of 'ecosystem services' through natural capital accounting. The Sustainability Accounting Standards Board has been founded to set standards for that kind of accounting, among other elements of sustainability reporting.

In closing on this somewhat esoteric macro level discussion of the impediments to the expansion of sustainable development in the industrial sector, my belief is that it is time for an evolution in capitalism. I see this occurring through both regulatory and marketplace dynamics, where the incorporation of values beyond short term financial gain to shareholders/ownership leads to a broader notion of wealth, capturing economic, social and environmental wellbeing over the long term. Clearly, some of this transition is occurring right now with the hard work of many committed sustainability professionals in multiple stakeholder groups. But there is much left to be done in this transformation. Seeing the surf industry solve its current economic challenges and begin to take a leadership role in this work would be extremely pleasing.

The engagement of a company with sustainability really stems from leadership. If a company's culture is built from the top down to incorporate the values and goals of sustainability, you mostly find things get done. Organisations are established, people are hired, systems are put in place, goals are set and measured and results are incentivised and rewarded. Behaviours follow leadership and cultural values. In an organisation where there are few or mixed messages and clearly higher priorities, trying to transform a culture to embrace sustainability becomes a unique challenge. Again, people throughout the organisation are evaluated and rewarded on how well they achieve the priorities they are given.

The properties/facilities manager is tasked with making sure the heating and AC are working and that IT has enough power to run the computing systems. Analyzing and evaluating renewable energy sources or dual flush toilets is not going to be at the top their list of priorities. Same for the IT team, the designers, the sourcing team and the retail crew etc. It's the rare individual who is willing to tackle, undirected by their boss, the subject of building elements of sustainability into their working world. So this is what you navigate on a daily basis, trying to build awareness, engagement, interest and action as best you can, knowing that you are making progress. This is the story of sustainability professionals in most corporations. You have good days and less-than-good days.

One element of the effort to build the values and culture that I think is way underutilised is athlete involvement. That's very powerful and in my view can drive a lot of change everywhere, at the consumer level, the retail level and internally at the product and operations levels. I think if a bunch of the top tier riders took some time to understand what it takes to build the boardshorts they wear, not to mention wetsuits, boards, tees, etc., and became advocates for lowering environmental and social footprints, that would be very powerful. This is what Conrad Anker, the head athlete for The North Face, has done and he's become a significant spokesperson for TNF on Sustainability. I understand it's tricky for the athletes, but I believe if the direction could be facilitated in a positive way by them, the industry would be more motivated to respond and change.

Unquestionably, the financial health of the surf industry is of paramount concern. You have to make payroll, pay suppliers, etc. etc. But what are all too often overlooked are the contributions sustainable development can make towards that. The perception is that these initiatives cost money and have low rates of return. The reality is that many of the initiatives save money and with certain capital expenditures have better rates of return than those made on riskier business ventures. The language of sustainability and the value it brings to a company needs to be translated into the language of business, from risk management, to efficiency, to product and materials innovation to brand reputation. We need to think about these dynamics as opportunities rather than problems. I think once those linkages are made at the governance levels of companies, then we'll see cultures, systems, priorities and outcomes change. I'm optimistic about the future and our ability to transform our production and consumption behavior in a way that will enable people and the multitudes of other species we're so dependent on to flourish for a long time to come.

So, in closing, what would I most like to see the surf industry start to tackle more earnestly in transitioning to sustainability? Through the work that's been done by leading companies in clothing, footwear and equipment industry, we have come to learn that the large majority of social and environmental impacts reside in the product supply chain, from raw materials through intermediary processing to final assembly and packaging. It is with this knowledge that I've come to focus most of my attention on where the greatest impacts and therefore the greatest opportunities are: the product supply chain.

For the surf industry, the transitions to sustainability rest in developing a much deeper and broader knowledge of materials and the manufacturing processes and its impact. This, most importantly, requires the science of lifecycle analysis to fully understand those impacts on the environment and then to move the supply chain to materials, processes, and technology that continue to reduce consumption, waste and emission impacts. Since the product supply chains for the clothing and footwear industry, including surf, are largely broad, overseas, complex and often shared, the ability for any one firm to transform the supply chain is very limited. As a result, a significant level of industry collaboration is needed to achieve the learning and move the supply chain needle to accomplish broader and faster sustainability goals and objectives. This is the transition I would like the surf industry to undertake. This applies to every product we use from boardshorts to wetsuits, surfboards to leashes, surf racks to board bags.

Am I optimistic? I'll say cautiously optimistic. I believe it's a rough road ahead as the surf industry struggles to right the ship economically. I think we'll get there, both from a macro and micro standpoint, especially as other apparel and footwear companies pioneer and forge ahead. But I have to admit, it sure seems like we should be leading the charge.

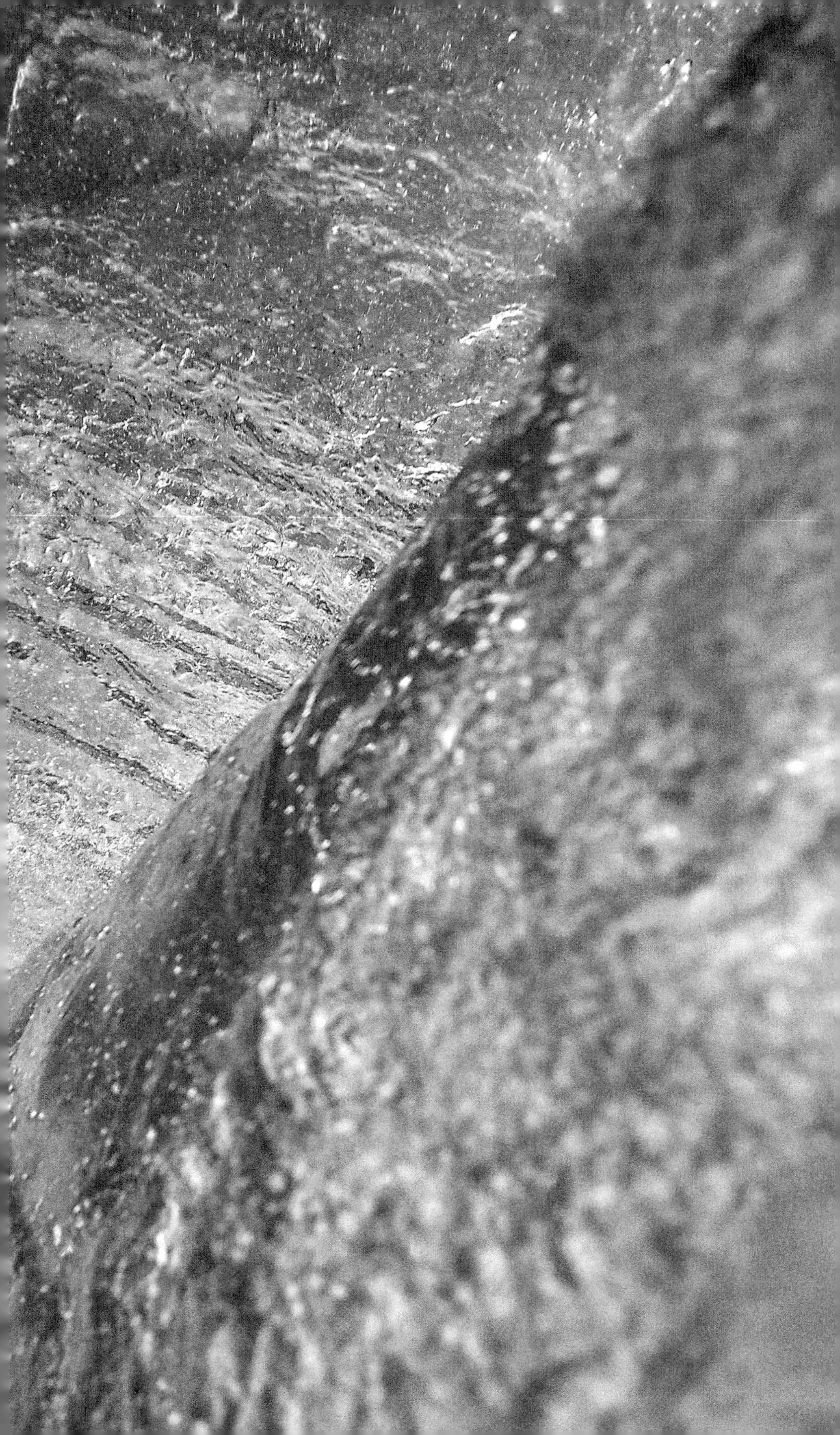

3.3

Transitions to Sustainability

Derek Sabori

When I walked into Volcom for the first time, back in 1996, I was instantly hooked. There was something in the air that made being there easy and, while it was a great summertime gig, I never imagined that things would come to where they are now. Seventeen years there? I wouldn't have guessed it, and not in a million years did I think that I'd have the word 'sustainability' in my title.

I grew up outside the Velcro Valley – about 30 miles outside it – and while these days, it doesn't seem that far, being a kid learning how to surf late in life (hey, back then, learning to surf at 12 was late in life!) and having to convince one of our Moms to make the trek from the North-East Orange County area down to Newport or Huntington Beach, it seemed a world away. A world that I wasn't sure I'd ever really be a part of – those of you that grew up outside the Action Sports industry, looking in, will know what I'm talking about.

It's not to say, however, that I didn't have my chance. I still regret that I hated sand so much and was too scared of the 'deep ocean' to take my very 70's 'hip uncle', who was living beach-side in San Clemente, up on the offer to go for a paddle and a little surf lesson when I was seven or eight years old. On many occasions, I refused the offer and begged my Mom to not make me go with him. Now, at forty-something I look back and shake my head. There are days too, when I'm out in the water and I might put a turn in that feels like something, which in my mind might look good if caught on film, and think… wow, I wonder what could have been? Who knows? What if I had caught the bug that early on? All right, all right, no chance, I'm sure, but hey a little daydream of life on the Tour is good for the soul. Regardless, I'm quite happy that the bug eventually caught me, but it wasn't until five or six years later that I was introduced to the pure stoke of surfing. I do have to admit something. The love of the ocean, the water, the journey – none of that is what brought me to surfing. Those are the things I learned along the way, but industry is what brought me to surfing. The look of it, the style, the music that I associated with it, the girls – that's what pulled me in. In fact, I think I can narrow it down to one best friend that I made in 7th Grade. He and his brother had something going on, something that I wanted to be a part of and dammit, it was surfing.

Once I had experienced it myself – that first wave that rose up out of white wash that then reformed and peeled perfectly and gently for what seemed like hours on the North Side of Huntington Beach – I was hooked. Absolutely, unapologetically hooked. It ruined any chances I had of being a collegiate soccer player; it launched my migration to coastal living and gave me the most important job of my career. I have not looked back since that first wave. I may have glanced from side to side on the occasional year, but surfing has become a part of my DNA and I'm a better man for it. It's a love that runs strong in my family and a love and culture that I will pass on to my children along with a love of family and friends, of art and music. To pass something on, though, it has to be there. It has to remain. I can only hope that surfing, the actual act of it, is something that my children will, in turn, be able to pass on to theirs.

For the record, I'm not a formally trained sustainability expert. I don't have a degree with the word 'environmental' in it, nor do any of my degrees have the word science in them. It was close though. My first two and a half years at UCI were spent in the School of Engineering and while the Physics and Calculus have served me well it was an elective course in the School of Ecology that had a major, if suspended, effect on my career path.

At the age of 20, I realised that no one had (up to that point) mentioned that cattle farming in Brazil had the potential to have a negative impact on the environment and our planet was astonishing to me. And Green House Gas? How in the world had no one mentioned any of these things? The importance of a rainforest? The true wonder of a balanced ecosystem? All now just being introduced? Well, as fascinating as it was, I continued to wander, leaving my engineer buddies to pursue a degree in Studio Art (OK, so I wanted to surf more).

I spent the next five years at university doing what I was supposed to. I learned, I experienced and I had fun, but I never really made much of a commitment to anything myself. I guess at that time, my commitment was to pack it all in, soak it all up and live for the moment. At times, I might have been accused of being a little carefree. As my waiting and bartending skills became better, and I earned more and I made some effort to support the Surfrider Foundation as best I could, but I didn't have my sights on anything much bigger than that. I cared, I know that; and I wanted the best, and understood that things could be better and that we were all a part of the bigger picture, but man, when the world seems that big, it's hard to pin down just what you can do to really make a difference. Since then, I think I've found what I can do to make a difference. Ten years on, a graduate who has worked in multiple roles at the company, I am a senior Director of Sustainability, reporting to the CEO, for the same company I began working for almost 17 years ago. It's a long ways away from my first days of answering the phone while the receptionist was out of the office for a week, but there's nowhere I'd rather be. I joke now, that I finally realise what I want do when I grow up.

Building a Sustainability Department, however, was a slow process and a team effort. There are some days when people ask me about it and refer to what I've built. I'm just the lucky one with the nameplate. I've been afforded the opportunity to be the face of it, but it takes a team. It needs good leadership, good camaraderie, an openness to change and commitment. And, it's a two way street. I call this the 'Grilled Cheese Effect' because the change, the commitment; it's like the heat that has to come from the top and the bottom to properly melt the cheese. You can have buy-in from the staff on the shop floor. You can have allies in almost every department, but if you don't have support – real support – from the very top, you're going to be paddling against the current. Building heat from the bottom up *and* the top down is paramount.

There's one other factor that has created this perfect swell and that's the dedicated resources that our parent group, Kering, have provided to help us drive this programme forward. In 2012, Kering (formerly known as PPR) announced that all the brands in the group would be creating an Environmental Profit & Loss and aiming for emissions, water use and waste reductions by 2016 alongside goals to monitor suppliers and to source paper and leather responsibly. While it's one thing to state some goals, it's another to back it up with resources, strategies, guidelines, workshops, and training. Again, I don't think there's much more I could ask for. In addition to the announced goals, there are many more in the pipeline that we are striving for internally.

So now what? Well, it's like one of those days where you're driving to your favourite spot for a 'check'. The wind blows fair, driving down the hill – check. You know there's a forecasted swell in the water – check. The tide? It's on a slow, steady rise – check. You make an inventory assessment in your head as you turn down the last street to your destination; boards, wetsuit, fins, leash, wax, sunscreen, fins – check, check, check. You find a parking spot quickly, run up to the vantage point for a look and yes! It's all there, waiting for you to do what you've been training for. It's time now to suit up, and for us to get out there and make something happen.

*Panel at Surfing's New Aloha: The Growing Trend of Giving Back conference in 2012
From left to right: PJ Conell, Derek Sabori and Jeff Wilson
(Courtesy of Gregory Borne)*

Sustainability in the Surf Industry

Rob Machado
Jessica Toth

We have many lifestyle options but we rarely see the direct impact of choices we make. The products we buy are available, shipped and on the shelves, ready for us to purchase. But maybe it is too easy to buy the coolest products without knowing what went into creating them. Before I buy something, I often wonder:

Do I need this item?
What is it made of?
How was it made?
How far has it travelled to get here?
What will be discarded from the purchase?
How will I use it?
How will I dispose of it?

These questions get at the product lifecycle – the cradle to grave life of the product. My goal is to try to select products with the smallest environmental footprint. We all make choices, consciously or subconsciously, but I think we have a responsibility to consider these questions and make the best choices we can. The industry where my choices have the most impact is surfing. So here I take it as my personal responsibility to ask what can I do to make each product more environmentally friendly. At every opportunity, I challenge my sponsors to produce the most sustainable products possible. My vision is for surfers everywhere – professional and recreational – to expect 100% environmentally-friendly products. I don't know what these products and features look like exactly, but I'm optimistic we'll get there.

I'm honoured to be in a position where my opinion is heard. As consumers, we can ask for sustainably sourced materials, environmentally conscious manufacturing, minimal packaging, and low-impact use products. Brands have many pressures like performance, materials sourcing, cost and pricing, marketing, packaging, transportation, and equipment life. As customers add sustainability to their expectations of individual products, we can force the overall transition to product sustainability in the surf industry and perhaps beyond. Our goal here is to highlight progress in surf products. By recognising current constraints, we hope to assess how much further brands must change to become 100% environmentally friendly.

I'm stoked to see all the headway we've made. Reading through the following analysis, I'd say we're halfway there. Some in the surf industry have embraced their role in this transition of products, setting goals and changing their brands. In my view, responsible stewards of the earth. All the companies in our analysis are leading by example. I want to see the transition trends expand and become 'business as usual'. That's what it's all about.

Sustainability Progress Challenge
The surf industry is dependent on the latest technologies. Foam replaced wood in surfboards many years ago because of its superior performance. Natural fibres were replaced by water-repellent synthetics. The next stage is to make products that can reliably perform while being environmentally friendly. Many of today's surf products are petroleum-based. The challenge now is to use technology to help us use resources sparingly, as well as to make natural and recycled materials perform as well as chemical-based products.

About This Research
For this research, we went directly to the relevant companies. They shared information about their current product lines and plans for the future. We learned about their frustrations and their successes in product design and development. Many are 'best-in-class', encouraged to tread lightly in making their products. This analysis is not an endorsement of these brands, rather, it is intended to provide insight into the industry's thinking and future direction.

Overview of Transitions in Progress
We found that the surf industry is keenly aware of its impact on the environment as well as its prominent position to lead change. In order to produce more environmentally friendly products, these companies are exploring alternatives to industry standards. They are:

- Comparing renewable and synthetic raw materials
- Sourcing and evaluating recycled and regenerated materials
- Fabrication processes, such as printing versus dyeing fabrics and using less noxious epoxies

The companies we studied have solid corporate social responsibility programmes beyond their environmentally conscious products. Reef gives 1% of Reef Redemption™ product sales to environmental and humanitarian programmes and operates out of LEED-certified headquarters. Surfyogis creates all products using only natural ingredients, such as chocolate and beeswax, and offers retailers display cases made from recycled teak. Dragon donates US$1 for each E.C.O. collection product sold toward an environmental cause[1]. While each is aware of the many issues surrounding their products' environmental footprints, our research uncovered some differences in the approach to limiting impact. As the table below shows, most emphasis is on finding more environmentally friendly materials.

Environmental Emphasis of Product Line
(first and second priority emphasis)

	Sustainably sourced materials	Environmentally conscious manu-facturing	Minimal packaging	Low-impact use
Channel Island ECOBOARD surfboard	2nd	1st		
Dragon Alliance E.C.O. sunglasses	1st		2nd	
Hurley Phantom boardshorts	1st	2nd		
Reef Redemption sandals	1st	2nd		
Surfyogis sunscreen	1st			2nd

Brand Specifics
Channel Islands
Surfboards are reputed to have the worst impact on the environment of surf equipment and apparel. The majority are made from polyurethane or polystyrene foam, which are petroleum-based products. They are not biodegradable or easily recycled[2] and their volume means they fill trash bins and landfill. In

addition, shaping and glassing processes involve chemicals that are harmful to the environment and hazardous to workers.

Recognising these problems, Channel Island joined the ECOBOARD Project established by non-profit Sustainable Surf. Sustainable Surf has a set of criteria a board must meet to qualify as an ECOBOARD. They aim to take advantage of green chemistry and renewable materials, in order to reduce the boards' environmental and toxic impacts.

Channel Islands offers each of their more than 40 surfboard models with the option of being made as an ECOBOARD. Their internal glass shop at the factory uses 100% ultra-violet (UV) cured coatings. That means there are no volatile organic compounds (VOCs) contributing to pollution. The shop produces 75% less CFCs (chlorofluorocarbons), which make up the vast majority of Southern California glass shops.

The ECOBOARD Project Benchmark
An ECOBOARD must be made from at least one of the following materials:
1. Blank: foam made from minimum 40% recycled foam or at least 40% biological content
2. Resin: epoxy resin made from minimum 15% biological content with low VOCs
3. Alternative Structure: A surfboard structure made from sustainably sourced biological/renewable material (aka-wood) that provides the majority of the surfboard's material and structural integrity – and therefore significantly reduces the amount of foam or resin needed to build the board
Additional charges apply to some ECOBOARD features, adding as much as 25% to the price of a finished board.

Feature	Detail	Upcharge
Marko recycled EPS foam	60% post-consumer recycled EPS foam	-
Entropy Resins	plant-based epoxy resin with 17% bio-carbon content	$125
Bamboo tail patches	replaces carbon fibre	$35
Bamboo full deck	increases overall durability	-

The ECOBOARD Project Benchmark can reduce the carbon footprint of a surfboard by 40%. The toxicity and VOC levels of the eco materials are close to zero.

Dragon
In 2009, action eyewear manufacturer Dragon Alliance began the E.C.O. (Environmentally Conscious Optics) initiative with the introduction of the Experience sunglasses line. It was originally a four piece eyewear collection. Due to its success, Dragon crossed categories and incorporated the technology into their snow goggles line.

E.C.O. eyewear incorporates new materials and manufacturing methods to create more environmentally-friendly products. The sunglasses and goggles collections are made from renewable materials, such as plant oil instead of petroleum. They also use plant-based rather than chemically derived epoxies. Packaging material includes a box made from FSC-certified[3] cardboard and a 100% organic cotton eyewear pouch, printed with water-based ink.

In the goggles line, Dragon uses bamboo as a natural hypoallergenic micro fleece material. They also reduced chemical resins, using an innovative gasket welding process. To close the product lifecycle loop, engineers, designers, and the in-house development team are looking for solutions to recycle old goggles and reuse polyurethane.

Trade-offs in using the environmentally friendly materials are few. E.C.O. sunglasses are lighter than plastic frame glasses. And the frame has less memory retention than typical injection-moulded plastic. Dragon feels that the overall benefits outweigh the few drawbacks.

Finally, Dragon is considering other ways to lessen the environmental footprint of their products through manufacturing and shipping. Their suppliers and vendors are sensitive to their impact. Though not yet quantified, the company believes the E.C.O. product lines generate less CO_2 throughout production and distribution.

Reef
Reef's stated mission is to provide surf products in a sustainable manner. In 2007, they launched the Reef Redemption initiative to formally integrate corporate social responsibility into product development, company operations, and giving programmes. Through this programme, Reef products use renewable, recycled, organic materials where possible. They also collaborate with local artisans in developing nations, such as Guatemala, Uganda, and Togo.

I challenged Reef to make the most environmentally-friendly sandal possible. The Machado Classic outsole is made from 100% recycled car tyre rubber. Leather processing is chrome-free, tanned without heavy metals, so less CO_2 is released. The sandals include 100% post-consumer recycled PET from recycled water bottles. Water-based glue emits 99.8% less VOCs as compared with traditional epoxies, and foam padding is a plant-based cellulose material. One tyre can make six pair of sandals and the company estimates that over 5,000 tyres have been reused to date.

Reef continues to look for environmentally conscious options. They recently introduced Coconut Stretch made from coconut husks. Compared with conventional fabrics, this renewable yarn dries faster and has greater UV protection. It is being used in Reef's boardshorts.

In addition, Reef is licensing Vibram® Ecostep rubber technology for use in their women's footwear collection. Ecostep rubber is made from 30% recycled scrap rubber, uses one-third less virgin material, and reduces scrap waste. Reef is also thinking about end-of-life disposal: where possible they are incorporating Eco-One™ into their EVA plastics. Eco-One™ is an organic additive that encourages plastics to biodegrade in biologically active landfill.

Surfyogis

Surfyogis is a small, private company in Bali. They make only two products – body oil and sunscreen. Their sunscreen, known as surfscreen, caught my eye for being as close to coral-safe as possible. The ingredients are chocolate, beeswax, coconut oil, and zinc oxide. As they point out, you can eat it. Australia's Therapeutic Goods Administration (TGA), comparable to the US FDA, has evaluated and certified Surfyogis' sunscreen as safe. They are in the process of getting FDA certification.

A 2008 paper, *Sunscreens Cause Coral Bleaching by Promoting Viral Infections*[4], published in the journal *Environmental Health Perspectives* reported that coral reefs are being damaged by sunscreen brought into the sea by swimmers. The scientists concluded that, even at very low concentrations, ingredients in sunscreen can cause the "rapid and complete bleaching of hard corals". They believe that 4000-6000 metric tons of sunscreen are left in the oceans. Subsequent articles in *National Geographic* and *NatureNews* heightened awareness of the problem.

The report found that as much as 10% of the world's coral reefs are threatened by bleaching from sunscreen[5]. Four ingredients found in common sunscreen – paraben, cinnamate, benzophenone, and a camphor derivative – were found to activate an otherwise dormant virus in algae, which caused bleaching. Surfscreen has not been tested on coral and Surfyogis does not claim to be coral-safe. In some of the articles about coral bleaching, however, all-natural sunscreens are recommended as a means of limiting damage to coral reefs and reef animals. Pollution and ocean warming are bigger contributors to coral bleaching, but, there is a link between the chemicals in many sunscreens and the health of coral reefs.

Case Study: Hurley
Overview
Hurley have taken the most detailed, analytical approach to sustainability. They are large, public company, and part of the Nike family of businesses. Nike had a well-publicised CSR problem in the 1990s when it was discovered that they were using child labour and sweatshops to produce their products. Brett Bjorkman, now a director at Hurley, was brought into Nike to fix the sourcing problem. Transparency has been the first step towards the solution. Nike and its affiliates disclose information on all primary suppliers on their website[6]. Hurley may be a good example to understand future transitions in the surf industry.

Water
At a recent in-house meeting, CEO Roger Wyett announced that *carbon emissions* are the concern for the previous generation, whereas *water* is the watchword of future generations. While you might not agree with that, the company is rallying round the cause, making water a priority. They generously support clean drinking water in developing countries through Waves for Water and Hydration Nation programmes, educating the public about global water scarcity using the tagline "1 in 6 do not have access to clean water". This message is a good fit since water sports are at the heart of much of Hurley's business.

Image and Transparency
Hurley is sensitive to its public image and consistently works to respond to negative attention. When Greenpeace highlighted concerns about toxins in Hurley's manufacturing effluent, Hurley began addressing the causes, aiming to eliminate all toxins in processes and products by 2020. Most impressively Hurley makes public its list of global factories, often including proprietary information such as products and contacts at each site.

To address sustainability issues, management uses an audit system for factories, rating them on a five-tier scale. They operate in 16 countries, from 69 factories with 129 mills feeding the factories. Working towards a goal of sourcing from 100% compliant factories, they divest from five to six vendors each year and add two to three new vendors each year. Today, Hurley does not know all the 129 secondary sources because many work directly with a factory without Hurley overseeing this but, by 2020, their aim is to be able to identify and audit all material suppliers.

Following the negative press from poor labour practices in Nike factories in the late 1980s and the 1990s,[7] Hurley, acquired in 2002, has a goal that all its partners and licensees have sustainable strategy plans in place. California-based Hurley follows the California Transparency in Supply Chains Act as well as adhering to California Prop 65 provisions, governing water and toxins.

Product Knowledge
To be able to track overall water use, waste, and carbon emissions, Hurley has to thoroughly know its products. Hanging up in Brett Bjorkman's office are a dozen items, each rated with a marker score according to the efficiency of material used and the sustainability of the materials and manufacturing processes. As head of Sustainable Business and Innovation, Brett is concerned with what it takes to create Hurley's products.

Their internally-developed scoring system, applied to all product categories, runs from gold to silver and bronze to yellow to red. By 2020, their target is to have all core product categories and new products rated bronze or better. They share lean manufacturing best practice among suppliers in order to remove waste. Examples of waste reduction methods include more efficient pattern-cutting and seamless weaving.

Hurley is also beginning to use a waterless dying process on rash guards and is evaluating other polyester products for the process. The fabric in Hurley boardshorts is made entirely from 100% recycled PET from plastic water bottles, and Hurley has a unique cotton regeneration process that salvages cotton scraps for weaving into new products.

It is exceptional for a company to rate the environmental impact of each product. In addition, Hurley evaluates the contribution of each material and each manufacturing procedure. They understand the trade-offs with each decision and consider how each product fits their overall sustainability goals.

Impact – Water Footprint
Their highly analytical approach, combined with concerns for water use, has led to insight, such as:

- A T-shirt created from non-organic cotton requires 655 gallons of water (649 gallons from agriculture and 6.02 gallons from manufacturing).
- Water use in manufacturing polyester is 0.1% of the water use to farm cotton.
- Creating recycled polyester uses 10% of water compared to creating virgin polyester.
- Printed boardshorts require less than 4% of the water to make dyed boardshorts.

This information is especially relevant for sales projections. By 2014, Hurley planned to sell 2.5 times more T-shirts than in 2010. If all shirts in 2014 were made from 100% cotton, they would expend 9.8 billion gallons of water during farming and manufacturing. Instead, their projected product mix enabled Hurley to create 2.5 times more shirts, using 12% less total water.

Goals

The value of knowing the impact of your products is especially evident in setting goals. Based on desired total water use, Hurley is able to project the ideal T-shirt product mix type by material. They plan to reduce reliance on farmed cotton, moving toward mixed material T-shirts made from regenerated cotton and recycled PET. Recognising that 70% of their environmental impact is from manufacturing, Hurley aim to move beyond factory compliance and towards gaining processing efficiencies. By 2020, using 2013 as a baseline, Hurley hopes to:

- Slash water use by 25% per unit by using more regenerated cotton, understanding their water footprint, and using water-free dyeing technology.
- Reduce waste in manufacturing processes by 10%.
- Reject toxics and achieve zero discharge of hazardous chemicals from factories.
- Cut energy and achieve a 20% per unit reduction in CO_2 emissions.

Summary: Transitioning into the Future

Our research found that the companies in our analysis are sensitive to their impact on the environment. Many of the products are used in the ocean on a daily basis, and the surf industry is making consumers environmentally aware.

The Bad News

We see that increased efficiencies and reduced waste mean more products can be made for the same or slightly less environmental damage. The assumption is that the rate of consumerism is growing; demand will only increase. A professional surfer may go through 50 boards a year while an average recreational surfer may need a new board annually. That's a very short product life for a durable good, made from mostly virgin, non-renewable materials.

We wonder if 8.6 billion gallons of water is too big a sacrifice for one company to be able to sell 15 million T-shirts in a year. If some products use 25% recycled rubber in one component, what about the other 75%? What about the same company's products without recycled components? If the price of environmentally conscious products is 25% higher, will consumers buy them?

The Good News
Looking at quantifiable progress, we are only beginning the transition toward 100% environmentally friendly, however, the wheels are in motion; progress has clearly begun. We believe that technological progress can catch up with consumer expectations of green progress in the surf industry. We estimate that a minority of surf industry materials are from sustainable sources. We suspect that the majority of companies and surfers are aware of the environmental impact of their sport.

Bridging the Gap
We want to get to 100% environmentally friendly and the sooner, the better. To get there, companies must continue on the technological path using less virgin material, looking for end-of-life repurposing, and promoting greater product longevity. Surfers are naturally in touch with the environment and they influence young, hip culture. Professional surfers may be the best messengers. By asking for sustainably sourced materials, environmentally conscious manufacturing, minimal packaging, and low-impact products, professionals will influence the buying decisions of recreational surfers and put pressure on the industry to transition more quickly. As all surfers add sustainability to their expectations of individual products, they will force the overall transition to product sustainability in the surf industry.

It's Time to Bring the Image of the Surfer into the 21st Century

Todd Woody

As the lull drags on at Second Peak and the sun slowly burns off the June haze, the silence of the lineup is broken when a pair of dolphins burst into the air a few yards away, inside the kelp beds strung across Pleasure Point. Heads swivel again as a sea otter pops up in the dolphins' wake and backstrokes its way past groms, long-in-the-tooth longboarders and twenty-something rippers. At last a set rolls through and I catch a glassy right toward the cliff-side house that Jack O'Neill built. There's a timelessness captured in these Santa Cruz moments – the surfer's up-close-and-personal encounter with marine mammals that have cruised these waters for millennia, the sandstone bluffs and the redwood-studded hills that have changed little since I was at school here in the 1980s. These waves too, first ridden 129 years ago when three visiting Hawaiian princes fashioned boards from redwood planks and hit the surf near Steamer Lane.

There's something else that has remained the same over the past half century – the image of the surfer. Whether appearing in surf magazines and videos or occasionally dropping into the mainstream media, the surfer invariably is presented as young, male, white and obsessed with speed. It's not a wholly inaccurate image but it's outdated and one that stands in the way of making surfing more sustainable. That starts with the surfboard, the iconic symbol of the sport whose materials date from the Gidget era – a hunk of toxic polyurethane coated in toxic polyester resin. Bad for dolphins, bad for otters and bad for shapers and surfers.

Paddle out into today's lineup in multicultural California, Hawaii, Australia and many other places, however, and you'll encounter a far more diverse wave tribe. Sure, the sun-bleached blonde, adrenaline-addled descendants of Miki Dora are still there in force. But there are far more women, 40-something groms, gay surfers and people of all races and ethnicities as well as parents surfing with their kids. There's the gray-haired grandmother riding a longboard

I often encounter in the lineup, the teenager I saw surfing a homemade alaia in San Diego and the middle-aged guy on a US$1,300 Danny Hess salvaged wood-and-recycled-EPS-foam board at Bolinas in Marin County, California.

A 2011 study sponsored by the Surfrider Foundation, entitled *A Socioeconomic and Recreational Profile of Surfers in the United States,* found that the typical surfer in the U.S. is 34 years old and university educated with an income of US$75,000. So much for the surf bum. At one of California's more iconic breaks, Trestles, the median age of a surfer is 37. Nationally, the average surfer owns four surfboards and has been hitting the waves for 16 years. At many breaks these days, you're as likely to see an Audi with a surfboard rack in the parking lot as a beater Honda. Or if you surf my home break at Bolinas, you'll spot surfboards strapped to the roofs of Tesla Motors' Model S electric sports sedan, battery-powered Nissan Leafs, Chevy Volts and biodiesel-fueled Volkswagen Jettas. In other words, surfers are going green and they got the cash to buy sustainable rides.

These are images that, for the most part, you won't see reflected in the media. If the wave tribe is increasingly large and diverse, the tribal council remains rather small and bro-ish. These are the industry insiders and influencers – the fashion executives, the surfboard manufacturers, the shapers, the pros and the contest organisers. If the tribal council continues to believe their primary audience and market are teenage and twenty-something guys – in other words, their peers or younger versions of themselves – then the appeal of sustainability as a selling point will likely be limited. If the wave tribe doesn't see itself or its values reflected in both the surf and mainstream media, they will likely tune out. Either way, the media disconnect makes forging a culture of sustainability around surfing more of a challenge, leaving many people in the dark about their options to surf green, whether they read *Surfer Magazine* or *The New York Times.*

In the course of reporting several stories on sustainable surfing and talking to ordinary surfers, I've been struck by both the lack of awareness about green options and the desire for them. Take Kirk Haney, chief executive of a biofuels startup in San Diego. A lifelong surfer who keeps a shortboard in his office, Haney grew up in the Northern California agricultural town of Salinas and surfed the cold-water breaks between Santa Cruz and Monterey. Now he and his business buddies – "Surfing is the new golf in San Diego," Haney says – are likely to grab their boards and jet off to Tavarua to surf Cloudbreak. "Would I pay more for an Ecoboard? Absolutely! But you got to get the surf shops to sell them," he tells me. "You're not even presented with that option when you go to buy a board".

Still, sustainability is slowly making its way into the local surf shop, the gateway to reaching the average surfer. I've come across the random Firewire Timbertek – a new wood-skinned, bio-resined board in Southern California surf shops. Walking into Patagonia's Cardiff outlet in San Diego, I find racks of Danny Hess surfboards as well as similarly constructed boards from local shaper Jon Wegener. "Most people coming in here are into the green thing but most probably buy for the aesthetics and performance," a Patagonia sales guy tells me.

As a mainstream environmental journalist who took up surfing in mid-life (or more aptly, surfing took over my life), I bring an outsider's perspective to the sustainability of surfing. My first exposure to the industry came in 2009 when I wrote a story for *The New York Times* on Green Foam Blanks, a Californian startup that developed a process for recycling polyurethane. The company's founders, two surf entrepreneurs named Joey Santley and Steve Cox, were attempting to get star shapers like Lost's Matt Biolos in San Clemente's famed surf ghetto to use the recycled banks. Surfing may be a US$7 billion global industry, but as I discovered reporting that story, it's largely a B-to-B business – bro to bro, as I put it – where personal relationships among a relatively small group of surf insiders influence the industry's direction. "Surfers are not going to sacrifice the performance of a light board for being green," Biolos told me back in 2009 in a shaping bay covered in chemical dust cast off from polyurethane blanks. He's right, but the comment underscores the focus, the obsession even, with pro-level performance and the fear that customers will shun any board that is perceived as 'too different'.

While surfboard design has undergone radical transformations over the decades, the razor-thin profit margins of the business have not encouraged experimentation and innovation when it comes to board materials. Top shapers depend on the top surfers they sponsor to drive sales when their winning moves are captured in a magazine photo spread or YouTube video. The pro surfers in turn are loath to put their standing at risk by riding a new type of board in competition. "It's an uphill battle as no one wants to roll the dice on their livelihood – whether it's the competitive surfer or the shaper barely making ends meet," Scott Bass, chief executive of The Boardroom, a trade show for shapers, told me in 2013.

The surf media and the apparel industry rely on the images of those same pros to sell everything from sunglasses to sandals in full-page ads. Surfing is hardly the only sport whose stars push product but the media's obsessive focus on pro surfers limits the opportunities to talk about sustainability among both the hardcore fans and those who consider surfing not so much as a sport but a way of life. That's not to say the surf media ignores sustainability – stories on Sustainable

Surf and other organisations working to green up the business have appeared in the major surfing magazines. And publications like *The Surfer's Journal* – for which I've written – cover surfing from a broader perspective. Online journals such as *The Inertia*, meanwhile, have brought new voices and views into the mix, as have citizen surfers who publish on Twitter, Facebook and other social media. Still, the sporadic nature of the coverage reminds me of a comment my editor at a U.S. national business magazine made to me when turning down a pitch some years ago: "But Todd, we just had a solar story six months ago". There's a similar challenge in getting surfing stories off the sports pages and to a broader audience. But coverage begets coverage.

After I wrote *The New York Times* story on Green Foam Blanks, I started getting pitches about other sustainable surfing initiatives. When I was on staff at another national business magazine, I wrote stories on another Southern California startup that is recycling polyurethane blank trimmings into a material that soaks up oil spills – an environmental twofer. That was followed some months later by an article I wrote on Michael Stewart and Kevin Whilden's work at Sustainable Surf to create an Ecoboard standard for surfboards that are made with recycled EPS foam, bioresin and other more sustainable materials as well as their work greening up pro surf contests. Those stories prompted some vigorous discussion on the magazine's website and even reached readers outside the surf media orbit – including a surprisingly number of business executives who surf. Twitter helped spread the articles to other surfers who follow my feed. Then I hit a wall. The word came down from New York to lay off the surf stories for a while, at least in the print edition of the magazine. That forced me to think about the different ways to cover surfing from an environmental angle. For instance, in Quartz, Atlantic Media's global business news site, I have written about the impact of climate change on surfing in the wake of scientific studies predicting that sea level rise will affect wave heights in different parts of the world.

By framing surfing as not just a sport for the pros, but as a wave of life that is an environmental story, a business story and a cultural story, sustainability becomes a far more interesting and multi-faceted tale that can have real-world impact. That requires embracing the wave tribe in its glorious diversity – kooks and all – even if that means slaying some sacred surf cows. When I ponder where sustainable surfing is going I think of that June day in Santa Cruz when I spotted a trio of 11 to 13 year old girls at Steamer Lane absolutely ripping it up while the boy groms cheered them on. That's the future.

Chapter Four
Critique

Chapter Three presented an industry-focused account of sustainability, as it exists today, within some of surfing's largest corporations. The overall perspective of this book views things from the sustainable development perspective as outlined in the introduction: complex, non-linear, and certainly contested. As such, any single account from any single sector will only present one piece of the puzzle. Chapter Four explodes the rhetoric of corporatism and capitalism and begins to deconstruct the whole concept of surf industry production and consumption. The commonality between the contributors in this chapter is that they all critique a system they see as betraying the ideals incumbent in sustainability both outside and within the surfing world. This is an important component of any discussion on transitions to sustainability; at its very core, it explores the need for the term sustainability that, if it does nothing else, suggests that humanity's current interaction with the environment and with each other is unsustainable.

As you will see, Shaun Tomson, former world champion and successful surf apparel businessman and the first professional surfer to publically and meaningfully support the Surfrider Foundation, is acutely aware of the complexities and contradictions that exist in matters of sustainability in surfing. Shaun's contribution, which reinforces surfing's innate spirituality and connection with nature and natural forces, strongly urges the surfing industry to revisit its roots, suggesting that the main brands have lost their way and that the industry may have reached a worrying saturation point.

Similarly, Scott Laderman emphasises corporate surfing's loss of connection to its roots. Scott also broadens this scope to discuss the impact of the capitalist system and the contradictions that exist as the rich get richer and the poor get poorer. Scott discusses globalisation's impact on the world and, with regard to surfing highlights, how manufacturing and production is often relocated to countries with minimal or no labour laws. Scott points to some interesting solutions to overcome these deep-seated issues.

Ted Endo, deputy editor of *The Inertia* at the time of writing provides a broad ranging critique of surfing culture both historical and contemporary. Ted suggests that surfing is a neo-colonialist force that is rife with deception and false imagery. Cori Shumacher, four times world women's longboard champion, describes the industry as Big Surfing. She also discusses worker exploitation with a strong emphasis on gender imbalance. She argues for stronger environmental justice perspective that really does encompass the three pillars of sustainable development. Mark Marovich talks of Shared Stoke and that it is this feeling and this connection which needs to be utilised in order to encourage a transition to sustainability

Finally, Pierce Kavanaugh describes the trials and tribulations as well as revelations of making the documentary *Manafacturing Stoke*. The insights provided by Pierce resonate very strongly with us as the editors of this book, the uncertainty, the doubt – but also the elation at the creation of something new. Ultimately, this chapter contextualises surfing within the broader socio-political environmental context of the world.

4.1

Pro Surfing and the Art of Inspiration

Shaun Tomson

Pro surfing started in 1976 with the formation of the IPS, the International Professional Surfers, which ultimately became the ASP – Association of Surfing Professionals. There was a group of us; a couple of Hawaiian guys, some Australians and South Africans, that thought there might be a future in what was then a new concept: actually making a living from surfing. It was amazing to be a part of it, see it all unfold, and ultimately kickstart the surfing industry; pro surfing really put the surf industry on the map. Out of everything pro surfing has done, and out of everything that pro surfers themselves have ever done, the single most important thing has been to inspire millions of kids to go surfing. The second most important thing is that it created a way for people with a passion for surfing, whether athletes, businesses people or simply stoked surfers, to make a living out of it. There are people out there that criticise the surfing industry, "Oh you're making money out of surfing with capitalistic intent", but I still think there is a purity of motive there. The business of surfing employs primarily surfers and that's a healthy and positive aspect of the surf industry.

Surfing companies have done terribly in terms of sustainability. There is so much green washing going in. Buying recycled-fabric boardshorts or T-shirt and then crying one's 'goodness' from the rooftops doesn't quite qualify as being sustainable. The surf industry started from grassroots and it happened within a year in Australia: Quiksilver started in 1969, Ripcurl in 1970. Ultimately, businesses are created to increase shareholder value for the stakeholders or the people that have invested money in them, and at a certain point the unique inspirational aspect of surfing that people were gravitating towards suddenly became an irresistible mass market. There's a purity associated with surfing that's very different to traditional team ball sports like basketball, baseball or football. The search for the perfect wave, paddling out into the unknown, it's just so different to traditional sports. The general consumer, especially young kids, really related to that because it was unstructured, free, more soulful. Surfing companies figured out a way to sell that lightning in a bottle and people loved it.

Ultimately, stoke wasn't enough to power the business. The management of the surfing companies just didn't have the skills to take it beyond the lifestyle level. Most of the guys were not MBAs, they had mostly come up through surfing, started these backyard businesses and then suddenly their companies were huge. A broad lack of business acumen really affected the stability of the industry, and bad decisions were made by some of the big brands. It seems every bad decision was motivated by a growth imperative and that is the way of Wall Street. Every single big brand has suffered as a result and many lost their focus. They didn't put back what they should have. Inspiration is at the core of all the companies, people gravitated towards them because they were inspiring brands, surfing was inspiring, but they never managed to get past the same old formula: put a pro surfer on a billboard, on a magazine and that's enough.

Today, people want creative engagement, people want inspiration, people want a cool store and, of course, people want a unique product. I worked for Patagonia for two years and it was also where I met Yvon Chouinard, now a good friend. We'd go surfing and he'd say to me, "You know Shaun, doing good is good for business". If more companies adopted that attitude they would see that, while a profit motive is very important, if your motive is also to do good, it can ultimately boost the bottom line. That's the way we are going to get profound change in the business of the surfing world.

Surf companies are at a critical point. They are at a crossroads and need to take a long hard look at where they've come from and where they are going. They need to ask themselves what their mission is. It shouldn't be just profit, sales and growth. Their mission should be to inspire people to surf. This doesn't mean I'm pushing for a gazillion more guys in the water, I mean inspiring people to relate to the surfing sensibility that is being connected to nature and freedom. People would come back and respond to that again in a positive way.

The surf companies have been abysmal supporters of the Surfrider Foundation. I was the first pro surfer to become a member in 1984 and for me it has been the best organisation I have ever been involved with. It is very disappointing to see how little support Surfrider has received from the surf industry. Sure, there is some money that gets donated from the Waterman's Ball every year but it is not like that many companies individually dig into their pockets. Without a clean beach and without access to the ocean you're not going to have a business. The 55,000 members of the foundation around the country are activists, hard core men and women who are out there fighting in their local areas to keep beaches open – if there's an issue Surfrider is there. Some brands, like Billabong, have supported Surfrider and every year the SIMA Waterman's Ball raises money and it is greatly appreciated, but it's not nearly enough. The brands should be a better support of core organisations like Surfrider and other enviro-groups like 'Heal the Bay' and 'Heal the Ocean'. There is a huge group of dedicated people out there who are just not getting the support from the surfing industry they need.

Pro surfers have incredible power to inspire thousands and thousands of kids across the country. You would think they'd want to use that power for good, but many pro surfers are totally disengaged from organisations like Surfrider. There are exceptions, for example, I had coffee with Dane Reynolds, one of the most popular surfers in the world, and he bent over backwards to help the Foundation. He said, "I'd be honored to support Surfrider, be in one of the ads, I'll design a hand-drawn Surfrider T-shirt". Other guys don't even return phone calls. Their agents don't even email you back. Not emailing back about Surfrider reflects the disconnect between pro surfing and the environmental and sustainability movements. Getting involved and helping costs nothing except a little time and the little things you do ultimately add up to big things.

Pro surfers, as a whole, need to realise that it's not just about the next wave, the next event – there is a responsibility to give back to the groups that protect their ocean. Certainly, there are guys who have a worldly, thoughtful view, like Kelly and Dane. By virtue of their success both have inspired a lot of kids in a very positive way. Kelly also has a powerful connection with nature. I interviewed him after he was in a final with Andy Irons, they were going for the World Title that year, 2005, I think. It was an incredible final at Jeffries Bay. The surf was eight foot, it was fantastic. They were both surfing to the absolute limit. Two minutes to go, Andy got this incredible wave right the way down the point, kicked out and started walking back up the beach, sure he'd won. Kelly needed a 9.3. I was doing the commentary for Billabong, so I was watching and the seconds counting down. Kelly got a wave but it didn't give him the score so he paddled back out. He looked tired, looked like he was paddling in slow motion. There was forty seconds to go and a set started coming in. The first wave kind of came through and he let it go by. I was like, whoah, what's happening here? The next wave came through and he let it go by? And then the next wave too? He had about nine seconds left and he took off and just blasted his way down the line, caught this incredible wave and got a 9.5 to win the final. It was incredible. I spoke to him afterwards, he said: "I was finished, I had no energy, I knew I needed one more but I couldn't do it. Then this pod of dolphins came by and I just followed them and they took me where

I needed to be". I thought, wow, this guy is just amazing, really connected to nature and plugged into the energy of the universe.

When I had my first company, Instinct, sustainability wasn't part of the thought process. However, the Patagonia thesis, that doing good is good for business, really does seem to work. If you have something that is perceived as being good, people will respond to it. When we had our company, Solitude, we were looking at some new ways of doing business that might be more sustainable. I read about this Dutch company that had developed a new digital printing process that was all water-based ink. There was no dying involved and there was direct print from the machine onto fabric, so it saved a lot of water and dye. We did shorts and they were the first digital printed shorts in the world and we were sure the customers were going to respond. At Patagonia, we did a study that showed that customers were not prepared to pay extra for environmentally sensitive clothing – they just won't. All things being equal, when you've got a $20 t-shirt that is environmentally friendly and a $20 t-shirt that's not environmentally friendly, sure they are going to buy the t-shirt that's environmentally friendly. But when you've got a $25 t-shirt and a $20 t-shirt, people aren't going to gravitate towards $25 t-shirt just because it is environmentally friendly or made by a sustainable company. Ultimately, at Solitude, we went forward with our focus on sustainability and we were successful with the product line because we felt good about it and a certain base of customers responded to it. Above all, I think you have to do what you think is good, and you have to do what you think is going to make a difference. I think that's a simple philosophy to live by, in and out of the water, and in and out of business.

One decision and one good turn can have a real impact down the line. I think the surfing industry is different to other businesses in many respects and I think it should be different. A person who surfs is connected to nature and so they should be making decisions that are for the ocean and not just for the bottom line. They should be, but they're not, and that's just the harsh reality of it. I think that some of the companies just lost their way. They need to go back to the mission of inspiring people to surf, they need to realise that it is an achievable and profitable mission. People need to be inspired, to metaphorically paddle out to the horizon and push their own boundaries. Go back to watering your roots, go back to where that company originally started from. Go back to inspiring people and I think the rest will look after itself.

4.2

Beyond Green: Sustainability, Freedom and Labour of the Surf Industry

Scott Laderman

On 24 April 2013, the eight-story Rana Plaza building collapsed in a suburb of Dhaka, killing more than 1,100 workers toiling in Bangladesh's massive clothing-manufacturing industry. With a toll far higher than the Triangle Shirtwaist fire of 1911 or the Ali Enterprises or Tazreen Fashion fires of 2012, it became the deadliest garment factory accident in history. This may seem like an unusual way to open a chapter in a book about surfing and sustainability. Bangladesh, after all, is hardly at the top of anyone's list of premier surfing destinations, and none of the major surfwear brands were reported to be using the Rana Plaza complex.

But it was a sobering reminder, if any were needed, that much of the clothing worn by Western consumers, including surfers, is assembled in often dangerous Third World factories whose workers earn the most meager of wages. As even a casual glance at the labels in surfers' clothes reveals, most of this apparel is made in countries hardly known for their generous pay or stellar working conditions, from Bangladesh, Cambodia, and Vietnam to China, Mexico, and El Salvador. This raises questions about precisely what we mean by sustainability.

Surfers like to think of themselves as environmental stewards, and it is easy to understand why they may do so when surfing is rooted in such an elegant exploitation of the natural world. Surfers channel the oceans' (or even lakes' or rivers') energy and conditions can vary depending on the tide, wind direction, or water temperature. Most surfers must travel in order to reach the waves – whether a couple of miles to their local break or overseas for a 'surfari' – and this has environmental consequences. So, too, does the manufacture of the equipment on which surfers rely: boards, fins, wetsuits, board shorts and bikinis, leashes, and wax. Former Quiksilver CEO, Bob McKnight, once put it in a comment with application far beyond surfwear, "We're all guilty. Making apparel is not exactly the most environmentally friendly industry"[1].

Sustainability should be about much more than the natural environment. It should also consider the social environment in which those who make surfing products must work. In a sport closely identified with freedom, what does it mean, we might ask, to have much of the surf industry so deeply invested in global labour practices that seem anything but free? And how is it possible to romanticise the people of the Third World, as so much of surf culture historically has, while at the same time exploiting them as the low-wage workforce for surf culture's material accoutrements? Much of the authenticity enjoyed by the surf industry derives from its local roots. When one thinks of O'Neill, for instance, one cannot help but think of Santa Cruz. The same is true of Rip Curl and Torquay. Those who started such operations were invested in their local communities and local people provided much of their labour. But as surf-related businesses grew and their markets expanded, many of these local connections were lost.

Quiksilver offers a case in point. The company originated, as did a number of surf-related brands in the '60s, with surfers hoping to subsidise their wave-riding habit – and they did. But by 2010, Quiksilver Inc. was a multi-billion-dollar corporation whose shares were traded on the New York Stock Exchange. While its roots may be in coastal Victoria and its headquarters in Huntington Beach, Quiksilver Inc. is incorporated in the tiny American state of Delaware. This might seem perplexing; after all, Delaware is not known as a centre of contemporary surf culture. The state does, however, boast at least one advantage for the modern shareholder: it is a haven for thousands of corporations with hopes, according to *The New York Times*, of "minimizing taxes, skirting regulations, plying friendly courts or, when needed, covering their tracks"[2].

If this seems inconsistent with Quiksilver's cultivated image as a hip, edgy projection of global surf rebellion, this may be because its multi-million-dollar marketing campaigns are second to none. Not only is the company cool, as its marketing suggests, but it is fundamentally ethical. Indeed, Quiksilver "recognizes the concept of corporate social responsibility and benevolence," it boasts[3]. Here, surfers might ask, what exactly do "benevolence" and "social responsibility" mean in an era of globalised labour? While most major brands continue to employ white-collar professionals in the United States, Australia, or other nations housing their corporate offices, much of the workforce that makes and assembles these companies' products is to be found elsewhere.

This has occasionally landed the surfwear brands in hot water. In 2003, for instance, *The New York Times* reported on the imposition of a company union in a factory producing gear for both Quiksilver and Billabong[4]. Then, in 2007, China Labor Watch revealed that Quiksilver had contracts with factories incapable of compliance with Chinese labour law[5].

To be sure, surfwear companies are not unique in this way. Much of the garment industry has looked to the developing world for the cheap manufacture of its goods. But the surfwear companies appear to want to have it both ways. They wish for their brands to be synonymous with 'freedom' – Quiksilver, through its subsidiary Roxy, claims to be all about "freedom, fun, and individual expression" – while at the same time taking advantage of the relative lack of freedom suffered by the low-wage workers who make many of their products[6]. In this light, it becomes difficult to square the freedom and self-expression touted by Quiksilver with what we know of the firm's labour practices.

In the late 19th and early 20th centuries, when the United States was in the midst of its industrial revolution, fierce debates erupted over the meaning of "freedom" and whether such freedom could survive the industrial economy. Many of those working in steel, meatpacking, textiles, and other trades, including countless new immigrants, like those immortalised by American writers Upton Sinclair and Thomas Bell, argued that their life stations increasingly resembled those of 'wage slavery'[7]. Business leaders countered that capitalism was not hostile to freedom because workers enjoyed the 'liberty of contract'. If a company's wages were too low or its workplace too dangerous, workers could exercise their right to rent their labour to others. Under the rosy gloss given to this arrangement by the captains of industry, companies would be forced to compete for workers' allegiance, which would mean higher pay and better conditions. In the real world, however, there were too many workers and not enough jobs. The companies thus exploited their disproportionate power to set the terms of employment.

Something similar is happening in the 21st century. Corporate globalisation has exacerbated a phenomenon that critics call the 'race to the bottom'. In a global economy in which nations compete to offer highly mobile businesses the most attractive investment climate, things many of us take for granted – rising wages, decent benefits, effective regulations, safe working conditions and the freedom to organise unions, all of which may cut into profits – become obstacles that hinder a nation's competitive advantage. This is why Bangladesh, where Billabong, Patagonia, Volcom, Reef, and other surf-industry members have all had products made, was, by 2013, simultaneously the world's second largest apparel manufacturing centre and the nation with the clothing manufacturing industry's lowest wages[8]. Such a global system is neither humane nor sustainable.

It contributes to the vast inequalities that separate the developed world from the less developed countries, and it furthers the income and wealth gaps within nations. This has consequences for the human beings who provide much of the surf industry's labour. So what is the solution? It is difficult to say, particularly given the general lack of transparency among the major surf-related brands about their current policies and practices. While production in the United States, Australia, and other more developed countries should still be encouraged, there may be no putting the offshoring genie back in the bottle. But reversing the race to the bottom is essential, and the industry could play a constructive role in this process. There are numerous possibilities: Quiksilver, Billabong, Rip Curl, and other industry giants could, for instance, immediately commit to providing a living wage to all workers making their products. This is not about meeting the companies' legal obligation to pay a particular nation's minimum wage. It is about paying wages that enable workers to meet their basic needs. They could also commit to universally honouring the international right of workers to organise independent unions and collectively bargain. A unionised workforce typically enjoys better pay and benefits, and it has greater power in the workplace to ensure that its rights are protected. Nations such as Bangladesh have made it exceedingly difficult for workers to form unions. The industry could endeavour to reverse such barriers, pledging not to move production to countries that fail to meet international labour standards, and it could use and support credible, independent monitoring organisations that make their findings publicly available. Groups such as Worldwide Responsible Accredited Production (WRAP) or the Fair Labor Association (FLA) are inadequate. WRAP focuses only on "compliance with local law" by claiming to respect "the unique culture of each country," which could mean an abysmally low minimum wage and an anti-union legal environment[9]. The corporate-funded FLA, meanwhile, has repeatedly proved unreliable, most recently through its notorious failures concerning the production of Apple products in China.

There will undoubtedly be challenges, particularly given the disaggregated nature of factory production but, with the collective support of its many members, the surf industry could use its influence to become a leader in pushing for higher wages and better working conditions. Only when surfers can feel certain that their way of life is not reliant on the exploitation of others can they truly find freedom in the waves.

4.3

Crimes Committed in the Spirit of Play

Tetsuhiko Endo

Like many of the myths told by the West and its apologists, the story of surfing is riddled with elisions. When viewed from afar they are easy to ignore under the good vibes and golden sunsets that have become the compulsive mantra of a decadent culture desperate to cast itself in a benign, soft-focused glow. But the closer you peer at the shrine of wave riding, the more apparent it becomes that the foundation is unsound and there are cracks in the edifice. Most will stop there and grumble about the loss of the 'old days', creeping corporatisation and the subsequent infestation of the sport by masses of poseurs and weekend warriors. Let us go further. Let us step inside the temple and take stock, scrutinise the false idols, the chipping paint, and the gaping holes that beckon to us with the pregnant whispers of an unaccounted-for past. It is only through a reckoning with this past that we can distill the worthy aesthetics and traditions that have been born from centuries of waveriding as a culture and art form from the elements that threaten to bring the entire edifice tumbling down under the weight of its own contradictions.

We start, as always, in Hawaii. The characters are also the same, from Captain Cook and the lusty, dusky, wave-sliding natives, to the writer-industrialist Alexander Hume Ford, the great author Jack London, and the unassuming waterman, George Freeth. It is the narrative we must reconsider, a narrative that London, in one of his articles on Hawaii, summed upped thusly:

"Not only did the Hawaiian born not talk about [surfing], but they forgot about it. Just as the sport was at its dying gasp, along came one Alexander Ford from the mainland. And he talked. Surfboarding was the sport of sports. There was nothing like it anywhere else in the world. They ought to be ashamed for letting it languish. It was one of the Islands' assets, a drawing card for travelers that would fill their hotels and bring them many permanent residents, etc., etc."[1]

If surfing can be said to have an original sin, it is encompassed in London's words. Though no apologist for the ravages of imperialism, he subsumes a century of invasion by foreign powers, coercive conversion to Christianity, economic exploitation, ravages by foreign diseases and the drudgery of the sugar cane fields into one phrase – "they forgot about it". An honest look at the History of Hawaii (the only true colony that the United States ever took) would not say that the Hawaiians forgot surfing. It would say that they were forced to forget. It would say that the colonisation of Hawaii, like the colonisation of nearly every other area of the world, was a project of cultural violence that disassembled the entity once known as 'Hawaiian culture' piece by piece, mixed it up and recast it in the image of its conquerors to serve the global market. When those whims changed, surfing was not recovered but instead reinterpreted and re-animated in some unsteady and half-baked iteration of its former self, pumped full of special interests, tourist kitsch, White Savior myths and bare-faced nostalgia, then sold to the world through Cosmopolitan magazine and beach demonstrations by coastal real-estate moguls.

Surfing is not the sport of kings, not as those pagan kings knew it. It is the ill-begotten child of colonialism and travel marketing, resurrected from the crucified remains of an indigenous culture to serve the global curio market as the king of the exotic commodities[2]. It is a Frankenstein messiah, promising salvation from the postmodern malaise (by way of the mysterious rapture of 'stoke') all the while inveigling us to buy another pair of board shorts to go with our all-in-one beach holiday. But surfing has not turned 'corporate'. It has been, in varying degrees, the pet project of corporate entities from its very re-inception in the 20th century, when Hume Ford saw that it could be used as an effective bate to market Hawaiin Holidays. As such, it functions on various levels. First and still foremost, surfing is the act of riding a wave. Second, surfing is a shared system of interests and beliefs. Finally, surfing is a symbolic system – bronzed bodies, shakas, and reef passes – that are regularly distilled and used to sell anything from package holidays to Coca Cola. In all three senses, surfing has grown apace with the neo-liberal economic developments of the 20th century, including the American exodus to costal properties (in their own country and abroad) and the explosion of the global mass-tourism market. Although it took root in certain places, notably California and Australia, what is exceptional about surfing is the way it spread from First World centres to often-tropical peripheries according to an almost purely classical model of colonialism.

Starting in the '70s it spread across the world on the backs of surf hippies, a class of people very similar to the one that Hannah Arendt calls "the mob" who spread the imperial dream of the great powers a century and a half before them. In the late 19th century, the mob was the "inevitable residue of the capitalist system", the "superfluous men" who fled every strata of European society, disaffected and fed up with their own economic and spiritual standing. They were the gold prospectors, white elephant hunters, the peripatetic traders, homesteaders, the administrators and soldiers. They ran the plantations and manned the maxim guns:

"Outside all social restraint and hypocrisy, against the backdrop of native life, the gentleman and the criminal felt not only the closeness of men who share the same color of skin, but the impact of a world of infinite possibilities for crimes committed in the spirit of play, for the combination of horror and laughter, that is for the full realization of their own phantom-like existence. Native life lent these ghostlike events a seeming guarantee against all consequences because anyhow it looked to these men like a 'mere play of shadows. A play of shadows, the dominant race could walk through unaffected and disregarded in the pursuit of its incomprehensible aims and needs."[3]

It is not hard to read late 20th century surf adventurers into this description. The expansion of 'surfing' could be seen as the by-product of an alliance between Western business interests (first in the form of drugs, later as swim suits and t-shirts) and the disaffected, countercultural residue of Western capitalism – young men who, fed up with the restrictions of postmodern suburban living, set out in search of one of the few remaining resources that no one had ever thought to exploit – waves. The difference, sometimes pronounced, other times less so, was that they did not bring a formal colonial apparatus with them. It would, however, be a mistake to say they came innocently.

If they had gone simply to ride waves, to enjoy a resource that no one else much cared for, then perhaps this article would be unnecessary. But as Joel Tudor once pointed out, the logic of surfing has always counted 'the scam' among its defining elements[4]. It has never just been about riding waves, it has been about finding a way to ride waves while not pursuing a job that would take you away from wave riding. It is rare for any dedicated surfer to describe his or her lifestyle in such boldly economic terms because it points to the central fact that the exotic rhetoric of surfing continually tries to mask: that the entire culture is based on a market driven, exploitative model. So where the surf mob went, tourism was sure to follow and the changes it would bring, through influxes of foreign investment, were profound.

Like many businesses before them, the business of surf expansionists started off rather questionably. Soon, surf camps sprang up and then fishing villages turned into surf ghettos from Newquay to Kuta beach. Today, we find ourselves in the era of the all inclusive surf resort – tiny outposts of pure colonisation clinging to the edges of places like Fiji, or swarming reef passes in the form of air conditioned yachts in the Mentawai Islands. They justify exploitation through a slight modification of that hoary cliché, terra nullius – "there were no surfers when we got here, erego the waves are ours". That such a logic should prevail, mostly unquestioned, by both those inside and outside surfing in the 21st century speaks to the shortcomings in both surfing as a social entity and the ability of academia to speak truth to power. Surfing is begging to be critiqued from a Postcolonial or Subaltern Studies standpoint, especially given that most of its driving imagery is culled directly from the contact zones of postcolonial encounter[5].

There are few cultures that so neatly pose the sticky questions of power that arise from the interaction between travel, transnational business, journalism and privileged leisure time than surfing. It stands alongside mountain climbing, as a living fossil – the missing link between outright colonial exploitation and newer, subtler forms of neo-imperialism. With the correct theorisation, it could produce the still-vague links that prove the transition from one type of inequality to another under the benign and totalising rhetoric of 'globalisation'.

The problem, of course, is that it is much more pleasant to join the mob than to stand against it. Some of the old empire's greatest and most eloquent apologists were formed in the crucible of colonial administration and so it is with surfing, as the smartest and most fervent are co-opted into the comforting aegis of the clothing companies and marketing firms who are able to subsidise a lifestyle of beachside leisure in return for reams of advertorial.

But PR cannot stand against a growing tide of public unrest. It cannot stand against Brazilians who are sick of being stereotyped, against Mentawaians who are fed up with being fleeced, against a general surfing public who are more globally aware than they have ever been and are quickly growing tired of the same old stories of deserted islands and perfect waves. The task before us is to break the culture of fear that surrounds any questioning of the sacrosanct myths of surfing. We must discard the deluded self-image of surfing as a 'counter culture' defined by a bland Australio/Californian homogeneity and look towards a future in which an already hybrid identity draws meaningfully and without exploitation on the new cultures that are beginning to influence it.

We can start this process in two ways. First, we must stop running our culture like an industry in which the bottom line always has the final say. It is time to define exactly how we benefit from the surfing industrial complex, and conversely, how it is corroding the very culture it seeks to deify. We have reached a point where our identity as a group is inseparable from a handful of large clothing brands whose thirst for profit has not only colonised the world, but it has colonised the very minds of surfers. This is not to say that board shorts, wet suits and, of course, surfboards are not valuable goods that are totemic to the pursuit of surfing. But once the acquisition of equipment outstrips the pursuit, once the gear itself is fetishised even more than the actual act of wave riding, then the transformation from sporting culture to consumer culture will be complete. We have not reached the point of no return but it is on the horizon and if we want to avoid it, we must begin to separate the essence of our pursuit from the commercial.

Secondly we must learn to turn away, every once in a while, from the beguiling pull of the watery horizon and train our gaze onto the shore. We must stop pretending that we move through terra nullius, unheeded and without footprint and instead begin to examine the ways that surfing has affected the places it has been transplanted, both for good and for ill. Bali, Costa Rica, Peru, and the many island outposts that dot the Indian Ocean and South Pacific; all have experienced the blessing and the blight of the surf bug. In the future it will be our responsibility, not as nationals of certain countries or denizens of First or Third worlds, but as torch bearers of the same culture, regardless of language, economy, and providence, to work together to ensure that our shared interests are protected and well-regulated. If surfers fail to look inward and make difficult critiques, they will find themselves stuck in an unending loop of cultural atavism in which the past is continually mined to feed the commercial gristmill of the present.

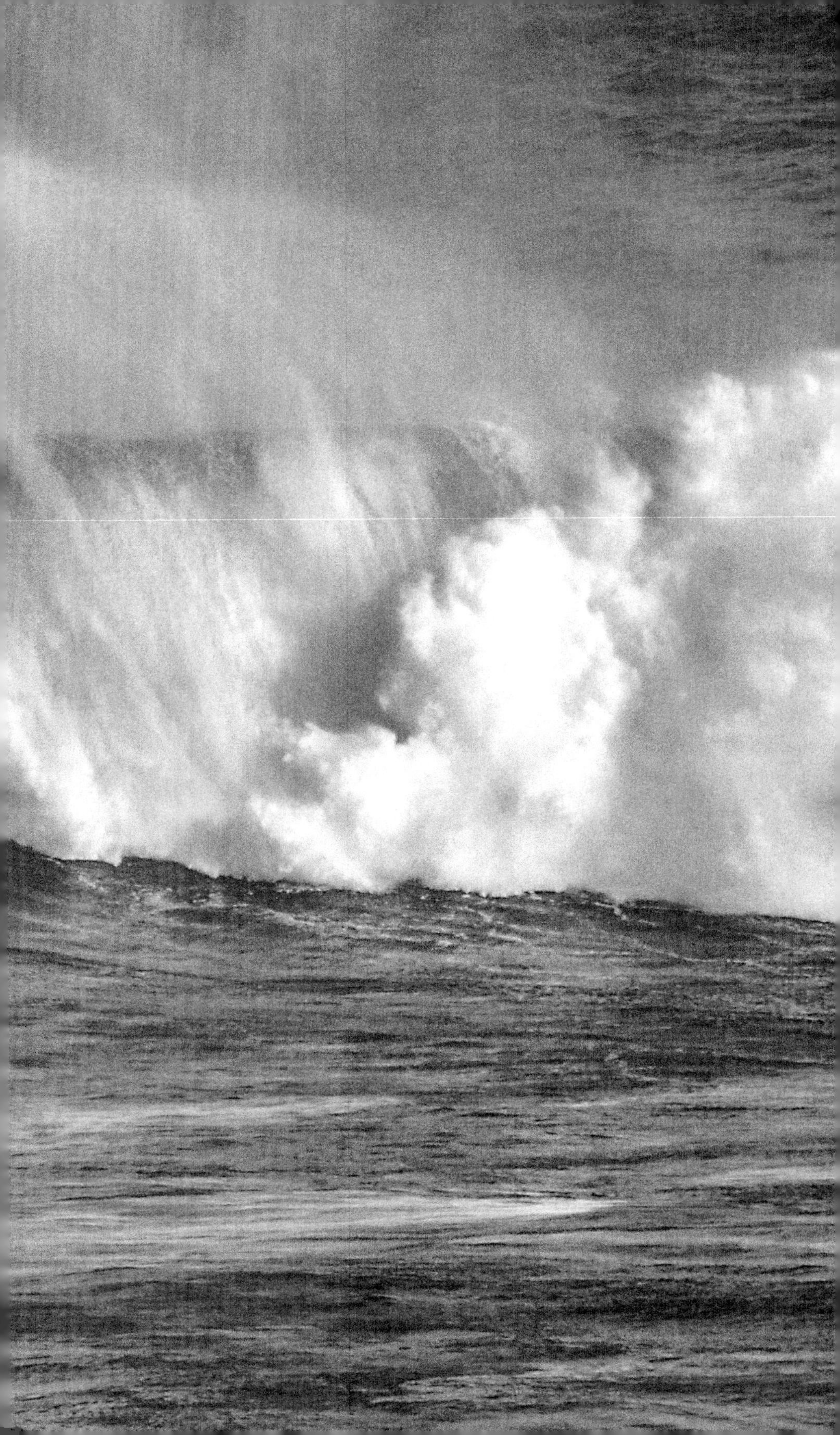

4.4

Shifting Surfing Towards Environmental Justice

Cori Schumacher

Being a surfer carries with it the dynamic experience of border-crossing. Each time we trespass upon the seas, we are crossing into territories once reserved for hardy adventurers, fisher-folk and warriors. Though the modern surf industry narratives might wish to recall historic identities in order to make surfing more heroic, most surfers connect with the activity of surfing more as exuberant play than anything else. Caught amidst this tango of defining such border-crossings are important nature elements that often get ignored by the surf industry when it creates products that appeal to consumers who can be coaxed into embracing the surfing lifestyle.

The ocean and its inhabitants are intuitive natural elements that are often used strategically in the conflicting narrative of the surf industry. An example of this is the use of the ocean-as-villain trope where surf warriors battle in competition. There has been much done to raise awareness of the ocean's health in a facile manner. This does not take into account the very processes used by the surf industry in creating the products that make it profitable. The single greatest challenge for the surf industry is the motivation to redefine and transition from simple environmentalism to environmental justice perspectives. That is, getting surfers and the surf industry to focus on production by working in a mode that values humans and nonhumans along with our environment.

Much has been written on the consumer side of surf industry growth, but we must look at the entire supply chain. If there is an embrace and respect of women does it apply to those who are making the clothing being sold to female consumers? Does it apply to the women and girls who are growing and harvesting the cotton that is used to make women's surf clothing? And what of the men and boys on the production end of clothing manufacture? According to the Free 2 Work organization, many surf clothing companies have not ensured

> **Big Surfing: A Space for Women?**
>
> We are able to objectively view the financial rise of the surf industry over the last several years and point to its direct connection to the embrace of the female surf-lifestyle market. The women's surf clothing market drove sales to their highest from the mid-1990s through to about 2008. Yet through it all, professional female surfers' sponsorship salaries remained substantially lower than their male counterparts, as did their prize money on the ASP world surfing tour. Though we do see relatively more female surfers in surf media, it remains a tiny percentage compared to representations of male surfers and is skewed toward a heterosexual male gaze.
>
> From 2008 to 2013, Big Surfing's profits descended and, as companies cut spending, women's competitions were the first on the chopping block. During this time period and continuing today, female surfers have increasingly been sexualized in marketing campaigns. The body type, skin color and sexuality that are celebrated/visible have been of one particular stereotype: thin and athletic (but not too athletic), white (with the sole exception being Hawaiian) and stressed as heterosexual. The surf marketing perpetrated by Big Surfing has done little to create an inclusive space for women, indeed it can be argued that it is actively constricting this space that blew open in the mid-1990s.

their clothing is made in a responsible or sustainable manner. Free 2 Work, a project that focuses on ending modern slavery, including child labour, has noted that some well-known surf brands score among the lowest when it comes to exploiting their workforce and supporting modern slavery.[1] Can we envision and carry out environmentalism that values all naturecultures?[2] For, if what is promoted as environmentally aware only benefits the companies marketing themselves as green to consumers, who can afford to purchase the surfing lifestyle, can we call this a positive social shift, 'sustainable' or even 'environmentalism'? The key questions to ask do not revolve solely around what privileged consumers receive as a consequence (a less guilty conscience), but how those who are struggling at the bottom of the supply chain benefit materially.

The same questions must be asked of how the big surfing brands actually benefit the ocean and its creatures. It does not matter if surf clothing companies raise money and awareness to benefit dolphins and whales if the very way they are making their clothing creates toxins that run from factories to the sea.

The surf industry has grown into a global business, organising much of its production internationally beyond closed doors. These transactions are not, however, beyond our ability to influence. Surfer-consumers with an eye towards environmental justice can hold brands accountable by asking: "Where was this product made?", "How was it made?", "By whom?", "How is the brand that has created this product for me, ensuring the equality, empowerment and safety of those making it, while working towards a more sustainable production standard?". Though the majority of surf companies have production standards in place, as illustrated by Free 2 Work's research, it is important that these standards are bolstered by transparent supply chains and publicly accessible, objective studies and research so the surfer-consumer can check these against their own values and ethics. Surf environmentalist ethics ought to stretch as far as the hands that pluck the cotton used to create our clothing and delve as deep as the sea that produces the liquid mounds we play on, but we will not be able to accomplish this if we, as surfer-consumers, do not first expand our imaginations past a vision of surfing as simple escapism.

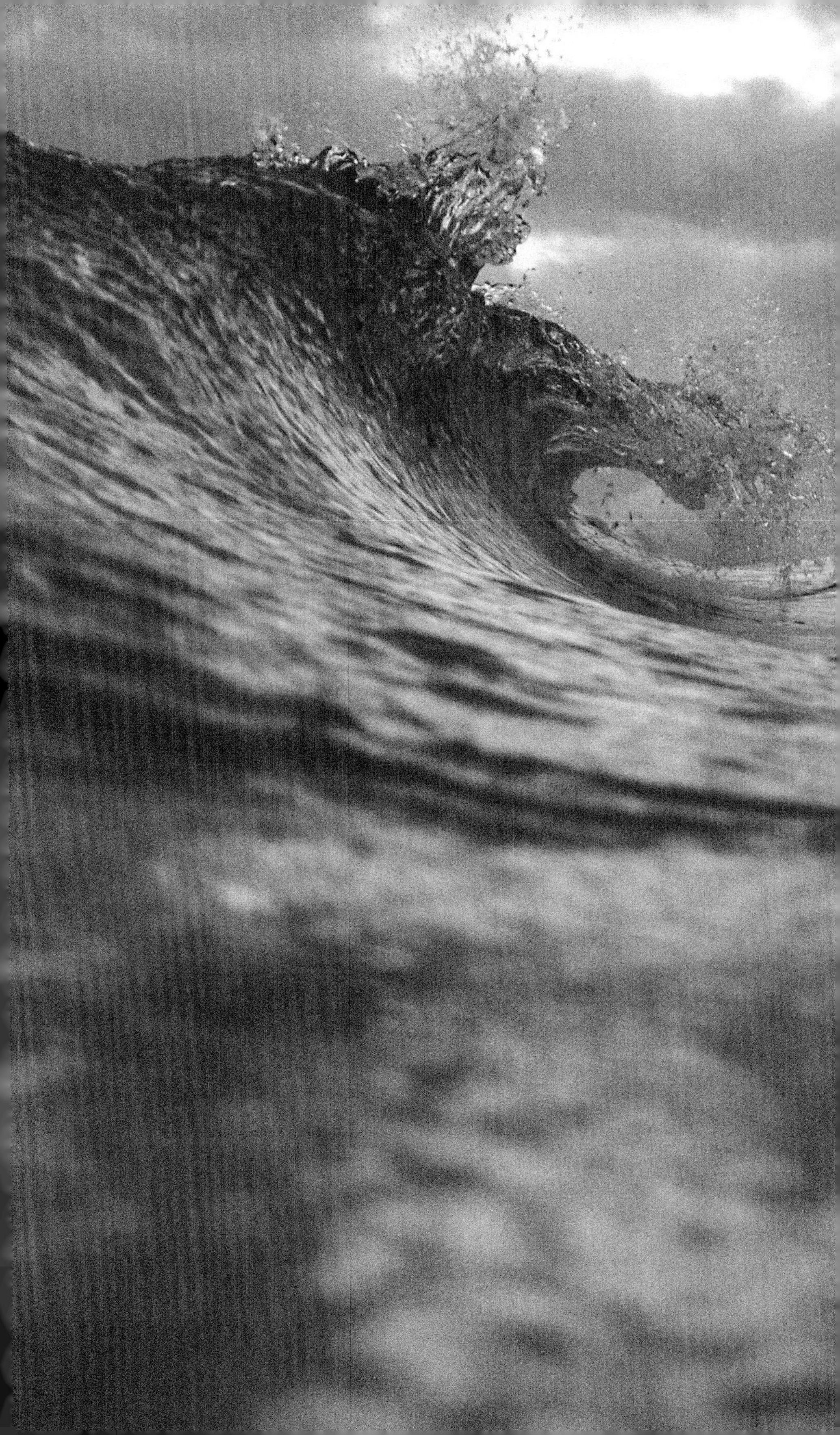

4.5

Shared Stoke: 'Only a Surfer Knows the Feeling'

Mark Marovich

Unique in the annals of surf marketing, a powerful tagline that moves beyond ad-speak to accurately reflect a spirit, seemingly without controversy, of the surfer and to the dreamer. But the slogan is innately controversial in being inherently dichotomous with the promotion and celebration, as presented, of the individual or collective 'surfer' above or beyond the outsider.

You know the feeling; you're part of the tribe, a global community living amongst the 'others', those who simply can't know the feeling but who subscribe to the dream or have had the dream subscribed to them? In this light, is this really the feeling we're after? From Madison Avenue to the Mall of America, Reunion Island to the Bakit Peninsula, the Silver Screen to Silver Strand, surf is alive! In our increasingly connected world, the surfing diaspora and surf dreamers alike are tangibly or romantically ensconced in nearly every corner. Taken as a whole, this community is numerically impressive, while the count of participating surfers is minimal in relation to society at large. The numbers don't tell the full story as our might is far beyond the count, a condition of the weight hoisted upon ourselves as progressive and exploratory individuals, and the weight bestowed upon us as the embodiment of cool by culture makers in the media. This individual and collective weight is immense and powerful and begets responsibility, the responsibility to move beyond us-and-them andto create a new feeling, this time a new reality, a reality of shared stoke.

'Shared Stoke' – the benefits accrued from the recognition and policy of mutual dependency between the physical and economic health of our communities and environment, on a global scale, and the health of our sport and industry.

How are we, as individuals, nonprofits and brands, doing as stewards of the dream? What can we do to move beyond 'the dream' to deliver the necessary ideal of shared stoke?

Statements and Missions

"Surfers are the natural guardians and spokespersons of the sea ... We base our lives in and around it. Surfers must be among the first to lead by example to create the critical mass of change that will inspire others to look after the ocean — our playground". - Dan Ross, professional surfer[1]

"By traveling to far-flung global surf destinations, the international surfing community is able to witness firsthand the daily struggle faced by the majority of the world's citizens. This interaction between the surfing world and the developing world presents a unique opportunity to create relationships with local residents and support the growth of their villages in a meaningful way". - ProjectWoo[2]

"Be the catalyst that transforms surf culture *and* industry into a powerful community that protects the ocean playground. We believe that surfing can become the premier showcase of people and businesses working together to solve environmental problems while having fun". - SustainableSurf[3]

"Build the best product, cause no unnecessary harm, use business to inspire and implement solutions to the environmental crisis". - Patagonia[4]

"...use apparel sales as a vehicle to provide care, support and financial resources to those in need". - Jedidiah[5]

With the current and prospective conditions of our environment, trans-boundary societal ills, and financial conditions around this blue planet, our pursuit of stoke hangs in the balance. We, as *knowers of the feeling*, must do our part to help break the barriers between us and the dreamers as our passion and the industry is at stake. Both Merriam & Webster deliver as a definition of the term bubble a 'delusive scheme'. While I'm not here to portend that the essence within 'only a surfer knows the feeling' is delusory or that it's a scheme against others, it does raise questions about what we have built around us and how we interact with the outside. Whilst we have the ability to create positive change on an individual and collective level by following the examples above, the real question is are we up to the challenge to move beyond where we are today and create shared stoke for all?

Exploring Sustainability in the Surf Industry Through Film: *Manufacturing Stoke*

Pierce Kavanaugh

September 2010
I got a message from my friend Gary that he was in San Diego to play some music at an event called the Cardiff Surf Classic and Green Beach Fair. He invited my wife, Petra and I to check it out. I hadn't heard about the fair, but it was such a beautiful day, one of those sunny late September weekends that even the most jaded Southern Californians realises just how good we have it. Not needing too much of an excuse to go to the beach, Petra and I were out the door in an instant. Strolling around the event, I soaked in the beehive of activity. It was a great turn out and the vendors were beaming. Towhead groms were carving skateboards in and out of everyone, mimicking roundhouse cutbacks on invisible waves. It flashed me back to a fond image of how I perceived North County while growing up. Surfers driving around in pickup trucks with their ladies, dogs and single fins hanging out of every open window. To me, North County always has a relaxed, hippie vibe to it, which I have always appreciated.

The Green Beach Fair featured everything from organic surf wax to homemade sunscreens with a central focus on recycling. As I meandered through the event I kept returning to the Enjoy Handplanes booth. It was manned by two Leucadia guys turning discarded surfboards and wetsuits into handplanes for bodysurfing. Not since the mystical Hand Gun from the late 1970s had I seen an actual handplane. Yet, here were all kinds of beautiful handplanes sitting right in front of me. Handplanes? Up here, in crumbly North County beachbreak? I was tripping out. I have been bodysurfing forever and I thought only about 20 people did it. Luckily, Gary began playing music so I could walk away from this booth quickly without telling these guys they were doomed. I mean, come on, nobody bodysurfs (this was nine months before the release of *Come Hell or High Water*).

So after quickly dismissing the future of handplanes, I left with the concept of sustainability in the surf industry nagging my subconscious. The seed for *Manufacturing Stoke* had been planted.

During my initial research, I was shocked to discover what a behemoth surfing had become. Since its infancy, surfing has grown into a $7 Billion dollar a year industry in the U.S. alone, with a massive percentage of revenue coming from apparel. I thought only Hollywood, Columbian drug lords, and Mark Zuckerberg made this kind of money. Surely with this kind of capital and profit on hand, the surfers on top of the corporate heap would have always factored environmentalism into every business decision they've made? After all, they are surfers first, right? In 2006 and 2007 there were even 'Green Issues' from Surfing Magazine where most major surf brands made sweeping declarations about their aspirations and commitment towards environmentalism.

The energy surrounding the Green Beach Fair signaled that something was going on – a paradigm shift, perhaps. I could detect a common, unspoken conversation simmering just below the surface. So why not, I thought, make a film on the current state of the surf industry? I can show these grassroots start-ups in conjunction with the established surf industry, and I was pretty sure a film had never been made on the subject. Usually, surf films are celebratory in nature with a bunch of exotic locales and beautiful waves but they rarely tell us more than we already know. I wanted to create a legitimate documentary about the surf industry that showed the good, the bad and the ugly.

The original concept was to create a short documentary film series revolving around different niche aspects of the surf industry in regards to sustainability. First would be surf wax, followed by shaping, wetsuits and, finally, clothing. I would conduct interviews with anyone who wanted to be involved – open to all. I just wanted discourse, no agenda. I just simply wanted to start the conversation. I figured the popularity of the Green Beach Fair warranted a closer look but I chose the short film format for two main reasons. I couldn't afford a feature film and frankly, I still didn't think people cared enough about the industry as a whole to watch an entire film. I recruited two close friends from film school, Geoffrey and Max, and persuaded them to bring any film equipment they had and to join me on a week-long shoot with a US$600 budget. Clearly getting paid was unlikely but I committed to feeding them and to beg, borrow and steal (returning said stolen items later, of course) to make this film happen. I then called Bird Huffman who put me in contact with my first interview. There was no going back.

November 2010

The first three interviews changed everything. John Baker Dahl of Wax Research, Matt Mattoon from Matunas Wax, and local Windansea grom phenom Lucas Dirkse had far more to say than I expected. We ran out of batteries, memory cards and daylight at all these interviews. There was passion, inspiration, angst, tension and hope. It was clear that this was much bigger than just a short film on surf wax. It turned out that people really do care about the surf industry and we had just opened up the floodgates. We downshifted, regrouped and resolved to do whatever it took to turn *Manufacturing Stoke* into a feature film, which meant: shoot sparingly until broke; scrape together cash for gas and film equipment rentals; repeat. John, Matt and Lucas unwittingly launched us on a five-month odyssey chasing more than 35 interviews the length of the California coast.

The initial interviews were nothing short of amazing. People were forthright and genuine in their concern for the surf industry. Every time we completed an interview it cemented the notion that this film was meant to be. One that stands out as a wake up call was with Glenn Hening who founded the Surfrider Foundation and has always been at the forefront of the preservation of our coastlines. Glenn can also come across as one of the scariest people on the planet. Luckily I had met Glenn before so I was somewhat prepared. I love Glenn and his intensity but he had me and my film crew backing away throughout the course of the interview – he was interviewing us! I get it, I was producing a film about one of Glenn's most fiercely held passions and he was challenging us. Incredibly informative discourse was punctuated with skeptical barbs revealing that he thought nothing would ever come of our film. His prods, pokes and doubts only motivated us – I was brought up a Catholic, so I recognise fire and brimstone. I will never forget leaving Glenn's house to take a lunch break between interviews; we were barely out the door when Director of Photography, Max, a little paler and wide-eyed than normal, grabbed my arm and whispered, "Pierce, now you have a film!"

During the first month of filming it became obvious that 'big surfing' wanted nothing to do with this film. Almost every phone call and email went unanswered. I called them all… Quiksilver, Hurley, Patagonia, Billabong, Volcom, Reef, O'Neill, etc. This was tremendously discouraging because I felt that in order to have a balanced film I needed representation from the industry. Sure, I was getting amazing interviews celebrating those on the fringe trying to deconstruct and recreate a surf industry with environmentalism as its ethos, but I still needed the voice of big surfing.

"SIMA ANNOUNCES LAUNCH OF SUSTAINABILITY COLLECTIVE"

I found this headline during my research and almost fell out of my chair. Here's what the rest of it said:

"Sustainability in the Action Sports Industry: Benefits and Best Practices Join the founding partners of the recently formed Sustainability Collective (an industry based advisory and resource organization) as they look at the current state of sustainable business in the action sports industry, offer practical – and realistic – tips on changes companies can make today, and where the industry can and should be in the near future. The session will include time for interactive feedback from attendees on what the industry's key needs are from this resource group.

Panelists:
Derek Sabori / Director of Sustainability, Volcom;
Jeff Wilson / VP of Sustainability Programs, Quiksilver
Roian Atwood, Manager of Environmental Affairs, Sole Technology".

The interview with Sustainability Collective has gotten me in hot water more than once, and with some really good friends, so let me be very clear about what transpired. In November 2011, the Surf Industry Manufacturers Association (SIMA) held an annual conference in Orange County and the formation of the Sustainability Collective was announced. Quiksilver, Volcom and Sole Technologies (Etnies) created positions to spearhead sustainable initiatives in their everyday business practices. Perfect timing? I was doing a film on sustainability in the surf industry and this group forms. It seemed too good to be true. So far, it has been impossible to even get my foot in the corporate surf door. We thought this may be a brief window of opportunity, so we scrambled. Soon we were on our way to Orange County, the epicentre of the surf industry. This was an opportunity for the brands to promote their newly formed union and, for me, it was an opportunity to dig a little deeper.

I interviewed Derek Sabori (Volcom), Roian Atwood (Sole Technologies) and Jeff Wilson (Quiksilver) together to get an overview of the Sustainability Collective and what changes they proposed for the industry. We had a great talk and these guys are really personable and I believe, given the chance, they could do great things, but I couldn't help but wonder, are their hands tied? Are they simply towing the company line?

I wanted the Collective to bring me over to their way of thinking. I was looking for a glimmer of hope so I interviewed Derek, Roian and Jeff individually to find out more about their company policies and their contributions to the Sustainability Collective. It appeared that Volcom and Etnies were doing well, initiating sustainable business practices, however, when it came to Quiksilver, it was kind of a train wreck. Jeff is a genuine guy who is dedicated to sustainability, but he seemed to find himself in the uncomfortable position of having to backpedal from Quiksilver's public claims to sustainability.

May 2011

Five months and 35 interviews spanning the gamut of the surf community later, what started as a stroll on a beautiful Cardiff day had turned my life upside down. *Manufacturing Stoke* premiered at Bird's Surf Shed in San Diego on May 21, 2011 and has since screened at over 20 international film festivals across the globe. It won a Best Film Award and a couple of Honorable Mentions. We pieced together our own grassroots tour on both sides of the country to bring the film to the people. We screened anywhere we could. Pizza parlours, libraries, surf shops, even the side of a barn. Little did I know that this would cartwheel us into our next endeavour. I walked away from production completely inspired. This cathartic process had me re-examine my own relationship with and within the surfing community. Truth be told, I hadn't been paying much attention to the surfing world for the last decade or so. It simply didn't speak to me. Sure I was in the water all the time, but I just didn't really care about mags, contests and other crap that came along with it. *Manufacturing Stoke* stripped my love for the ocean down to its bare essentials. I realized I didn't need much more than that.

Pierce grilling the panel at the 10th Annual Surfing Arts Science and Issues Conference, Surfing's New Aloha: The Growing Trend of Giving Back, in February 2012 (Courtesy of Gregory Borne)

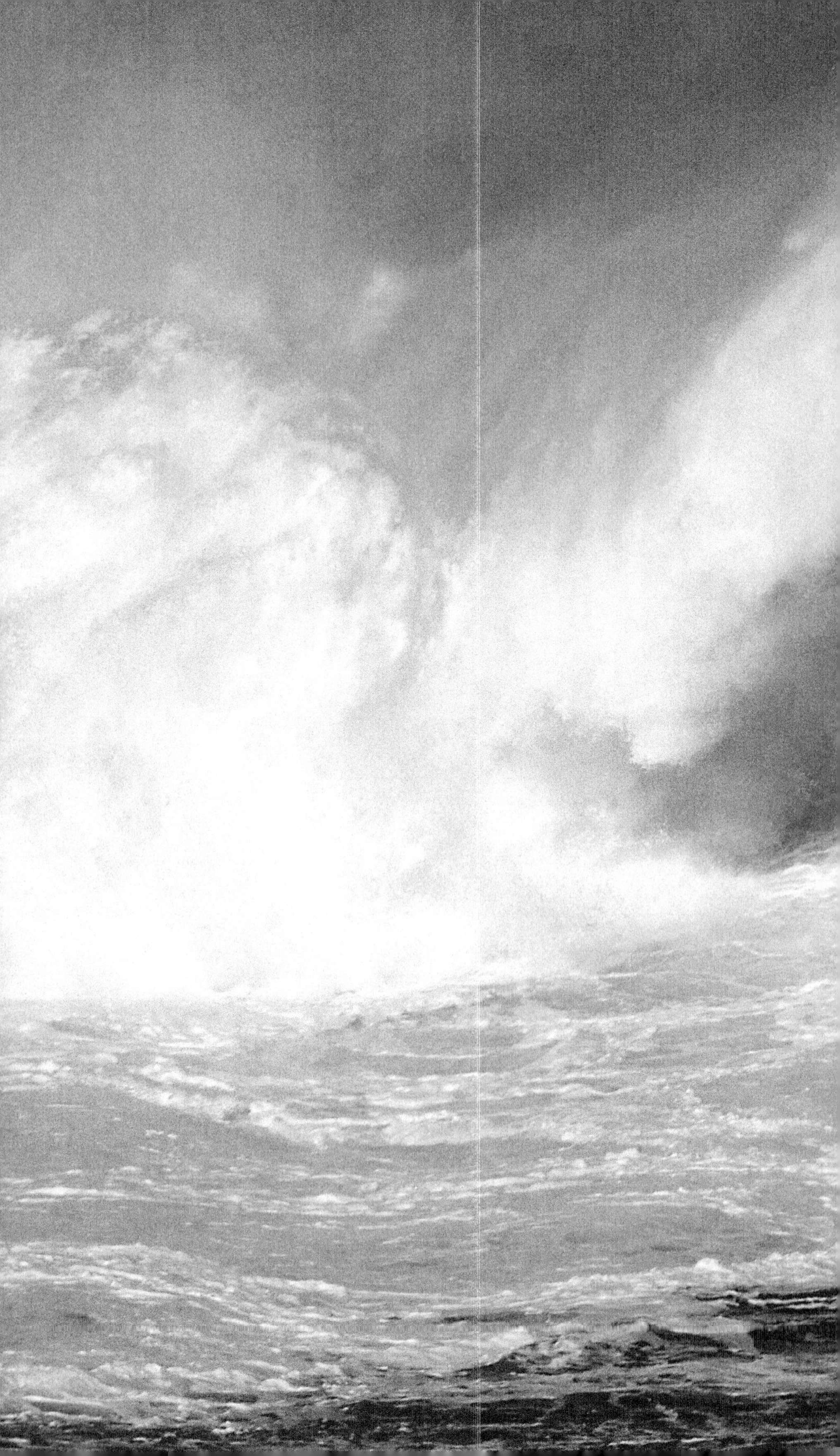

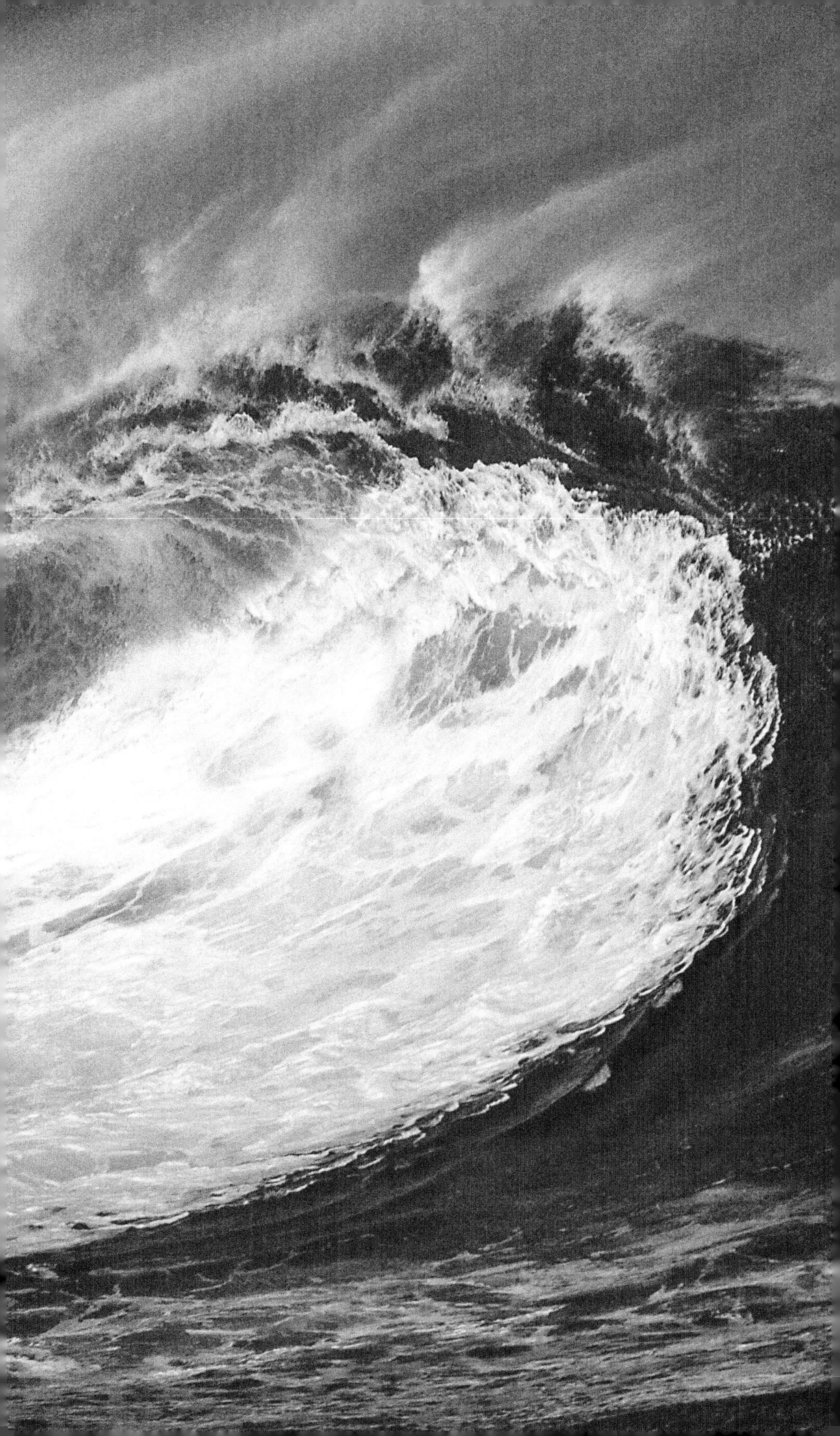

Chapter Five
NGO Response

Chapter Five builds upon the previous chapters' picture of what sustainability means in surfing and what issues may be contributing to a transition to sustainability through some unique insights from the captains of the surf industry and leading thinkers in the surfing world. Chapter Five provides a series of responses to the challenges of sustainability. Each contributor in this chapter represents unique leadership roles from the world's largest surfing NGO, arguably the industry leader in technological innovation in surfboard manufacturing, a five time Irish surfing champion, PhD and founder of Waves for Freedom. This chapter also includes insights from an innovative organisation that preserves and highlights the history and culture of surfing in the UK. Finally, Chapter Five provides us with a commentary from arguably one the most success organisations in promoting and implementing sustainability in the surfing world, Sustainable Surf.

Together, the contributors for this chapter discuss diverse issues all responding to the challenge of sustainability in their own ways. Jim Moriarty and Chad Nelson of Surfrider Foundation discuss econometrics, and the role of stewardship and partnerships. Nev Hyman goes on to discuss Firewire's innovative processes, his personal commitment to sustainability and empowerment, and how this has inspired and contributed to his NevHouse initiative.

Easkey Britton offers a perspective that compliments the contribution of Cori Shumacher in the previous chapter, by discussing the important role of gender ethics in the surfing world. She does this in a comprehensive way from the origins of surfing in Hawaii, and personal role models such as Rell Sun, through to the importance of Surfing Development Organisation (SDO) and media in transitions to sustainability.

The Museum of British Surfing, the first and only surfing museum in the UK, emphasises the importance of history and culture for sustainability as well as expanding this to emphasise the importance of climate change and sea level rise to the surfing community. Connecting to the social realm, they also highlight their activities in educating youth by linking surfing to the environment. Finally, Sustainable Surf discuss how they are transforming surf culture towards sustainability. They talk about the underlying philosophy of their work as well as the programmes they have developed that have led to them receiving the 2014 Surfer Magazine's 'Agents for Change Award'.

Devastation caused by Cyclone Pam in Vanuatu, March 15, 2015 (top) and a NevHouse prefabricated home made from recycled plastic, offering solutions (bottom) (Courtesy of Jessica Williams)

5.1

Surfonomics: Using Economic Valuation to Protect Surfing

Chad Nelsen

Less than two miles off Huntington Beach, one of the most iconic surf towns in Southern California, the oil tanker *American Trader* was positioning itself for a routine connection with the offshore birth of the Golden West refinery in February, 1990. The captain made a critical error in gauging the water depth and punctured the vessel's hull with the anchor. Over 400,000 gallons of crude oil spilled into the sea. After a couple of days, the oil washed ashore polluting 14 miles of the Southern California shoreline from Alamitos Bay to Crystal Cove, closing the beach and many popular surfing areas for 34 days.

The ensuing legal battle lasted over eight years and resulted in a jury awarding the State of California US$18 million for damages resulting from environmental damage, beach closure and loss of surfing. As part of that lawsuit, economists on both sides argued about the value of beach going and surfing to determine the value of lost recreation as part of the damage assessment. This is one of the first documented cases of surf valuation entering an official decision making process. Dozens of other surfing areas impacted by coastal development, such the Killer Dana that was buried by a boat harbour, have not had that benefit, but surfing was likely to have been undervalued due to lack of empirical research on the economic values of surfing.

Almost 25 years later, our knowledge about the value of surfing has improved and there is a small, but growing, body of research on the economic value associated with surfing that can be used to aid decision making that may impact surfing resources.

Using Economic Values in Decision Making
Throughout the world, there is increasing development pressure along the coast forcing difficult decisions to be made about coastal issues and trade-offs between the conservation of existing natural and recreational resources

and development interests that could impact them. These decisions are often driven by economic arguments. Arguments for development can use known market forces such as the value of their development, increased tax review and the creation of jobs. These decisions often result in trade-offs that impact the coastal environment and the flow of recreational and ecosystem services that are supported by a healthy and accessible coastline. The economic impacts of coastal tourism are well known and are one of the most important drivers of the coastal economy in California and around the world[1]. Like other open access public resources, much of the economic value of coasts and oceans lies outside traditional markets because there is no fee for direct participation and therefore no observable value. Less is known about these non-market values of coastal recreation or how coastal management decisions will impact these values.

The non-market value of coastal recreation can be described as the amount users would be willing to pay for recreation on the coast. Information that accounts for both the market and non-market values associated with coastal conservation and recreation are required to make decisions regarding public resources that are ultimately best for the welfare of the public.

Non-market Values of Coastal Recreation
Research on non-market valuation has evolved over the last 30 years. There is a growing body of research on coastal recreation, but most of it is centered on beach-going[2]. Coastal recreation is a diverse set of activities that include going to the beach, surfing, walking, swimming, shore fishing, kayaking, snorkeling, diving and many other niche uses. Most research on the economics of coastal recreation has grouped all of these participants as beach-goers. However, these groups make choices regarding their recreation based on different beach attributes, have distinct behaviour patterns and different economic impacts and values associated with their recreational choices. See Nelsen, Pendleton, & Vaugh (2007)[3] for an example regarding surfing. As a result, management decisions affecting coastal resources will impact these users differently.

Capturing Data About Surfers
Methods to better understand coastal recreation and determine the non-market values require capturing data on the visiting and behavioural patterns, demographics and spending habits of coastal recreation by interviewing individual users either on-site or off-site[4]. Compared to the large general category of general beach-goers, many of these niche activities attract a small

population of avid visitors (e.g. scuba diving, surfing, standup paddleboarders) that represent a disproportionately high number of visits, local spending and non-market values for the size of the user group.

In some cases, entire user groups may be missed when assessing the value of coastal recreation or not studied at all. This is the case with most niche coastal uses like surfing. This can occur because the subset of users is too small to be captured via traditional population-wide surveys or they use the coast differently than typical beach-goers (different times, locations and seasons) and are missed by on-site surveys[5]. To adequately intercept a sufficient number of respondents of these activities requires a large number of survey respondents in a randomly chosen sample pool, or targeted methods can be used to identify potential respondents from these groups.

In these circumstances, researchers are faced with a trade-off between developing a survey methodology that captures a large, random population of users that is representative but may not capture important niche uses (i.e. surfing) or developing a targeted survey (e.g. opt-in Internet-based survey instrument) that may not be perfectly representative but will still capture important recreational, demographic and economic data that can aid decision making. When weighing up potential advantages and disadvantages of Internet-based surveys, it is less important that the survey is perfectly representative but instead how any disadvantages compare to other alternatives (e.g. other survey methods or no data at all) or if information collected will address the necessary management questions.

Choosing a Survey Methodology

Traditional survey modes such as Intercept surveys, Random Digital Dialing (RDD), or mail back survey instruments are more widely accepted and well vetted in the literature, and provide the ability to extrapolate to the larger population[6]. They also have disadvantages: they are expensive and time consuming to implement, especially when considering large areas with numerous access points. They may require a prohibitively large sample size to capture small but avid user groups or they may capture too small a sub-sample to provide statistically robust results.

Internet-based survey modes also have clear advantages and disadvantages. Those used for economic valuation are not yet common in the literature and therefore less accepted by academics or agencies. They often suffer from a lack of repetitiveness because the survey frame is not known and therefore can not be extrapolated to the larger known population of users[7]. Internet-based surveys may also be biased because the demographics of Internet users may be different from the general population.

Despite these disadvantages, the detailed information provided from Internet-based survey instruments may still answer important questions that can aid coastal zone decision-making. For example, Internet-based survey methods can aid in revealing the spatial extent of specialised coastal uses. In turn, this data could be used to identify specific locations for intercept surveys. Internet-based surveys can also provide targeted demographic and economic information on the users captured, which has value even if not expanded to a larger population. Further, Internet-based surveys made provide insights and raise question that motivate further research using expanded Internet-based research (e.g. representative Internet panels) or traditional methods.

Surfing Case Studies

Two previous decisions that affected surfing resources did not benefit from empirical research on the consumer surplus value of surfing, likely because surfers are difficult to survey. Surfers are hard to capture because the population of surfers is relatively small, their distribution is clustered and they can be difficult to intercept[8].

As mentioned previously, the 1990 *American Trader* oil spill closed access to popular beaches and surfing areas at Huntington Beach. It was possible to transfer empirical consumer surplus value from previous studies to determine the appropriate mitigation fee for the lost value for beach-going, but surfing proved more difficult. Although, surfer visits were counted using extended survey hours to capture their use (6.30 a.m. to 6.30 p.m.), surfers were not intercepted or surveyed to determine the consumer surplus of surfing. Instead, the consumer surplus of a surf visit was first estimated as equivalent to a nearby water park (US$16.95 in 1990) and then later as 25% higher than an individual beach visit (US$18.75 in 1990)[9]. Neither of these values were based on empirical data. Second, when seeking mitigation for the impact to a popular surfing area in El Segundo that was degraded by the construction of a groyne and beach fill, the California Coastal Commission referred to Chapman and Hanneman's (2001) water park entrance fee to value surfing when determining the lost consumer surplus. In both cases, the consumer surplus value of surfing was likely to have been undervalued due to lack of research on the economic values associated with surfing.

In contrast, when the California Coastal Commission was considering a toll road that could impact surfing at Trestles, in San Onofre State Park, an Internet-based survey was used to quickly and inexpensively gather data on surfers visiting Trestles to show that it is used by a relatively small (compared to beach goers at other popular beaches) group of avid surfers who are willing to travel long distances and generate annual economic impact on the City of San Clemente, ranging from US$8-12 million as valued in 2006[10]. In this case, the non-market values of surfing at Trestles were not included because that research had not been completed at the time of the decision. Inclusion of the consumer surplus values would have further demonstrated the high value of surfing at Trestles during the decision making process. Surfing at Trestles is valued at US$80 per person per visit, with an annual economic value of US$26 million in 2006[11]. The results on economic impact, not economic values, were provided to the California Coastal Commission and were considered during their determination regarding the construction of a toll road that would impact the quality of the waves at Trestles. In this case, the economic impact associated with the surfing resource at Trestles was considered in the decision making process and played a role in the denial of the project and protection of the waves[12]. The use of economic information on surfing to inform decision making is still the exception when management decisions that could affect surfing are made.

Surfonomics Research
To date there are a limited, but growing, number of research projects around the world that are focused on the economic values associated with surfing. A 2007 study of South Stradbroke and Bastion Point in Australia found that surfers spent AUS$20 million and AUS$231,000, respectively, on surfing at these specific surf breaks each year[13]. A 2008 study of Mundaka in Spain found that surfing has an estimated positive economic impact of up to $4.5 million per year to the local economy, in a town of approximately 1,900 people[14]. A 2009 study on Mavericks[15], famous big wave surf spot in San Mateo, California found that the average visitor to the area receives a benefit of US$56.7 per trip, which amounts to a total annual economic benefit from the Mavericks region of US$23.8 million[16]. These studies show that surfing areas are strong economic drivers and have a high economic value to local communities and to visitors. Other studies are currently in progress in Baja California, Mexico, Bali, Peru, Costa Rica and France (results pending).

Conclusion
Every day coastal zone managers are making decisions that impact coastal recreational amenities. Many of these decisions have economic information on the benefits of coastal development, but few have information on the market and non-market economics of coastal recreation. Efforts to value coastal recreation lack non-market values of coastal resources and recreation, which can tilt decision making towards the benefits of development over the conservation of public resources. This is shown in cases in California involving surfing (Killer Dana, Pratte's Reef, *American Trader* oil spill).

Coastal management decision makers are challenged by the lack of readily available economic information on coastal recreation, especially surfing. Additional research on the economics of coastal recreation and, more importantly, academic work that provides practical tools for coastal decision makers, will provide a better balance when making trade-offs between conservation and development of coastal resources. Most importantly, improved understanding of the non-market values associated with the coast will help ensure that public coastal resources do not continue to be undervalued in decision making in the future. The next time an oil spill closes a beach to surfing or a project is proposed that will impact surfing, we are much more prepared to make economic arguments than in the recent past. That said, there is still much to be done.

5.2

Protecting the Waves We Love So Much

Jim Moriarty

Surfing, as a culture, is at risk of losing the very thing it's centered on – good, clean waves. We sit on top of one of the world's most wonderful natural forms, waves. Yet it seems like we're failing to see or act on the wave degradation and loss happening. Let's keep things simple, the lowest common denominator regarding what surfers should care about are the following:

a) No wave should be lost.
b) All waves and coastlines should be accessible.
c) All nearshore ocean waters should be clean.

These are not novel or extraordinary ideas. These ideas frame why Surfrider came into existence 29 years ago. These issues are why our grassroots network as grown as large as it has all over the world. Yet, let's be real, we surfers are not all on that same page because the reality offers a biting contrast to the above statements. Waves are being lost. If you live in Southern California you hear older surfers speak of "Killer Dana" which today is a large harbour and you also feel the ongoing struggle to "Save Trestles" (a wave which is still not protected even though it's located within a popular State Park). As we all know, things are much, much worse outside the United States. Waves in places like Madira, Portugal or northern Baja, Mexico are threatened and then lost and only a few people are even aware. The simple truth is it's much easier to kill a wave in a developing country than it is in a developed country.

Places on our coastline are increasingly inaccessible. 60% of the state of Maine's coastline is private, you cannot access the ocean. Beach access fights are Surfrider's second most popular campaign type in the US. Outside the United States things are, again, worse. When a hotel goes into a pristine coastal area in the developing world one of the first things done privatizing the coastal access.

Hotel owners want to promote the fact hotel guests will have their own, private, trash-free beach experience.

Water is not clean and there is very, very little intelligence to know how dirty it is. The Obama administration defunded the BEACH Act in the United States and, with one pen stroke, essentially killed funding for clean water testing. At the grassroots level, Surfrider activists perform thousands of water tests every year via its Blue Water Task Force. We routinely confirm dirty water and work with various entities to have such issues addressed. Beyond Europe, US water and a handful of other First World nations water quality testing is rare. Public access to water quality testing results is even more rare. Connecting this with surfing, the San Clemente High School surf team must get Hepatitis shots in order to participate on the team. At a recent professional tournament in Brazil the winds shifted as the women's competition started. Raw sewage from nearby poor communities drifted into the lineup and made every surfer ill. These scenarios should make all surfers pause.

Surfing, our culture, has allowed these straightforward concepts to slip. We are allowing waves to be lost, access to be taken away and water quality to decline. However, there *is* hope and that hope is the surfing culture evolving into something that is more reflective of wave stewardship than wave domination. A parallel can be found in a neighboring sport. In the early days of rock climbing it became clear that the same people receiving joy from climbing peaks were the same people that were destroying the rock. The first climbers were literally hammering pitons into the rock and that act changed the experience for every climber that would follow, including them. It became clear that this culture had to change or the very thing they were drawn to, clean, climbable rock surfaces, would be lost. Surfing culture must move from being short-term oriented: this year's rising grom, this year's boardshort, this year's race for the title, this year's free surfer to demanding a long-term, sustainable future. Change is hard but change is also absolute. Surfers need to follow the example set by climbers. We need to preserve what we love so dearly so it's there tomorrow and the day after.

5.3
Sustainable Transitions: From Firewire to NevHouse

Nev Hyman

The Nevhoue team with The Hon. Joe Natuman, Prime Minister of Vanuatu (Courtesy of Nev Hyman)

I spent 35 years of my life making surfboards using toxic and quite horrible chemicals but was lucky enough to last 25 years in that career and not really be around them. I just shaped and had factories away from where I worked. But that doesn't discount my distaste for the fact that surfboards are manufactured out of some pretty toxic chemicals. So, in 2005, as a company, we decided to make a more environmentally friendly surfboard using materials that were better for the environment. The end result of that decision was the most environmentally friendly surfboard of that period in the world. This was recognised when we won the Surfing Industry Manufacturing Association (SIMA) award in Eurosima. We were very aware that we needed to improve. Part of that improvement was finding the right people to help realise that vision, for example Mark Price from X Reef Bazil, a brilliant brand marketer, but also an environmentalist in his own way.

The proof is in the product and today we have the most environmentally friendly surfboard on the planet, Timbertek. Back in 2005, I remember boldly standing up at a trade show in San Diego, probably a little bit too boldly and maybe a little bit to cockily and urging the audience to move away from Polyurethane (PU). I emphasised the need to move to more sustainable and user-friendly materials, not only for the environment but for indigenous workers, that are more often than not, an exploited workforce. Sadly, PU is as strong as it has ever been and whilst I'm not trying to put the nail in the coffin on PU, there still needs to be more effort to embrace epoxy bio resins that are now available. However, there is no denying that Firewire's competitors are using it, and pro surfers continue to win on PU boards. If you step back and look at the bigger picture, it's not the end of the world when you consider how many surfboards are used against, say, how many cars are made for example, so from this perspective it has very limited impact on the environment. What's really excited me about the evolution of Firewire is that, due to the complex but flexible nature of our manufacturing technique, we are able to play with other materials so much easier than any other surf board manufacturer, making it easier for Firewire to embrace more sustainable manufacturing techniques and materials.

Firewire surfboards are unique in a number of ways. Firewire boards aren't moulded so we can vacuum form any material in, on and around the board and we are not restricted by a hand shaped blank. We are always scouting for the best new, environmentally friendly materials. With Timbertek, we are using a sustainable timber Paulownia using the same construction schedule with the 12 millimetres of timber around the rail to give the flexural properties that you need for performance. So we have a board that surfs the same, if not better, than our FST performing boards. We have Sally Fitzgibbons, Felipe Toledo and other guys from California like Timmy Reyes who are performing well on the Timbertek. They're lightweight, super strong and a little bit stiffer, meaning it springs back quicker, so you get this really lively, electric feel. The only thing chemical about that board is the EPS core, which is the least toxic of all surfboard cores.

From a sustainability perspective, we extend this ethos throughout the lifecycle of the development of the board, having a positive impact on the local environments and communities that we operate in. For example, our factory in Thailand is the cleanest, most advanced surfboard factory in the world. The workers in the factory doing the lamination don't have to wear masks because there's very little fibreglass when the boards are sanded which means there's very little, if any, fibreglass particles flying about in the air, which is the most prominent hazard in the surfboard factory.

Furthermore, we are constantly striving to find new ways to raise the bar. We have recently introduced a new surfboard packing regime. Think for a moment of the thousands of surfboards that are transported globally every year. They use plastic, cardboard and other materials which will eventually end up in landfill. With 15,000 to 20,000 surfboards coming out of our factory this is a phenomenal amount of waste. If you go into a retail outlet which has just received, let's say, a delivery of 20 surfboards, there's a pile of waste with only landfill as its home. We recognise that this is not an acceptable part of the lifecycle of the surfboard so we have developed a system whereby there is no plastic in the packaging of the boards. We're doing as much as we possibly can as a company, but we're doing it in a way which is profitable so we are able to support our pro surfers and investors. We also support things like the Stoke Foundation which involves giving boards away to indigenous communities around the world or to surfers who simply can't afford new boards. The sustainable aspect of Firewire is so relevant to the mantra of the company. We are not doing this for the publicity, but are getting plenty anyway.

To a certain degree, there is a lesson here for the rest of the surfing industry. So far, we're the only surfboard company that's actually been successful at manufacturing volume, high performance surfboards that are significantly more sustainable to the environment, and all of this has happened in about seven years. Our competitors have, over the last eight years, tried to emulate us in their own way and they have been very successful at it. A good example would be Fibreflex. AABlot of technologies have been developed, but ultimately no one has gained the ground that Firewire has because we have a superior manufacturing technique (entirely CAD CAM). There are no 'ghost shapers' in Firewire. The boards come off the system 98% finished.

I had an epiphany about two years ago when I was sitting in a coffee shop in Helsinki, Finland. I was sitting there, watching all the beautiful 6.2 Finish girls walking by whilst designing boards for Michel Bourez from France that he was going to ride at Teahupoo. When I had finished, I hit send and, at that moment, thought, Oh my God I am never going to see or touch that board. This realisation was a turning point for me personally as I have always been so hands on, especially on team boards. Fast forward to today and, at the time this contribution was written, I received an email from Filipe Toledo who urgently needs a new board. I put my conference call on hold. I design his board in five minutes and send the file to Nathan on the Gold Coast who turns the AKU file into a 3D model. Then he sends this off to Thailand where the board gets machined and vacuum bagged three times and when it comes off the machine the last time, it's 100% finished its accurate to 0.5 millimetres. The only thing that the proverbial shaper has to do is run 120 grit around the rail to take off the bearings, double check the edges, which are already cut in by the computer, thinning the tip of the nose down by about three to four millimetres. Today every other shaper on the planet that is using a computer system like AKU-Shaper or Shape 3D and APS 3000 is doing this as a result of that earlier epiphany. They're all using a programme that I pulled together using CAB designers like Jimmy Freeze and Emanuel Vimlin from Shape 3D. The idea was that dumb shapers like me could actually use these 'Auto CAD' style programmes. So here I am now, in my wine cellar in Seminyak doing boards for the world's most innovative surfers.

The future of sustainability within the surfing industry must be innovative and make strides in a similar way to Firewire, who is in the unique position of being able to use materials that others can't. The original Timbertechs, just as with the original Firewire (Sunova), all had to be handmade. Now we are making more than a hundred boards a day. When someone has a great idea to build the board in a sustainable way, you would be hard pressed to actually do it. My worry is that until somebody does what Firewire has done, the industry is going to stay where it is. That's why, seven or eight years later, the whole industry is still using polyurethane. It's not going to change until another company is able to take the lead alongside Firewire.

Nevhouse
Years ago, I invested in a European plastics recycling company called JET. I thought if I was going to invest in something, I might as well invest in something that helped to clean up the environment that we surfers rely so much on. The technology was amazing as you could take the seven codes of co-mingled plastic and put it all into a unique extrusion machine which popped out transport pallets, posts and floorboards, etc. Unfortunately, the company didn't really take off as well as I'd hoped as the end products weren't really 'sexy' enough; they didn't capture much needed investors imagination, even though the environmental aspect was warmly received by many. In 2012, I was in Bali, having a great time surfing whilst researching opportunities for JET. I was with

this group who were doing work with the Indonesian government regarding homes for the poor required in Lombok, and was asked the question, Could we build houses out of plastic waste instead of just flooring and posts. Of course, I said, "Sure we can!" but after looking into it, I realised that the JET system I was using couldn't actually do what I said it could. I knew that if I could turn post-use plastic into houses for the poor I'd have no issue selling the concept, so I hired Leyland Williams, a Polymer Chemist from Canada and Ken McBryde, Principal architect of Innovarchi and now Hassel in Sydney who is an expert in Indigenous housing. To complement his brilliance, we hired ARUP, the globally renowned engineering firm and ultimately designed a house culturally specific to Indonesia. This is a flat-pack, erect and dismantle in two days, inexpensive home. It is resistant to bacteria, low or no maintenance, earthquake, wind and fire resistant and will last generations. Diverting waste from landfill, off the streets and out of the rivers and turning it into houses for the poor is a very compelling story that captures everyone's imagination as it ticks every box whilst bringing positive attention to charitable causes and government initiatives to bring attention to the millions of homeless globally. Why is this process so special? Simple. You can't make the unique profiles that houses are constructed from out of traditional materials like wood, concrete, composites, aluminium, or even virgin plastic, as it would be just too expensive. Our secret is inexpensive or zero cost post-use plastic materials combined with pretty amazing chemistry to provide the structural integrity required to build a home.

Another important application we are exploring now is Transitional Housing for refugee and disaster relief. They can be erected in two days and left permanent, or de-constructed, flat packed again and moved on. What's more is that they are culturally relevant to their host nation and community. Our team intimately assess the cultural and architectural requirements for each region/country, resulting in a house destined for or built in Fiji, Jamaica or Papua New Guinea, which may be a different house than for Indonesia, Brazil or Sudan. However, the profiles that make up the house remain the same. There are multiple applications within Third World scenarios according to the demographics, right through to First World applications like Groovy Granny Flats and Eco Surf/Dive Resorts Surf.

The aim for 2014 was to complete our research and development facility in Totonto, Canada and a showcase plant in Bali and/or PNG, meaning that pilot homes were available in May. Governor Pastika of Bali is so enamoured by the project that he invited me to his home village in north east Bali in 2013 to witness the handover of a traditional concrete block home provided by the government to a poor family. He wants Nevhouse to replace the traditional construction as soon as possible. We also took the Governor to another family who are living in squalor in Denpasar 20 minutes from the official Governors residence. 29 people, 10 families, two of those incestuous resulting in seven severely disabled children who had never left this house of horrors in their lives. He was visibly shaken and instructed his housing/social Minister to get these people out of here and build them another house immediately.

Our commitment is to provide two houses for these people at no charge. This is a prime example of how diverse the problem is, yet how ready we are to tackle it. We have the product and the team. We are looking at a plan where in a few years time we will have plants operating in over a hundred countries around the world, which we hope will result in the quantifiable diversion of plastic waste from the environment to homes for the disadvantaged. Few are aware of the fact that millions of tons of plastic waste is shipped annually in 40ft containers from First to Third World countries, particularly China. Just consider the carbon footprint of that!

China is putting up what has been called a 'Green Wall' due to the poor quality and organic contamination of waste, which is causing backlogs in the USA, Canada, Australia and Europe. We are looking at creating a new market for the materials waste management companies which need to offload. For example, partnerships with companies like Waste Management Inc. in the U.S. and Visy in Australia who ship waste to China, could divert it to PNG or Indonesia. This is PR gold for companies who are proud of their mantras of Reduce, Reuse and Recycle: "We are taking YOUR waste and making houses for the poor". Currently, large waste management companies do not publicise that they are relocating waste from First to Third World countries. However, in this scenario these companies now have an economically viable alternative that produces social and environmental benefits for all involved.

The innovation and technology does end with Nevhouse. It actually becomes the hub of a broader network, encompassing energy, water, sanitation and other infrastructure, that will enable a house or an entire village to be built completely off the grid in a sustainable and renewable way. We have formed a group of complimentary technologies to implement this objective and we are always looking to improve the existing recycling process. We are all so pumped on the idea that we can actually do something good for people less fortunate than ourselves, whilst effectively diverting plastic from landfill and our precious rivers, lakes and oceans. Doing well by doing good.Ferum volorae

5.4

Just Add Surf: The Power of Surfing as a Medium to Challenge and Transform Gender Inequalities

Easkey Britton

Surfing is the driving force in my life and my lens to focus with. Like many of the authors in this book, surfing is a compulsion, an addiction, what I live for and can't live without. It keeps me in a constant state of restlessness, my mind and body always searching for the next wave. How can we translate the values of surfing to address some of the issues at the core of the sustainability of our oceans and the lives of those who live in relation to the sea? This piece shares some of my own personal reflections as well as case studies from surf and development NGOs to explore how the apparently simple act of surfing can transcend global inequalities, becoming a powerful creative medium for empowerment. We cannot discuss sustainability without considering gender. When I say gender, I mean both men and women, the relationships men and women have with the sea and each other. As Anca Sandescu, a former gender intern at UNOY Peacebuilders said, "If you do not deal with gender issues, you do not deal with the sustainability of societal transformation". With females under-represented at all levels in sport, including surfing, when we talk about gender it tends to raise the issue of *women's* participation in the sport. This piece looks at what drives these gender inequalities in surfing, focusing on the important role surf and development programmes can play to overcome gender barriers, not just in surfing but also for society as a whole.

The Importance of Role Models
According to recent research on gender equity, sport and development, a lack of female role models is a key issue for female participation in sport. This is not for a lack of role models but rather the result of differing media access

and coverage in sport as well as gender norms – how society expects men and women to behave. These norms permeate our beliefs, attitudes and behaviors and can strongly control the accepted and expected roles for women in different cultures and society. The report emphasised the importance of female athletes and leaders sharing stories to inspire, create visions for girls and open doors for new opportunities, so they can re-imagine future possibilities[1].

When I was a kid growing up on the remote northwest coast of Ireland there was little or no surf scene, and I relied on my annual birthday subscription to what was then the only women's surf publication, *Wahine* magazine. That was my way of connecting with what other women and girls were doing in surfing. One of the first issues I got had a beautiful image of a Hawaiian woman on the cover and inside was the story of a remarkable modern day surfing queen and water warrior battling breast cancer. Her name was Rell Sunn, called 'Queen of Makaha' by her friends. From that moment, she became my role model. It is no surprise that Rell's Hawaiian name, *Ka-polioka'ehukai*, means heart of the sea. She was a real embodiment of the aloha spirit of surfing and inspirational in terms of bringing kids into surfing and pushing the standards of women's surfing at a time when they were getting little or no support. Her philosophy of aloha and respect for the *mana* of the ocean has influenced my whole life. Growing up in the ocean and traveling the world surfing, Rell heard all kinds of great stories: "As a woman, I swore they would not be stories that belonged only to men. That women could tell these same stories". An all-round water woman, her constant love was surfing and she talked about its power to heal, "When you get in the water and catch a wave, you own your life again. Surfing gives you great inner strength". In early January 1998, aged 11, I found out the devastating news of her death. Rell had lost a 15-year battle with cancer aged 47. She was a woman who blazed an unconventional path and breached the predominantly male domain of surfing, opening the way for other women. A woman I had never met, yet she taught me the importance of sharing your passion.

Fast forward 15 years and women's surfing has exploded in many respects, closing the 'gap' with the guys. One 'gender norm' that is certainly being challenged is the view that you need to have *balls* to charge. Women are going wave for wave with the worlds best male big-wave chargers at some of the heaviest breaks in the world, proving that the ocean (whatever about society) does not discriminate. Keala Kennelly on winning the Billabong XXL award in 2011, famously quipped, "When you ride one of those big waves it doesn't matter what you got between your legs!". It's inspirational to see other woman in their element in what for so long has been thought of as a wholly male domain. When in fact women have been charging for a very long time, further back than we can dream.

Masculine or Feminine? Tracing Our He'e nalu (Surfing) Roots
Modern practice of sport has largely been an environment of testosterone charged masculinity and surfing is no different. Little has been said and much forgotten about some of the first surfers being women. The earliest records of people surfing, captured in the drawings from Captain Cook's voyage in the 18th century to the Hawaiian Islands, show Polynesian women surfing together with men. The first explorers from the western world commented how agile and skilled they were riding the crests of waves in unrestrained beauty and joy, equal to their male-counterparts. On the south shore of Oahu, at Waikiki, the surf spot now known as Outside Castles was called Kalehuaweke by the Hawaiians to commemorate an incident in which a commoner dropped into the same wave as a Hawaiian chieftess, which was a major taboo. To save his own skin, he offered her his lehua wreath to placate her.

There is another Tahitian myth about Vehiatua, the woman surfer with hair made from wind who could command the waves. Unfortunately, their naked freedom and power in the ocean and lack of subservience to men did not go down well with the missionaries and, once again, Eve was banished from the Garden of Eden. After 125 years of Hawaiian-European contact, surfing went from a national past time and way of life to a sport only engaged by a handful. However, even on its deathbed, surfing was still practiced in its darkest hour by the very few. One of these few was Royal Hawaiian Princess Ka'iulani, who reportedly rode a seven-and-a-half foot alaia koa surfboard[2] in the 1880s and was described as an "expert surfrider", and "last of the old school at Waikiki" by early 20th century surfer, Knute Cottrell. Our true surf heritage has somehow been lost in translation. There is still little recognition of the gendered nature of sport and that females are under-represented at all levels (athletes, coaches, managers, media, industry)[3]. It is for this very reason, the side-lining of women in many modern sports, that women may actually become more liberated from the constraints of gendered notions of what the feminine ideal is (or should be) if they engage in the sport. It can lead to empowerment within their community and contribute to positive health and welfare outcomes[4]. However, Saavedra (2005) warns, "equal opportunities do not necessarily result in equal outcomes".

What Happens When You Share Your Passion? The Transformative Power of Surfing

Surfing has spread to all corners of the globe, crossing geographical and cultural boundaries. However, the local context or environment in which people are able to practice surfing varies wildly, as do the diversity of men and women who surf. It is by traveling that the surfer opens him or herself up to the diversity of these realities, from Ireland to Iran. It's argued that sport becomes a mirror of society[5] and a surfer friend of mine once told me that a wave is a mirror to our souls – it reflects our commitment, our fear and willingness to face it. As a result, this 'mirror effect' has opened the eyes of some traveling surfers to the local realities in countries where, as outsiders, we can visit and enjoy 'surf paradise' but quickly realize the opportunities for those with this amazing natural resource on their doorstep to access it might not exist.

Often in collaboration with local leaders or community-based organisations another type of NGO is established, surf and development NGOs (referred to as SDOs in this piece) where the aim is to promote empowerment and community development through surfing. After an online review of some twenty SDOs, their important potential in breaking down gender norms or 'taboos' and engaging with vulnerable groups, especially women and girls, became immediately apparent. What follows are a short selection of case studies highlighting some of the gender dimensions in surf and development programmes[6]. The focus is primarily on developing countries where the impact of surfing is poorly considered and the relationship between women and surfing in these regions even less so. That said, similar issues persist in my own culture and society in Ireland and other so-called 'developed' nations where the number of adolescent girls continuing to pursue the passion they discovered in their childhood drops dramatically in comparison to boys[7]. This study, therefore, has relevance for women's participation, not just in more developing countries, but globally.

I've recently returned from a journey that just a short while ago I never could have imagined possible – a country where we don't immediately think of female pioneers and leaders in sport, and certainly not surfing. My journey first began in 2010, when I followed my passion to place called Baluchistan which has a stretch of wave-exposed coastline in the southeastern part of Iran. I saw the potential of a place that was unknown as a surfing or even tourist destination and knew I had to come back and dive deeper below the surface. I felt it was a unique opportunity, especially as a woman, to take a look through a different lens (surfing) at what is so often portrayed as a threatening country. My first visit, captured in a short film, caught the attention of other young women in Iran who also surf – pioneers and leaders in their own sports who wanted to learn more about surfing and share their passion for sport, which is not always easy to practice in their country, but they can't live without it. As a result, in 2013, I co-founded Waves of Freedom, an initiative and film project with director Marion Poizeau, that has grown from a desire to connect with others through surfing and learn from them what it's like to follow a passion in a country which is far from familiar. The aim of our return journey was to engage with young women through surfing, exploring what they think about the experience and to examine how women surfing there is perceived by men and women, locals and foreigners, leaders and youth and what is the potential for that region.

The motivation for this project is driven by the desire to pull back what I like to call 'veils of the unseen', to encourage open-minded travel and tolerance, and to understand something familiar from a totally different perspective and to share a passion. It's about reclaiming what once was very much a feminine pursuit and sharing the values that surfing can teach us, especially the importance of our relationship with the ocean and each other. The seed of surfing in Iran is taking root, surf history is in the making and it is being shaped by stories of pioneering female sports athletes who want to teach other girls surfing; a mother who overcame her fear of water, her husband standing by the waters edge holding their baby while she rode her first wave to shore; a political leader who sees hope and potential for change; fathers who want their daughters to know the stoke of surfing; girls and boys learning from each other; a village who fell in love with the sea and wants to become the first surf centre in Iran, creating Iran's first surf club at Ramin.

Surfing is the genesis or seed that provides the structure and principles for the majority of these SDOs, often introduced by traveling surfers who took the time to share their passion. For example, a core principle of Robertsport Community Works (RWC) in Liberia is, *to express the unique values inherent in wave-riding - individualism, camaraderie, non-materialism, and an appreciation for human kind's historic relations with the Ocean.* RCW is a non-profit organisation that aims to create community-based tourism initiatives that focus on conservation and surf tourism. In 2009, local surfer and Director of RWC, Elie Calhoun, helped establish Mama Liberia sewing co-op and sister project within RCW founded on the belief that "when a woman profits her family profits". RCW represents both men and women and its primary activities are promoting education, environmental activities and surf development (e.g. surf clubs, equipment, lessons, tourism). The project also carries out other development activities such as capacity building, promotion of gender equality, small business development, adult literacy and self-help programs. The potential to contribute to gender equality in SDOs is high. Take for example the widespread positive impacts on women's empowerment and decision making at the household and community level in Robertsport for women in the Mama Liberia sewing co-op, where women now have control of their own income and ability to contribute directly to the education and wellbeing of their household and community: "My husband used to beat and abuse me, but the Community Chief said that because I used my sewing money to build my house, that he had to leave and I could stay" (Miriama, co-op member). Elie explains the importance of promoting equitable participation from all parts of the community in their approach to community-based development, "it infuses everything we do [...] also having equitable problem-solving mechanisms that fairly resolve issues to maintain group cohesion, this is huge for us, a big part of what we do". It is the creation of an enabling environment, where not only opportunities are created but also a person's capacity to act and do what they could not otherwise do changes, in turn changing the traditional definitions of gender roles[8].

Like Mama Liberia, some projects are specifically aimed at women and girls, such as *Cubanitas Surf* in Havana, Cuba. Established in 2006, the organisation is mostly focused on young girls, initially learning to swim and then surf, with the aim to bring new opportunities and an educational culture about environmental care to Cuban women, to show the benefits of promoting women in surfing and other ocean activities. The primary focus is on education and environmental activities, healthcare and surf development (e.g. surf clubs, equipment, lessons) which includes beach clean ups, therapies for children with disabilities, education about marine life, and swimming and surfing lessons for kids. At the heart of these SDO projects is surfing, the reason for their existence, yet their impact extends far beyond the simple act of wave-riding. According to Yaliagny Guerrero Prieto from *Cubanitas Surf*, "it's the solid base where all want to go, and is the perfect final result for mixing the ocean, environmental care, culture and a healthy life style". Another important element is the bonds and positive relationships between the sexes that the ocean can create, "mixing girls and boys for surfing and swimming lessons creates competence that stimulates both genders, mostly the girls to push more for a better result. Having both genders at the same time educates young males to respect what girls are capable of".

Despite this, many challenges facing women's participation persist. For the

Cubanitas, it is difficult to get girls to participate and their partner projects, Royal 70 and Havana Surf, which attract a far greater number of male participants. The greatest obstacles for female participation, as well as the more obvious basic material and infrastructural needs, are socio-cultural barriers (i.e. social acceptance and gender norms), as Yaliagny explains, "in a Latin country it takes time to change the 'rules' where being the 'macho man' is considered the main aspect. Also the limitations of a country like Cuba makes all the surfing equipment more difficult to get, there are no surf shops on the island". A lack of recognition or support at a national or government level was highlighted as an issue, as well as the need for building stronger community networks: "We would love to have more support from women's organizations or any kind of sponsorship to go further in our goals and make the sport more common between girls in the island and beyond". Another issue is safety. Women and girls are often most vulnerable when it comes to health and safety risks,[9] a risk which can be increased as a result of social and cultural stigma. Obviously, creating 'safe' spaces for people, especially women and girls, to meet and work is crucial. Working with an SDO in South Africa, Emi Koch, founder of *Beyond the Surface International*, explained how a young girl in Durban had to stop surfing because she became pregnant. Her pregnancy was the result of being raped, a daily occurrence on the streets. "I think of these women when I think of strong, beautiful surfer girls. These girls wear oversized clothing sporting boys boardshorts in the water for extra coverage to prevent unsolicited attention or darkened skin from the sun".

Despite having the opportunity to surf, deeply entrenched cultural belief systems can really limit the ability to engage with young women through surfing. In India, at the Kovalam Surf Club, established by passionate surf traveler Jelle Rigole from Belgium in 2005 as part of a bigger NGO, Sebastien Indian Social Projects (SISP) who explained that when it comes to equal rights for both sexes it can sometimes feel like fighting a losing battle. Participation of girls in surf lessons for local kids is low and irregular. The biggest issues are social acceptance and safety in a society where the world contracts for girls when they reach adolescence and leisure activities are not considered important where[10] there are already competing obligations for women in the home. When good connections are built up over time between the project leaders and local families, a girl can be motivated to keep surfing, but on condition she maintains her fair skin. With India's strict caste system, tanned skin is associated with people who live outside in the sun, or in other words, the poor living on the margins of society. Once puberty kicks in these aspiring surfer girls are forbidden to mix with boys for fear of bringing shame to her family or causing problems when finding a 'good' husband. Their duties in preparation for becoming a 'good wife' take priority. It becomes clear that, although very important, simply creating opportunity and making resources available is not enough. Improving the conditions necessary to enable people to do what they could not otherwise do is essential. Unfortunately, as Jelle's comment highlights, this ability to influence change in one's life differs greatly for men and women: "As I see it now, it is still impossible for a local girl from a very traditional, below-the-poverty-line family, to continue surfing and even schooling after puberty has been reached. We've been trying new ideas over and over, but nothing seems to change this very archaic tradition... I hope time will bring a wind of change".

Sustaining the stoke
Change is possible and it can happen in the most unlikely of ways. Emi Koch sees surfing as a tool for youth empowerment, especially for girls. Emi shared her recent experiences of the empowerment local women felt surfing for the first time in a small fishing village in India. While filming *Beyond the Surface* with other international female surfers and Ishita Malaviya (India's first-woman-of-surf), they met with a group of local female basket weavers. The local women asked the group what they did and if they could try it too so they all jumped into the water in their colourful saris. A man, screaming and shouting, came running towards a woman who had just successfully ridden her first wave all the way to the beach. Worried looks were exchanged, he came up to her and cried, "Do it again, do it again! That was amazing, you must go back out and do it again!".

Once you get in the water, the rules and norms of society dissolve and the power of the ocean to connect and spread happiness is huge. However, coming ashore again can be a challenge. These 'rules and norms' have been carefully built and protected for centuries, if not millennia. It's hard to believe that just adding surf can change anything, that the simple act of wave-riding could break them. I hope it will start with sharing these stories, the aim of which is to show that other possibilities exist, to challenge and transform gender and social inequalities, to bridge our fear of the unknown and embrace the unfamiliar. It is from exposure to "counter-stereotypical images" and the "delinking of negative associations with these images" that change happens[11]. This, combined with the willingness of the media to show that other possibilities exist, is an important way to challenge and transform gender inequalities, creating space for new ways of doing and more opportunities for men and women. Finally, it is not possible to achieve any of this in isolation. As a global community of surfers and a human race connected by the oceans, there is tremendous potential to connect with each other and provide practical and moral support, accelerating change. For example, beginning with grass-roots initiatives like Ramin Surf Club and helps the seeds for hope grow in forgotten regions of the world, which are rich in cultural heritage, humanity and heart.

In conclusion, I present some suggestions to help integrate gender equality in surf and development programmes more actively and explicitly and to begin to transform gender norms, as well as strengthening relationships for social good[12] This list of possibilities and priorities are a synthesis of some of the successes and needs of the SDOs who participated in this study:

1. 'Step zero' – recognising the importance of carrying out gender analysis prior to project or programme implementation and throughout the programme as well as training and awareness raising for staff.
2. Claiming and creating a safe space that is both practical and symbolic.
3. Improving access to resources (both material, e.g. equipment, and social, e.g. leadership and moral support).
4. Providing incentives (e.g. 'no school – no surf', transferrable skills for employment, education and access to health care).
5. Holistic approach – identifying 'gatekeepers' and lobbying and involving local authorities are a must (e.g. working with the tourist police in Kovalam, official recognition by sporting authorities in Cuba).
6. Capacity building and support to include and integrate with other women's organisations and groups.
7. Participant driven programmes – the importance of co-creation throughout planning, implementation and evaluation stages (e.g. Mama Liberia, Ramin Surf Club).
8. Creative and collective solutions linking surfing and other activities (e.g. health care, child care, education, language courses, environmental awareness, micro-finance projects, access to credit, business skills, IT training)
9. Mentorship programmes and role models who challenge and transform gender norms. Female role models from the local area are essential catalysts for change (e.g. Ishita in India). It is important that

their stories are shared in the media globally and locally to open the door for others to follow.
10. Urgent need to address the major research gaps in gender, surf and development, in particular the need for transnational research to better inform policy to support best practices.
11. Recognising that 'gender' is both male and female, it's about the roles and attitudes of men and boys as much as it is about women and girls.

In the end, what all these stories have in common is connection, the power of surfing to connect. Without connection, passion is an empty vessel. On my last day on this beach in Baluchistan, I felt strangely at home even though it was so far from my own. We stayed on the beach until the sun set and I was cold, wet, salty and exhausted, but I didn't care, I didn't want to leave. When we were leaving the water one of the young Baluchi men turned to me and said I was like "his big sister… that we've become sea sister and sea brother". I couldn't believe it, he had echoed the words of Rell Sunn: "If you share the ocean, well then you're completely bonded because that's like being blood brothers or blood sisters. And Aloha is to keep giving that love and feeling it come back, until there's nothing else you have to give"[13].

Andy Abel, Justice Nicholas Kirrowom, CMG Nicky Wynnychuk and UK surf team including Dr Easkey Britton of Waves of Freedom at Tupira Surf Club during hand over ceremony of pink nose boards to member of the Tupira Surf Club by SAPNG as part of its policy on empowering women.

5.5

Museum of British Surfing, The Long View: Charting Britain's Surfing History

Peter Robinson
Andrew Coleman

The Museum of British Surfing opened to the Public in April 2012 at its new permanent venue in Braunton, North Devon. Previous to this three-year development project, the museum had a nine-year record of successful touring exhibitions. Since 2004, its displays have been seen by close to half a million people around Britain – and the museum has received loaned items from across the globe, including the world's oldest surfboard from Hawaii. Then, in June 2009, The Museum of British Surfing was established as a registered charity.

As my founding gift, I donated what is believed to be Europe's largest collection of surfing memorabilia. The Museum now holds, in trust for the public, a unique and internationally important collection of over 1,000 surfing artefacts, which trace more than 230 years of British surfing heritage. The collection is comprised of more than 200 British surfboards, some a century old, and hundreds of items of memorabilia such as clothing, surfing kit, promotional products and film and print archives. The collection has now started to attract public donations and the museum has been able to acquire a small number of key items from its own funding. Nationally significant, the collection celebrates the surfing history of Britain, a culture at the heart of North Devon coastal life. By creating an important national collection, The Museum of British Surfing aims to improve the local tourist 'offer' and help persuade more British surfers to surf at home.

Within three months of opening, the Museum won a National Collections Trust Award for its Sustainability Policy and work within the local community, which has been embedded into the everyday activities of the Museum. Being located at the centre of a World Biosphere Reserve and an Area of Outstanding National Beauty means it can provide an insight into the natural processes that shape the coastline and the threats from climate change and marine litter.

Probably the single greatest challenge to the sustainability of surfing in Britain is the likelihood of rising sea levels, as a result of climate change. While there is a lot of uncertainty about the magnitude of this, the best current estimate predicts a rise of around one metre by the end of the century, which means that Britain will have a new coastline, and many surf breaks will no longer exist. This means that, assuming that the number of surfers remains the same as today, breaks will become overcrowded, causing a greater potential for conflict in and out the water. Other challenges that face British surfing include competition of access to costal and marine resources as well as onshore and offshore developments that can threaten waves and costal processes.

The Museum of British Surfing is striving to connect surfers to the natural environment by organising and supporting beach cleans and raising awareness about the costal environment through exhibitions. These exhibitions track the development of surfing technology from wood, through to polyester and back to wood again. Given the technological developments in surfboards and the desire to travel to breaks, surfers probably have a greater carbon footprint than the average person, which is why connecting surfers to their environment is so important. The museum's 'long view' of Britain's surfing history allows it to show how surfing can be enjoyed in a low-carbon way, by highlighting the connections between the natural environment and the sport. Leading by example, the Museum drives down its carbon and environmental footprint, while also supporting local economic and social development.

5.6

Transforming Surf Culture Towards Sustainability: A Deep Blue Life

Kevin Whilden
Michael Stewart

Surfers and the surf industry need to understand that our current lifestyle choices and business practices are causing serious and direct threats to the surf breaks, coral reefs and beaches that make up our ocean playground. At stake is the long-term viability of surfing as a sport and the marine ecosystem habitat for the many beautiful and wondrous plants and animals that share the ocean with us. There are many human-driven impacts on the ocean's ecosystem, such as plastic litter, agricultural and sewage water discharge, over-fishing and coastal habitat destruction. However, the most significant and widest-reaching impacts to ocean health are caused by the emission of carbon dioxide from the burning of fossil fuels for our energy use and manufacturing needs.

Atmospheric CO_2 levels are rising at an extraordinarily rapid rate and have passed the 400 parts per million (ppm) milestone, which has not happened in millions of years. This results in multiple global ocean impacts. The oceans uptake about 25% of the CO_2 emissions through chemical absorption, which causes ocean acidification. The rate of acidification is now happening ten times faster than has ever occurred in the geologic history of the Earth[1]. This will have terrible consequences to calcifying organisms that will no longer be able to make their shells and skeletons, such as coral reefs, mollusks, and plankton. In parallel, 90% of the heat gain from global warming occurs in the ocean (only 10% goes to the atmosphere), which further causes heat stress to corals and also changes global ocean circulation patterns that drive global climate and ocean nutrient distribution. Finally, sea level rise is caused by melting glaciers and ice caps and by the thermal expansion of the warming ocean.

These global issues have direct and immediate impacts on surfing. The scientific outlook for coral reefs is bleak as a result of ocean acidification and ocean warming, with 90% of coral reefs threatened with extinction by the year 2030[2]. Likewise, the conservative projection of one foot of sea level rise by 2050[3] will cause major negative impacts to developed coastlines. For surfers specifically, this rapid rise in sea level will swamp out many surf breaks globally, creating a condition of 'permanent high tide' that will diminish the quality and frequency of good surf.

The challenge of reversing all of these negative environmental trends is why we started Sustainable Surf in 2011 – a not-for-profit organisation based in California, USA. We firmly believe that the first step in solving these global problems starts with reducing the impacts that we can control as individuals. This is how we can live an authentic 'ocean friendly' lifestyle that achieves proper respect and gratitude to the gifts the ocean gives to us. We also believe that this is the first step in achieving a meaningful political solution. If surfers can start to live a low-carbon lifestyle and if the surf industry can develop low-carbon products and practices, it may be possible to engineer a transformation in society itself to more rapidly engage with the CO_2 problem and its solutions.

After two years of operation, we're already showing success in creating a transformation within surfing. Our procedure is to identify key barriers in the culture and business of surfing that are preventing transformation toward sustainability. We will then develop programmes that educate and enable actions to directly break these barriers. Our premise is that transformation can build its own momentum after the initial barriers are broken, and then will no longer need our intervention and effort. Ultimately, we believe a sustainable future makes inherent sense to nearly everyone and our task is merely to catalyse the transformative forces that have difficulty competing in a business-as-usual society.

Creating Transformation with Sustainable Surfboards
A good example of our systematic approach to catalysing societal transformation is found in our programme, The ECOBOARD Project. A modern surfboard is created with many toxic petrochemicals, has a very high carbon footprint and is fragile with a generally short lifespan. Alternative surfboard materials with reduced toxicity and carbon intensity have been available since around 2008, however these materials have made extremely low sales in the surfboard market. Surfboard builders would not use them and surfers didn't know they

could order boards made from them. This is surprising given the generally high level of environmental awareness of many surfers, and the sustainable heritage of the original wooden surfboards used by ancient Hawaiian culture.

At the launch of the ECOBOARD Project, we recognised three primary barriers. First, would the sustainable surfboard materials perform as well as toxic modern materials? If the resulting sustainable surfboard had lower performance, durability, or good appearance, then it would never make any significant market penetration. Second, could the sustainable materials be used with existing surfboard manufacturing techniques? Third, would surfers order boards made with sustainable materials? Most surfboard builders make a high percentage of custom surfboards and they would be highly unlikely to refuse work from a customer that specified sustainable materials. Thus achieving manufacturer familiarity with these materials would be driven by customer demand, and not by manufacturer choice.

At the early stage of programme development, we worked with two innovative surfboard material manufacturers to create products that had no limitations in terms of performance, visual appearance and durability. Marko Foam developed a post-consumer recycled EPS blank called E-Foam in 2009 that made very little market penetration. In 2011, we helped them work with a few talented shapers to identify the best formulations for high-performance shaping and surfing. Legendary Southern California shaper, Timmy Patterson, and pro surfer Mike Losness, were instrumental in this R&D process.

The end result was an EPS blank made from 25% post-consumer recycled polystyrene foam, with identical surfing performance. It was slightly more difficult to shape in comparison to virgin EPS, but this difference was relatively minor and any competent shaper with sharp tools would have no problem using it. As a result, it has a 20% reduction in lifecycle CO_2 emissions and contributes to keeping waste EPS foam out of landfills, oceans and beaches. To create a viable sustainable resin, we worked with Entropy Resins, which had developed a plant-based resin made from the waste of pulp and biofuel production. Their initial product had good performance but was yellow in color, which is a non-starter in the commercial surfboard industry which values a bright white board. In 2012, Entropy developed a bright-white resin with 17% bio-carbon content and which can be used with standard epoxy surfboard production techniques. After testing with innovative surfboard builders like E-Tech Boards and Firewire Surfboards, this product was released to the market as Super Sap CLX. It has a 50% reduction in lifecycle CO_2 when compared to standard epoxy resin.

By the end of 2012, the first two barriers had been broken. A sustainable surfboard could be made using recycled EPS foam and plant-based epoxy resins, with an overall 30% reduction in lifecycle CO_2 emissions. It had high performance, light weight, bright white visual appearance, and actually had increased durability versus traditional polyester resin and polyurethane foam surfboards. The next step in sustainable transformation required educating the surfers and manufacturers to use these materials. To do this, we created the first consumer-facing standard for a sustainable surfboard, called the ECOBOARD Benchmark, which specifies sustainable materials that can be used to make an ECOBOARD. Surfboards made with at least one of the qualifying materials are eligible to carry the 'Verified ECOBOARD' label (above).

Our goal with the ECOBOARD Benchmark and label was to create an easy-to-follow method for both surfers and manufacturers to buy or make a sustainable surfboard. In February 2013, the Surfing Industry Manufacturers Association (SIMA) officially endorsed the ECOBOARD Project Benchmark as the recommended standard for sustainable surfboards. Many leading surfboard manufacturers have joined the ECOBOARD Project, such as Firewire Surfboards, Channel Islands, Lost Surfboards, Stretch Boards, T. Patterson Surfboards, Super Brand and more. Most have a section on their website devoted to the ECOBOARD Project, and they are all happy to make ecoboards as a custom option. Various pro surfer team riders are also testing ecoboards and all have reported excellent performance.

Industry acceptance of the ECOBOARD Project continues to grow. We estimate that overall sales of ecoboards are increasing at a rate of 400% per year. In 2014, Firewire Surfboards announced that they would make a switch to producing 100% ecoboards. Finally, there were several material manufacturers that planned to bring new, sustainable materials to the market in 2014, thus giving board builders and surfers many new options to make (or buy) an ecoboard. All signs point to a growing momentum for sustainable surfboards. We estimate that a large percentage of surfboards will be ecoboards within three to five years and the market transformation is occurring right now. The real question is, how much credit can Sustainable Surf claim in engineering

SUSTAINABLE STOKE: TRANSITIONS TO SUSTAINABILITY IN THE SURFING WORLD

Environmental Benefits for an ECOBOARD Surfboard
Analysis for 25% recycled EPS and 20% bio-carbon epoxy resin

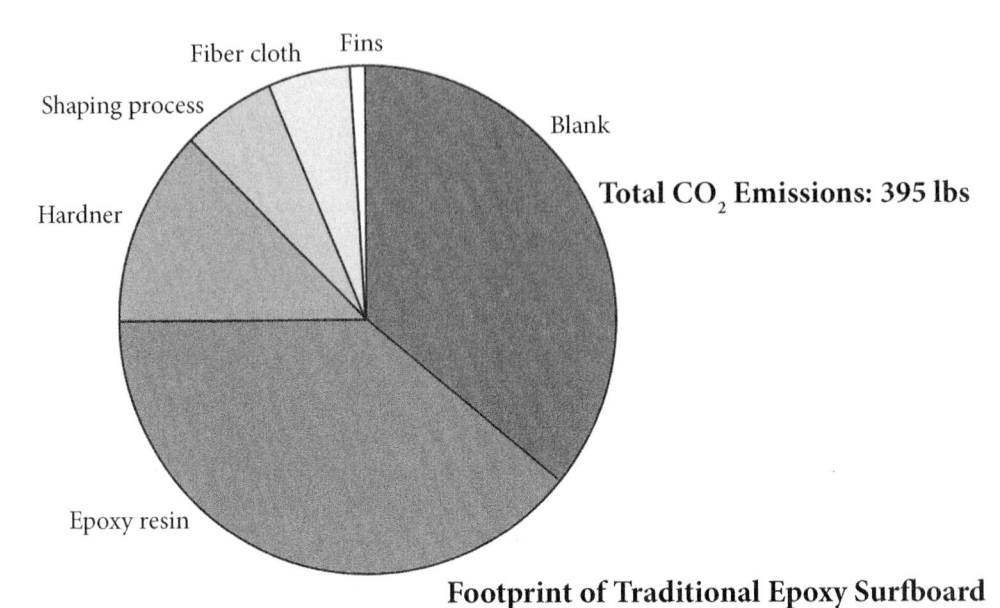

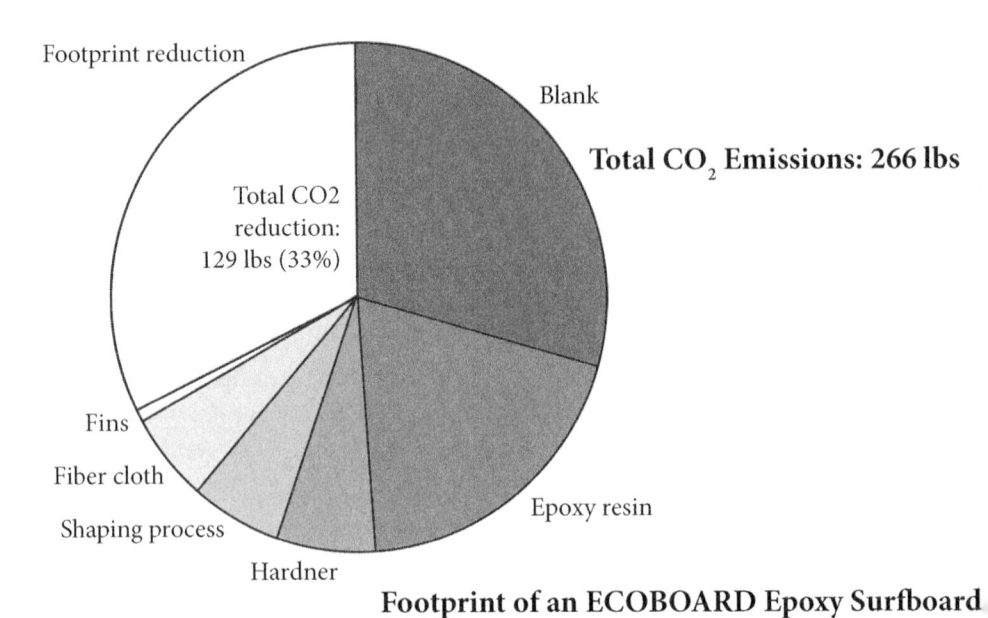

Total CO_2 Emissions: 395 lbs

Footprint of Traditional Epoxy Surfboard

Total CO_2 Emissions: 266 lbs

Total CO2 reduction: 129 lbs (33%)

Footprint of an ECOBOARD Epoxy Surfboard

this market transformation? Certainly, we did not invent the materials needed to make a low-carbon surfboard, however, we do believe that we have played a crucial role in the exponentially growing rate of adoption of sustainable materials. Our conversations with surfboard builders proved that they were aware of the sustainable materials and had even tested them. However, they had a limited intention of using them because they perceived very low market demand and/or they had earlier tested lower performance versions of the sustainable materials. Our programme gave them a way to build sales of ecoboards, and our persistence encouraged them to continue trying the materials as they improved. In some cases, we even had to order personal surfboards to get them to test the materials again. All of these efforts provided a platform for a SIMA endorsement that would not threaten their members.

Living a Deep Blue Life to Reduce Societal CO_2 Emissions
Solving the CO_2 problem is an enormously complex and difficult task that requires the engagement of all levels of society (individuals, business, government, science and religion). Current CO_2 emissions are rising faster than ever, with unmistakable consequences, yet society is no closer to implementing serious solutions. We believe that the most immediate and significant barrier preventing action is the lack of a desirable 'low-carbon' lifestyle that can serve as positive motivation for individuals to reduce the emissions they control. Achieving this will benefit businesses that are leaders in reducing their emissions and will support the development of political willpower on the issue.

We aim to use the popular appeal of surfing to establish a direct link to a desirable ocean-friendly and low-carbon lifestyle. Our challenge is to: (1) create a community of people who authentically engage in the available solutions and (2) then quantitatively demonstrate their collective impact. If we can do this in the surfing community, it has the potential to have significant influence on society because of surfing's influential role in popular culture. Surfing is used to sell all kinds of products because it creates a positive association. We believe that surfing can be even more effective at selling a positive vision of a sustainable society that is fun and desirable.

Our newest programme, launched in mid-2014, is the Deep Blue Life initiative. It is designed to educate surfers on the very real threats that are scientifically measurable to oceans, reefs and coastal communities, such as ocean acidification, ocean warming and sea level rise. This programme will also demystify how those three issues will manifest in the average surfer's life, by putting the negative effects within the context of the surfing lifestyle. Ocean acidification and warming will be connected to the health of coral reefs, the waves they create and the ecosystem for fish and mammals they provide. Sea level rise will be connected to the loss of surf spots and the diminished quality of rideable waves due to a condition of 'permanent high tide'. These threats (and solutions) will also be connected to societal impacts such as climate change, extreme weather, droughts and coastal flooding.

The Deep Blue Life programme is not simply another list of '10 things you can do to save the planet'. It is a complete and simple strategy of specific daily actions that have the largest potential for producing a positive and measurable benefit to the ocean health. At the core of this programme is the idea that without a healthy surfing habitat, (including beaches, reefs, water and marine life) the surfing lifestyle will cease to exist. The personal choices we make can have significant positive benefits on ocean health. However, there is no comprehensive educational resource on these choices designed specifically for surfers and coastal residents. Deep Blue Life fills a void in the surfing community by directly addressing the most significant threat to the oceans, reefs and coastal environments: human CO_2 emissions from the burning of fossil fuels.

Human CO_2 emissions cause ocean acidification, ocean warming, sea level rise and climate change, which are already having a direct and measureable impact to our oceans, reefs, and coastal communities. The oceans are acidifying ten times faster than the fastest rate in geologic history. Recent surveys show an 80% decline in coral reefs in the Caribbean and a 50% decline in the Pacific and Indian oceans. Likewise, recent increases in sea levels are causing increased damage to coastal communities, particularly in combination with storm events, such as Hurricane Sandy, which had one foot of additional storm surge due to global sea level rise alone[4]. As sea levels continue to rise, this problem will only be exacerbated.

The solutions presented by Deep Blue Life will have both environmental and personal benefits. For example, reducing the household water footprint will save money for the individual, reduce sewage and storm drain pollution as well as reduce CO_2 emissions (water usage accounts for 8% of California's total CO_2 emissions). Furthermore, reducing the household plastic footprint will save money on disposal fees, reduce CO_2 emissions and marine plastic pollution. The multiple benefits from each solution, such as saving money on bills, will increase the amount of individuals willing to participate and take action. This provides a positive path for messaging and promotion, rather than the negative path of discussing threats from CO_2 emissions. Ultimately the positive message will be the most powerful and will create the necessary synergy with the positive appeal of the surfing lifestyle that has the potential to transform society.

A key aspect of the Deep Blue Life programme design is to provide attractive solutions that are directly associated with major environmental problems. This helps break the barrier of societal apathy to problems that seem too big for individuals to solve. We can more rapidly drive awareness and action in response to current events like the 500-year drought in California, extreme weather events anywhere and various news and scientific reports of ocean devastation.

The attractiveness of solutions will be further enhanced by the powerful connection to surf culture. Famous surf athletes like Rob Machado and Greg Long are now ambassadors of Sustainable Surf and the Deep Blue Life programme. They will help promote their healthy, ocean-friendly lifestyle and look for additional positive solutions to the major problems that threaten oceans. With their help, a 'deep blue life' will be seen as more engaging, fulfilling and desirable.

A key component of Deep Blue Life is a social media campaign that will utilise the hashtag: #deepbluelife. Surfers will be encouraged to post their actions to their social media, and demonstrate how they are living a #deepbluelife. We believe that this message will resonate with the surf community and will be widely adopted, particularly since our pro surf ambassadors will be promoting this with their own actions.

To help individuals to live a more ocean friendly lifestyle, these are the core strategies recommended in our Deep Blue Life programme:

1. Health Management: includes better food choices (local, organic, sustainably sourced), exercise and recreation and a healthy state of mind (relaxed and mindful).
2. Waste Management: includes the Four R's – Refusing, Reducing, Reusing, and Recycling – to limit the impacts of daily consumption on strained natural resources.
3. Renewable Energy: includes using renewable energy like solar, wind, wave and biofuel. Also includes energy efficiency strategies. Many of these strategies actually have a 'negative cost' because the money savings are greater than the installation cost.
4. Cleaner Transportation: options include bikes, skateboards, electric/hybrid vehicles and even vehicle sharing.

5. Community Building: get involved locally and seek out environmental/social groups that can share resources and ideas.
6. Carbon Footprint: reduce CO_2 emissions with the above strategies and then offset the remaining emissions that are difficult to minimise or eliminate (e.g. air travel, car travel, home energy use).

If surfers can implement the above ideas in their daily lives, they will achieve a dramatically reduced impact on the ocean and climate and their CO_2 emissions will be significantly less than the majority of people who are not concerned about the issue. They will become the true leaders in society on reducing carbon emissions.

Overall, reducing human CO_2 emissions and solving climate change is perhaps the most difficult task that human society has faced. Now, the only thing that is clear is that very little progress has been made in the past two decades since climate change became a major issue. Global CO_2 emissions are rising faster than ever before and have exceeded the worst-case scenario from the Intergovernmental Panel on Climate Chance (IPCC) projections in 2007. The CO_2 problem is much more intractable than other global environmental threats that were solved by multi-lateral agreements, such as ozone depletion by CFCs and the Montreal Protocol. Solutions must now be looked for in unlikely places and perhaps a small cadre of surfers living a Deep Blue Life can be the catalyst that engages society to start dealing with the problem effectively and finally. More information on Sustainable Surf and our programmes can be found on our website, www.sustainablesurf.org.

Rob Machado with Kevin Whilden and Michael Stewart of Sustainable Surf (top) and Michael Stewart and Michel Bourez after Michel won the first major surf contest using a "verified Ecoboard", in double overhead surf at Sunset Beach Hawaii in December 2014. His Firewire surfboard is glassed with Entropy Super Sap resin (bottom) (Courtesy of Sustainable Surf)

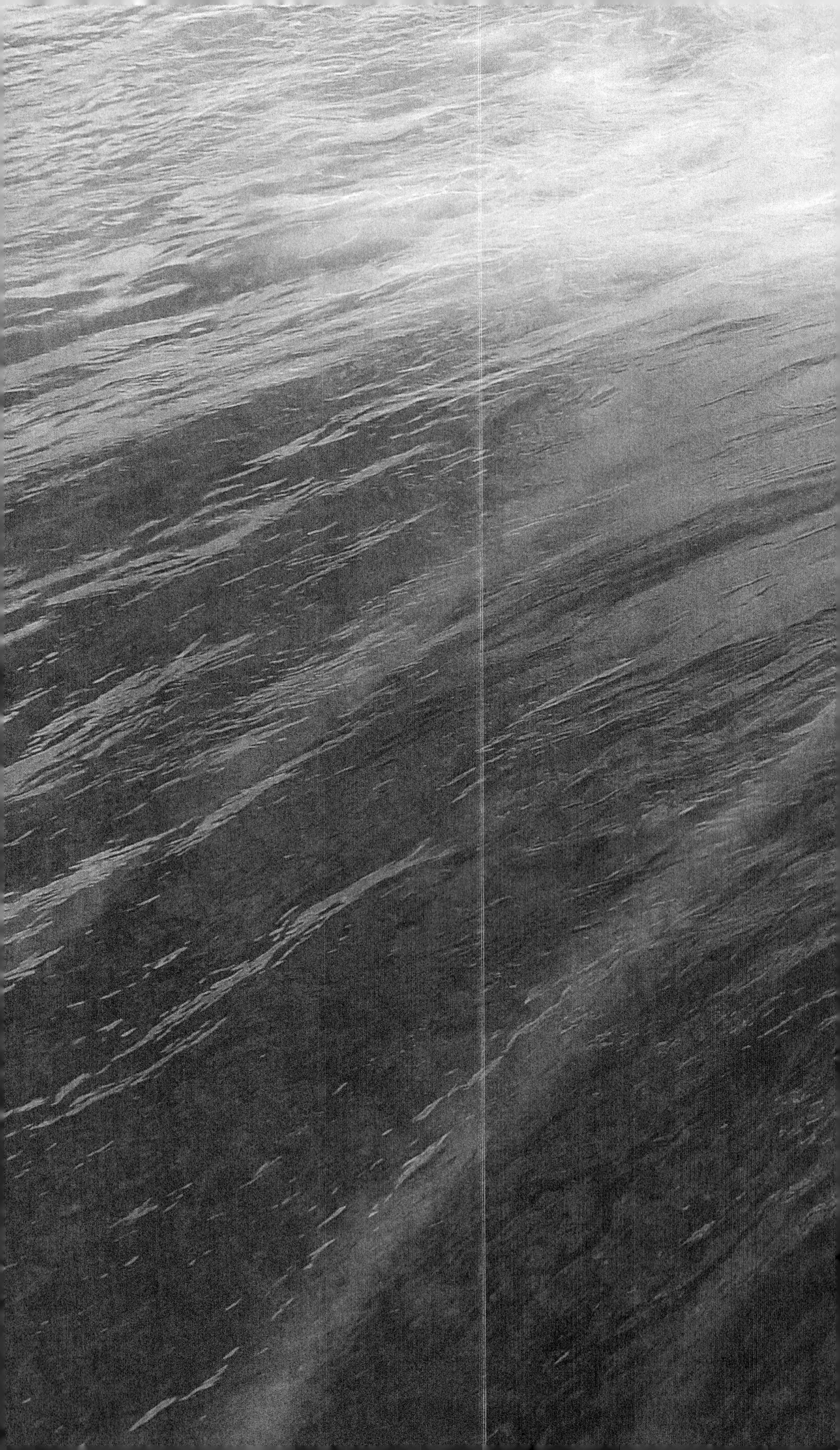

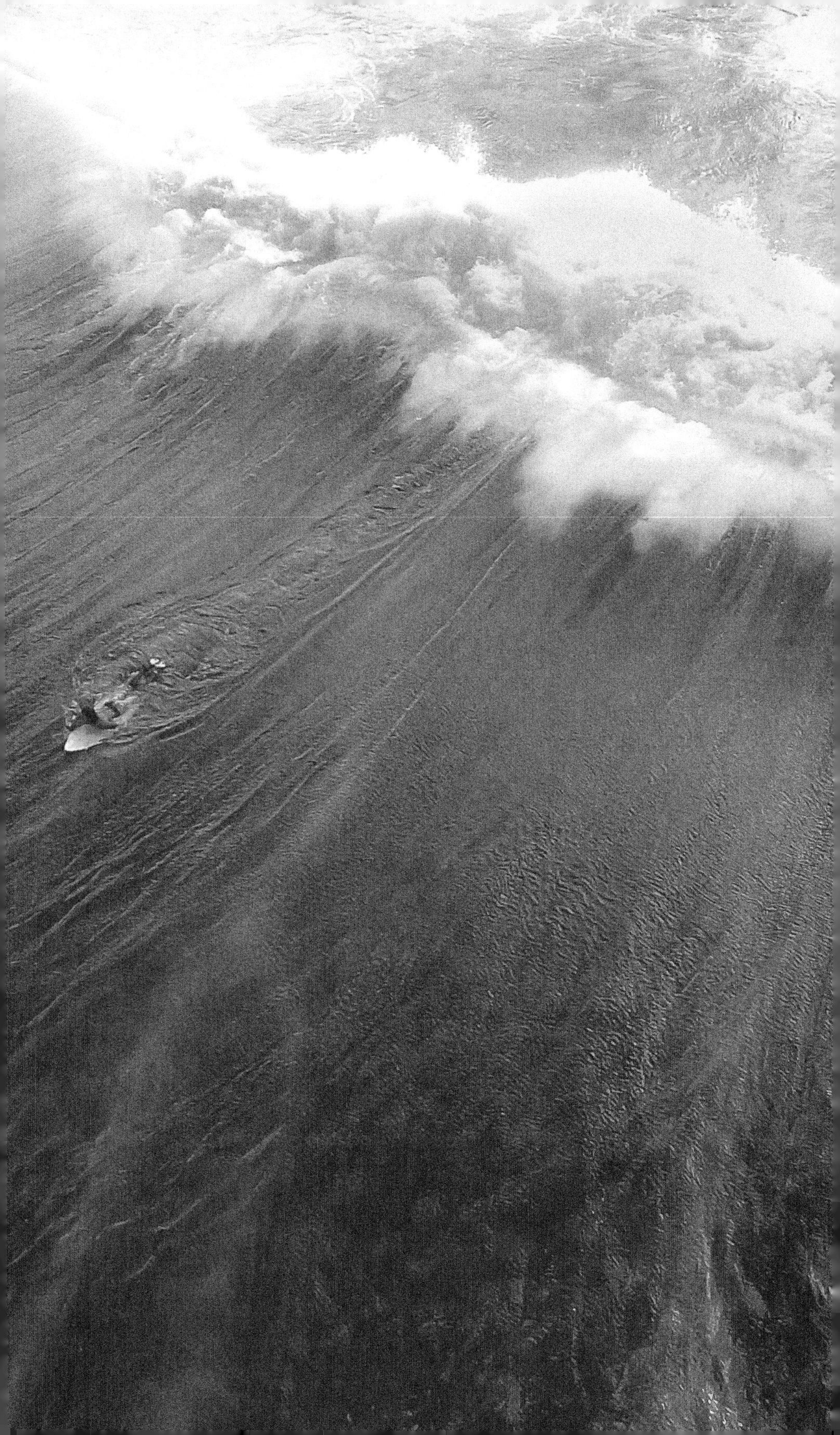

Chapter Six
Case Studies

This chapter offers case studies that address a broad range of issues relating to sustainability. It opens with Emi Koch exploring her inspiring experiences that led to the formation of Beyond the Surface International that focuses on motivating at risk youth. Emi explores how her interaction with the surfing industry has enabled her to develop her vision and help communities around the world.

Sean Brody discusses his amazing journey that has led to the foundation of a surf School in Liberia. Sean's personal commentary provides incredible insights into the realities of establishing a surf retreat in a culture foreign to his own, and the associated trials and tribulations. Sean emphasises the importance of community engagement and gaining support from multiple stakeholders at the national and local levels. But Sean also emphasises the importance of serendipity and the situations that can arise from chance meetings that cannot be planned for or anticipated. Following this, Andy Able and Danny O'Brien explore the creation of the first surfing club in Papua New Guinea and the impact this has had on local communities. Expanding this discussion, Andy explores the formation of a sustainable model of surf tourism that can avoid the pitfalls of unregulated and rapidly expanding surf tourism in other parts of the world.

Again, following on this exploration of good practice from lessons learned by trial and error of surf development, Serge Dedina highlights the Baja Boom the destruction it brought on local coastal communities and Wildcoast's role in preserving these communities and coastal resources. Serge and his fellow authors emphasise the need to 'open up' the toolbox of methods needed to preserve coastal environments. Finally, this chapter presents a piece by Professor Malcolm Findlay, founder the first ever degree programme focusing on surfing. This personal account of the rise and fall of the Surf Science and Technology programme at Plymouth University highlights the incredible educational value of surfing. It also highlights the stigmas that accompany surfing and the need to push through these stereotypes.

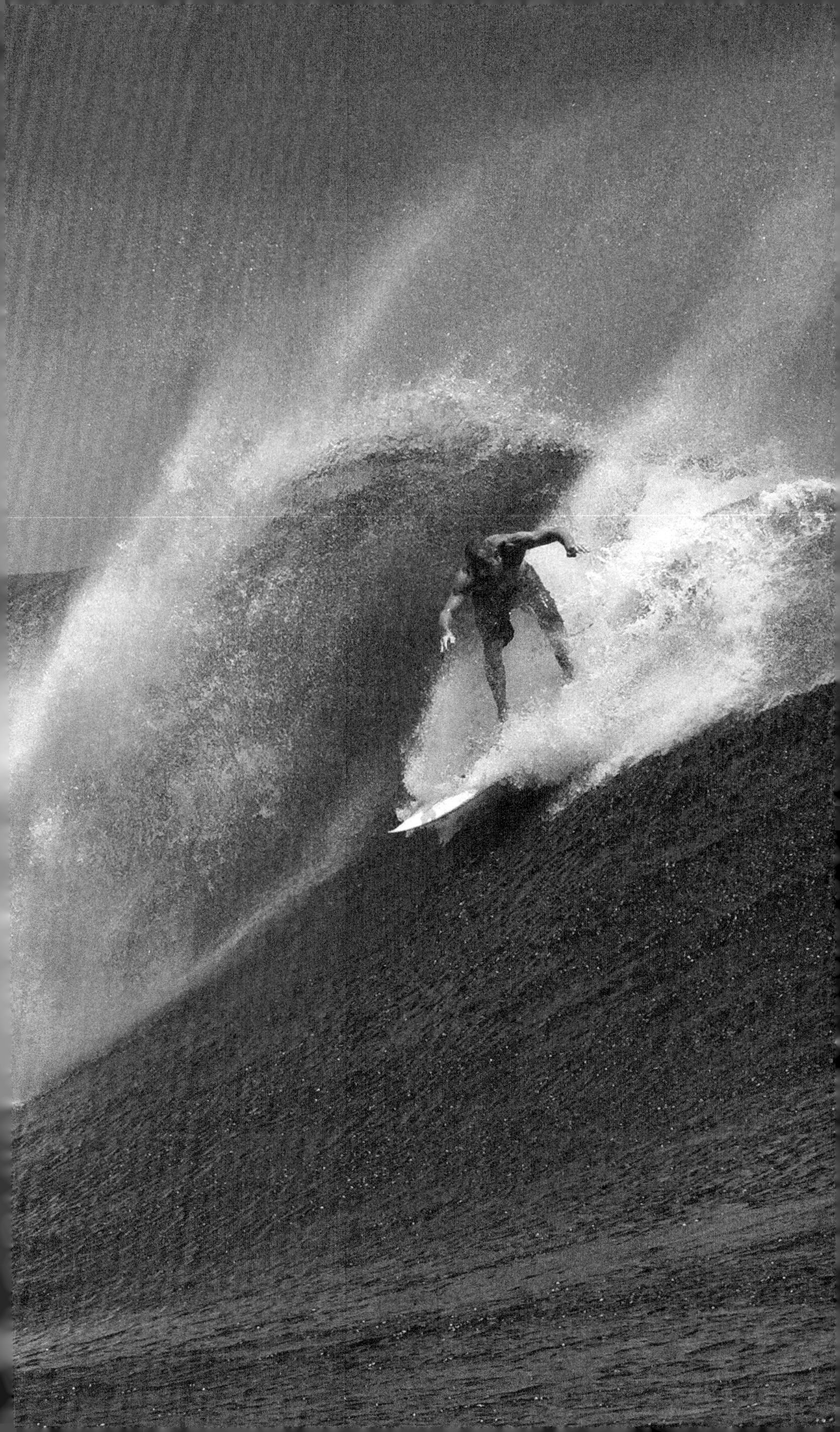

6.1

Grommets of the New Age

Emi Koch

An orange moon sits like an ancient deity, keeping a peaceful watch over a sleepy fishing beach, close to Pondicherry on the eastern coast of India, near Chennai. The waves are pounding the shore, the fishermen behind us roll out cigarettes like mantras and surf cinematographer Dave Homcy's *Brokedown Melody* is being projected onto a plain white Lungi (traditional South Indian mens wear that looks somewhat like a skirt rolled up into shorts). I sit with Ramesh, nestled in my lap and Krishna, sitting tall and attentive to my right – two little boys I have come to love like little brothers, both transplants from Karnatika whose families own souvenir shops that cater to mostly Russian tourists on Lighthouse Beach in Kovalam. Ramesh and Krishna, along with the rest of their families, rely on the incredible efforts of the Sebastian Indian Social Projects in Kerala for schooling and general assistance as they struggle to rise above the Indian poverty line. What these boys lack in Indian Rupees, they gain in their talent in the water as two of the best surfers in the Kovalam Surf Club. What started as a small incentive programme to keep kids in school by Belgium social worker, Jelle Rigole, eight years ago has now turned into a sustainable programme, gaining worldwide attention, calling international filmmakers to corporations in the surf industry to keep a close watch on these rising stars because the next generation of surfers will be from the places you will least expect.

    The act of surfing has now reached parts of the world farthest removed from surfing's Polynesian origins or its current well-known and overcrowded popular breaks. And because of enthusiastic young people, surfing is flourishing beyond belief. For the past five years, thanks to the generous support of giants in the surf industry such as Billabong and Vans Shoes, I've dedicated my life to traveling to the 'out-of-the-ways' around the world to experience how the simple act of riding waves has positively impacted the lives of thousands of youths around the globe. If the history of the world was only recorded using government-sponsored paperwork, no one would ever know these kids even existed. But because of surfing, a form of self-expression that cannot be manufactured and exported like uniformed garments in a workshop, these groms' incredible stories of hope, struggle, hardship, love and pain are being told using the medium of wave riding. Inspired by the groms I have met on remote beaches in Peru, South Africa, and India, I have used the resources developed in my small NGO, Beyond the Surface International, to support other nonprofits, startup initiatives and programming that use surfing to attract and inspire these youngsters.

Beyond the Surface International (BTSI) is a global platform for surfing clubs and coastal community development organisations focused on motivating at-risk youth through wave riding and ocean fun. BTSI was founded on the belief that the innate ability for human beings to have fun, play and laugh can be harnessed to fuel individual empowerment, community advancement, and larger social changes. Initially, BTSI helped sponsor three amazing NGOs: WAVES for Development in Lobitos, Peru, Umthombo Surf Club in Durban, South Africa, and the Kovalam Surf Club in Kovalam, India.

BTSI now sponsors even more innovative initiatives and collaborative creative projects with platform members to be implemented in coastal communities worldwide, led by youth organisation members in their local villages and cities, to spark and sustain dialogues across the planet. Thanks to the generous support of multinational corporations and leaders in the surf industry such as Billabong Girls, Vans Shoes and local San Diego companies like Sun Diego Boardshops, Bird Rock Coffee Roasters, and Surfindian, and even companies outside the industry like Urban Outfitters, BTSI has been able to go far beyond what I ever thought was possible. In the coastal communities where BTSI engages with the youth, wave riding is flourishing, but it is still unaffected by mainstream surf culture. As a consequence, the stoke these kids have is as pure as it gets; the purest form of stoke I've ever seen. They couldn't care less about the big names on the World Tour. Their favorite surfers are their friends and their favorite boards range from the one with the middle fin missing to the big blue one. The issue with community development work is that it has become just that – *work*. But the idea of the youth and community developing to their fullest potential is fundamentally embedded in the innate ability we have, as humans, to forge meaningful relationships and long lasting connections. When governments or established entities in the NGO world lose sight of this ability, that is when efforts made in the name of community development fail. That is the problem with charity.

Giving kids access to a surfboard and setting up a platform for them to share their thoughts and ideas will not keep them out of jail. But, one thing I know is that, years from now, these groms will remember that one wave, or that one day at the beach where they stood up on an epic right, did a cutback, wiped out, and wiping their hair from their faces and snot from their noses, they wheeled around to look at me with my arms raised in celebration, a priceless and most genuine expression of stoke saying, "Did you see that?!". I know I will too.

Every individual has something valuable and significant to share with the world and we, as members of the surfing community and industry, have the ability to protect and cultivate environments, facilitate programming, and support innovative initiatives that use surfing to provide young people with opportunities think for themselves, nurture their own voices, express themselves, and be heard. In a world with so much meaningless chatter, surfing remains one unique, thought provoking and nonviolent method to spread a positive and nurturing message to a greater audience and facilitate communication. And wave riding knows no volume control.

Today, I receive so many emails from young surfers all around the world asking to volunteer through Beyond the Surface International and go in the direction of sharing waves as opposed to just surfing as a solo adventure. It creates a spirit of connectivity to one's neighbour in the water that is alive and I am encouraged that the future of surfing, both for the surfing community and the industry that it supports, will be positive, inclusive and benefit everyone who remembers the stoke of their first wave.

*Lines marching in at an undisclosed spot in Liberia
(Courtesy of Sean Brody)*

6.2

Sustainable Stoke: Liberia

Sean Brody

When I first came to Liberia in 2009, my motive was quite clear: get the waves, get the shot, get paid, go home. Commissioned to photograph a surf trip for a National Geographic TV show *On Surfari*, I intended to come home with a stellar array of imagery that showcased the pristine coastline, the epic left hand point breaks and the spirit of adventure that accompanies such a surf trip. West Africa – Liberia in particular – is not a typical surf trip for an average surf traveller. It requires getting off the beaten track, getting out of your comfort zone, and letting the unknown variables fall into place.

We got dialed in quite nicely by one of the only expat surfers in the country at the time, Keith Chapman, a dentist who had originally come to Liberia on Mercy Ships (a floating hospital that pulls up to port and offers health care and surgeries to populations in need). He disembarked, started the first dental clinic in Liberia and raised a family of two daughters and two adopted Liberian sons, with his wife in the developing nation. Chapman contacted Shane McIntyre of *On Surfari* about the sand bottom point breaks of Liberia. So a few weeks later, we were off to Africa. Our accommodation consisted of safari-style tents that were located in an ideal spot, facing the surf, with the community behind us. We got to know the preferable tides, winds, swell direction and lighting conditions. We were able to watch the surf and get right on it when the waves were pumping. It was great! Everything I was looking for in a surf trip and destination, so I initially thought.

I returned a year later with a few friends and we were not able to stay in the same place, facing the best wave, but rather we stayed about a mile up the beach as it was cheaper. I arranged to rent a 4x4 from a South African living in Liberia to cut the walking time down significantly. The vehicle was delivered, but it was not in working order. It had flat tyres, spark plug problems and a myriad of other complications. We worked on fixing it every day with little success. There was one problem after another, so we were trekking up the beach daily with surfboards and camera gear in tow. Each day, during our hike back after hours of amazing surf, we would agree that we would definitely have the vehicle working 'by tomorrow'. On about the third day, I had an epiphany: the broken down 4x4 turned out to be the best thing that could have happened. As I walked along the beach each day, I met local people and developed a rapport. The sweet old ladies would teach me short sayings in Vai, the local dialect; I would pull in fishing nets with the local fishermen and be rewarded with fish and the kids would call my name and come running up the moment I became a silhouette on the horizon, to give me a fist bump or Liberian handshake. At these moments, I realised there is much more to a surf trip than ideal surfing conditions. The beauty lies in walking through the community, meeting the people and integrating into the local culture. When I returned the following year, the people I had met made me feel like a long-lost friend and I was warmly welcomed and invited into homes for family meals.

In 2010, I started Surf Resource Network to help implement small community development projects in Robertsport. The focus is on youth mentoring, water safety training, health, sanitation and job creation. By 2012, with my friend and business partner, Daniel Hopkins, I decided to open Kwepunha Reteat, a social impact business in Robertsport. The intention was to help grow the sustainable tourism and hospitality industries in Liberia and to partner with Surf Resource Network to continue implementing community development projects.

The following are a few components of the model we are implementing in Robertsport, Liberia and a few lessons we have learned a long the way.

NGO X Social Impact Business

The unique quality of our model is the fact that we have a double-edged sword: we are operating both a social impact business and an NGO, simultaneously and complementarily. The more successful the business becomes, the more direct benefit goes to the local community. If we simply had a social impact business we would be helping to create jobs, but not directly exerting our influence and expertise on health and education. At Kwepunha Retreat, we are dedicated to donating 15% profits back into community based initiatives. Rather than donating to another non-profit organization, we are able to directly implement and monitor initiatives first hand; plus there are no NGOs operating on a full-time basis in Robertsport, so we have to create the initiatives ourselves.

Combining Sustainable Surf Tourism with Community Health

There is a direct correlation between sustainable tourism and community health. They go hand in hand. Tourists don't want to see the beach used as a toilet. At the same time, when money is being spent in a destination there should be exponential improvements to the health and sanitation infrastructure. Additionally, a healthy population equates to a more productive work force and a more successful student body, which ultimately stimulates the economy. Less working days lost to illness and more energy means more money to be earned and less money to be spent on treating the sick. The more sustainable the tourism, the healthier the local community should become. At Kwepunha Retreat, this is our main vision. Local communities should benefit when new tourism develops in their region.

Community Support: From the Bottom Up

The most common question I am asked is, "How much did it cost to start Kwepunha Retreat?" But the more relevant question to ask is, "How many years of relationship building did it take before the community invited you to start a business?" Anyone with a pile of cash can attempt to build a business or to start a project, but unless they have the full support of the community, the project is doomed before it gets off the ground. I spent four years keeping promises, learning people's names, spending quality time, eating local meals, mentoring the youth and sharing laughs with the locals of Robertsport before we attempted to start a social impact business there. We have been welcomed with open arms and their community has become our community.

From the Top Down

In addition to being fully embraced at community level, our project would not have progressed without the full support of the local government. We have built and maintained great relationships with the Superintendent of Grand Cape Mount County and the Mayor of Robertsport. We have even been introduced to the President of Liberia, Madame Ellen Johnson Sirleaf, to talk to her about surfing as a new sport in the nation and as a viable economic driver. She had heard of the Liberian National Surfing Championships that we host each year and commented, "I've heard of this surfing thing, and I support it".

Stakeholders

When coming to a new destination and opening a social-impact business, there are many and various groups of stakeholders to consider and it is important to address the needs of what is most important to them. Some of the various stakeholder groups in Robertsport consist of not only the local surfers, but also the fishermen, the market women, the youth groups, the community chiefs, the religious groups, other local businesses, the neighbours, the local government, etc. In order to ensure we appeased all of these various stakeholders, we created a Five Year Community Health Plan under the consultation of Dr. Dave Jenkins, founder of SurfAid International. It is important to talk everything through before acting. Get to know who the stakeholders are and introduce yourself. Learn the challenges of the community and let your intentions be known, but be very careful to not make promises (or say something that may be perceived as a promise) that you cannot keep. One phrase that has worked well for us is, "We are trying to understand this challenge, so we can think of some possible solutions as a group".

Surfing Tourism as a Stepping Stone

Surfing tourism does not require the level of infrastructure that other forms of tourism requires; perfect waves are a natural resource that is as good as gold when combined with warm water, lack of crowds and friendly locals. Surfers do not need the luxuries of the developed world, such as flatscreen TVs, air conditioning – or even running water – to enjoy their tourism experience. Surfers will sleep in the sand if the surf is pumping and in the case of Robertsport, the waves are as good as it gets.

In Liberia, there is no other real draw for tourism due to the lack of infrastructure. What we have seen in other coastal destinations with similar challenges (lack of health care, education, jobs) is that the surfers come first. They want to buy a cold beer, have their clothes washed and somewhere to eat, etc. As the surfers spend money locally, the infrastructure tends to improve and this paves the way for other forms of niche tourism, such as ecotourism, adventure tourism, eventually even family tourism. As long as there is a model in place where the local community can benefit exponentially from the increase in tourism, then surfing can act as a pivotal stepping stone for other forms of tourism, which in turn stimulates other industries.

At Kwepunha Retreat, we can't control the development that comes into the town of Robertsport but, as early adopters, we are able to demonstrate a model to the local community where they can see the benefits of tourism. This way, when an investor wants to come into the community with the intention of benefiting solely the foreign investors, the local population does not have the wool pulled over their eyes. They understand the value of what they have and they know that there is a model that works, which all comes back to community support. The local community is less likely to support a project that does not have a direct and measurable benefit to them.

The Ripple Effect
As more surfers trickle in, the local surfers are starting to see the benefit. Many have become surf instructors, some have lead nature hikes and one local surfer is now a surf photographer. It is not just local surfers who benefit, however, from the newfound surf tourism, but also the travelling surfers who require some facilities. Additionally, the local Women's Sewing Co-Operative is starting to make surfboard socks; local carpenters are shaping alaia surfboards and hand planes and traditional canoe carvers are making miniature canoe handicrafts to sell to tourists. What really appealed to me about Robertsport was that it was a blank slate. Tourism was virtually non-existent, which gave us the opportunity to do things right from the start, as opposed to trying to rewind negative effects of tourism years down the line.

Many organisations operate in communities where tourism has existed for years, or decades, and they try to rewind issues such as environmental problems or try to create benefits for the local population, when there is already a model in place that has written them out of the equation. By having the support of some of the world's leading experts in sustainable surf tourism, we are able to address certain issues before they get out of hand and that really appeals to us. We have been trying to gain credibility and exposure for our project. So far, we have not received any funding, but media exposure and support has added credibility to our project and has allowed us to grow organically, attracting like-minded individuals and organisations.

Adaptability
A unique challenge of opening up a surf retreat in Liberia has been learning to adapt to the various niche markets that now frequent our destination. We are geared towards accommodating travelling surfers. Due to the large population of expatriates that live in Liberia, the high number of NGOs, the volume of United Nations staff and the presence of other development organisations in Liberia,

we have quickly become a popular destination for the young development worker crowd to escape the bustle of Monrovia by coming to Robertsport at the weekend. Our atmosphere and business model has been easily adapted for this niche market and many of these guests have even taken up surfing, taught by local Liberian surf instructors. We have quickly become the best option for accommodation in town, so we have a plethora of guests, each with their own needs and requirements. Everyone from surfers to the President's executive staff, to high religious leaders, to ex-generals from the Liberian civil war have stayed with us. We have learned to be flexible and adaptable, understanding that many of the Liberian guests prefer a Liberian menu. We are able to cater to the young backpacker/development worker/travelling surfer crowd and simultaneously offer a more exclusive experience to private groups. By serving multiple niche markets, we are able to grow the business and the social impact as surf tourism starts to trickle into the country.

Liberian Surfing Federation
The presence of Surf Resource Network and Kwepunha Retreat in Robertsport has allowed us to help the local surfers form the Liberian Surfing Federation and we continue to mentor and advise them as they grow as a club. The support of the local surfers is huge when it comes to sustainable surf tourism; they will ultimately dictate the vibes in the water and its reputation as a surf destination; so the practice of good vibes and surfing etiquette from the inception of the sport in Liberia has created a pleasant surfing experience for everyone.

The Liberian Surfing Federation is about to have their fifth Annual Liberian National Surfing Championships, which is an accomplishment for this young surfing culture. Previous competitions attracted more than 35 local competitors (men, women, and juniors) and drew a crowd of spectators of 1,000 people or more to witness the two-day event in an isolated fishing village. The competition has become very important to the local surf community and is a year-round topic of discussion.

A new and admirable Board Share System is being implemented by the Liberian Surfing Federation. Young local surfers, who participate in a monthly beach clean up, attend the Liberian Surfing Federation Meeting and who maintain good grades at school, are eligible to borrow boards on a daily basis. They don't take the surfboards for granted and they are held responsible and accountable for them. Due to the limited number of surfboards in the country, this model works quite well, not only to keep the surfboards in better condition so they last longer, but also to let the surfers try a variety of boards to see which suits their surfing best. Sharing waves with the local surfers is a rewarding experience and watching them grow and mature as a group makes all the challenges worthwhile.

A little Help From Your Friends
To get involved with an existing project, like Kwepunha Retreat or Surf Resource Network, or to create a project, it is important to remember that there is a plethora of individuals and organisations that share a passion of giving back through surfing. The Center for Surf Research at San Diego State University and the International Surfing Association have been a huge help to us at Surf Resource Network and Kwepunha Retreat.

Leave the 4x4 at home and meet the local people
There is more to a surf trip than epic conditions... culture, friendships, knowledge and peace of mind await. Perfect waves are just the icing on the cake.

Sean Brody (right), during his time as ISA Africa Development Adviser, along with the President of Cape Verde, Jorge Carlos de Almeida Fonseca. Brody delivered a presentation about developing the sport of Surfing in Africa during the 2014 CISA Convention for African Sports Development, which was held in Cape Verde (top).

2012 Liberian Surfing Championships, Benjamin McCrumuda, being chaired up the beach after the dramatic final by some of the other members of the Liberians Surfing Federation, along with Kwepunha Retreat founders, Sean Brody and Daniel Hopkins (bottom) (Courtesy of Sean Brody)

6.3

Negotiating Communties: Sustainable Cultural Surf Tourism

Andrew C. Abel
Danny O'Brien

In the mid-1980s, young Papua New Guinean, Andy Abel, broke his leg in a motocross accident. The result was a trip south to Australia, for surgery and extensive convalescence. Leaving his tropical Papua New Guinean home became something of an awakening for the teenage Andy, a third generation member of one of Papua New Guinea's most esteemed pioneering missionary and political families. The Abel family can trace its history back 122 years ago when Andy's grandfather, Reverend Charles William Abel of the London Missionary Society, landed on Kwato Island, Milne Bay Province in 1891. His late father, Sir Cecil Abel KBE, OBE, was a Cambridge educated political scientist who served with the Allied Forces during the Battle of Milne Bay during World War II. He later went on to work with Papua New Guinea's founding Prime Minister, Grand Chief Sir Michael Somare, and other pioneering leaders, to gain independence for Papua New Guinea in 1975 after 70 years of Australian administration.

Andy spent three months convalescing on Queensland's Sunshine Coast. The monotony of not being able to run around was maddening at first, but eventually, Andy began to look forward to his daily ritual of sitting on the bluff at Alexandra Headland, mesmerised by the waves below and the surfers riding them. Inspired by the surf, when he got home, Andy's father allowed him to return to the Sunshine Coast to finish off senior high school. But high school wasn't what Andy had in mind; his thoughts were decidedly more aquatic in nature. Surfing went on to become Andy's obsession, and he excelled at it. At the same time though, he couldn't ignore what was happening back in Papua New Guinea during the mid-1980s. Resentment over copper mining in the state of Bougainville, and the indigenous view that foreign owners were excluding locals from decisions relating to mining benefits, had erupted into armed and brutal conflict. A secessionist movement led by former surveyor and leader of the Bougainville Revolutionary Army (BRA), Francis Ona, ensued. Thousands were killed, and the protracted conflict effectively halted 40% of Papua New Guinea's national income.

By the late-1980s, Andy was 19, with little experience or money, wide-eyed with a dream. Surfing gave Andy a new insight in terms of how he saw the world, especially his homeland. But the Bougainville conflict also had a deep and lasting effect on his thinking about local versus foreign ownership of resources, and how these relationships should be managed to benefit traditional resource custodians. His new mission in life was to return to Papua New Guinea with surfboards, to establish the foundations of modern surfing.

The Challenge: Surfing, Surf Tourism, and Sustainability
Papua New Guinea lies north of Australia, and its economy relies heavily on agriculture, mining, fishing and logging. Despite its wealth of natural resources, 40% of the nation's 6.3 million people live in poverty; health care, education, communication and transport infrastructures are notoriously lacking (Australian Government, 2010). Nonetheless, Andy recognised his homeland as a diverse country of over 600 islands, more than 800 unique dialects and traditional cultures, with abundant marine, forest, and wildlife resources. He saw surfing as a sport with the potential to empower village communities, and his vision was one where surf tourism would provide a commercially viable alternative for remote villages to alleviate some of the crippling poverty they were faced with.

Surfing is not entirely foreign to the traditional Melanesian way of life. Villagers along the northern coasts have, perhaps for thousands of years, used planks of timber from broken canoes, called *palang* in pidgin English, to fashion surfboards similar to the Hawaiian *paipo*. These communities still perform a pre-colonial ceremony designed to cause the sea to rise up and provide good quality surf[1]. Modern versions of surfing arrived in Papua New Guinea during World War II when Australian troops stationed in Aitape established a surf club. While small groups of surfers were exploring the East Sepik coast in the 1960s, it was not until 1988 that Andy began laying the foundations for village-level surfing and a related surf tourism sector around the northwest provincial capital of Vanimo[2]. Nonetheless, despite a precedent for surfing in Papua New Guinea, in the eyes of national, provincial and local levels of government, organised surf tourism was indeed a foreign concept. Conversely, Andy saw its potential as niche cultural tourism capable of contributing to the nation's economy and overall GDP.

Papua New Guinea has a complex fabric of matrilineal and patralineal customary laws that govern the use of land and fringing reefs. In referring to surfing resources – fringing reefs and their immediate surrounds – the phrase 'traditional resource custodians' is used in preference to 'landowner', because in the dominant Melanesian culture, familial clans are seen as merely the current custodians of surfing resources that are to be passed on to succeeding generations. Indeed, 97% of Papua New Guinea's land and fringing reefs are subject to these traditional laws. Another important element of this cultural equation that tends to be taken for granted on the ground is the inclusive role that women play in all communities. Much of Papua New Guinean society is regarded as matrilineal, with women as the custodians of the land and fringing reefs. Therefore, even though men are the nominal heads of families, when it comes to land and reef matters, it is the women who call the shots.

It was in this complex sociocultural milieu that Andy set about forming a sustainable basis for surfing in his homeland. In its purest sense, the challenge before him was to lead the establishment of an industry that was committed to helping generate income and employment for traditional resource custodians, whilst ensuring low impacts on traditional cultures and the natural environment.

Getting to Work

The policies, ideas and eventual model that drove Andy's thinking on surfing development catalysed in 1987 during the Bougainville crisis – a war between the traditional land and resource custodians on one side, the Papua New Guinean Government on the other with its military and the CRA Mining Company. Bougainville's traditional resource custodians were marginalised from decisions concerning the exploitation of their mineral resources; they thought their concerns were being ignored by the National Government and CRA Mining Company. Francis Ona, leader of the Bougainville Revolutionary Army, mobilised and shut down the huge Bougainville copper mine that represented 40% of Papua New Guinea's GDP at the time. The losses amounted to hundreds of millions in foreign exchange earnings, taxes, and jobs. Two generations of children were deprived of basic education and health services and over 10,000 lives were lost on both sides of the protracted conflict.

Andy saw that, regardless of the scale of investment, if Papua New Guinean resource custodians are marginalized and exploited for their natural resources and wealth, they will shut down any operation – big or small. The fact that the Bougainville copper mine remains closed, 26 years on, is an unambiguous testimony to this. The mine remains shut despite the combined efforts of the United Nations, a host of NGOs, and the national governments of Papua New Guinea, Australia and New Zealand, to have it reopened. During 1988, Andy had the lessons learned from Bougainville in his mind, but he also drew deeply on his upbringing. Andy was raised in his mother's matrilineal customary society of Milne Bay Province, and also had the inspiration from his father and grandfather's unwavering service to country to draw on. So he began to plan how surfing and surf tourism could be introduced in a way that did not denigrate traditional values, but would build meaningful socioeconomic and community building outcomes for his young, evolving country. To achieve this, there were no precedents, role models or textbooks to draw on. There was simply a modern version of an old sport and uncharted waters that had to be tested at a calculated risk. This with a people steeped in traditional customary beliefs dating back tens of thousands of years, which they still live by.

Andy's first step, with the assistance of a small group of volunteers, was the establishment of the Surfing Association of Papua New Guinea (SAPNG). The SAPNG was founded with no national or provincial government financial assistance. It struggled for years to be taken seriously by all levels of government and related agencies. So Andy had to employ some lateral thinking in order to bring surfing to remote village communities. He was certain of one thing: he did not want to be remembered as the architect of destruction of his country's rich cultural traditions by replicating the surf tourism models he saw in countries such as Indonesia.

Indeed, most surf tourism operations in Indonesia's Mentawai Islands in the mid-2000s were foreign owned, so most profits went overseas and developing surfing participation at the village level was actively discouraged, lest it defile the surf tourism product. Ponting[3] argued that proactive discouragement of local surfing was a measured reaction by the surf tourism industry to what it perceived as a threat to the imperative of uncrowded surf. Based on the quality and *uncrowded* nature of the breaks they access, Ponting noted that many operators were charging five-star prices for three-star accommodation and service. So once surf breaks become crowded, the basis of five-star prices becomes seriously compromised. So rather than institute mechanisms for self-regulation, some Mentawai surf tourism operators instead sought to discourage local uptake of the sport of surfing. In illustrating this, Ponting quoted a surf magazine editor who explained his experience in attempting to give surfboards to local children that were interested in learning how to surf. His tour operator prevented him from doing so, stating: "If you do that, next time you come back here they'll be out there"[4]. So not only were Mentawai communities excluded from decision making about the commercial aspects of surf tourism, they also faced opposition to experiencing the stoke of surfing.

Essentially, the situation in the Mentawai was a classic tragedy of the commons. Of a common pool resource: multiple individuals acting in their own self-interest will eventually destroy a common pool resource. The Mentawai surf tourism industry, dominated by foreigners, simply went around the host communities and circumvented any local protocols. Meanwhile, the Indonesian Government failed to enforce any legislation or regulations, so the foreign controlled industry was left to do as it pleased, at the expense of traditional resource custodian host communities.

Andy knew he had to avoid this situation at all costs. His evolving vision was one where Papua New Guinean host communities were recognised as full and willing partners in the surf tourism enterprise, rather than the "exotic curios" they had been relegated to in Indonesia[5]. He also knew that, at the village level, the sport of surfing would captivate his people, just as it did him. But the SAPNG needed an alternative model around which to build the enterprise... Enter the Abel Reverse Spiral approach to sustainable surf tourism.

The Abel Reverse Spiral Model
In contrast to the top-down, foreign-led approach in the Mentawai Islands, Andy devised a more bottom-up, community-centered approach that would develop surfing as a community level sport in tandem with commercial surf tourism – what he called the Abel Reverse Spiral Model. Figures 1 and 2 (opposite) illustrate the logic of the model, with Figure 1 depicting the approach to surf tourism employed in other countries in which influence and decision making are driven in a top-down manner that excludes traditional resource custodian host communities. By contrast, Figure 2 portrays the reverse spiral approach in which host communities are *the* central players in decisions regarding the use of their surfing resources.

By the early 1990s, as Papua New Guinean surf tourism evolved and expanded from its Vanimo base to New Ireland Province, Andy refined the model with the help of a couple of brothers from Kavieng – Shaun and Nick Keane – and the now 13-member SAPNG board. The Keane brothers built Nusa Island Retreat in Kavieng and saw the reverse spiral model as a transparent, structured way to maintain mutually beneficial relationships with local resource custodians.

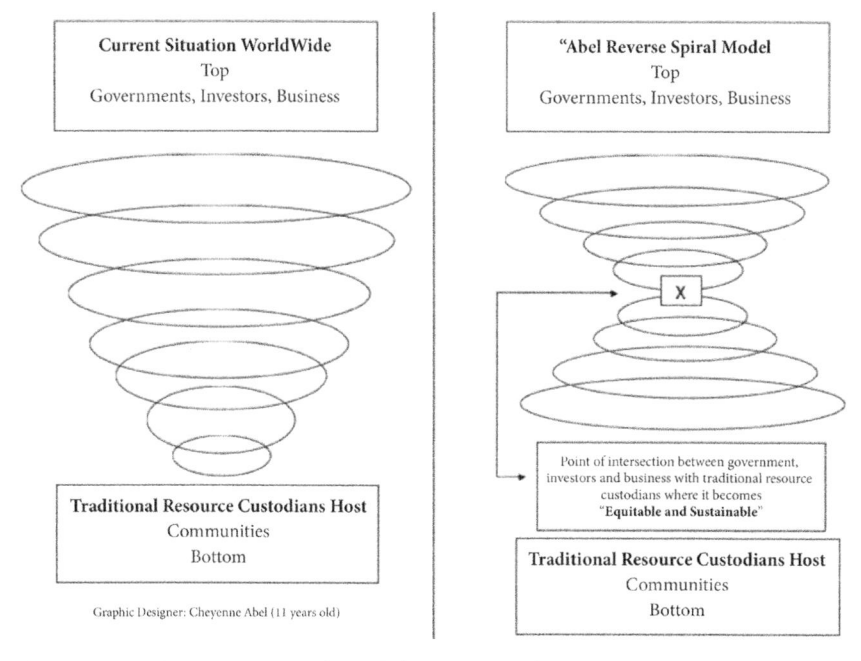

Figure 1 & 2 Top Down Approach vs Abel Reverse Spiral

Nusa Island Retreat is now the longest running and most popular surf tourism resort in Papua New Guinea. With new surf areas being discovered, regional Surf Management Plans (SMPs) became necessary, but at the core remained the assurance that influence spiraled up from host communities, rather than down from big business, government and external stakeholders. Figure 3 (overleaf) depicts the evolved reverse spiral model and the key stakeholders in Papua New Guinean surfing. Influence is depicted as spiraling up and out from Surf Area Communities in the bottom left corner of the figure.

The SMPs are a formalised attempt to sustainably manage surf tourism, and aim to guarantee that, "the PNG surf experience remains unique […] to ensure direct benefits to surf area communities"[6]. Regional alliances made up of community leaders, locally owned surf tourism operations, and the surfing clubs in each respective surf zone, administer the SMPs. The alliance in New Ireland Province, Nui Ailan Surfriders Alliance (NASA), was formed to promote the sustainable development of surfing and to administer the SMPs in the province's four designated surf zones. When asked how he would define sustainability in Papua New Guinean surfing, a former NASA Secretary highlighted the central role of surf area communities:

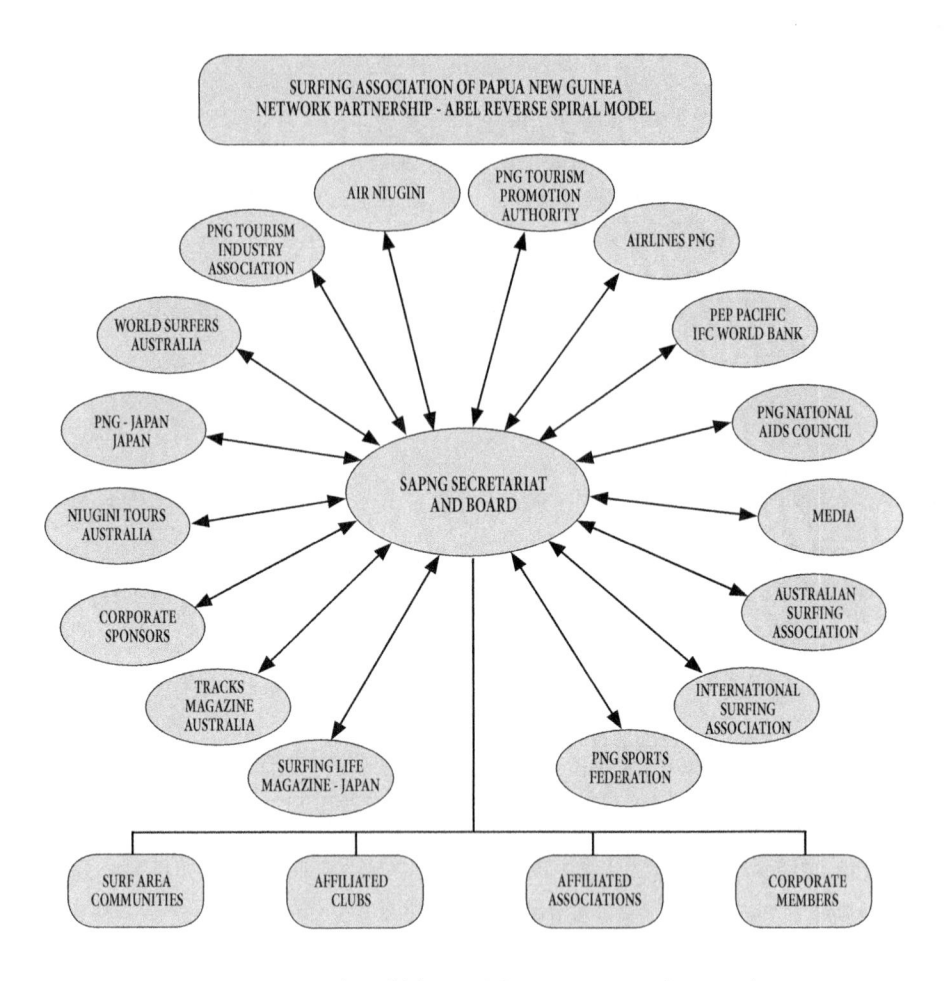

Figure 3: SAPNG Reverse Spiral Model (SAPNG Strategic Master Plan, 2006)

"Sustainability would be the locals remaining happy because, really, if they decide they don't want anybody surfing their reefs, then bang – it's over! They have total say over how their resources are used, and that's exactly as it should be[7]".

A key component of the reverse spiral model is an extensive consultation process with traditional resource custodians. Before the establishment of any commercial surf tourism venture, Andy, in his role as SAPNG President, consults with local communities on their interest in hosting surf tourism. The consultation process involves SAPNG representatives meeting with local clan leaders, elders and Village Planning Committees (or VPCs, which are locally elected bodies that are the common mechanism for decision making in regional village communities). Then, with local permission, Andy and other SAPNG representatives make public presentations at village meetings and run question and answer sessions, all of which are aimed at explaining the sport of surfing and the nature of surf tourism. So rather than resource custodians being relegated to the periphery of the surf tourism equation as in some other parts of the world, the SAPNG's consultation process ensures host communities' central role in the process.

Where a community agrees to host surfing, the SAPNG first helps them establish an affiliated surf club to develop village-level surfing. This happens before the commencement of any commercial operation. By getting them in the water and actually learning to surf first, locals get a clearer understanding of the sport, which puts the horse squarely in front of the cart in terms of local ownership of the surfing enterprise. Dependent on local capacity and infrastructure, regional resource custodians, surf clubs and the SAPNG all agree upon a quota system that effectively limits the number of surf tourists per day per zone to a mutually agreed upon number. In most surf zones, the daily quota is 20 non-local, visiting surfers per day. Importantly, locals can surf as much as they like. Each surf tourist then has two fees integrated into their lodging packages. The first is a one-off levy to the SAPNG of AUS$50 that contributes to the SAPNG's administrative costs and surf sport development activities throughout the country.

The second is a daily fee of AUS$10 per surfer per day which goes to the respective regional surf alliances. This second fee is reticulated back to the surf areas to fund community development projects as identified by host communities themselves. To date, these projects have included initiatives such as the purchase and/or construction of school educational facilities, water reticulation projects, and aid posts. These agreements are negotiated over a period of time and ratified between the parties before the first commercial paying surfer is allowed to surf the area. The agreements are then reviewed before the start of every season and consolidated by the SAPNG, with information passed on to registered wholesalers and marketing agents around the world.

Empowering Communities

By 2006, two live-aboard surf charters began operating around the St Mathieu Islands. Coastal youth, building upon pre-existing wave riding skills, adapted readily to the new wave riding technology. The SAPNG currently boasts

10 affiliated surf clubs throughout Papua New Guinea in Vanimo, Wewak, Madang, New Ireland, and Port Moresby; with Manus, Bougainville and Aitape coming on stream in 2013 with ground work established in partnership with the traditional resource custodian host communities.

The most recent Papua New Guinea Tourism Master Plan (2007-2017) identifies nature-based tourism resources that predispose the country to competitive advantages in the niche market of sport tourism. Indeed, diving, trekking, game fishing, surfing, climbing, canoeing, caving and rafting are each identified as, "critical components of the future development of tourism" in Papua New Guinea[8]. Of all of these sectors, surfing is the only one with a formalised, community-centered strategy to address the challenges of sustainability. For this reason, the Papua New Guinea Tourism Promotion Authority commended the SMPs to the country's other tourism sectors as an exemplar of how to, "ensure [tourism] benefits are provided to landowners and host communities"[9].

Clearly, the SAPNG must be doing something right. Not only was there the endorsement from the Tourism Promotion Authority but, in 2006, the World Bank partnered with the SAPNG to assist in the draft of its first ever formalised strategic plan. The very next year, in 2007, the country's Grand Chief and Prime Minister, Sir Michael Somare, was on site in Vanimo to open the first ever Papua New Guinea National Surfing Titles, where he also announced a PNG100,000 Kina grant to build a new two-storey school building in the host community. As Andy reflected on this significant milestone: it wasn't soccer or rugby or cricket or anything, it was surfing that brought the Prime Minister to Lido village in Vanimo and in lieu of what he saw, he donated PNG100,000 Kina to a double-storey classroom which is all built now. And in the eyes of these village people, who've been deprived of basic services for 34 years, they're going "Wow! These surfers are actually delivering where government is failing!" We receive the money from the levies and then reticulate it down into the community, so it bypasses the bureaucracy and politicians, etc.[10]

Also in 2007, the Governor General Grand Chief Sir Paulius Matane, on behalf of the Papua New Guinea National Government, bestowed on Andy the Order of the Member of Logohu (ML) for his 21 years of service to his country for the promotion and development of surfing and surf tourism. This was a clear recognition from the highest level of the land of Andy's leadership in bringing tangible benefits through surfing to remote village communities. Then, in 2008, one of Papua New Guinea's Supreme Court Judges, Justice Nicholas Kirriwom, solicited Andy's help to establish surfing in the village of his upbringing in Ulingan Bay, Bogia District, about two hours drive north of Madang. When Justice Kirriwom and Andy met in late 2008, the seeds were sewn for Tupira Surf Club to come into existence. On visiting the region, Andy was blown away by the beauty and consistency of the waves, and Justice Kirriwom was intrigued by the sheer athleticism of the sport. He was also hopeful that surf tourism could provide an alternative to his community's reliance on local, foreign-owned logging operations, which had wreaked environmental carnage in the region for decades, with very little local benefit. In surfing however, he could see social and economic benefits reticulating directly back to Ulingan Bay communities, with no environmental downside. When Justice Kirriwom then put the idea of surfing and surf tourism to Ulingan locals, it was embraced wholeheartedly. And as Justice Kirriwom explained shortly before Tupira Surf Club hosted the 2011 National Surfing Titles, the prospect of achieving these benefits without the environmental carnage he'd seen from logging was especially appealing:

"Surfing is clean and healthy, and promotes a healthy environment. The idea of bringing in surf tourism was to try to prevent further logging operations in the Bay. The loggers used the Bay as a log-pond where they loaded their logs onto the ships. We had so much damage – heavy pollution in the water, no fish in the Bay, the marine life was just devastated. So that's why we worked for so many years to stop this, and then this idea of surfing came along and we thought this was a better way to use our marine resource to better ends all 'round'[11]".

As graphically illustrated in the 2011 award winning documentary, *Splinters*, which was directed by Adam Pesce and produced by Emmy Award winner, Perrin Chiles, women remain central players in Papua New Guinean surfing. Indeed, in a country where women's access to sport participation and resources has traditionally been limited, a key outcome from village-level surfing development has been the involvement of women and girls in the sport. Women and girls now represent around 25% of all club members throughout Papua New Guinea's 10 surfing clubs. When asked about the changes unfolding in her community as more women and girls take up the sport, one community leader explained that,

"It was a little bit difficult for girls before, because the mothers would demand the daughter's presence to help them with house chores and other things. But I guess the parents are slowly coming to realize that surfing is not only a sport; it's developing the minds of young children to learn other things and to meet other people [...] So I think parents are coming to realize that this sport is not only for boys, it's also for girls. And they want the girls to learn something, you know, that the boys are also learning[12]".

Conclusions: The Company We Keep

It has been a long and bumpy road to legitimacy for the SAPNG, but the seed that was planted and nurtured over 26 years ago has grown into a solid tree that is fruit bearing and sprouting in newly identified surfing destinations around Papua New Guinea, in partnership with the respective traditional resource custodian host communities. The SAPNG model of development has traversed the complex terrain of traditional land and property rights, diverse cultural values, traditions and heritage across Papua New Guinea and married this with the aesthetics of global surf commerce, without denigrating the way of life of the indigenous people and ensuring through this partnership protection and preservation of fragile environment and reef ecologies. The Abel Reverse Spiral Model with its SMPs is still going through refinements with regular consultative meetings and self-regulation among stakeholders, but it is working and evolving under the SAPNG as the governing authority of surfing and surf tourism in Papua New Guinea. The SAPNG is delivering tangible benefits and opportunities to host surfing communities that have embraced the sport and surf tourism as an integral part of their daily lives.

And, if the company we keep is any indicator, then the endorsement of the Papua New Guinea Tourism Promotion Authority, the involvement of the World Bank, attracting Emmy Award winning filmmakers, a Chief Justice, and 20 local and international corporate members, and Andy's award of the Order of the Member of Logohu from the Papua New Guinea National Government, must surely indicate that the SAPNG is doing something right. Nevertheless, the challenges of sustainability remain. This is why the SAPNG is now fighting to have the regulation of surf tourism mandated into law through an Act of Parliament. When this bill is completed with the support of current Prime Minister O'Neill, and ratified into law, the SAPNG will become the first surfing body in the world to have its own Act of Parliament. The lessons of the Mentawais illustrate that market forces are not enough and human nature tends to work against us. In Papua New Guinea, the SAPNG made it a fundamental priority and duty to empower surfing's traditional resource custodians by establishing organisational structures consistent with the provisions of the laws available under the PNG Constitution, so that surf tourism compliments surfing development as its core activity and sport. As the pioneers of everything surfing in Papua New Guinea, this was to ensure that surf tourism could not become a threat to itself and to the traditional resource custodians that choose to welcome it into their communities.

The SAPNG mission is clear in ensuring the creation of a legacy to protect the aspirations of traditional resource custodian host communities for now and future generations. This mission is consistent with the SAPNG's constitution and powers vested in the SAPNG Board: to protect the rights of the people and to ensure that surf tourism development does not make host communities bystanders and servants in their own land. It is our collective duty and challenge as surfers, regardless of race, creed, color or profession, to ensure that host communities are party to the planning, implementation and management of the surf tourism resource from the bottom up, and are an integral part of the surf tourism product and, as a result, tangibly benefit in direct and indirect ways from it.

Andy and first Prime Minister of PNG, Grand Chief Sir Michael Somare GCMG, CH, MP, in conversation about SAPNG at the 2007 Inaugural National Surf Titles in Vanimo where he committed K100,000 (AUS$40,000) towards a double story classroom (now built) and a public holiday for public servants and the community in honor of what SAPNG has contributed towards nation building.

6.4

Surfing and Coastal Ecosystem Conservation in Baja California, Mexico

Serge Dedina, Eduardo Najera, Zach Plopper and Cesar Garcia

A surf trip to Baja California, Mexico, used to be all about finding uncrowded waves, clean water and a no-worries escape from Southern California. South of Punta Baja, more than 200 miles below the U.S./Mexico border, the Pacific shoreline is dotted with small fishing settlements. There is almost no pollution, coastal access is unimpeded and security means wearing rubber wetsuit booties to avoid stubbing your toes while walking out to surf cobblestone pointbreaks.

The coastline between Tijuana and Ensenada is a prime example of how fast a once spectacular and public coast can be transformed into one of the world's worst examples of unplanned, inaccessible, and polluted coastal corridors. Much of the coastline is fenced off behind private development; fences and concrete walls often illegally impede coastal access to the host of quality surf spots.

In Rosarito Beach, the shoreline is hidden behind garish high-rise condominiums and hotels; more than 25 defunct high-rise buildings litter the coastal zone between Tijuana and Ensenada. In addition to blocked beach access, coastal pollution also reduces the region's surfing options. A few miles north of Rosarito Beach, up to 30 million gallons of wastewater is spewed onto the beach every day, contaminating the coastline for miles. The sewage wafts through the line-up at Baja Malibu, a beachbreak listed by *Surfer Magazine* as one of the best surf spots in the world.

For conservationists, the coastal corridor of northern Baja California coastline is an example of how we have failed to develop and implement the necessary legal tools required to protect coastal ecosystems that also happen to be surf spots. In many cases, it can also be the narrow-mindedness and self-interest of surfers that is an obstacle to adequately protecting these breaks. In the case of Baja California, many surfers have been happy to invest in development projects that have mangled the coastline and blocked access to surf spots in return for having exclusive access to waves.

Coastal ecosystems and marine features that produce quality waves are best conserved for the future through their proactive protection. This is what we have carried out over the past decade, aiming to preserve the ecological integrity of some of the last wild and undeveloped stretches of Pacific shoreline on the Baja California Peninsula. Our action has been varied and includes placing legal protective buffers around the coastal zones through private land acquisition, conservation easements and public conservation concessions where responsible public access and use is permitted. Our efforts have not been intentionally designed to preserve surf spots. Rather they have been carried out with the objective of preserving globally significant coastal and marine ecosystems. Our conservation endeavors have helped to preserve a multitude of world-class point breaks and reefs that litter our conservation sites. On the peninsula's central Pacific coast, in the Valle de los Cirios Area of Protected Flora and Fauna, we have preserved 26,142 acres and 31.4 miles through private acquisitions and conservation easements. This includes seven prominent points, five wetlands and eleven continuous miles of the region's least disturbed coastal zone. Additionally, through the application of federal coastal conservation concessions, carried out in partnership with Mexico's National Protected Area Commission (CONANP), we have preserved more than 324 miles of coastline that includes one UNESCO World Heritage Site and the world's last undeveloped gray whale lagoon. We are working on securing an additional 780 miles of coastline through concessions with CONANP that would preserve at least two more UNESCO World Heritage Site and a multitude of quality surf breaks.

Baja Boom
Surfers that assume an undeveloped coastline will remain that way forever overlook the fact that wave-rich desert regions, like the Baja California coastline, or the northwest coast of Australia, are rich in resources that are attractive to industrial and tourism developers. Mega-development and industrial projects proposed in these regions require giant tracts of cheap land (which is often owned by cash-strapped rural ranchers, farmers and fishermen) and coastal access in order to be profitable.

What we learned from the aggressive and haphazard coastal development in northern Baja is that surfers must be conservation visionaries in order to preserve the coastline and marine features that create quality waves.

The threats to the Baja coast and its surf spots originated in the 'Baja Boom', opening the once locked up coast of Baja California to a wave of speculators and developers. The sudden rush to develop the coastal zone of what had been a long and isolated desert region was the result of changes to the Mexican constitution in 1992 which allowed land under the control of collectivist *ejidos* (land collectives) to become private and for sale on the open market. For the first time, many white sand beaches and pristine coastal desert of Baja California could be purchased. This resulted in the 'Baja Boom', a race of speculators and multi-national corporations buying and developing the coastline of the peninsula from 1995 to 2008.

The Boom detonated with the announcement, in early 1995, that the Mitsubishi Corporation planned to develop a 500,000 acre industrial salt harvesting facility adjacent to Laguna San Ignacio, the world's last undeveloped gray whale birthing lagoon. As a result, conservationists, who had ignored Baja California in the mistaken belief that the peninsula could never be developed, rushed in to defend it.

The 'Baja Boom' reached its zenith during rule of President Vicente Fox from 2000 to 2006. Among the proposed projects included a plan by President Fox to build a network of marinas and resorts, an *Escalera Nautica* or Nautical Ladder, at over 20 of the most remote beaches in Northwest Mexico. Fox announced the project a year after his predecessor cancelled the Mitsubishi salt project. Beaches along Baja's central Pacific coast, barely on the radar, even for surfers, due to their isolation, were being offered up as future marina locations. Hand-painted signs posted along Baja California's trans-peninsular highway announced land for sale at the distant proposed marina sites. Property owners, desperate for cash in Baja, even posted 'Developer Wanted' signs along the highway.

Although the Baja California Peninsula has one of the most expansive networks of protected areas in the world, covering roughly two-thirds of its land mass, concessions can still be granted for even the most destructive land users. Land or beach concessions, within natural protected areas, can be granted by the federal government on the basis that in Mexico the first 60 feet of beach, inward of the high-tide mark (also known as Federal Maritime Coastal Zone or ZOFEMAT) and land areas without a legally recognised owner, either private or communal, are considered to be national assets subject to be concessions for resource exploitation for the 'common good' or 'development' of the nation.

The Vizcaino Biosphere Reserve and the Valle de los Cirios contains much of the peninsula's prized Pacific and Sea of Cortez coastline, making areas of global biological significance targets for development. When the only new marina associated with the *Escalera Nautica* project was built (and then abandoned) at Santa Rosalillita in the Valle de los Cirios, and Mitsubishi was granted its concession to the northern shore of Laguna San Ignacio, it became apparent to WILDCOAST that additional layers of protection were required to conserve these critical ecosystems. Federal protection was not enough.

Valle de los Cirios
After observing the way multi-national corporations and land speculators were making bad deals with poor people to buy their land, we reasoned that conservationists could make equitable transactions with those same communities to preserve their land. Instead of removing people from the land and coastline they depend on for their livelihoods through ranching and fishing, we developed a programme to ensure that land deals would respect residency, access and, in some cases, secure the tenure status of local resource users and residents who are often the best environmental stewards (in many cases fishing communities and ranchers don't always own or have legal rights to use the land they work on).

The Valle de los Cirios Pacific Coast is one of the most isolated coastal stretches on the Baja California Peninsula, making it one of the few remaining coastal 'wildlands' left in North America. The encompassing protected area, the Valle de los Cirios Area of Protected Flora and Fauna, is named so for the Cirio cactus or Boojum tree, an endemic plant species found only along this stretch of the Baja California Peninsula and in one select location in the state of Sonora. WILDCOAST identified an 88-mile (53,420 acres) coastal corridor, defined by the Ejido San Jose de las Palomas, within the protected area, for long-term land conservation efforts. Priority conservation sites along the Valle de los Cirios Pacific Coast include coastal wetlands and surrounding watersheds, point complexes, undisturbed shoreline and other important habitat areas. To protect these locations, WILDCOAST is pursuing a combination of private and public land conservation strategies.

Since 2006, WILDCOAST has been carrying out direct land purchase and conservation easement opportunities with landowners in Ejido San Jose de las Palomas. The long-term project vision is the conservation all major point-complexes, wetlands and other key shoreline areas in the region to protect habitat, maintain open public coastal access and develop on-site environmental stewardship among the region's tenants and visitors. To date, WILDCOAST has protected 31.4 miles of coastline.

Currently, we are carrying out management and stewardship activities on protected properties. We have placed informational signage at key visitor areas with information on camping best practices. We have worked with the local municipal government to clean up old waste sites, removing 9.5 tonnes of discarded debris in 2012. There is still much work to do regarding waste management, including fish camps and removing invasive plants that compete with native species for water and significantly impact the wetlands and watersheds that dot the coast.

Federal Zone Concessions
As a response to the Escalera Nautica and other badly planned coastal development projects, we partnered with CONANP to expand its efforts to preserve the Federal Maritime Coastal Zone, or ZOFEMAT, adjacent to the peninsula's federal protected areas (areas that do not include the ZOFEMAT). This unprecedented policy initiative comes from the frustration of CONANP from having to fight off development threats such as the Escalera Nautica and the Mitsubishi salt project in and adjacent to federally protected land.

Since 2008, WILDCOAST has partnered with CONANP to protect shoreline through ZOFEMAT conservation concessions in critical coastal areas on the Baja California Peninsula and Sea of Cortez. The ZOFEMAT within Mexico's federal protected areas can be set aside for conservation through jurisdiction transfers to CONANP called *acuerdos de destino*. Before WILDCOAST's involvement, the federal agency did not have the funding or staff capacity to carry out required field surveys, topographical studies, mapping, photographic archiving or applications processes.

With WILDCOAST's logistical and technical support, CONANP is protecting critical shoreline in undeveloped coastal areas in the Valle de los Cirios, the Vizcaino Peninsula, Bahia Magdalena, Laguna San Ignacio, the Sea of Cortez and Cabo Pulmo (on Baja's East Cape) through this strategy. So far, more than 324 miles of coastline have been conserved with an additional 768 miles in applications in the process.

WILDCOAST provided CONANP field crews with GPS devices, tablet PCs, cameras, other equipment and logistical support to carry out the extensive field surveys required to solicit *acuerdos de destino*. Field surveys are an essential component of the ZOFEMAT *acuerdos de destino* process that requires rigorous fieldwork to obtain the data necessary to compile applications. WILDCOAST expedited and streamlined this process through this logistical and technical support.

For many of the fishing communities of the region who harvest fish through marine concessions granted by the federal government, the ZOFEMAT conservation concessions have helped to secure the protection of their coastline that, in the past, has been threatened by development. In the case of Punta Abreojos, for example, a fishing village with a population of approximately 1,000 residents, the ZOFEMAT conservation concessions will help to prevent future projects like the planned jetties and marinas proposed by Mitsubishi and the National Trust Fund for Tourism Development (FONATUR, a semi-public sector organization) that would have wiped out valuable lobster and abalone grounds, in addition to destroying point breaks and reefs surfed by locals and visitors alike.

Conserving the Future
The legal tools that we have applied to preserve coastal and surf spots on the Baja California Peninsula are only some of the methodologies available to surf conservationists in order to preserve surfing areas. What is clear from our work is that conservationists need to apply as many different tools as possible to preserve coastlines that will forever be targeted by government agencies and multi-national corporations for development.

In the case of our project areas on the peninsula, we have demonstrated that conservationists can and must work with local residents so they can continue to safeguard the coast for future generations and demonstrate to government agencies the value of sustainable management. Surfers must carry out conservation projects that enhance local tenure status and coastal access for all. Surfers cannot afford to wait for someone else to do the job of preserving their coastline for them. The task of coastal conservation is the job of everyone who enjoys the recreational opportunities: both fishing and wilderness experiences that an intact coastline provides. In order for surfers to continue riding the waves they love, they must be strategic, smart and realistic when it comes to preserving waves and the coastlines that sustain them.

… 6.5

Embedding Surf Stoke in Academia

Malcolm Findlay

On 4th March 2012, surfing lost one of its pioneers, but this one never stood on a surfboard, rarely went to the beach and couldn't tell Duke Kahanamoku from Kelly Slater. Colin Williams was born in 1948, so could well have recorded much of the momentous development that took place in surfing up until his untimely passing, had he not been largely oblivious to all of it. His introduction to surfing didn't come until March 1998, when serendipity placed him in the coastal town of Newquay in Cornwall, on the same weekend as the British National Student Surfing Championship. This event had grown from humble beginnings in the early 1970s to one of the world's biggest surf contests, with over 600 competitors and a vast entourage of followers and supporters from about 150 different educational institutions.

Colin, a stout and affable geologist, sporting a dense white beard, was a Senior Manager at Plymouth University and, well known for his insight and creativity, had been given a 'roving brief' to generate new ideas for academic study programmes. The advent of the New Labour Government in the UK the previous year had seen the launch of an ambitious strategy aimed at increasing the number of young people entering Higher Education. Prime Minister Tony Blair had made a famous speech about, "Education, Education, Education"[1] and the class barrier eroding principles of the 1997 Dearing Report[2] were to be embraced across the UK's HE sector in what was being called the "Learning Renaissance"[3]. Colin's mission was to enable the University to engage with this agenda. When he realised that his progress through the narrow, surf-shop lined streets of Newquay was being impeded due to a student throng, Colin, who rarely took any time off work, felt the cogs in his brain begin to turn – if this many young people are turned on by surfing and it's the basis for a niche economic sector, could it be used to underpin a study programme?

It's at this point, while I was teaching and researching at Plymouth University's Institute of Marine Studies, that I made my entrance. Upon his return to Plymouth the following Monday, Colin asked around the University for someone with whom he might discuss his idea. "You need to talk to the guy who runs the Fisheries Science Department", someone told him, "he often turns up late to give his 9am lectures with dripping wet hair and we know why". Colin and I discussed the idea on the Tuesday afternoon and I was immediately on board; we formed a development a team and our ride on the wave of surfing academia began.

Surf Science and Technology: The Underpinning Ethos
On a personal level, I align with a description the first World Surfing Champion, Midget Farrelly, gave of himself back in 1964, the year he took the title: "Not that I'm a fanatic – a surf nut. I don't spend my time camping on the beaches thinking of nothing else but the surf"[4]. Our initial research into the possible market for a surfing-based academic programme showed that a great many people, male and female, were cast in that same mould. Our survey work confirmed a variety of reasons why people are gripped by surfing, including the physical experience of riding waves, the opportunity to commune with nature as well as the surf culture itself. We also confirmed that surfers have other lives, wanting to develop intellectually and enhance their career prospects; it would never be enough to focus simply upon the act of surfing alone. We had to identify, as accurately as possible, what these people wanted from a surf-related degree and of equal (or perhaps greater) importance, what prospective employers might need of our graduates.

The data from the many questionnaires, interviews and focus groups we ran suggested clear potential for recruiting a viable number of students to a programme that, being constructed around surfing and the surf industries, had authenticity but also held credibility through a diet of study that was academically rigorous, challenging to the intellect of students, and relevant enough to underpin genuine career opportunities. Importantly, the potential students we identified were bright and capable but, nevertheless, often on the periphery of Higher Education, unsure whether it was right for them or they were right for it. In talking to these people about the proposal, we seemed to be whetting appetites for degree-level study through an academic offer that tapped into an interest in surfing and this was the essence of the idea – attracting students who would not otherwise have gone to university and optimising opportunities to achieve to their academic potential.

Stoking the Curriculum
The late 1990s saw the concept of 'transferrable skills' taking hold in UK higher education[5]. Modern industries needed a range of qualities in the graduates they would recruit and people were moving between jobs with increasing frequency, so there was an acceptance across the sector that it was no longer appropriate to deliver degree courses with an extremely narrow focus. This helped our cause immensely. We continued to explore the market, drawing information from the surf industry and assessing whether we had the staffing, facilities and capacity to assemble a curriculum that would meet the needs of graduates while, at the same time, allowing them to adapt to other careers; in education, finance, public relations and so on. Our aim was to develop a programme of study where much of the learning was done in context – instead of a dry and abstract lecture on rip currents, for example, we would take our students to the beach and throw oranges into the water at the shoreline, tracking the progress of the oranges and explaining why they went where they did.

I spent months calling in favours from people I knew in the surf industry and making new contacts with others, gathering information that would shape the curriculum for this globally unique initiative. The evidence showed that, as well as the larger, well-known companies, the surf industry was supported by a vast array of small enterprises in which the operators were required to 'wear many hats'; perhaps designing and ordering in the morning, selling and marketing in the afternoon and organising finance and managing human resources in the evening. We had to cater for all of this while maintaining our focus on surfing.

In planning a delivery model we drew upon expertise among the University's staff, both in the Institute of Marine Studies and the wider institution, to generate four themes; Environment, which would include components in Ocean and Atmosphere, Waves and Beaches, Environmental Issues, and Marine Meteorology, culminating in specialist work in Coastal Management; Business, including Finance and Business Functions, Marketing, and Export and Import Procedures, tied together through specialist projects in Trade in the Surf Industries; Technology, which embraced Materials and Manufacturing, Design and Quality Management as well as offering the opportunity for students to make surf-related equipment; Performance included Human Biology, Sports Performance and Surfing Skills Analysis. Running alongside this very broad curriculum were supporting modules in Enterprise and Professional Skills and the History and Development of Surf Recreation.

Through these early stages, we were plagued by a constant nagging doubt. Were we trying to cover too much? As the French artist, Eugene Delacroix once declared, "the artist who aims to achieve perfection in everything achieves it in nothing"[6]. But we persevered, working to create a structure that allowed seemingly disparate aspects of the curriculum to relate to each other in a coherent way. The great advantage of this was that we were able to use surfing as the core, around which we built a progressive three year student experience with each modular component relating to the others in meeting a set of overarching aims and objectives. The end product was a broad ranging, evidence-based curriculum, centred upon the surf industry but at the same time endowing graduates with skills that could be applied in a wide range of contexts, therefore broadening career opportunities.

As we distilled the curriculum and delivery model, we inevitably found that the programme did not suit everyone. I recall meeting with Nat Young (the second World Champion, in 1966) and outlining the proposed curriculum for what had assumed the working title of, 'Surf Science and Technology'. Young repeatedly posed the same question – "what about the *spirit* of surfing, where is this in the programme and how will this be nurtured?" I knew what he meant; he wanted to know how we were embedding 'surf stoke' in a credible academic offer – something that had not been done before – and it was a fair point. I furnished a reply based upon the contention that wherever you gather a group of people with a common bond, 'stoke' will abound but I admit that, at the time, this was founded upon hope rather than any supporting evidence.

How the World Received BSc Surf Science and Technology
The latter part of 1998 and start of the following year saw frenetic action among the programme development team, culminating in a series of rigorous programme approval events. These involved detailed scrutiny both within the University and in the presence of independent external validation panel members drawn from academia and industry. In effect, the Approval Panel for a new academic programme is acting on behalf of every student who might enrol and every employer who might take on one of its graduates and our inquisitors, quite rightly, took the job seriously. We were put through our paces, defending and justifying every word in the extensive documentation we had submitted to scrutiny but finally, in March 1999, Plymouth University approved the Bachelor of Science degree in Surf Science and Technology and gave the go-ahead to advertise twenty places on the degree for September that same year.

As soon as the first advert appeared, the workload of the University's Public Relations Department doubled. Media enquiries flooded in, at first from the UK then, like a storm swell marching across the open ocean, from around the globe. Colin and I were being interviewed by newspapers, magazines, radio and TV stations and, due to time differences, were having to take shifts so we could address the Australian, American and Japanese interest at unearthly hours of the night from here in the UK. For a couple of months, we had full-time support from a marketing and press officer, not something the average academic would need (short of having developed an engine that runs on seawater). The University had a press coverage company called Durrants, who picked up every mention of the degree and this was sent on to us, revealing that, as well as the 'broadsheets', almost every small town newspaper in the UK was carrying the story. For TV news editors, it seemed to be one of those handy stories that could be formed into a piece to be slotted in their bulletins on 'no news' days, when no local politicians had resigned because of inappropriate behaviour, no factories had closed and no local cats had managed to get stuck in a tree.

As news spreads, people naturally began to form views, sometimes based upon fact but more often, on their preconceived ideas of both academia and surfing. Coverage ranged from lengthy, well-considered articles to the plain moronic, illustrated in the cartoon (opposite) from, of all sources, the *Times Higher Education Supplement*.[7]

In the early days of media interest, the pendulum seemed to swing wildly between support and detraction. In March 1999, comments such as, "If Plymouth offers surfing because people come to the region for the surf, will we get football studies at Manchester University?"[8] and "These surfing profs should be given gold stars for pushing forward the parameters of education; they have taken a subject that will engage young minds and framed a course that will stretch them"[9]. As the debate matured, however, the case for what we had set out to achieve began to win the day thanks in no small measure to more considered commentary from enlightened academics, such as Professor Sir Roderick Floud, who at the time was President of Universities UK. Professor Floud was reported in *The Times* as saying the degree was providing employers with the skills they wanted[10] and this was followed by a stream of very positive comments posted on the newspaper's website by members of the public.

Every so often though, someone would take a swipe at "the surfing degree", as the detractors liked to call it. One particularly venomous attack came from a speaker at the annual gathering of the Professional Association of Teachers in

University degree in catching the tube

the UK[11]. Subsequent to reading about this I contacted the individual concerned with an invite to come to Plymouth and review what our students were doing in the course of their studies, in fact I even offered to cover his travel and subsistence costs, but I never received a response. When we did manage to get those with negative preconceptions to visit, things often turned out differently, for example when Sam Kiley, a prominent television and print journalist came to Plymouth with a Channel 4 film crew. Kiley would later tell me that his original intention was to portray Surf Science & Technology as a 'Mickey Mouse' degree in the course of a programme for the highly respected *Dispatches* current affairs series. Sam's visit coincided with one of our annual Contemporary Issues in Surfing conferences and, after witnessing our students delivering insightful presentations and high quality debate, he abandoned his original idea and shifted his focus to postgraduate provision at another University.

The media circus ran for around three years, with interest waxing and waning as momentous events, such as 9/11, came and went leaving gaps in news columns and TV bulletins that had to be filled. Oddly, as though it was somehow the final say on the matter, an article, penned by a journalist named Sally Palmer, appeared in a science magazine called *Focus* in July 2003. I was waiting at Bristol Airport for a flight to the Canary Islands – to a UK surfer the equivalent of a U.S. surfer's trip to Hawaii and had gone to the news-stand to get something to read during my journey. There, in pole position on a revolving stand, was a copy of *Focus* featuring a piece on Surf Science and Technology[12] (August 2003). Ms Palmer, with whom I'd done a telephone interview that I couldn't even remember some months previously, gave a balanced and analytical account, concluding that, "scientific and technical skills were being taught to a high standard, with practical applications for a burgeoning industry".

Cloning the Degree

Within weeks of the programme being advertised in 1999, and amidst the initial media interest, proposals for 'clone' educational programmes emerged. The first came from a nearby institution, Cornwall College, where a Diploma level course was proposed that would link with the University degree by allowing students to progress to gain a full honours degree with the University. We worked with Cornwall College in developing a 'reverse engineered' curriculum for this, allowing seamless progression and a mutually beneficial financial arrangement. Over subsequent years this proved a successful relationship with some excellent students joining the Plymouth Degree, gaining good awards and going on to forge a variety of successful careers. Elsewhere in the UK, the Swansea Institute for Higher Education in Wales worked to develop a programme in Surf and Beach Management, with elements directly copied from the Plymouth programme, but this was never actually launched. As word spread internationally, we heard of institutions in Australia, South Africa and the United States that were developing similar degrees to Surf Science and Technology but few, if any, made it to the point of actually offering a coherent study programme. The sticking point seemed to be that, while these institutions had ready access to Plymouth University's programme documentation, few had the array of staff expertise that needed to be brought together to deliver the curriculum forming the Plymouth Degree.

In 2002, we were approached by Edith Cowan University in Western Australia. Colin and I flew out there and, dressed in Quantas tee shirts worn because the

Airline inconveniently managed to lose our luggage, discussed possibilities with one of the Deans, Professor Elizabeth Hatton. We agreed a franchise deal, in which our Degree would be delivered by Edith Cowan at its Bunbury Campus in the world-renowned Margaret River surfing region. This was widely regarded as something of a coup for a UK University to export a surfing programme to Australia, exemplified in comment in the Times Higher Education Supplement, "Plymouth might consider offering a course in coal retailing to a prominent city in the Northeast"[13], a play upon the irony of selling coal to Newcastle in the UK, where it is, or at least was, intensively mined and shipped across the country.

So, Who Wanted to Study Surf Science and Technology?
It appears that Oscar Wilde had it just about right when he said that, "The only thing worse than being talked about is not being talked about"[14]. Although media coverage of the nascent Surf Science and Technology degree was on balance positive, the significant amount of negative publicity did not appear to deter prospective students. Within a very short period of time from the programme being first advertised, over 800 applications had been received. Trite headlines such as, 'On the Crest of a Wave', 'Surf's Up', 'Making Waves' and 'Take the Tube to Work', regardless of what the article subsequently went on to convey, had grabbed attention and prompted potential applicants to find out more and commit to making their applications.

Among those applying for places there were some excellent candidates, presenting with high calibre qualifications in relevant subjects such as Physics, Mathematics, Technology, and Business. Many applicants had left school with university entry qualifications but had not been inspired to enter Higher Education at the time and had instead gained significant work experience. Some applications were rather speculative though, for example the one in which the applicant had no work experience and possessed only a "Certificate in Hot Air Ballooning" – he didn't get offered a place on the course!

What was very clear from the start was that, although not every applicant could be described as emanating from a background from which access to University was rare, we were clearly reaching a great many prospective students who would not otherwise have considered Higher Education. By way of just a couple of examples – there was Ross Pomeroy, who had been working in a Tax Office until he heard about the Surf Science degree and, with no formal university entrance qualifications, enrolled on a Higher Education access course with no other intent than getting progressing to Surf Science and Technology.

Ross went on to gain first class honours then gained a doctorate in Advanced Composites Manufacturing before accepting a university lecturing job himself. There was also Chris Jones, who, while in the Army had been injured in a helicopter accident and was pensioned off. Despite having a bad leg, Chris enrolled onto Surf Science and Technology, gained a good degree and went on to postgraduate study before becoming a teacher at a specialist science school.

What Was Successful?
Over the years, we had excellent engagement with and support from the surf industry. No other academic programme, certainly among the hundreds on offer at Plymouth University, had such a broad range of interaction. Students had the opportunity to interact with, amongst a great many others, the following prominent figures from the world of surfing; Derek O'Neill (initially CEO Billabong Europe, later Billabong Worldwide); Phil Jarratt (prominent author and Quiksilver Marketing Manager); Alex Dick-Read (Founder/Editor of *Surfers Path*); Chris Hines (Founder of Surfers Against Sewage); Professor Kerry Black (Founder of Artificial Surfing Reefs Ltd); Dave Reed (Pro Surf event organiser and Founder of the UK Pro Surf Tour); Perry Hatchett (ASP Head Judge); Dr Tony Butt (Internationally recognised surfing oceanographer); Carlos Burle (Renowned Brazilian big wave rider); the late Bill Bailey (Founder of Bilbo Surfboards and UK surf pioneer); Roger Mansfield (Author – *The Surfing Tribe*); Eric Davies (Former Head of UK Marketing for Salomon Surf); Tom Kaye (CEO of Finisterre); Carey Brown (Founder of C-Skins wetsuits); and the list could go on and on.

Regular visits were arranged to Billabong Europe, Quiksilver Europe, Euroglass, and the ASP Pro Event Site, all in south west France and closer to home, to GUL International, The UK National Surfing Centre, and a range of historic surfing equipment collections. Students also had the opportunity to build boards with oversight and guidance from luminaries such as Luke Young (UK 'Shaper of the Year', 2012) and the highly experienced and entertaining, Steve Bunt of Best Ever Surfboards. Students took advantage of retail, manufacture and distribution placement and internship opportunities with Quiksilver and Billabong in France, Volcom in California and a range of local opportunities in the UK. The first External Examiner for the programme, whose role was to oversee quality and standards of assessment, was Dr Nick Ford of Exeter University, co-author of *Surfing and Social Theory*[15], an excellent addition to the body of academic surfing literature.

It may have been the result of the novel curriculum and the ethos of learning in context, but perhaps, through the medium of the Surf Science and Technology degree, we have tapped into a particularly innovative and creative population of students. During their second year, students engaged in Trade Fair, where they worked in groups to develop and market business ideas. Some of these were nothing short of ingenious; a self-bilging polypropylene fleece pouch for hand warming, a new design of carbon fibre kiteboard and a beachfront surf wax dispenser adapted from a tampon vending machine, as a small selection from hundreds.

One of my personal high points came during a visit I made to the Action Sports Retailer Trade Show in Long Beach, California in 2001. At the time, this was the main exhibition for surf industry manufacturers, distributors and retailers so I went regularly to pick up details of the latest products, make links and explain the concept behind the Surf Science degree wherever the opportunity presented itself. The show also included a 'Legends' stand, where some of the most prominent figures in the development of surfing took the opportunity to meet delegates, as well as selling their books and posters. I spoke briefly with Greg Noll, Mike Doyle and the late Leroy Grannis before meeting Professor Ricky Grigg, the famed big wave rider and oceanographer, who was so enthusiastic about what we had set out to achieve that he gave me a copy of his book, *Big Surf, Deep Dives and the Islands* inscribed with the words, "To Malcolm Findlay, a pioneer of surfing academia".

What Was Less Successful?
Like any new academic area, BSc Surf Science and Technology evolved and developed in its early stages. The degree was stoked by enthusiasm and a generally positive vibe and by the mid 2000s it had gained credibility and built momentum but there were, nevertheless, some deep-seated problems.

Not every member of the University's staff was fully behind the programme; some still felt that engaging in what they perceived to be a populist and academically "lightweight" subject area was somehow beneath their scholarly dignity. The default response from these members of lecturing staff was insistence upon delivering a curriculum that suited their own, often tightly focussed, research interests notwithstanding that these might be of only peripheral relevance to the ethos of the programme and, perhaps worse, of little interest to the students. This effect was particularly acute when it came to finding supervisors for students' final year research projects and led to drastically inequitable allocations in which enthusiastic members of staff became massively overburdened while some academic colleagues luxuriated in the time and space to indulge in personal research interests. The irony of this situation was that, by 2003, Surf Science and Technology was producing an income of just under £1 million per year for the University, internal redistribution of which was used to preserve the esoteric research careers of precisely those who were brushing aside their obligations to students and colleagues. This was a serious failing, especially on the part of one particular Departmental Manager whose priority appeared to be seeing his name appear on co-published research papers rather than ensuring equitable workloads among staff.

Plymouth University's Institute of Marine Studies quickly came to see Surf Science and Technology as something of a 'cash cow' yielding significant income that was used to prop up less lucrative areas particularly, as noted above, some aspects of research. In contrast, less alacrity was evident when it came to providing resources for the programme. In fact, it took three years of campaigning before a dedicated technician could be appointed for the programme, and then only when the potential consequences of a student drowning were hammered home to the Institute's senior management. Committed members of teaching staff were forced to resort to their own strategic research accounts, some built up over years, for the purchase of essential equipment and the costs of fieldwork and visits were often agreed only with great reluctance.

By 2006, a new fees regime had been introduced in UK Higher Education. As for every other Higher Education course, students enrolling on BSc Surf Science and Technology faced having to pay a significant contribution to the overall cost of their tuition. For Surf Science and Technology this seemed to herald a subtle change in the type of students applying for places on the programme. Perhaps the consequence of debt aversion in mature students who had work experience, or maybe due to changing perception of surfing and its supporting industries, but the composition of the Surf Science cohort gradually changed and, by 2010, when the Browne Report[16] recommended that every student should pay at least £21,000 (US$33,600) towards degree tuition fees, the vast majority of new recruits had just left school. The underlying problem with this change was exemplified during induction sessions when increasing numbers of fresh students would report that they had chosen the programme as a 'lifestyle choice' rather than extolling it as exciting opportunity to engage in Higher Education or a career-changing experience, as had been the case only three or four years previously.

Is the Stoke of Surf Academia Sustainable?
The increasing popularity of surfing has clearly been wrapped up in the emergence of lifestyle sports in general, the growth of which was well described by Rinehart[17]. Much of this growth was taking place at roughly the same time we were embarking on our Surf Science and Technology journey, so there is little doubt that we were caught up in and carried along by a much greater wave. The question is whether this wave has surged as far up the beach as it can before drawing back into the ocean, i.e. is this level of academic stoke sustainable?

Recruitment to the Surf Science and Technology programme declined from 2006 onwards, perhaps the result of the new UK student fees regime, or the general economic climate (or maybe both). In 2004, it was reported that surfing had contributed £100 million to the Regional economy of South West England during the previous year[18]. No repeat of the survey has been pursued since but the fortunes of prominent surf industry names may offer some clue as to where the industry has gone. In 2005, Quiksilver's share price peaked at over US$16 before tumbling to less than US$1 in the global economic crash in late 2008. Quiksilver has shown a modest recovery to the US$4-6 range in early 2013[19] but its rival, Billabong, has fared worse. Closing at a high of over Aus$14 in May 2007 its share price then slumped badly, hinted at a recovery in 2010 before meltdown to less than US$1 in late January 2013[20]. In South West England, one of the companies that had strongly supported Surf Science and Technology, GUL International, went into administration in April 2011 as a result of reduced sales and problematic exchange rates[21]. It may be that sustainability of the Surf Science and Technology degree is inextricably linked to the visible prosperity of the surf industry, measurable in terms of figures such as these. After all, with tuition fees now at £9,000 (US$14,500) per year, graduates need well-paid jobs and the transferability of degree skills to other professions is often poorly understood by prospective students.

The Browne Review cited one of its aims to be rendering Higher Education sustainable in the UK. It may be that invoking the terms of this Review has helped put a certain version of Higher Education on a sustainable footing but it does not appear to have underpinned the original mission of BSc Surf Science and Technology, which was to draw into Higher Education students who would not otherwise have considered it. The Review states that "the system is put on a more sustainable footing by seeking higher contributions from those who can afford to make them, and removing the blanket subsidy for all courses – without losing vital public investment in priority courses".[22] BSc Surf Science and Technology is unlikely to ever be regarded by the government as a 'priority course' in the way that degrees in Nursing or Engineering might be. In a sluggish economy, consumers quite naturally reduce non-essential spending and this was probably the precursor to the decline in share prices of the most prolific surf industry brands. With increasing numbers of prospective students joining the Surf Science and Technology degree as a lifestyle choice such a qualification had perhaps become a discretionary investment. Perhaps the pool of prospective students, often mature and with family and financial commitments, whose appetite for higher education could be sparked by such an innovative offer, was easily drained or maybe they were retrenching to more conservative and recognised qualifications, perhaps with external accreditation (accountancy, law, etc) – an understandable reaction in constrained economic times.

Maybe the decline in recruitment to the Surf Science and Technology programme was merely a reflection of the surf industry's general loss of stoke. In 2012, Derek O'Neill, described as a "lifelong surf fanatic"[23] and a generous supporter of the Surf Science and Technology programme, was replaced as Chief Executive of Billabong by a chain-store retail specialist who has never surfed. In early 2013, Bob McKnight, who cut his business teeth selling surf shorts from his car boot between surf sessions, was replaced as Quiksilver's Chief Executive by the former Chairman of Disney Consumer Products. At the time the degree was conceived, surf gear was mostly sold in surf shops, involving contact and conversation with shop staff, who were often surfers themselves; online shopping has changed this. A significant element of the Surf Science curriculum covered nearshore oceanography and meteorology, but a plethora of websites now dispense surf predictions that seem to render such understanding unnecessary. It's not difficult to argue that losing these kinds of connections has diluted the level of stoke at the core of the surf industry.

Academic study programmes need to evolve and develop, otherwise they become stale and irrelevant, the consequence of which is becoming unattractive to students. The fundamental requirement for this kind of constant development is committed and enthusiastic staff. I moved on to manage the University's regional partnerships in 2006 but little effort was made to find a replacement Programme Leader with true passion for surfing and credible knowledge of the industry. The original concept of 'learning in context' became diminished, with visits, fieldwork and guest speakers being increasingly replaced by conventional classroom and laboratory teaching which is cheaper and requires less time-consuming engagement with industry. Without someone to fight the corner and argue for relevant curriculum, contributing lecturers resorted to rehearsal of their personal research interests, regardless of how peripheral these might be to the central thrust of the degree. By 2010, although it was still offering students a rigorous academic experience and a valuable qualification, it could easily be argued that Surf Science and Technology had to some extent lost its way.

Epilogue
In 2011, in an effort to reduce its Higher Education funding burden, the UK Government introduced Student Number Control, which strictly regulated the numbers of students each British University could recruit.[24] This effectively put the brakes on the previous decade's aspiration to vastly increase numbers of university entrants, essentially driven by financial austerity following the economic crash of 2008, but perhaps also with a smattering of political dogma around reintroducing exclusivity in Higher Education. As in most Universities, this prompted a strategic revision of Plymouth's portfolio of programmes, in which Surf Science and Technology was identified as something of an 'outlier' operating in concert with, but separate from, other degrees. Fearing that this signalled vulnerability on a number of levels (this was not, after all, a 'priority' course and recruitment had declined) a decision was made to phase out the BSc Surf Science and Technology programme from 2012 and reallocate the student places to related degrees. The last cohort of students is due to graduate in 2015.

I'm saddened by the way things have panned out. We'll never know whether Colin Williams' original concept, sparked by the stoke of accidentally landing among a gathering of surfers in the late nineties, could have been sustainable in the long term, given a consistent educational environment and appropriate staff or whether it was always going to be a 'Marilyn Monroe' initiative – burning brightly but briefly. Whichever is the reality, the legacy of Dr Colin Williams lies in the continuing contribution the five hundred or so graduates over the fifteen year lifespan of the programme are making to both surf-related industries and the professions to which they gained access though the Surf Science and Technology degree.

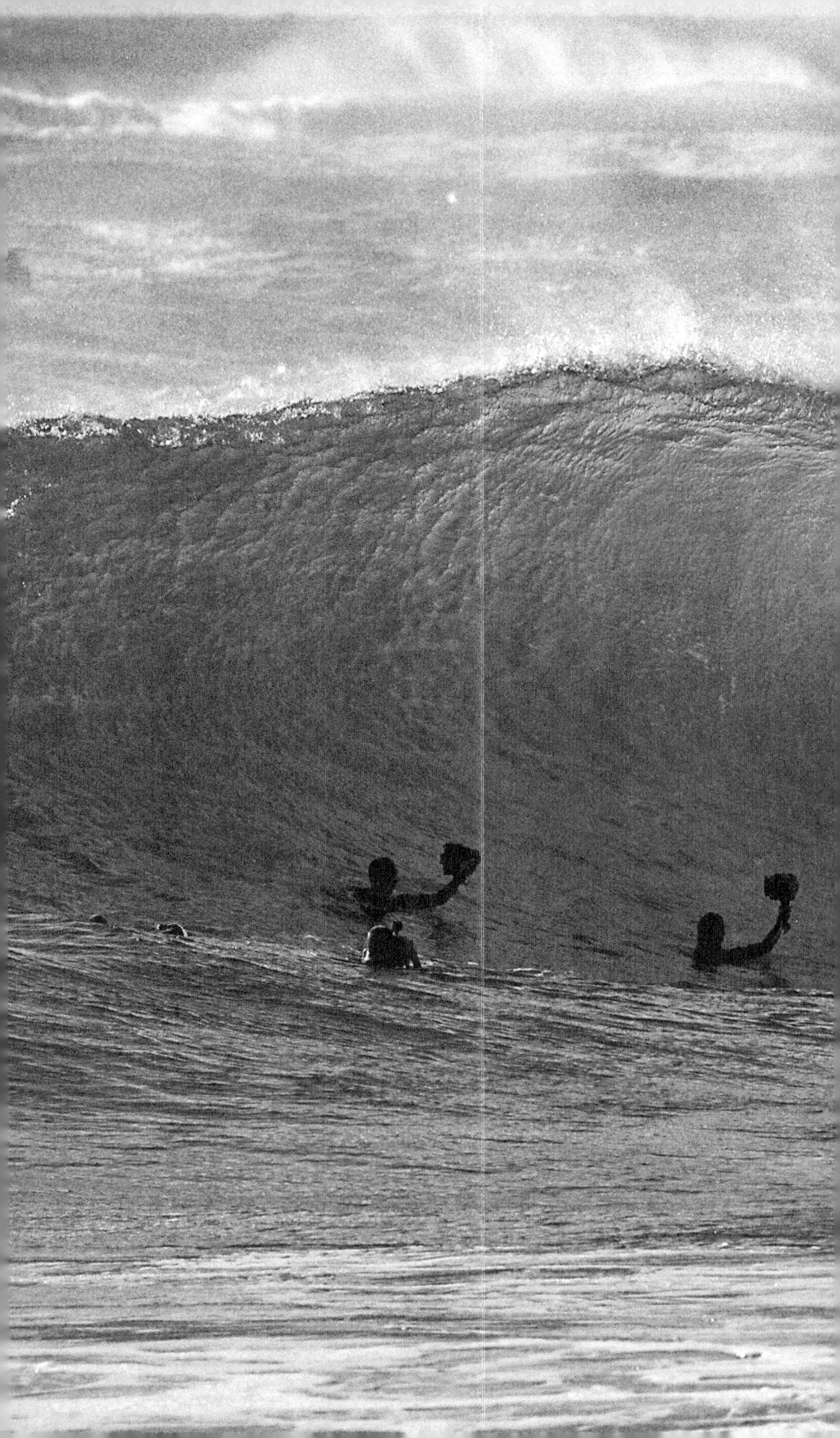

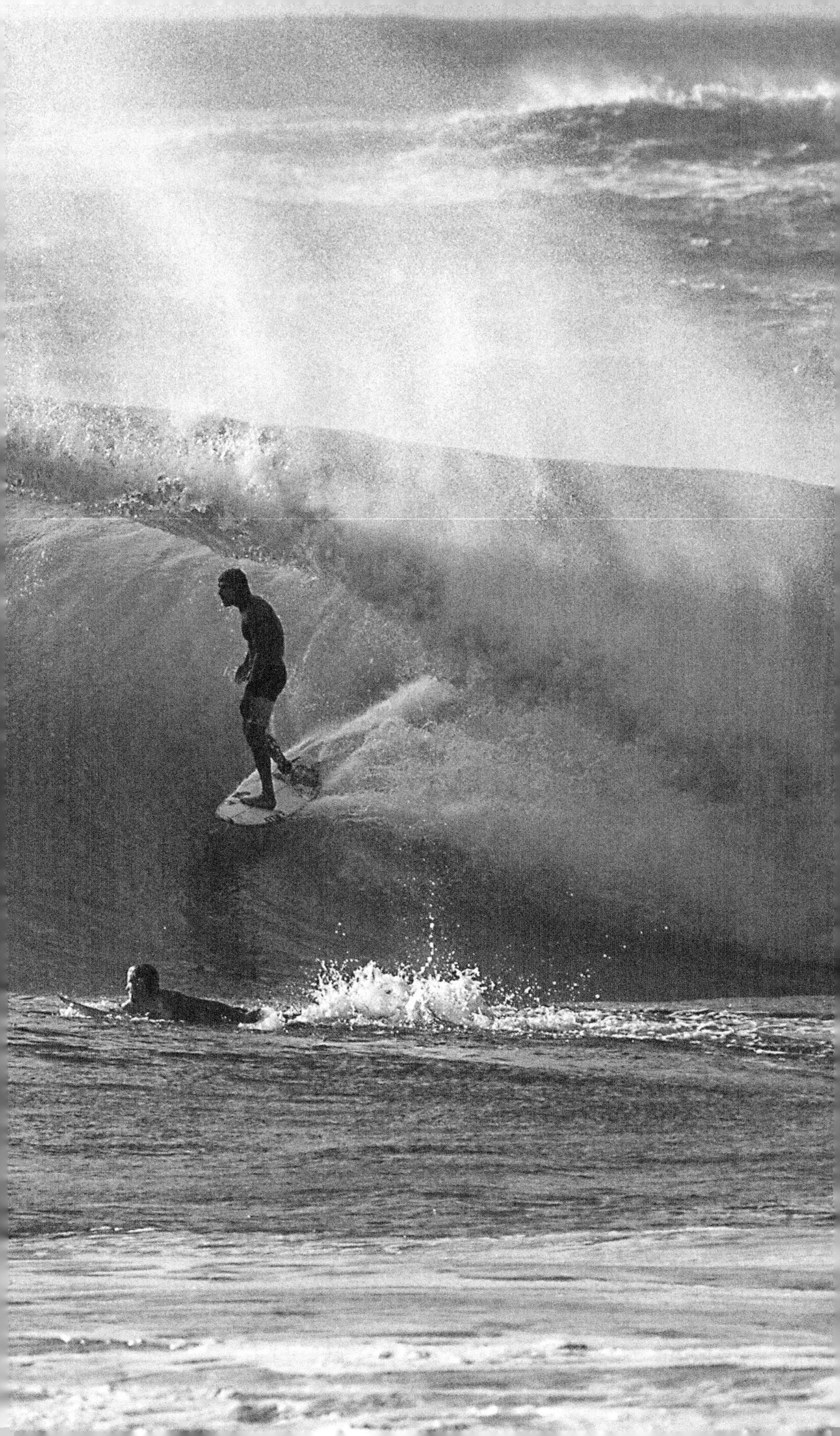

Chapter Seven
New Knowledge & Solutions

Whilst, to a certain degree, all contributors touch on this throughout the book, it is in this chapter that we introduce authors who we consider to be presenting new knowledge and solutions. To kick this off, co-editor Jess Ponting outlines a number of initiatives that have grown through the Centre for Surf Research at San Diego State University. Jess's contribution is broad ranging and begins by breaking through the stereotype of the surfer, emphasising the uniqueness of sustainable surf tourism as an activity and as an area of academic study. It traverses the boundary between theoretical discussions, policy analysis and practical solutions. Jess emphasises that there is still a need for mainstream surfing research in the surfing world and this is an important component.

Michellle Blauw discusses the importance of surf craft. Michelle highlights the formation of the Australian Surf Craft Industry Association and the importance of nurturing this dying craft in order to sustain local economies.

Tony Butt provides some primary data and commentary to explore the elephant in the room – namely, surf travel. Based on Tony's analysis, he can be seen to expose some of the myths and underlying assumptions of sustainability within surfing and offers solutions and actions. Tony also highlights some of the barriers for integrating sustainability into surfing and the difficulty in effecting change and creating positive behavioural change. This phenomena is often described as the value action gap, where the idea that providing information and education on a particular issue will lead to a corresponding rationale and positive change in people's behaviours. What psychological, sociological and other research indicates is that the process of creating change is much more complex and convoluted than we realise. Indeed, if the literature around behavioural change settles on one salient point it is that there is no single model; there instead needs to be a raft of initiatives and actions that are capable of facilitating transitions to sustainability. Examples of this have already been presented in this book so we will let you draw out your own conclusions on what these might look like. What is clear though is that having a benchmark or baseline from which we can work is essential.

Emma Whittlesea presents an analysis of the Green Event Pathfinder that can provide this benchmark. It does so by exploring multiple aspects for the Boardmasters Surf and Music Festival in Cornwall, UK. Emma highlights that it was surprising to find that respondents to the research felt that the most important areas for improvement were around recycling and waste management even though measures had been taken to promote each of these. Again, this adds to the complexity of achieving a greener event. Certainly, the Pathfinder initiative was an important step towards making these transitions a reality.

Sam Bleakley applies a sustainability lens to the Maldives, emphasising a comprehensive approach that includes biological and political sustainability, whilst Ben Freeston explores the role of Magicseaweed in potentially contributing towards a transition in surfing. More than this though, Ben cautions against the arrogance of 'the surfer' as a unique subset of humanity, and that the things that draw us to the ocean and the beauty of the natural environmental are open to and appreciated by all.

7.1

The Audacity of Stoke: Surfing the Ivory Tower

Jess Ponting

The 'audacity of stoke' requires some explanation. My journey into academia was not pre-planned or deliberate, it was more gravitational. As a moderately feral, dreadlocked and nose-ringed graduate of the Australian Nation University's School of Resource and Environmental Management, I signed up with the Overseas Service Bureau, the Australian equivalent of the U.S. Peace Corps and the UK's Voluntary Service Overseas. My goal was to be involved in the front line of protecting the natural environment. My enthusiasm for conservation started as ripples emanating from the first Rio Earth Summit and the resulting documents that comprised *Agenda 21*. I saw this as an invitation to 'go forth and protect' in a brave new world of global environmental politics, where success was measured and reported in terms of square miles of protected land and seascapes.

Unfortunately, little thought was given to what this wave of preservationist zeal meant for communities that agreed to preserve their resources. In some areas it precluded traditional uses and flora/fauna harvesting; it was almost never tied to an effort to leverage the preserved resource as a sustainable driver of social and economic development. The approach was verbally slapped down at my first community meeting in the remote village of Tongunjamb in the Waskuk Hills of East Sepik Province in Papua New Guinea, a few months before my twenty-third birthday. Alternatives had to be found and sustainable tourism, a relatively new concept in 1996, was one alternative that would enable a protected forest and a living culture to generate a sustainable income, without requiring the irreversible destruction of both.

Each day in Tongunjamb resembled the pages of a 1920's edition of *National Geographic*. I had the opportunity to surf great waves on the islands near the provincial capital of East Sepik Province, Wewak, but for the most part I was far up the Sepik River, relegated to mind surfing the tiny, endless barrels spinning out of the wake of motorised dug-out canoes. After a year, I wanted to reconnect with the ocean, so I left Tongunjamb and spent the better part of the following year travelling over land and by ferry through the Indonesian archipelago, surfing the best waves I'd ever seen. I noticed that surf tourism was supporting remote rural coastline communities throughout Indonesia. More often than not though, this came at the expense of the environment, society and culture. It seemed to me that if lessons from community development and sustainable tourism could be transferred to surf tourism development then surf destinations wouldn't be destined to reinvent the same rickety, misshapen, malevolent wheel and travelling surfers could stop inadvertently wreaking destruction on communities that live near world-class surf breaks and their environment. This realisation ultimately led me back to university. I figured that the worst thing that could happen was that I'd end up being an academic.

Identifying the Problems and Opportunities
Sixteen years later, the Center for Surf Research at San Diego State University was created with a view to addressing the key sustainability issues in surf travel and Martin and Assenov[1] claimed that surf tourism has developed its own distinct literature. They cite 156 pieces of surf tourism research published between 1997 and 2011 to support this claim. Surf tourism literature is multidisciplinary, evolving, and covers a range of issues including the growth of surf tourism as an industrialised tourism system, surfing tourist space, demographics, behaviour and market segmentation, event management, and sustainability.

Despite the growing interest in surf tourism from the academic community and given the immense value of surf tourism and its impact on thousands of coastal communities around the world, our understanding of the size and scope of surfing and surf tourism is startlingly limited. Lazarow and Nelson[2] estimated there were 20 million surfers globally, while Warshaw[3] estimated only five million. International Surfing Association President, Fernando Aguerre, estimated 25 million with five million surfers in Brazil alone[4], and O'Brien and Eddie[5] presented a figure of 35 million surfers, 15 million of these might be considered active and surf several times a week. In the U.S., a lingering social stigma that can be traced back to Sean Penn's all-too-convincing portrayal of Jeff Spicoli in 1982 film *Fast Times at Ridgemont High*, positions surfers on the fringe of society – juvenile delinquents of questionable social value and surfing as unworthy of academic scrutiny. Despite the lingering stereotype, American surfers have, according to one study, a median age of 34 years, a college education or above, are employed full time earning at least US$75,000 a year, make one hundred visits to the beach each year and spend US$66 per visit.[6] It is worth noting that, at the time of writing, the President of the United States and the Australian Prime Minister are both surfers.

Surfers are known to be a very mobile group. Barbieri and Sotomayor[7] found that 91% of 135 respondents from a variety of countries had taken a surf trip in the past five years. Of those, 82% had taken more than two surf trips; almost 40% had taken more than 10 surf trips, and almost 20% had taken more than 21 surf trips in the past five years. Surfing and surf tourism is known to take place in many thousands of destinations in 160 countries[8] and the value of some well-known surf breaks has been calculated using travel cost analysis and ecosystems services methodologies. Uluwatu in Bali, Mundaka in Spain, Mavericks in northern California, and Stradbroke Island in Australia were found to generate US$8.4 million[9], US$4.5 million (2008)[10], US$23.8 million (2009)[11], and US$20 million respectively. A more comprehensive methodology of value assessment estimated that surf tourism brings in almost US$820 million in revenue to Australia's Gold Coast each year, with the same area's broader surf industry worth more than US$3 billion annually[12]. O'Brien & Eddie estimated the value of the global surf industry including surf tourism at US$130 billion[13].

Clearly, surfing and surf tourism is large and growing and it impacts thousands of coastal communities around the world in ways that we are only just beginning to acknowledge. In my travels through Indonesia in the mid 1990s, I was struck by the disconnection of many surf tourists from the reality of daily life for the Indonesian communities hosting them. Surfers tended to favour an alternative reality, informed by the discourse of surf magazines and surf movies; very few of those acknowledge local people, much less give them a voice. This appeared to influence the nature of surf tourism development that followed and the role of local people in that development. The Center for Surf Research engages the audacity of surf stoke to transcend stereotypes and reject the status quo of surf tourism development. The aim is to surf the ivory tower of academia into the mix and find solutions to problems through empirical research and the application of knowledge and evolving best practice. Six key areas have been identified as holding promise for helping to drive positive change in surf tourism, including: developing a theoretical framework for understanding the social processes at work; practical analytical frameworks for assessing surf tourism management models; sustainability certification for the surf tourism industry; an education programme targeting sustainable surf tourism management; a system for the world championship tour of surfing and its spectators to engage with surf destinations; and establishing a platform for the dissemination of knowledge and ideas. These key areas are discussed in detail below.

1. Theoretical Framework

At the theoretical level, there has been a need for a framework or theoretical lens to view and make sense of the process of surfer colonialism as the frontiers of the known surfing world are pushed back. This became the focus of my PhD research and resulted in the conceptualisation of a process of 'Nirvanification' that describes the apotheosis of many surf destinations from remote, rural, impoverished, fishing villages to the new centre of the surfing universe[14]. The Nirvanification process has four stages that take place in parallel. The first phase is the social construction of Nirvana that leverages four symbolic elements that act as anchors to temporarily secure Nirvanic space: perfect waves, uncrowded conditions, cushioned adventure, and a tropical, pristine environment. The second phase of Nirvanification involves threats to the symbolic elements of Nirvana from embodied experiences of place that contradict Nirvanic discourse. For example, poor weather, substandard surf, overcrowding and exposure to local living conditions. The third phase of Nirvanification involves protecting Nirvana through the deployment of a series of myths, so tourists feel comfortable on a luxury surfing adventure within sight of people struggling to feed their families, whose resources they are exploiting without compensation. The fourth phase of Nirvanification is the development of alternative discourses, of which there are many[15].

Due to the impermanence of tourist space, which is constantly re-produced, re-performed by tourists, the tourism industry, and hosts and re-negotiated, agency exists and change is possible[16]. Surf tourists are increasingly having embodied, tactile experiences co-performed with local communities in the liminal space of surf tourism that require emotional and cognitive processing. Surf tourists' embodied experiences of place are driving a growing awareness of local space and this is beginning to alter perceptions and expectations of Nirvana. Surf corporations complicit in the Nirvanification of the Mentawais are aware of the shifting discourse and are repositioning their marketing regarding their role in the islands. For example, Billabong and Quiksilver have become major SurfAid donors. Through its non-profit foundation, Quiksilver produces media that directly threatens Nirvanic discourse and myth, documenting and publicising the predicament of Mentawai villages destroyed by a tsunami in 2010 and challenging surfers to engage with relief efforts. Surf tourists' embodied experiences in the liminal space of the Mentawai have resulted in a reimagining of meanings and the development of new performances. This has come at the expense of Nirvanic myth, which is now struggling to retain a foothold in the Mentawais. In the absence of effective regulation of the industry to shore up the quality of the recreational experience, to ensure that local communities benefit from surf tourism and, to protect the natural environment, the Mentawais will have a surf tourism industry, but Nirvana will transition to the next surfers' dreamscape.

The importance of this work is that it gives a frame of reference in order to try to understand some of the social forces at work in the construction of Nirvanic surfing destinations in some of the world's least developed places. It also provides hope that surfing does not need to continue to repeatedly make the same mistakes, that addressing issues of social justice does not preclude issues of a commercial nature – the surfer's dream of Nirvana can also function as a means of engagement with local people and poverty reduction. Many surf tourists are able to conceive of a paradise for tourists in which local populations are known to be struggling, as long as their actions as tourists in that space are thought to be a part of the solution to those issues rather than exacerbating them[17].

2. Practical Analytical Framework

At the policy level, there have been no practical analytical frameworks to help assess the relative sustainability of surf tourism management plans. As a result, decisions were being made all over the world about the exploitation and management of precious surfing resources with almost no understanding of their implications. The Framework Analysis for Sustainable Surf Tourism (FASST) was originally built on recommendations stemming from data gathered in the Mentawais in 2003[18]. This was framed in the context of a successful model of surf tourism development in Papua New Guinea[19] and further developed and coined as the framework analysis for sustainable surf tourism in the context of deregulation of the surf industry in Fiji[20]. The five interrelated principles of the FASST are:

1. A distinct move away from economically neo-liberal approaches to development;
2. The need for formal, long-term, coordinated planning that recognises limits to growth;
3. Systematic attempts to foster cross-cultural understanding;
4. Village-level surf-sport development;

5. Contribution to poverty alleviation.

The principles are normative rather than prescriptive, and are designed to provide a framework for analysing the sustainability of surf tourism development in less-developed countries across different geographical, cultural, political, policy, and regulatory settings. The fundamental premise is that the more deeply these principles are enmeshed with the management and regulatory mechanisms of a destination, the more sustainable a surf tourism system is likely to be.

3. Sustainable Surf Tourism Certification
At the level of individual surf tourism businesses, owners often don't necessarily understand what sustainability is, or how to integrate it into their business. In order to address this situation, CSR has developed a partnership with a certification programme for surf tourism properties – the Sustainable Tourism Operators Kit for Evaluation (STOKE) Certification. STOKE is based on the Global Sustainable Tourism Criteria which represent the consensus output of decades of work by professionals around the world to develop a universal sustainable tourism 'language' organised around four key areas: sustainable management, socioeconomic impact, cultural impact and environmental impact. Since tourism destinations each have their own culture, environment, customs and laws, the criteria are designed to be adapted to local conditions and supplemented by additional criteria for the specific location and activity. Over a three-year period, the Center for Surf Research worked with surf resort operators in Fiji, Indonesia, Costa Rica, and Hawaii to adapt the criteria to fit with the generally smaller-scale surf resorts that are always located in fragile coastal and marine areas, often adjacent to indigenous people struggling to find their way in the 21st century. In addition, an entirely new set of criteria were developed specifically for surf-tourism services and surf-break protection.

The goal of STOKE is to make it easy and cost effective to access information about sustainability best practice and, if required, to provide a consulting service to design and implement these practices. Additionally, the certification of surf resorts will enable consumers to make more informed inter- and intra-destination decisions (certified properties will be able to display a STOKE Certified logo on their marketing material) and make it easy for surf resort owners to implement sustainability initiatives and have these recognised and leveraged for market advantage. STOKE certification has further advantages over mainstream sustainability certification and labelling in that the mainstream tourism market is so diffuse that it is virtually impossible to deliver messaging about a certification programme to a sufficiently large share of the market to result in measurable marketing advantage. The majority of the surf tourism market, by comparison, can be relatively easily reached through several key magazines and websites. STOKE utilises sustainable tourism student interns in its administration and operations. In the process of developing the certification programme, students are able to spend time in Fiji, Hawaii, Costa Rica, Mexico, Indonesia, and Panama working with general managers of surf resorts. These experiences were crucial learning opportunities for the students involved, however only one or two at a time were able to benefit from this. The following section is a response to the need to increase this kind of educational opportunity to educate the next generation of surf travellers and surf tourism operators.

4. Sustainable Surf Tourism Study Abroad Classes
Until the Center for Surf Research developed its programmes with Groundswell Educational Travel, there was no educational programme available tailored to specific knowledge and techniques for surf tourism management. There was no programme available to accomadate students' passion for travel, surfing and coastal environments, or curricula on sustainability generally. Groundswell represents my third attempt to establish a long-held dream to deliver the coolest college courses ever conceived; the programme is underway, though still in its infancy. The dream is to develop it to serve students from all over the world and to deliver a world-class education in world-class surfing destinations all over the world. The curriculum is based on Nirvanification Theory, the Framework Analysis for Sustainable Tourism, and STOKE Certification evaluation training. Programmes are specifically designed to deliver benefits to the environment and communities of the places we visit. Bocas del Toro on the Caribbean Coast of Panama was the first Groundswell Travel destination and was successfully followed by Nicaragua and Costa Rica. We are actively reaching out to academics and universities around the world to develop this programme and to develop a network of surfing academics who deliver educational opportunities for students and advocate for fragile coastal and marine environments, and for the people that live there.

5. SurfCredits

The loudest voices in the surfing world – pro surfers and the Association of Surfing Professionals' (ASP) World Championship Tour (WCT) – make almost no noise about the sustainability of surf tourism, an industry they help to drive and grow. Sport and event-management has begun to focus on how economic and social benefits to stakeholders can be maximised, both during and after events – even how sport and sporting events can facilitate community building and enduring social legacies in communities plagued by war, poverty and other forms of social injustice. Despite developments in the theoretical realm, surfing contests are yet to develop a coordinated approach to ensure that the surfing World Championship Tour is positioned for positive economic and social impact in event destinations. In 2014, a new company, ZoSea Media, which has staff with senior level marketing and operations managers from mainstream sport broadcasting, took over management of the WCT, having purchased the ASP in 2012. Promising to bring a more consistent and professional approach including a considered corporate social responsibility strategy.

In 2012, an initiative called SurfCredits, initially a collaboration between the Center for Surf Research and several other non-profit organsiations that has grown into its own non-profit entity, was successfully launched at the 2012 Volcom Fiji Pro. Prior to this, while some event sponsors undertook corporate social responsibility (CSR) initiatives on an ad hoc basis, the WCT had no formal approach to CSR. SurfCredits was designed to function as the individual contest sponsors and the ASP's formalised mechanism for CSR at WCT events.

The broadcast platform for the WCT is an online webcast of each event, and increasingly a delayed and condensed television highlights package. SurfCredits utilises the WCT's webcast and broadcast platform to employ an online donation system that links surfers, destinations, audiences, athletes, communities, aid projects, and sponsors to benefit host communities in WCT event destinations. Webcast viewers of WCT events are asked by contest announcers to donate to pre-vetted non-profit organisations that are doing important humanitarian, conservation, or research work in communities where events are held. In return, donors have the chance to enjoy gifts and prizes, the most significant being a stay at a surf resort in the contest location. SurfCredits has been at four WCT events raising over US$30,000 for non-profit organisations and giving away six surf trips to locations such as Fiji, Hawaii, Costa Rica and Indonesia. Initial results show great promise. When effectively activated, the SurfCredits model works and is capable of raising tens of thousands of dollars per contest with almost no cost to the ASP and sponsoring brands. A recent unpublished survey of 1000 purchasers of SurfCredits found that engagement with SurfCredits made 83% feel more positive about the philanthropic efforts of the ASP, 84% feel more positive about the sponsoring brands, 78% feel more positive about ASP athletes, and 95% felt more tangibly connected to destinations, their communities, the environment, the contest, and the ASP.

Qualitatively, respondents commented on the symbolic progression of the ASP that SurfCredits represented, the following comments from the survey demonstrate the point: "So awesome to see the commercial arm of surfing finally giving back"; "Great way to progress contests out of the 'we came, we conquered' era". In addition the quantitative data was also reflected in qualitative comments: "It sounds cheesy but I really do feel more connected to the place and people as well as to the contests, the surfers who support the causes, and the announcers who promote them, knowing I already have my contest T-shirt locked down and my entry in the draw, all for a great cause". SurfCredits was invited to make formal pitch to the ASP for activation in the entire ASP WCT from 2014 onwards. SurfCredits was incorporated into the Vans Triple Crown of Surfing for the first time in 2013, however the ASP has not yet committed to a broader application of SurfCredits moving forward.

6. Public Forums & Research Community

Given the size and scope of surfing, it remains surprising that many universities shy away from legitimising its study. I have been asked to help legitimise PhD students' work on surfing and surf tourism to a skeptical, non-surfing faculty. There is a real need to surf the ivory tower. While the development of the Center for Surf Research and related research centres at Plymouth University in the UK and Bond University in Australia herald a change, there are still obstacles for researchers and academics to ply their various disciplines to the betterment of the sport and the communities it touches around the world. The Center for Surf Research is attempting to drive change in this area by creating a community of surfing researchers, by listing graduate and undergraduate research opportunities, internships opportunities, and volunteer opportunities for students from SDSU and for students everywhere. We have consolidated the research done to date on surf tourism in an evolving bibliography that is available to the public, and we regularly stage conferences that bring the surf industry, academics, students and the general public together to discuss issues surrounding surfing, surf tourism and the sustainability of both. In 2011, we staged our launch/conference 'The Audacity of Stoke: An Intellectual Jam Session on Surf Philanthropy'. In 2012, we staged the 10th annual Groundswell Society Conference with the theme 'Surfing's New Aloha: The Growing Trend of Giving Back'. In 2013, we co-produced the 'Surf Park Summit' and moderated a panel that discussed the sustainability of the burgeoning Surf Park industry. We hope to establish a cross-disciplinary society of surfing academics to encourage greater application of surfing's best thinkers to the problems of the interface between the sport, environment and community.

Conclusion
With some notable exceptions, the gatekeepers of the ivory tower have excluded surfing, forcing surfers to mask their true passion with broad, diffuse research that partially incorporates surfing environments and its impact under some other, less controversial, title. There is ample evidence to suggest, however, that we are seeing the audacity of stoke – if I can paraphrase Rabbit Bartholomew – bust down the door so surfing can benefit from academic exploration. The six key areas for driving positive change outlined here represent just one institution's efforts to this end and are symptomatic of broader transitions to sustainability in the surfing world being driven on many different levels, within and without academe, the surf and travel industries, and political power structures.

7.2

Surf Craft: Essential for the Future of the Surfing Industry

Michelle Blauw

Surfing and the 'bronzed Aussie' are an iconic part of Australian culture, just like cricket and the Opera House, but sadly the grass roots of this Australian way of life is under severe threat. The Australian surfboard manufacturing industry has been around for over 50 years and has grown into a vast trade, exporting millions upon millions of dollars of surfboards around the globe and spawning big multinational surf brands such as Billabong, FCS, Quiksilver and Rip Curl to name just a few, not to mention the barrage of Australian World Surfing Champions over the years. Australia is already globally recognised as the leader in surfboard and fin design, just look at Simon Anderson and his invention of the thruster (three fin set-up) in 1981 which revolutionised surfing by changing the way shapers looked at their designs and the way surfers looked at their equipment and what they could do on a wave.

And then there's FCS (Fin Control Systems) which was the first removable fin system in the world invented in 1995 by another Australian surfer and now is the largest supplier of this type of system in the world. From surfboards stem surf tourism, world class surf contests and many of the multinational Australian surf labels who started out making surfboards and eventually grew into the global giants they are today. This industry however has long grown out of its 'cottage industry' status and little has been done within the industry, or outside of it, to change this, bringing it to the next level. Without a healthy, thriving 'surfboard' industry there won't be a future for the 'surf' industry in Australia, an industry which generates in excess of AUS$11 billion a year revenue.

Currently, there is no formal recognition of surf craft making as a trade, no formal training, no apprenticeships and no qualifications. This, in turn, is not enticing any new blood into the industry and not enabling any of the highly skilled and experienced individuals from within this industry to pass on their skills and knowledge to others. Basically, without training, apprenticeships and qualifications being put into place, this is a dying trade. For these reasons, the Association of Australian Surf Craft Manufacturers, their suppliers and retailers, was formed to unify and work together to achieve certain goals to save the trade and our industry and then work on strengthening it to continue to be world class players on a global scale.

Surfboards are at the root of this highly lucrative industry tree. We need to nurture the roots for the tree to survive but perhaps it's already too late. The damage is too great as many board manufacturers are shutting their doors or moving their operations off shore where it is cheaper to manufacture. If nothing is done, surfers won't be able to order a custom surfboard direct from the local shaper within five years and this would be a sad day indeed! The Australian Surf Craft Industry Association (ASCIA) formed in 2009 has been working tirelessly with local government, city councils, consultants and the members of the Association to form a Certificate III in Surfboard Manufacturing.

"Following extensive industry research into the training needs of employees and new entrants into surf craft manufacturing, it is apparent that there is a need for structured training that leads to a national qualification. This will assist current manufacturers in taking on apprentices" – **Gold Coast City Council, Economic Development Branch.**

Through research, we have explored the possibility of creating an entirely new qualification or using an existing qualification. It seems, however, that 23 out of the 24 units required to make up the Certificate III in Surf Craft Manufacturing can be taken from existing nationally recognised training packages and only one enterprise unit is needed to make the requirements. This has allowed us to move forward swiftly and the next step is to identify a registered training organisation (RTO) to deliver the course.

From the humble beginnings of a group of passionate surf craft manufacturers getting together to discuss industry needs, to the incorporation of the Australian Surf Craft Industry Association, to now being a few steps away from delivering the first Certificate in Surfboard Manufacturing, we have come a long way. None of this however, could have been achieved without the time and dedication of a handful of individuals who's efforts will ultimately determine the future of surf craft manufacturing in Australia and beyond.

7.3

Surf Travel: The Elephant in the Room

Tony Butt

The effects of environmental degradation, including the effects of global warming induced by carbon emissions, will probably be more immediate and more profound on us surfers than on other members of the rich nations of the world. We are more sensitive to things like sea-level rise, storminess, coastal flooding and coastal pollution because we spend our lives right there, on the coast – on the 'front line'. The very source of the waves we ride is the weather and the climate; so we really ought to be concerned that the weather and climate don't get altered so much that it ruins the coast and the waves. We are going to be on the receiving end of all these problems, but we are also one of the causes of the problems in the first place.

I'm going to focus on surf travel, first addressing the question of whether or not all the travelling we do actually makes us less environmentally friendly than we should be. Then I am going to suggest how we might be able to lessen our environmental footprint associated with travel and hence not only help save ourselves from the immediate consequences of environmental degradation, but also become good role models and persuade other, non-surfing members of the community, to become more environmentally aware.

Vehicles and Aeroplanes

Until the industrial revolution, all the travelling we did was either on foot, on the backs of other animals, or using wind power (if we travelled across the ocean). On land, the fuel we used to propel us along came from the food we ate or the food we gave to our horses, camels or elephants and because of the way our digestive systems had evolved, burning carbohydrates faster than food grows was physically extremely difficult. As a result, the speed with which we travelled was governed by the speed at which we could burn those carbohydrates. Travelling was, therefore, sustainable.

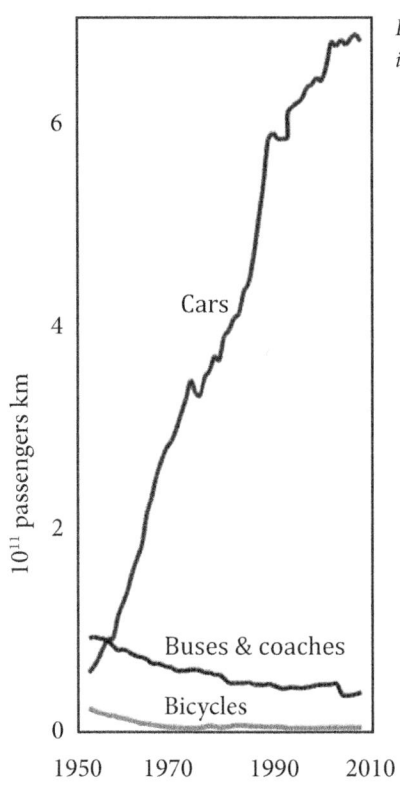

Figure 1: Use of cars, buses and bicycles in the UK since 1952[1]

The last couple of centuries have brought trains, cars, buses and, eventually, aeroplanes – all powered by fossil fuels. Today, our world is completely dominated by these vehicles and we couldn't imagine what it would possibly be like without them. Think of all the possible forms of transport you could use for a surf trip; walking, cycling, horseback, bus, train, boat, ferry, car or plane. Most of these, apart from the last two, are rarely used for surf trips and, if they are, they are invariably combined with either the car or the plane. Those two are the most convenient forms of transport for us, but, at the same time, the least environmentally friendly. Their use has increased dramatically in recent decades and continues to increase, not just among the surfing population, but throughout the entire population of the rich countries of the world.

Our use of the car has been increasing rapidly in the last half century while the use of public transport has decreased considerably (Figure 1). The graph does show some hope though – since around the mid-1990s, although the use

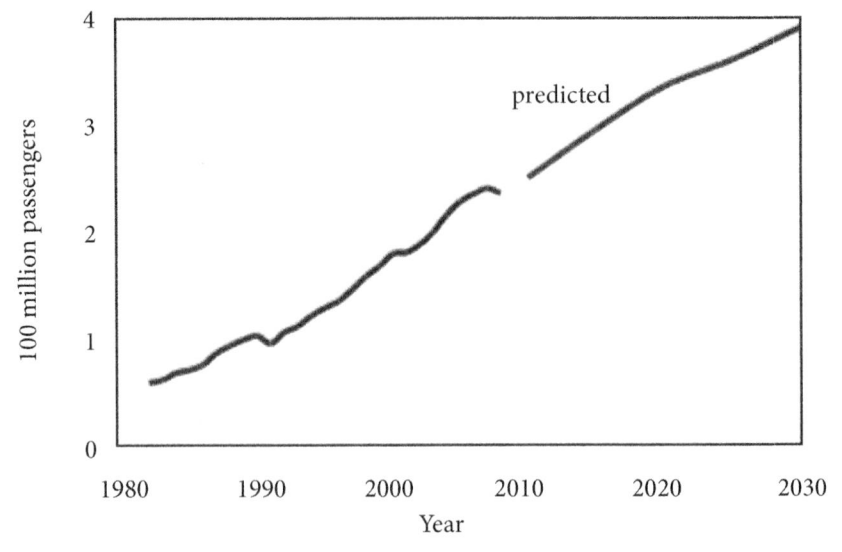

Figure 2: Number of passengers passing through the U.K.'s airports from 1982 to 2008, then predicted from 2010 to 2030[2]

of the car has still been increasing, that increase has slowed down. At the same time, the use of public transport is not decreasing at such a fast rate as it was a few years ago. But that is not good enough: that graph needs to start to show a sharp decrease in the use of the car and a sharp increase in the others. If we are to stand a chance in the next few years, the use of the car must fall below that of public transport, like it was until about 1955.

Due to the immense distances we can cover in a short amount of time, flying around the world is extremely popular. Half a century ago, most of us travelled from one continent to another by boat, which could take months. Then, a few years later, air travel went 'mainstream' and everything changed. Now we take it for granted that you can get to virtually any point on the planet within 24 hours. Figure 2 shows how air travel increased between 1982 and 2008, and how it is projected to grow in the next few years.

The result of planes taking us so far in such a short time is that they burn vast amounts of fossil fuels and are therefore a major contributor to global warming and resource depletion. Nowadays, there are super-cheap short-haul flights everywhere and it just doesn't make sense to do it any other way. As far as long-haul surf trips are concerned, well, to get from one continent to another we have almost always used the plane. Whereas before, we would arrive somewhere and

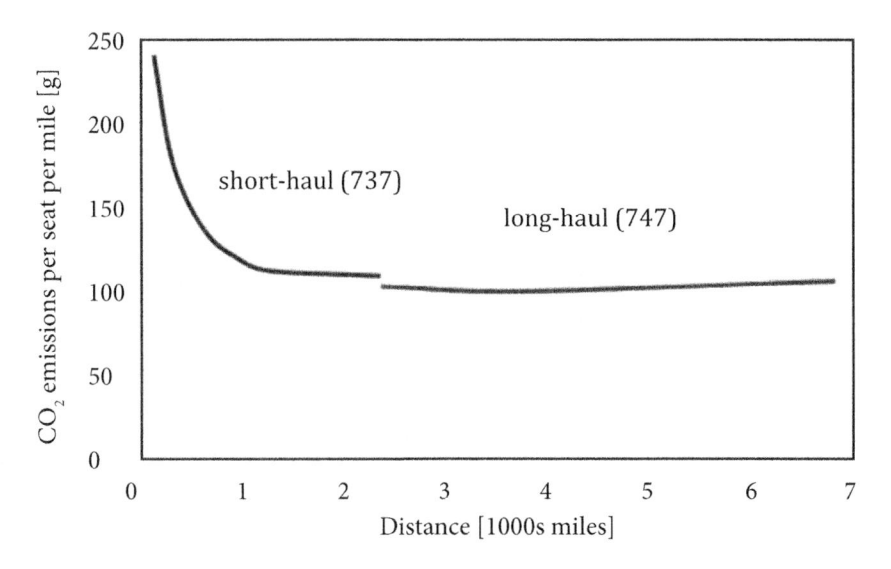

Figure 3: Approximate carbon dioxide emissions per mile as a function of flight distance: You can see that it is much better to take one long-haul flight than lots of short ones[4]

wonder what we were going to do for the next six months, nowadays we go on seven-day package deals to the Mentawais – something unheard of 30 years ago. The surfing elite – those whom we aspire to emulate – go from Hawaii to Maverick's to Ireland, or from Western Australia to South Africa to Chile, just for one swell. There are two reasons why flying is probably the most effective way of pushing your ecological footprint sky high. Firstly, the emission of greenhouse gases per person per mile is around the same order of magnitude as if you were to drive that distance on your own. But we tend to cover a lot more miles by plane which is, of course, the point of flying. The other reason is that the overall effect planes have on global warming is thought to be a lot greater – more than double by some estimates – than just the emission of greenhouse gases from their engines. Among other things, the vapour trails produced by high-flying jets modify the natural clouds, resulting in extra heat being trapped in the atmosphere[3].

Short-haul flights have the most significant effect on the environment. Getting the plane off the ground, up in the air in the first place takes an immense amount of energy. Therefore, the fewer times you can take off and land, the better. So, ten 1,000-mile flights are much worse for the environment than one 10,000-mile flight. Figure 3 shows how the amount of greenhouse gases emitted per mile increases drastically as the length of your flight decreases. Another negative effect air travel has on the environment is from the airport itself. Apart from atmospheric and acoustic pollution, airports take up a massive amount of natural land and their constant expansion contributes to land destabilization and reduced biodiversity, just the same as building a city.

So it looks like our ecological footprint, due to travelling, has increased dramatically over the last few decades and is continuing to increase, principally due to the fact that we are using much more carbon-intensive forms of transport, particularly flying.

The Survey

Are we surfers more or less environmentally friendly than the average citizen? Ideally, it ought to be less. One reason is that surfers ought to be more environmentally aware than most people because we depend on a very fragile part of nature (the coast) and we'll be the first to notice when things start to change, such as episodic coastal flooding, increased storminess or rises in sea-level. Another reason is that surfing, stripped down to its bare essentials, is a low-carbon activity, similar to walking or cycling. The act of riding waves itself doesn't burn any fuel, doesn't result in any emission of greenhouse gases and doesn't cost you anything apart from some wax and the wear and tear on your board and suit. When I started surfing I remember thinking how wonderful it was because of that very reason. Of course, at that time, I lived in a city and rode my bicycle to the same beach every day.

So, just out of curiosity, in 2009, I decided to check my own ecological footprint. At first I was convinced that I was an environmentally-friendly surfer and that I practiced what I preached. But when I got the results, I was shocked. My footprint was above average. I couldn't understand it – I had energy-saving light bulbs in every room of my well-insulated flat, I hardly used the heating, I recycled practically everything and bought locally-grown produce, plus I worked from home. Alright, I *did* drive my car around a bit looking for surf, but I live less than 20 km from most of the spots I surf and had a very efficient car. As it turned out, the big problem was the one long-haul flight I take once a year. As soon as I took that out of the equation my footprint went right down.

The next logical step was to look a little further and try to get some information on the footprints of surfers in general, not just myself. So I put a survey on the internet. It was pretty simple and was designed to find out how much travelling surfers do, by road and by air. The values I got from the survey would then be plugged into an eco-footprint calculator[5], together with average-citizen values for all other factors not attributable to travel (such as whether you use low-energy bulbs etc.). That way, I could avoid asking too many boring questions and, by keeping the other factors constant, I could directly test the effect of travelling on surfers' carbon footprints.

These were the questions asked:

(a) In what part of the world you live?
(b) What size car you drive (if any)?
(c) How far you drive in a year?
(d) How many short-haul, medium-haul and long-haul flights you take a year?

The area of the world where you live was divided into four categories:

(i) North America, including Hawaii,
(ii) Australia/New Zealand,
(iii) Europe,
(iv) Rest of the world including South America, Africa, Asia, and the Pacific Islands.

The carbon-footprint calculator needed an exact figure for the number of kilometres per year travelled by air, which I calculated from the average distances of long, medium and short haul flights. Then, to allow direct comparisons between distances covered by road and distances covered by air, the number of road kilometres per year was 'normalised', working on the principle that bigger cars emit more carbon for the same number of kilometres. For example, a typical 4x4 emits about 1.8 times as much carbon as a typical two-door mini; 1,000 km in a 4x4 would have the same effect on your carbon footprint as 1,800 km in a two-door mini. The results in the following graphs show averages for each geographical area. Where I've put 'average citizens', these are 'official' figures, obtained from the website containing the footprint calculator. Where I've put 'surfers', I mean those people who filled out the survey, not *all* surfers. As I discuss in a minute, a survey like this cannot hope to capture the entire surfing population of every area of the world.

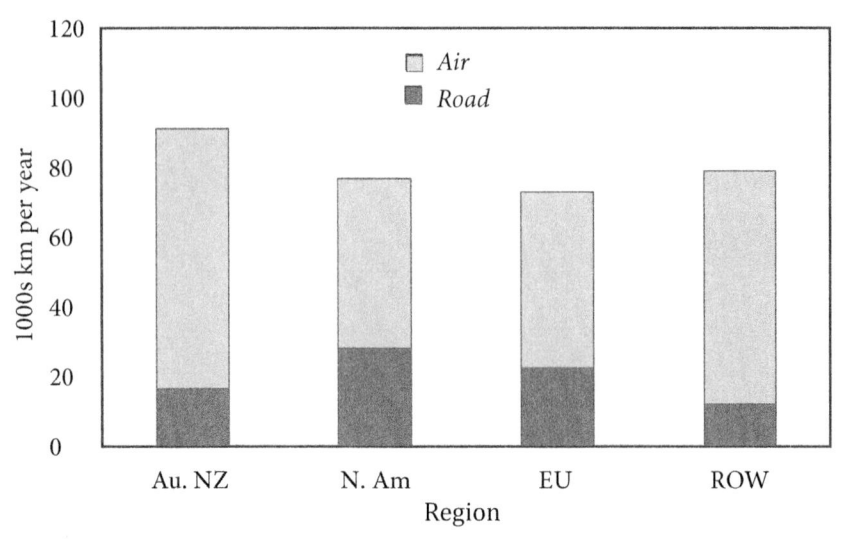

Figure 4: Average number of kilometres travelled by you, by air and by road. The road kilometres are normalized to be equivalent to those driven by a small 2-door car.

First of all, looking at the average number of kilometres travelled by air and by road (Figure 4), it seems that those living in Australia and New Zealand tend to travel the most. This is not surprising, since surfers living in those areas are quite isolated from the rest of the surfing world and are, traditionally, avid travellers. North American surfers tend to drive more than anyone else, or at least drive bigger cars, which is no real surprise either. You might be wondering why the overall number of kilometres from the rest of the world (ROW) is so high, when this category represents the poorest areas. I suspect that most of the respondents are far more affluent than the average citizen in those countries and therefore have enough money to travel just like us in Europe or North America. In summary, the results from this plot seem to be fairly logical, which suggests that the data is accurate.

Next is the centrepiece of the experiment: the carbon footprint graph (Figure 5, opposite). Looking at the graph, the first thing we can see is that, in all cases, the carbon footprint of the survey participants is higher than that of the average citizen, which suggests that surfers emit more carbon into the atmosphere than normal people. In fact, combining all the geographical areas, the surfers' average footprint is 32.8 global hectares (gha), compared with 16.8 gha for the average citizen – almost twice as much. The biggest differences are in the poorer countries, with a massive 35.2 per cent difference between the footprints

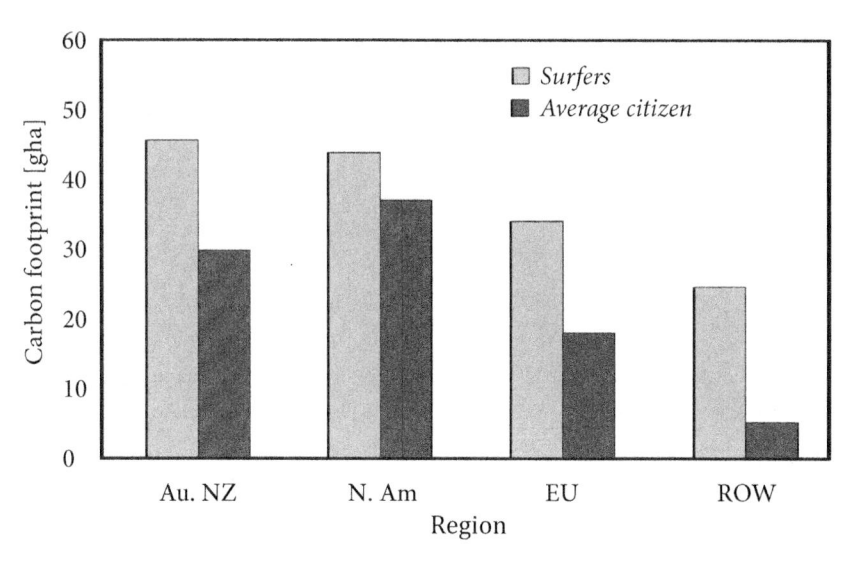

Figure 5: Carbon footprint in global hectares (gha) for surfers (survey participants) in each geographical area compared with the carbon footprint of the average citizen in that area.

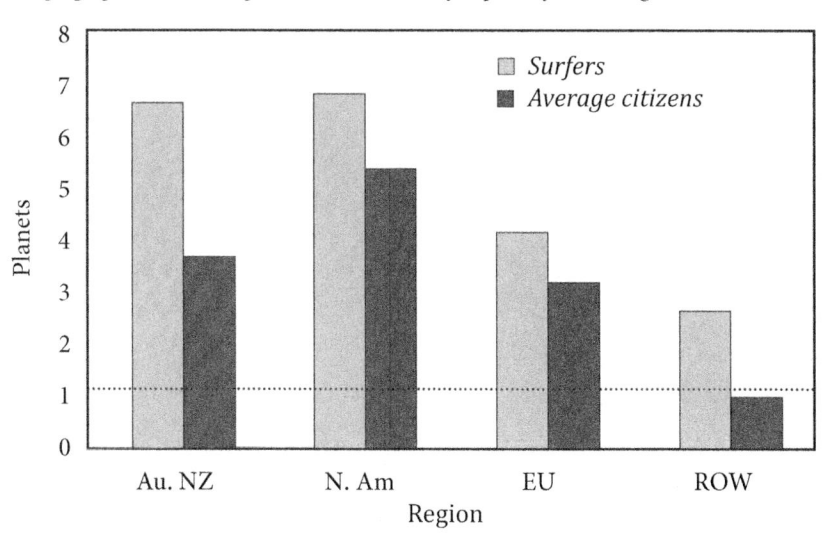

Figure 6: Number of planets we would need if all the citizens of the Earth consumed the same as the average surfer or the average citizen in each geographical area. The dashed line is just to show how the results compare with a sustainable (one-planet) level of consumption.

of surfers and average citizens in the ROW, compared with a modest 18 per cent difference in North America. This is probably because surfers living in poor regions of the world are bound to be more affluent than the majority of the people around them, otherwise they wouldn't be able to surf, or indeed have an internet connection to fill out the survey in the first place.

Figure 6 shows the number of planets we would need to support us if the entire world population consumed the same as (a) surfers and (b) average citizens, in each geographical area. For example, if everybody in the world consumed as much as the average North American surfer, we would need about 6.8 planets to support us. Put another way, North American surfers are using up the Earth's resources 6.8 times as fast as those resources are being renewed. This survey took into consideration the whole ecological footprint, not just the carbon footprint. I assumed that surfers are no different from average citizens when it comes to other factors that influence the ecological footprint, such as the amount of household waste we generate or the amount of second-hand clothes we buy, so the only influencing factor is the amount of travelling we do. In all cases, the figures are higher for surfers than for average citizens and are all above the sustainable limit of one planet. In summary, the results of this simple survey suggest that, as surfers, the contribution to our ecological footprint due to travelling is higher than that of the average citizen.

It might be understandable that the African surfers taking part in this survey travel a lot more than most Africans, because African surfers are much richer than the majority of African citizens. But North American surfers are even worse than other North Americans, who are already eating up the Earth's resources faster than anybody else in the world. Of course, this survey was very simple, with many assumptions made. It might turn out that the contributing factors other than travelling – those that I have simply assumed to be the same for surfers as for everybody else – are actually much less for surfers. If those factors had been added into the survey they might have been low enough to offset our high carbon emissions from travelling, putting our carbon footprint below that of the average citizen. But I doubt it. To compensate for the greenhouse gases generated by a small amount of travelling requires a lot of effort elsewhere.

Another point, which could make things even gloomier, is that the data is probably skewed towards a smaller carbon footprint than is realistic for surfers in general. That is to say, the real carbon footprint for surfers might be even bigger than this survey suggests, because data from the high-end consumers amongst us is probably quite scarce. Those surfers with the biggest carbon footprints, such as those who know they are consuming excessively but don't care, or those who simply don't believe in global warming, would have been the least likely to waste time filling out this survey. In conclusion, according to the results of this study, we, as surfers, seem to be a long way from the ideal environmentally-friendly citizens we make ourselves out to be, and the main reason for that seems the amount of travelling we are doing by car and by plane.

What To Do About It
It seems that travelling is the one thing that makes us surfers less environmentally friendly than average citizen. To be absolutely sure we were contributing as little as possible to global warming, and, therefore, to ensure the preservation of the coastline and the continuation of surfing, perhaps we should stop travelling altogether. Perhaps surfing should only be done by those who live within walking or cycling distance to the coast. Would this work?

The problem is that, if you are a surfer, travelling and all the experiences that go with it, is also one of those things that you will probably value more than any amount of material possessions or home comforts. If we had to give up travelling altogether, surfing just wouldn't be the same. If we couldn't travel, we would lose out on the peripheral aspects that come with travelling – things that get absorbed by us effortlessly – a knowledge of the cultures and languages of the world, an openness and tolerance towards people of those different cultures, and, ironically, an enhanced awareness of the fragility of our environment. If we didn't travel, we would find it even more difficult to appreciate the frailty of our environment and the finiteness of the planet and so, we would be even less inclined to reduce our ecological footprint and persuade others to do the same.

So, is there a way out of this paradox? Is there some way we can still keep travelling, continue to soak up foreign cultures and tropical barrels, and continue to appreciate the miracle of our environment, but without destroying the very environment we have learned to value? One thing we could do is mitigate the environmental destruction brought about by our travelling by creating a corresponding environmental 'construction'. In other words, put back the biodiversity we removed, or remove the greenhouse gases we pumped into the atmosphere. As long as we could exactly compensate for our environmental damage in this way, we could take as many short-haul flights as we wanted and it wouldn't matter. Some surfing organisations and clothing brands that sponsor large surfing events, plus a few individual pro surfers, justify their huge environmental footprints by taking part in some mitigation scheme. This not only makes them feel better about it, but encourages us to imitate them.

The most well-known form of environmental abuse mitigation is carbon offsetting. This is a scheme that is supposed to neutralise the greenhouse-gas emissions associated with a particular activity by contributing just the right amount to a scheme that soaks up the greenhouse gases that your activity emitted. Typical ways of doing this range from the distribution of energy-saving light bulbs to developing countries, to replanting the Amazon rainforest. When you book a flight, for example, sometimes you are given the option to pay a bit more and 'offset' that flight, so that its effect on the environment is neutralised.

Of course, it is not that simple. If the effects of greenhouse-gas emissions and global warming are a long way from being understood by the best scientists in the world, so how can we possibly say that any mitigation schemes will work? In short, we can't expect to reverse the effects of our environmental interference by interfering with it even more, especially since we don't understand how it works. Therefore, mitigation schemes are not really getting to the root of the problem. They do nothing to encourage us to reduce our environmental damage – in fact all they really do is make us feel less guilty and relieve us of a responsibility.

A much better idea than mitigation might be to really try to reduce the ecological footprint of our travelling, not by giving up travelling altogether, but by simply changing the *way* we travel. This could make a big difference to our footprint and, at the same time, maintain our environmental awareness, both of which would feed off each other. Putting more emphasis on travelling as an adventure in itself, rather than as a means to an end, might be the solution. Instead of getting to and from some spot as quickly as possible, collect up seconds of tube time as if they were marketable commodities, perhaps we should step back a little and enjoy the journey. Until a few years ago, most of us didn't have the slightest clue about global warming, resource depletion or loss of biodiversity, but we tended to automatically travel in a more environmentally friendly way. It wasn't just the fact that air travel and cheap short-haul flights were less available then, it was also seen to be much more clever and cooler way to travel a long way for a long time on as little money as possible.

If you could find uncrowded surf using limited resources, you were a hero, like those guys in the magazines. Instead of flying half way round the world to chase one swell, quivers of boards, jet-skis and helicopters leaving a trail of greenhouse gases behind them, those guys would be on the road for a long time, discovering hidden pointbreaks in remote areas, living among the local population and sending back fascinating stories to the magazines just when we thought they had been lost forever. We wanted to be just like them. Nowadays, you might say that things are obviously different: you might think that all the places that were undiscovered 30 years ago now have surf camps or are serviced by organised boat trips. But you will find that there are plenty more undiscovered, unsurfed or forgotten surf spots, even today. There are countless examples of recent 'discoveries', many of which are very close to existing surf populations – spots that have, for some reason, been ignored or perhaps missed by local surfers and other travellers.

So how can we convince other surfers to want to travel in a more environmentally-friendly way? One thing we can do is 'un-sell' modern air travel and all the hassle that goes with it. If you think about it, air travel is pretty stressful. When we have to put up with the same madness over and over again, the novelty tends to wear off. For example, how many times have you been stuck in that queue before the x-ray machine, checking your watch every few seconds, wondering if your boards are going to make it to the other end, and perhaps imagining being dragged off and tortured in your own country for being a terrorist? In the end, you just want to get it over with and get to your destination. Usually, that part of the trip just fades away as a bad memory instead of being an integral part of the experience. At the same time, we can try to 're-sell' the idea of travelling on a low budget in novel ways, perhaps using examples of surf spots that have been discovered recently and the amazing adventures that people have had on the way. My own stories are humble ones but, even now, I am still discovering unsurfed big-wave spots in a part of Europe that has had a thriving surf population for many decades.

Recently, some great examples of novel ways of travelling have been published, including the award-winning 2010 film by Cyrus Sutton, *Stoked and Broke*[6], and Christian Beamish's extraordinary book *Voyage of the Cormorant*[7]. But is anyone actually taking any notice, or are these and other excellent pieces of work just part of some underground movement, followed by people who have already had the right idea for years? Even though some of us already realise that travelling in a more sustainable way can be much more fulfilling than all that jet-setting, it still seems that the vast majority of surfers are either not receiving the message properly, missing the point or are simply not interested.

For example, my survey was conducted through *Surfers Path*, a publication with a global readership of over 50,000. I was expecting a response from at least a couple of thousand individuals, but I obtained less than 200. In 2011, I published the definitive *Guide to Sustainable Surfing*[8], downloadable free through many websites and available for one euro from Amazon. Again, there was very little response from the general surfing population. Just to show that it is not just me, as part of a special 'green' issue[9], the staff of *Australian Surfing Life* magazine sent out messages to the top 45 professional surfers asking them if they could provide tips for young surfers about how to be environmentally aware. Out of the 45 surfers they only got two replies. It seems that the message isn't getting out to surfers, so logically it is not getting out beyond surfers into the mainstream 'public' media. Sometimes it is maddening how journalists fail to notice the blindingly obvious. For example, this quote from a website describing a BBC documentary:

"But the ocean isn't just about food. In ancient Hawaii, chiefs used surfing competitions to show off their power and prowess. Nowadays big-wave surfers do the same, monitoring conditions around the world to ensure they are in the right place at the right time when the giants come rolling in. If only all our relationships with the sea were so benign. [...] And since the oceans absorb 50% of the carbon dioxide that we release into the atmosphere by burning fossil fuels, we are continually increasing the acidification of the oceans"[10].

So how do those surfers get there 'when the giants come rolling in'? By bicycle? Turning back to the problem of convincing the surfers themselves, why is it such an effort to change their behaviour to something that is obviously to their advantage? Is it something to do with the way the message is being put out there? Or is it something deeper, something to do with the very nature of surfing?

I stated earlier that travelling in a more sustainable way needs to be portrayed as something really cool and exciting, something that is done by surfing rolemodels that all other surfers will try to emulate. At the moment, it is not being portrayed like that. At the moment, the majority of the material out there only serves to make people feel guilty about what they are not doing and what they should be doing. Most surfers can't be bothered to read something that is going to make them feel bad about themselves and take their fun away.

The other problem, of course, is the vested interest by large multinational clothing companies that control the images put out in the media of our role models, and, therefore, try to control the behaviour of the people who follow those role models. This includes making people buy a certain brand of wetsuit because they want to be like a certain pro surfer who is wearing one. But perhaps, albeit inadvertently, it also makes people wish that one day they could be just like their heroes in the magazines and spend their lives chasing swells from Hawaii to Australia to Southern America and back again.

So, there is another layer to this complicated problem. We surfers could be a shining example of a social group that manages to enjoy life at a much smaller environmental cost than most others – role models for the non-surfing population to follow. But the elite pro surfers are also role models for surfers. If they don't change, most of us won't change, and then we can't persuade the rest of the population to change.

Tony surfing ten minutes from his home
(Courtesy of Oliver Kingshott)

7.4

Greening Events: The Case of Boardmasters Surf and Music Festival, UK

Emma Whittlesea

"I'm really stoked that Relentless are getting behind this and surfing is helping to save a bit of Amazon at Boardmasters with Cool Earth. The rainforests are vital for the oceans, so it definitely gets my backing."
Ben Skinner, British and European Multiple Champion Surfer from Cornwall

Green Event Pathfinder Project

Cornwall is a county in the South West of England that welcomes around 4.5 million staying visitors each year[1], more than eight times Cornwall's population of 532,300 people[2], and hosts over 150 hallmark events annually. Major events are seen as economic drivers, contributing significantly to the economy in Cornwall and adding to the cultural appeal of the county. In 2011, VisitCornwall (the official tourist board for the county) wanted to support local events to become 'greener' and to help them measure and manage their environmental footprint. A 'Green Event Pathfinder' project was set up in partnership with Cool Earth and Boardmasters. The aim was to explore the sustainability of an event and evaluate the environmental impact and use the results to guide and encourage better practice in the sustainable management of events across Cornwall. The event that was chosen was the Relentless Boardmasters Surf and Music Festival, which attracts around 15,000 visitors and 100 music acts annually.

The Boardmasters Festival was chosen as the 'pathfinder' event for two main reasons. Firstly, it is Europe's biggest surf, skate and music festival and takes place annually in Newquay, with 2011 being its 30th Anniversary. Secondly, the festival was already committed to reducing its environmental impact, so there was active interest in sustainable activities already underway. Actions that were already in place before the pathfinder project include Reduce, Reuse, Recycle (the Three Rs) practices, working with public transport providers and local contractors, and creating partnerships with local environmental charities. The most notable activities and commitments identified by Sports Vision (the event organisers who are now known as Vision Nine) for the 2011 event were:

1. Partnership with National Express nationwide to promote public transport use to the event.
2. A bus service from Newquay town centre to the festival site.
3. A direct footpath created between the site and Newquay town centre to encourage walking.
4. Local contractors used wherever possible to minimise transport and support local business.
5. Event bicycles used wherever possible.
6. Partnership with 'GoCarShare' to promote car sharing.
7. Green Car Tax of £5 per day or £8 for the weekend for those driving to the event which was donated to Cornish Charity, Surfers Against Sewage (SAS).
8. Where practicable, waste is sorted on site and recycled.
9. Event branding is reusable.
10. Reduced number of PVC branding used by third parties.
11. Promotional material printed from sustainable sources.
12. All catering uses recycled packaging and recyclable utensils.
13. Beer and cider is served in recycled bottles.
14. Organic and local based caterers are used wherever possible.
15. Partnership with key environmental organisations including, Surfers Against Sewage, the National Trust, and RSPB.
16. Undertake a daily beach clean at Fistral Beach.

The festival was held over two main sites at Fistral Beach and Watergate Bay and the focus for the 2011 'pathfinder project' was the Music Festival at Watergate Bay. The research collected environmental impact data from visitors, staff and for the operational aspect of the Music Festival. Views were also gained from visitors to inform environmental improvements to future events. The data was collected through a face-to-face on-site visitor survey conducted with 533 visitors to the Boardmasters Music Festival over two days of the event. The gender split was 41% male and 59% female, with an average age of 20 years. The survey explored their demographic profile, accommodation and travel choices, spending patterns and thoughts on environmental improvements.

The operational data was obtained from the event utility providers and data on the impact, profile and behaviours of staff was estimated by Sports Vision who managed the event. In addition a carbon and ecological footprint assessment was made using REAP Tourism[3], a resource and energy accounting tool using data derived from the survey and staff profile.

The results showed that 87% of participants stayed in the Newquay area. Low impact accommodation was predominant, with 77% camping, 7% staying with friends and relatives, 5% caravanning and the remaining 11% stayed in a combination of hotels and hostels. Visitors travelled an average of 294 miles, with the most popular mode of travel being the car, which accounted for 84% of journeys, with an average car occupancy of three people. The next mode was bus (8%) followed by train (5%). Excluding the cost of entry, people expected to spend £140 over the weekend, spending most on accommodation.

Participants were asked if they were more likely to attend Boardmasters in future if they knew that the event was organised sustainably (1 being 'Strongly Disagree' and 5 'Strongly Agree'), the average score was 3.8 suggesting that environmental improvements are beneficial, not only for reducing negative environmental impact, but also to retain and attract visitors. Furthermore, participants demonstrated environmental awareness, with 89% providing suggestions for future environmental improvement. The detailed survey results provided lots of ideas, but the most popular improvements were the need for improved waste and litter management (30%) and improved recycling facilities and information (29%). This was followed by the need to reduce congestion and the number of cars (12%), improve energy management and the use of renewables (11%) and improve toilet facilities (11%).

It is surprising that the most popular areas for improvement are around recycling and waste management when existing practices were in place to promote Reduce, Reuse, Recycle principles, but the results showed that festival goers were under the impression that there wasn't any recycling at the event, calling for more obvious signage and information. Additional suggestions for improvement included waste segregation, provision of compost bins, more recycling bins on-site and at the campsite, and improved litter management using more litter pickers and 'litter police'.

Linked to the litter and waste management improvements were suggestions to reduce the amount and type of plastic packaging (8%) which included: less plastic and more biodegradable and eco-friendly food packaging; provide only re-usable cups; have a cup return and collection policy; and take a deposit on drinking glasses to reduce littering. A number of respondents commented on the need to reduce plastic and promotional gifts, with suggestions to "stop giving out pointless carrier bags" and for "no advertising leaflets".

Despite efforts to reduce the transport impact of the festival, the number of cars and associated congestion was identified as a notable area for improvement. Suggested solutions included, improved provision and promotion of public transport and shuttle buses to and from the town, encourage car sharing by providing free parking for 'full' cars (although the average car occupancy is high at 3), develop a 'park and ride' scheme, and incentivise public transport through train and coach concessions.

Energy use also featured as a common area for improvement, suggestions included the use of sustainable energy sources like wind turbines, solar and bicycle power. Some respondents also wanted to see improved management of energy, such as turning stage and ride lights off in the day and querying why generators were left on all night. Alternative fuels such as biodiesel for generators and fines for idling engines were also mentioned.

Other ideas for improvement included carbon offsetting and 'green police' to monitor and manage negative environmental impacts from the event (for example to check people take tents home or to provide a tent recycling area). There were also suggestions to provide compost or eco toilets, use recycled products such as toilet roll, provide free tap water and more covered seating, use e-tickets, encourage more 'fair trade', provide spiritual and 'green' stalls, have less fast food and use local food providers and suppliers. Despite Boardmasters attempts to 'green' the festival and develop sustainable practices it was clear that there are still many areas for improvement. There is a need to improve visitor information and communications as respondents were unaware of the existing efforts such as recycling and alternative travel options to the car.

The Festival's Environmental Footprint

The total water footprint was estimated at 115,000 litres, split between the camping area (staff and public) which consumed 78% of the total water (90,000 litres) with the remainder being consumed by the festival site (25,000 litres). The total waste removed was 45.54 tonnes, of which 9% was recovered/recycled (4.16 tonnes). Food bins were provided but it was contaminated and the electricity consumed was estimated at 117965 kWh.

The total carbon (CO_2) footprint of the Boardmasters music festival was estimated at 1395 tonnes. The impact per visitor day if staff and operational impact are included is 24.47 kg[4] CO_2. The predominant contributors of the emissions from the event were food (38%), followed by 'other' items including shopping (29%) and travel (22%). The emissions impact of the events operations was only 4% of the total emissions with the remaining 96% being visitor and staff emissions. In addition, the REAP Tourism tool was used to estimate the ecological footprint at 761.31 global hectares, equating to 133.56 global square metres per visitor day. Methodological improvements for future environmental monitoring of Boardmasters would be to expand the coverage to both sites by including Fistral Beach activities, to set up data capture and monitoring systems beforehand and to utilise a staff-and-service provider survey to gather more detailed information on behaviour and resource consumption.

Benefits of the Pathfinder
"It is great that event organisers are taking the lead voluntarily to reduce impacts and to measure and manage carbon. This is a rapidly growing area of regulation, but an important one that can save money, our environment and communities. We hope this pilot can be rolled out and can pave the way for other events in Cornwall."
Malcolm Bell, Head of Tourism at VisitCornwall

The Pathfinder Project protected an area of rainforest with Cool Earth that was an equivalent size to the festival venue, securing around 8,000 tonnes of CO_2, more than five times the 'music festival' CO_2 impact and saving the habitat of 17 endangered species. The project findings were used by VisitCornwall to improve awareness of the impact of such events and encourage better practice and sustainable management of events across Cornwall. This was supported through a leaflet produced in partnership with Cornwall College to provide guidance for event organisers.

The specific outputs, in terms of environmental 'footprints' and 'visitor views', provided a baseline of suggestions for future environmental management while partnership improved the visibility of Boardmasters' commitment to sustainability. The 'pathfinder' project was endorsed through interviews and quotes and received a lot of press coverage which included West Briton (4/08), Atlantic FM interview (05/08), BBC Spotlight coverage (11/08), ITV coverage (12/08) and the Western Morning News (12/08). Cool Earth benefited through the protection of 40 acres of rainforest, actively engaging with 18 volunteers who undertook the surveys and talked to event goers. They received £654 in donations at the Cool Earth stand, had over 19,000 Facebook 'views' of the photos taken in The View area and the rate of fans increased by 3000% post event. The festival organisers also took the Cool Earth theme to the arena by protecting a tropical tree in the name of every artist performing at the event along with competing surf champions.

Cool Earth charity director, Matthew Owen said the partnership between VisitCornwall and Cool Earth was a huge step forwards in minimising the environmental impact of the events industry in Cornwall: "Boardmasters is the first event in the UK to take charge of its carbon footprint in such a high impact way. The protection of 40 acres of rainforest will see the same amount of CO_2 saved as 200,000 people flying from London to Newquay."

7.5

Making Cultural Pearls Out of Political Grit

Sam Bleakley

Like many, I surf for primal reasons – the untiring challenge of how to fit into the curve of a wave and best engage with its rhythms and surprises. There is little cerebral about this passion that the ancient Greeks called *thumos* – the emotional contact between a person and their environment which is at its peak, an artistic performance, a dance. It is right to worry about sustainability as a conscious management of the earth's resources, to leave a legacy for future generations and this extends to cultural legacy. Every generation has a duty to generate aesthetic capital and push the boundaries of creativity. Every generation must give their performance a unique twist to enrich their culture, to ask, what is it to fully explore *thumos*? Surfers get close to the grain of the sea and understand its smooth or fickle nature better than most. But many breaks have been so thoroughly mapped that they have become striated: take-off points, sections and tidal factors have become common knowledge rather than local knowledge. Hence the lure of outsider spots to outsider surfers, where the smooth spaces are nomadic, shape shifting and alluring.

The Maldives, in the Indian Ocean, have, for some, become striated space, well mapped, rehearsed, with predictable performances. But serendipity remains a big factor in surfing across these 1,192 island atolls. They sit atop a huge,underwater coral mountain range, their outer polyps alive and glowing with a phosphor, a living skin providing treadmills on which spin perfect cylindrical waves. But below Paradise is an ecological and sustainability timebomb. While the reefs are generally thriving, recent rising sea temperatures have literally cooked some of the coral to death. The atolls lie too low to deal with the one metre of sea level rise predicted over the next century. The highest point, of 2.3 metres, is the 'lowest high point' for any nation on earth. This is the fragile and terrifying front line of climate change and the conscience of a carbon footprint will become generational.

In 2008, a remarkable, far-sighted leader, Mohamed 'Anni' Nasheed, won The Maldives election, ending 30 years of autocratic rule by Maumoon Abdul Gayoom. Anni saw beyond the country's immediate horizon and set out to leave a remarkable legacy. He raised global awareness about sea level rise using imaginative tactics, such as hosting an underwater cabinet meeting with ministers using air tanks and communicating through hand gestures. He set up debates to combat plastic pollution to develop sustainable waste management on tourist resorts and he campaigned to buy land abroad to build a new 'Maldives' in replacement of the old homeland when it disappears. Anni was educating for adaptability and threw in free health care for good measure.

But Anni faced fierce political opposition because supporters of the former president Gayoom still dominated his parliament. Following a variety of political events, Anni resigned. The situation in The Maldives is still uncertain, and surfing here has to come face-to-face with issues concerning biological and political sustainability. Yet, upon arrival in The Maldives, you cannot sense this deep political tension. Malé, the tiny and overcrowded capital, built on tourism and tuna fishing, continues to float as if beyond human stain. One million visitors arrive each year, and most go straight to their resorts, never reaching the capital. The airport island of Hulhule is where a rash of budget accommodation is being built. This is a new-town project spearheaded by Anni to ease the strain on Malé. There are a variety of surf breaks accessible by *dhoni* or seaplane to the north and south, first explored by the late Australian Tony Hinde. He began surfing The Maldives in the 1970s and initiated a new and open-minded era of surf tourism at Pasta Point on Chaaya atoll.

The water is so clear at Pasta Point that it is often hard to make out the shape of the wave. When surfing, I imagine that I am breaking free from the grip of the ocean that is provided by its oily, thin skin and, as I leave the water, the skin heals and forms over behind me. This is not a fiction, or a poetic fancy – the uppermost one millimetre of the ocean, effectively its skin, is a gelatinous, sticky film full of microbial life unique to this layer that may be important to the wellbeing of the planet. While research on this is in its infancy[1], the general consensus is that gas exchange, central to the carbon cycle, such as absorption of methane, occurs here. It could be that the sea's skin, like the rainforest canopies, plays a critical role in regulating gas exchanges that ultimately affect global warming. My conceptualised breaking out from the skin of the sea could be a sensation of one skin rubbing against another.

I am an ocean lover who was bitten by a bug of which the consequences are impossible to shake off, so I have worked to shape an occupation as a professional competitor, travel writer and academic out of this beautiful habit. Part of my career is about relating surfing to music, improvisation and performance, including surfing whilst listening to jazz music on a waterproof mp3 player[2]. This has been extended to the use of metaphors in writing, for example comparing long-fetch Indian Ocean swells to jazz drummers who set up their kit and play booming rolls on the tom-toms, as set waves thunder in. The aim is to translate this type of surfing into text on a page and to give travel writing an element of surprise. I try to consolidate my work in travel, surfing (and subsequent writing) as a parallel process, so my travel writing captures the fluidity and surprise of surfing. This forms a platform for my work, for cultural sustainability, weaving previously disparate elements into new wholes that are, by nature, elastic.

As the local surf culture develops and grows in The Maldives, it is important to remember that it is against a bitter, more pressing background of dying coral and rising seas, volatile politics and brittle pearls. But these local surfers can also be champions of sustainability. It will be a shame if the environmental spark of former president Anni fades, but some lights burn so brightly that they are forced to live with intensity, not longevity, like a hot coal in a rainstorm. Travelling surfers can also do a great deal to raise awareness of the political and environmental work of Anni. But, as 'surf travellers', we have to remind ourselves that we have not discovered any new surf breaks. We are guests, sometimes uninvited, of those who already live there. We enter a circle of hospitality that must be honoured and not broken. As Jacques Derrida[3] says of hospitality, it is an impossible condition, an aporia, yet must be enacted as if it were possible. It is always a work in progress. The host can never offer unconditional hospitality because the guest is unpredictable. But a guest, such as a travelling surfer, can help the host offer hospitality simply by being tolerant of difference and aware that there is much to be learned through suspending one's own cultural baggage. Transition to sustainability offers a perplexing mixture of the disappointing and the promising. Our passion to surf, perform and travel must be part of this process, helping to make cultural pearls out of political grit.

Tim Marsh of Safari Surf, Jess Ponting, and Carl Kish – co-founder of STOKE Certified on location in Nosara, Costa Rica
(Courtesy of Jess Ponting)

7.6

The World Wide Web

Ben Freeston

The lifestyle most of us enjoy is unsustainable if we continue to live as we currently do. If there's one big mistake most of those of us who identify as surfers make, it is to imagine that surfing is more important than it really is. The planet is neither going to be destroyed by surfing nor saved. We've created this mythos that what we do is somehow different to the rest of the population, or that we somehow operate on a deeper level, in respect to our relationship with the environment. It is a mistaken arrogance to assume the reasons I drive to the beach, fly abroad or perhaps covet a house overlooking perfect surf are fundamentally different to those that seek the same simply to enjoy the sight of the sun setting over the ocean or to breathe clean, sea air.

If we accept this, then we have to accept that the issues over sustainability are bigger and more complex than the tokenism that represents sustainable surfing so far. However, waves themselves are an endlessly renewable resource. I can't be the only surfer to have stood, looking at great surf and wondered how many waves, over how many thousands of years must have rolled over the same reef, unridden. But, of course, even this renewable resource can come under pressure from a growing population.

At Magicseaweed, I like to think we are reducing impacts. We reduce the costs of finding good waves, but the reality is more nuanced. Reduce the costs and people tend to simply consume more. For surfing, that means more people on the roads and more people in the water. Whilst the impact of the internet on this has been somewhat exaggerated (ignoring other critical factors like population growth, wetsuit technology, aggressive lifestyle marketing campaigns and increased leisure time), it's undoubtedly a contributing factor. With surfing we see the same issues with competition for our resource as any other. Crowds breed intolerance and aggression. They cause us to retreat into our private domain, to hoard and to become less welcoming of strangers. Managing these issues has fallen, in a large part, to local surfing communities. Some have adopted an aggressive form of localism, with varying degrees of success. Most have attempted to implement some kind of system based on status in the local surfing community. It seems a shame that, in my experience, the internet, rather than serving as a tool by which local and potential visiting surfers could perhaps communicate, has become a soap box for those who wish to see the situation reduced to it's lowest common denominator. The internet is particularly good at this and surfing is, again, far from unique.

At the same time, the internet has also pushed back boundaries to travel and exploration. Sure, the unknown and unknowable have rapidly diminished over the last century or so, but how many of us now get a chance to explore and experience waves and cultures we'd otherwise never have encountered? Does a remote wave in a hard-to-reach Third World destination have more value than the empty, unridden fodder of dreams most of us will never fulfil, or as the realistic and perhaps positive intersection of the surf traveller meeting and supporting a fledgling local surfing community. Not just with the jobs and income that it might generate but also the intangible benefits of people conversing about a common experience across the boundaries of language and culture.

Perhaps if there's one thing surfing the internet and surf forecasting does have the potential to deliver, it's a positive insight into this interconnectedness. Strong winds around Greenland create powerful ocean currents that are part of a global circulation, pushing cool water south. Warm water currents from Hawaii are part of the same system and are ultimately part of the circulation that creates our North Atlantic Gulf Stream. These global ocean temperatures force the development of atmospheric patterns.

Ocean temperatures in the Pacific affect the development of pressure systems over the Continental United States which in turn influence the position of the North Atlantic Jet Stream. The position of this influences in turn the location and strength of powerful winter storms. A large storm might pass up the East Coast of the United States creating solid local short period waves from Florida through to New York. Undergoing cyclogenesis at higher latitudes, it can deepen and create solid groundswell arriving almost simultaneously from Norway to Senegal. Perhaps a sense of this can be a positive factor. Perhaps a better understanding of these patterns can give surfers an implicit knowledge of a Gaia Earth in a way that can help foment change that stretches beyond simply how we choose to participate in our sport. In this we hope that Magicseaweed might have made a tiny, positive contribution.

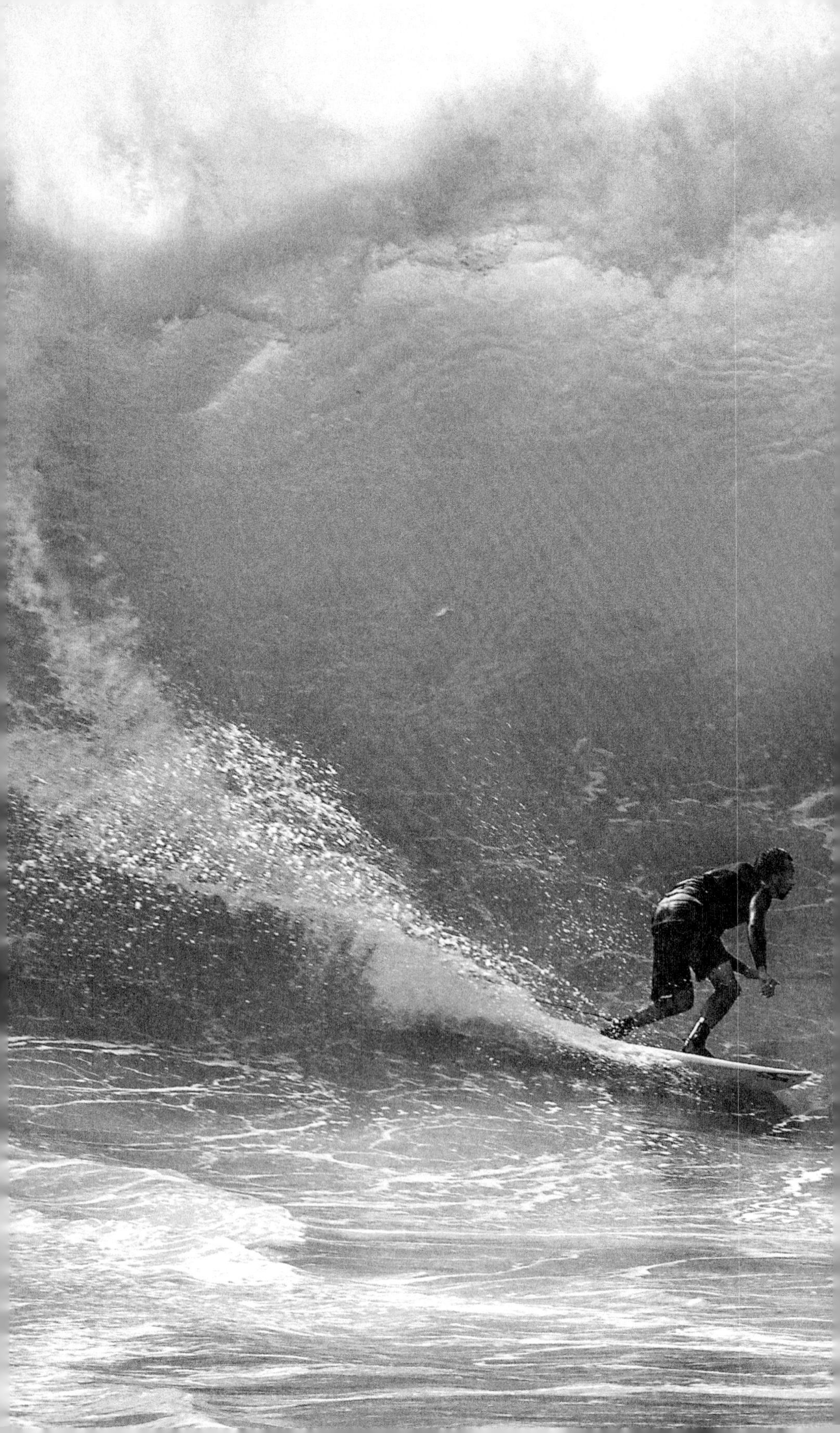

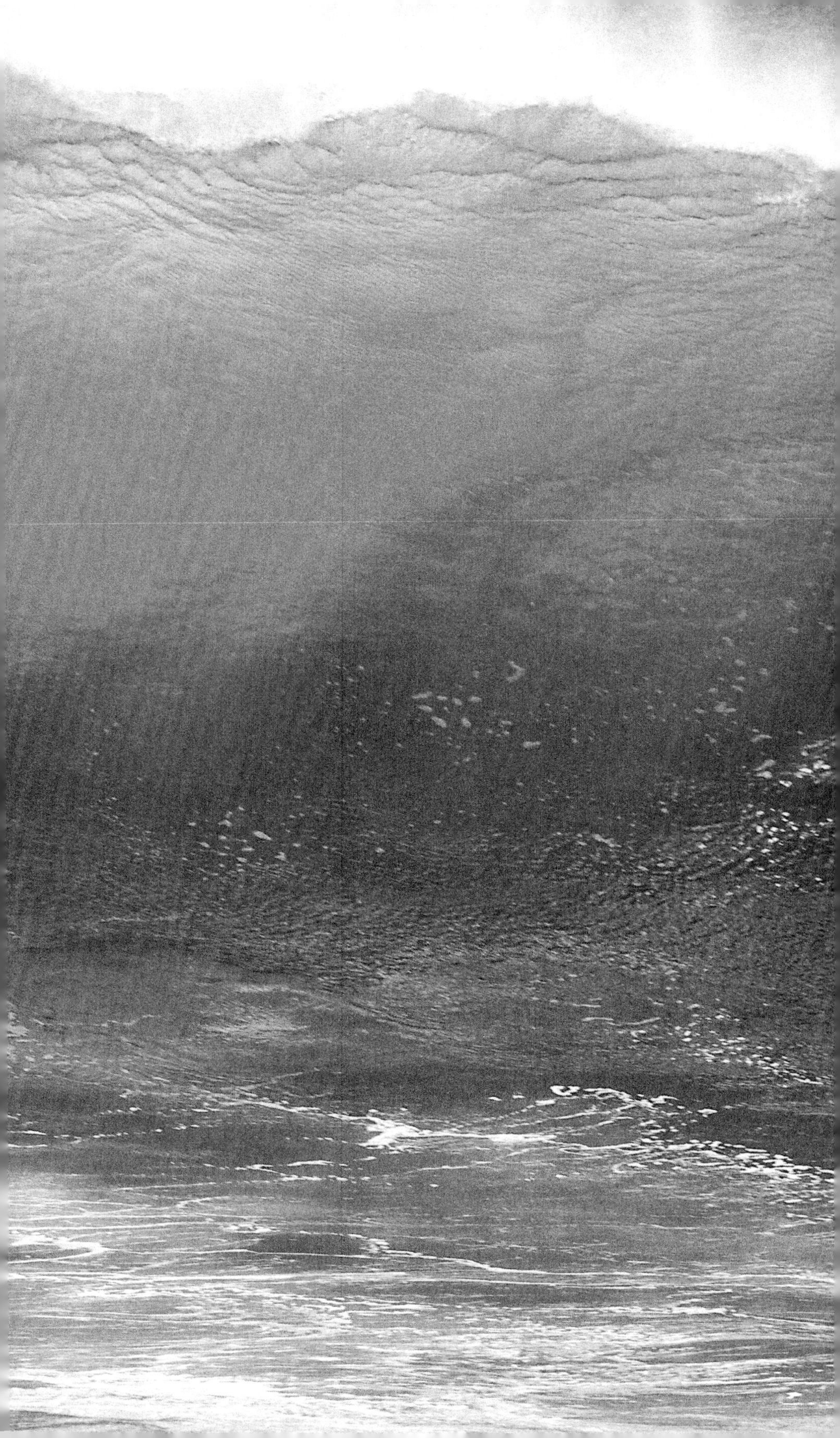

Chapter Eight
Call To Political Power

A common theme throughout this book has been that surfing is capable of driving positive change. Just the same, the following sections talk very specifically about political action and power and how surfing as a political force, both from within the political system and from outside of it, can effect a transition to sustainability on a local, national and international scale. This chapter draws on some seminal figures that have promoted change through surfing.

It begins with Kevin Lovett who talks as much about the internal struggle, the politics of the self, as he does about the external political world. Kevin's piece strikes at the heart of the underlying tensions that are apparent throughout this book as we struggle to achieve a sustainable future. It highlights the important role of knowledge and the varying forms of knowledge that need to be considered – not just scientific but spiritually and locally embedded as well – whilst at the same time being sensitive to non-locals as we construct our own realities. Kevin weaves this narrative into tangible issues relating to the Indonesian Marine Protected Areas.

Glenn Hening as an 'eloquent provocateur' provides a sweeping deconstruction of the surfing world providing an insight onto the mind of the founder of the worlds most successful surfing non-profit organisation. This is followed by Chris Hines who, through the foundation of Surfers Against Sewage, changed national legislation leading to measurable improvements in water quality around the UK. Chris's writing illustrates the power of surfing and its ability to change the world. Hugo Tagholm echoes these sentiments and outlines current initiatives that SAS are driving forward that connect on the ground action to the highest political levels. Hugo emphasises the importance of employing the full spectrum of activities to create change from campaigning and lobbying, to grass roots activism, all of which contribute to creating new legislation. This is demonstrated through SAS's recent success in creating the Protect our Waves all parliamentary Group. Brad Farmer founded Surfrider Australasia and is a pivotal figure in the creation of National Surfing Reserves. Brad emphasises the importance of leadership within and beyond the surfing world and the need for these leaders to be able to embrace commensurate solutions that are driven through the establishment of effective organisations. Brad points out that, very much like the term 'sustainable development' itself, surfer organisations can be oxymoronic, a contradiction in terms and points to the urgent need for new legislative and community level governance to be implemented.

The final contribution of this chapter, and deliberately so, is from 1968 world surfing champion, co-founder of the first professional world tour and professional surfing organization, and former Hawaiian senator Fred Hemings. Fred's writing provides a remarkable and inspiring insight into the how he instigated change at the highest political level. Discussions on the need to protect the environment are balanced with cautionary examples of the unintended consequences of environmental activism.

Fred goes on to discuss his pivotal role in the creation of the Papahanaumokuakea Marine Sanctuary in 2006. This sanctuary formed the foundation for the Pacific Remote Islands National Marine Monument being proclaimed a national monument on January 6, 2009. On 25th September 2014, President Obama expanded the area of the reserve to 490,000 square miles. To put this in context this is three times the size of California and nearly four times the area of all national parks on land in the U.S. In all, the contributors to the final chapter do not point to finality but instead the need for ongoing political debate that begins with our love and passion for surfing.

8.1

Stoke in a Sea of Uncertainty

Kevin Lovett

From a quantum physics point of view, it seems we cannot get by on dreaming alone. In order to create our change we have to actively collapse waves of infinite possibilities to actualise such change. In so doing, as Ghandi suggested, we ourselves create the change that we wish to see in this world.

It is so easy to become caught up in Maya, the world of illusion, and not realise that we are essentially creating the world ourselves every moment and with every breath. Engaging our imagination momentarily allows us to create our own virtual world; what would be the result if our brains were in fact GoPro cameras that not only stored visual information as memory, but also constantly broadcasted such information through an interconnected network that linked the space between elementary particles? If the combined visual information, projected by people, could then be downloaded through our mind back into our computer-like brains, the creation of a virtual holographic world would be complete. This is a model where certain quantum physicists find compatibility with the stages of mysticism, where concepts such as the illusory appearance of materiality and the nature of God as consciousness can be openly discussed. In order for us to lead responsible lives, we must become aware of what is happening around us. Increasing our awareness will allow us to make better choices, which will not only positively impact our lives in the present but will also assist people in fulfilling their ultimate potential.

Information is the only currency of exchange that matters in our world; with relevant information, we are able to convert it into knowledge through the medium of education. When we integrate that knowledge into our own lives through experience, we transform the original information into wisdom. Wisdom assists us to change the course of our lives and to ultimately dissolve the separation between not only ourselves and others but also ourselves and our natural environment. Wisdom, like gold, is the only means of transferring wealth through time. That is, if one considers real wealth being our emotional, physical and spiritual health. The life of a short-term pessimist, but a long-term activist in optimism, is not without its challenges, particularly in terms of dealing with the doubt that can be generated when looking deeply into the overwhelming difficulties that currently confront us. The doubt I refer to lies in my wavering certainty as to whether we can continue to evolve to reach our full potential, without manufacturing a paradigm shift in the management of the planet.

Dr Amit Goswami, a contemporary thinker in science and spirituality, is an advocate of 'monistic idealism', the philosophy that defines consciousness, not materiality, as the primary reality. The call for a paradigm change in the world can be achieved, he says, firstly through generating a quantum change within oneself. This is not a startling new view, as shamanic traditions and esoteric religions have been instructing followers in 'the way' since the dawn of time, however, having this view interpreted by an innovative thinker from the world of quantum physics carries additional affirmation. Goswami's view confirms our individual ability to change ourselves and, in doing so, we change the world around us. The quantum world recognises the existence of unlimited possibilities, which are collapsed via downward causation in the mind of the observer, becoming an experience, which is actualised through upward causation from elementary particles to atoms, to molecules, to cells, to subjective consciousness, creating our own virtual world of materiality.

Understanding the nature of the required quantum leap, and the factors which is required to support a paradigm shift, can be explained by Dr Goswami through comprehending non-locality. Non-locality is a connection among potentialities outside of space-time that can affect events within space-time. Surfers of all descriptions have experienced non-locality at some stage, whilst locked inside a spinning watery vortex, deeply tubed, innately aware of the intricacies of their present position yet simultaneously connected to everyone and everything within the waking state of consciousness. Essentially, we create a virtual reality for ourselves within a multiverse of consciousness that includes matter. Our conditioning is all that separates us in the material world. But dreaming about change is different to creating change and, for this, we have to follow our elders not only in words, but also in deeds. Those who have made a quantum leap in not only thinking, but also in doing have already outlined a variety of solutions to our present social and ecological conundrum.

"I have a response to people who say you can't go back. Well what happens if you get to the cliff? Do you take one step forward, or do you do a 180 degree turn and take one step forward? Which way are you going? Which is progress?"[1] Questions with answers provided by Doug Tompkins, a true legend of the fall line, who, along with his climbing partner and visionary, Yvon Chouinard, innovated the cleanest line connecting living over the last 50 years. Both 'conquerors of the useless' continue to show leadership now, when it counts the most. Doug has pioneered environmental activism, establishing among many endeavours, the Foundation for Deep Ecology and the Conservation Land Trust. However, as we face a global dark night of the soul, what kind of attitude does a man like Yvon Chouinard bring to the table? "The word adventure has gotten overused. For me, when everything goes wrong, that's when adventure starts"[2]. So our challenge to deliver more responsible management of our planet's natural capital could very well be the greatest adventure of our individual lives. Tompkins and Chouinard recognised the personal responsibilities that came with working within a 200-year-old busted industrial business model that could no longer be sustained ecologically, socially nor financially.

Yvon Chouinard, together with his longterm Patagonia business partner, Vincent Stanley, outline their cogent views on personal responsibility in their book *The Responsible Company*.

"We are still in the earliest stages of learning what we do for a living both threatens nature and fails to meet our deepest human needs. The impoverishment of our world and the devaluing of the priceless undermine our physical and economic wellbeing. Yet the depth and breadth of technological innovation of the past few decades shows that we have not lost our most useful gifts; humans are ingenious, adaptive, clever. We now need to more fully engage these gifts to make economic life more environmentally responsible, and less destructive to nature and the commons that sustain us."

The old model of scientific, economic, social and philosophical materialism also heavily infected surfing through the development of the industrial surf complex. The ignorance of flogging to death products generated within a tired, imperfect, profit-based business model was lost on most of the owners of surf corporations who grew up in the '70s, when surfing faced a previous fork-in-the-road moment. Professionalism and profit chose one path whilst those who had been bitten by the wanderlust bug chose the path less travelled (mostly to metaphorically lose themselves in order to ultimately find themselves).

Some subconsciously blended business with their emerging environmental spiritualism to create a wellbeing-supported lifestyle pursuit. Luckily for us, they have innovated a new path forward that has identified core stakeholder needs, essential to the long-term management and maintenance of the economic integrity of Gaia. Surfing is all kinds of things to surfers, but at its heart it is an unwinding path towards personal self-transformation.

Tom Blake, the quintessential surfer, recognised early on that his surfing experience bought him into a deeper relationship with life itself; he undoubtedly glimpsed the innermost essence of the vast expanse, seemingly dedicating his life to understanding the singularity of existence. In the *Voice of the Wave*, Tom illumined that:

"The physicist knows all atoms to be of such a complex nature as to still defy the scientist, still harbor secrets. Each has within it that divine and godly principle, that minute part of the vast mass and energy system of the universe. Each water molecule, and there are billions in the smallest wave, is a model of order, harmony and rhythm; thus, the atom becomes a key point of reference to logic, to right action, in judging the wave as well as all problems in life."

In 1974, following a year spent traversing the world's oceans, Larry Yates immortally articulated the esoteric and mythological site of transcendence that he discovered, cradled deep within the spirit boat of his surfing experience.

"Somewhere, in the midst of this ancient sea, surrounded by the intense energy and sparkling beauty of her ocean waves lies the forgotten Island of Santosha. It is more than just an island. It is many Islands and it is this Island Earth on which we live. It is a state of mind, a state of being and land of forgotten dreams. An Island bound by the spirit of the sea and living within the spirit of Man."[3]

Indonesia contains the world's largest archipelago; its exotic, equatorial environs manifest numerous secluded surfing locations with the potential to encompass the ethos of Larry Yates' dreamlike Santosha. From the early 1970s onwards, the Indonesian surfing experience became metaphorically known as 'the dream'. From the depths of mysticism, we understand that causes and conditions produce future results, and that foresight is gifted to a solitary few, but who could have predicted the impact in remote Indonesia from the 40-

year search for Santosha that continues to this day? Surfing materialism in the '80s was focused purely on profit-driven outcomes and, in doing so, failed to economically assess what would be the long-term impact of their actions in their feverish promotion of semi-remote Indonesian surf locations. The future socio-cultural challenges or consequences of a sudden spike in visitor levels on remote and fragile environments occupied by predominantly disadvantaged communities were never even considered.

The '80s exploitation of 'the dream' by the surf industry complex was achieved by the commodification of ineffable dreamlike images of saturated beauty, which symbolically alluded to Larry Yates' Santosha treasure map. These images were printed by the millions on over-priced T-shirts and boardshorts, labelled, 'Paradise with an ocean view'. 'The dream' was sold using thousands of square meters of advertising space, countless videos and cover shots to bog standard consumers, who purchased the branded products, and ultimately carried them over time to comfortably appointed surf slums dotted throughout the archipelago.

Retrospectively, looking over the past 35-40 years of surf travel in Indonesia, we've all contributed in some small way to an interconnected network of surf slums. Cautiously looking forwards, we now learn from hindsight that today's secret spot is potentially tomorrow's surf slum. Personal responsibility has to appear in the future of surf travel. Jess Ponting, one of the editors of this book, comments in relation to slums like Sorake in Southern Nias: too often "we create a legacy of soiled destinations, disheartened and distressed communities and missed opportunities to replace poverty with sustainable livelihoods"[4]. The good news is that change is occurring and it's being generated, in part, by a new breed of surfing-related scientists who are feeding the international surfing community precious information which will affect visitor behaviour and undoubtedly impact positively on local communities.

Consultative parameters, used to assess the limits of acceptable change in these economically and resource deprived surf-based communities, can be included in a responsible tourism management model tailored for such locations. Long-term management models are required to address unique stakeholder needs within communities that, for the most part, remain trapped in a subsistence poverty cycle. Included in the management model would be plans for the rehabilitation of some of the archipelago's iconic surf breaks such as Uluwatu, Bali and Lagundri Bay in Southern Nias. The Country Director of Conservation International in Indonesia is the visionary Balinese, Bapak Ketut

Sarjana Putra, who recently shared his creative insight into the current and future challenges existing within the world's largest archipelago in a paper titled *Indonesia: Integrating National Surf Reserves into National Marine Protected Areas (MPA) System*.

"Failure to adopt a more responsible development programme going forward may result in Indonesia losing opportunities to successfully manage the economic value held in its large number of prime wave assets now seen as natural capital for the country's *blue economy*. In terms of risk minimization one of the potential solutions to the avoidance of this potential lost opportunity is to immediately begin the process of integrating surfing area development into an imaginative strategy that will build a long-lasting management of our national marine protected areas (MPAs). Our MPA system has a target of 20 million hectares of MPAs to be established and managed in Indonesia by 2020. By pursuing this course of action, surfing areas can become zoned and given a clear legal support in local, provincial and national governance. Indonesia will start this approach by concentrating initially on its most iconic existing surf locations which have already become overwhelmed and threatened by uncontrolled rapid development such as the Uluwatu Bukit Peninsula, Bali. This can then be extended as the lessons learned and success gained can then be applied to other surf areas in the country.

"Uluwatu, on Bali's Bukit Peninsula, was cemented in surfing history when Rusty Miller and Steve Cooney paddled out for the filming of Morning of the Earth in 1971. The combination of perfect reef formation, consistent swell, and seasonably predictable winds has led to Uluwatu becoming one of the most highly visited waves on the planet. The main surf area is located within close proximity to the most famous and sacred ocean temple of Bali, the Pura Luhur Uluwatu. The Uluwatu region therefore has cultural significance for more than just surfers. The draw of Uluwatu has led to an expansion of surf tourism across the entire Bukit Peninsula with more than ten breaks surfed regularly. Additionally, the marine resources and fisheries of the Bukit Peninsula are biologically diverse, as the area also functions as feeding grounds of Olive Ridley and Green turtles as well as dugongs, also key sightings are made of large schools of dolphins as well it is also a migratory route of Sperm and Breedy's whales. These facts make the Bukit Peninsula not just important from the viewpoint of being a valuable surfing area but also it shows the Bukit to be a high priority region for marine and cultural conservation, which is critical to the livelihoods of local people.

"Unfortunately, the surf, coastal and marine resources of the Bukit are under increasing threat. Tourism has brought rapid and unplanned development and with it, erosion, sedimentation, sewage, marine debris, and over-fishing for seafood, ultimately degrading the environmental and sociocultural resource itself. Uluwatu and the Bukit are now at risk of becoming a tourism 'boom to bust' story, with major threats all acting on the site's natural value highlighting a clear lack of planning and management. The Bukit area's development mirrors the unplanned and sporadic development of the entire island of Bali which currently faces extreme threats to the natural capital which if left unchecked will subsequently ruin the island's natural assets.

"Fortunately, there is now an opportunity to advance sustainable management of the Bukit Peninsula as part of Bali's growing network of Marine Protected Areas (MPA) that is mandated by the Indonesian coastal act number 27/2007 on integrated coastal management, act number 31/2004 on fisheries and also legally strengthened by the Bali Government regulation (PERDA) number 16/2009 on the 20 year Bali Spatial Plan. The Perda 16 provides strong policy for a no development zone within a 5 km boundary of the Uluwatu Temple. This protection is, if well enforced, necessary for sustaining not just the ecological services of the Uluwatu area but also the socio-cultural beliefs and values of the Balinese stakeholders. Within the framework of the MPA network, each MPA will be designed to protect the unique biological, cultural, economic, and recreational values of each site. This will ultimately contribute to the overall responsible management of Bali's marine resources which in turn will encourage and support sustainable livelihoods for local communities.

"For practical reasons, at least one appropriately sized MPA would have to be established in each of Bali's regencies which would incorporate applied sciences in their zonation system and be well managed by the local capacities. By establishing a well managed MPA network, Bali would be able to demonstrate in practice the "ridge to reefs" concept (Nyegare Gunung – the ancient Balinese mantra for guiding the decision making for sustainable development) and also Tri Hita Karana philosophy (Balinese philosophy in sustainable development based on the balance between people, nature and God) and this should therefore create a new greener path for managing the current and future development impact on Bali. Both of these concepts need to be well translated in practical terms in order to guide how the ecological connectivity ("cause and effect"), which exists between the ridges and reefs, can be prioritized in order to control Bali's development and successfully manage the island's resource sustainability.

Uluwatu and the larger Bukit Peninsula have therefore been identified as a high priority for management within this network of managed areas.

"What does a MPA mean for resident and traveling surfers, local communities, government and business? An MPA encourages all users to develop an awareness of our surrounding natural environment and how we interact with it on a daily basis. It challenges the psychology of travelling surfers along with tourists and business managers in that it encourages them to take responsibility of their actions and behaviours while they are visiting or operating businesses within our well known and semi remote surfing areas. By having a management board for the surfing area/MPA, the local communities will have more voices/chances to integrate their socio-cultural values into the development plan of their areas. They will become empowered to manage their own natural capital, potential revenue can be raised locally for maintaining their community/cultural infrastructures (such as the village temples, public service restrooms for surfers/tourists, garbage bins and area management) and this could create green jobs. Through the development of user based fees or tariffs similar to that of visiting a national park or a ski/snowboard resort the surfers/tourists would assist the locals in creating a responsible management for green and clean surf areas which will benefit all stakeholders. Transparent, accountable and professional management of such funds would ensure that a fully functional surfing reserve could operate within a high quality and functional MPA. The government would benefit from this on many levels as they can then promote the values of the *blue economy* which is supported by matching commitments from tourists/surfers/businesses that help fund the programs. All user experiences are enhanced by the establishment of a long-term vision which would ensure that similar quality experiences are maintained for future generations.

"The successful implementation of an 'Uluwatu Surf Reserve' model can lead to a similar framework being transposed to other significant surfing areas in Indonesia such as Grajagan, East Java, Lagundri Bay in Southern Nias, Lakey Peak in Sumbawa and to the Mentawai Islands of West Sumatera. The incorporation of all surfing areas into the national MPA management system will see Indonesia create a new innovative pathway towards managing the natural capital of our archipelagic nation and at once greening the development of the blue planet".

Pak Ketut concluded his above vision with an inviting Balinese call to adventure: "Come and join me, lets make this happen". I am heartened by Pak Ketut's surfing reserve vision for Indonesia. I trust that I will see it come to fruition in my lifetime, as I feel it is an extraordinary opportunity for us to address the needs of all stakeholders in threatened Indonesian surfing environments; it creates something both functional and unique, which goes well beyond the flag naming status awarded to surfing reserves in several western democracies. A call to adventure always entails a quest. The quest to create a responsible world simply mirrors our own personal quest to find ourselves. These are serious matters indeed and in such circumstances it is good to have the advice of the experienced Yvon Chouinard, to keep everything in perspective: "It's kinda like the quest for the holy grail. Well, you know who gives a shit what the holy grail is. It's the quest is what's important". To nourish and nurture us in our combined quest, we have only to tap the source of stoke which sustains all of our pursuits both in and out of the water. On the Surferspirit Surfrider website of Hawaii, I recently found the wellspring from which stoke arises in the following shamanic description of our ancient art of expression.

"He`e Nalu, means to slide on churning water, to start anew, In Hawaiian, surfing is called he`e nalu. Literally translated, it means, 'to slide on churning water'; however, its significance is reflected in the deeper meaning of one of its root words: nalu, which also means 'amniotic fluid'. When we are born we can be thought to he`e nalu. To the Hawaiian sensibility, surfing is a means of celebrating life. To go into nalu is to return to the womb, to cleanse, and to leave it, is to be born anew. The ancient Hawaiian ritual of Pi kai, or Pi wai, is the practice of cleansing in water to wash away negativity and impurity"[5].

Stoke is like a tap root that connects us to the amniotic fluid of consciousness in Goswami's Ground of Being, to the quantum state of mind where the surfer, the board, hand glide or body, together with the wave and the ocean, momentarily all dissolve into one. There are many waves it seems; in the quantum world, they say that all light is either in particle or waveform. Light carries energy and information; maybe all three are indivisible. It seems highly likely that the small, physical wave we ride (as a part of a bigger ocean) is just a mere ripple, upon a universal confection of an infinite variety of waves, containing both spirit and matter, in the Great Mother of Consciousness. It could be said that all sentient beings are surfers of the standing waves of possibility.

If one substitutes master mythologist Joe Campbell's 'bliss' for 'stoke' then we can sublimely connect with Campbell's prescient advice that resonates deeply in surfers of all generations: "If you follow your bliss, you put yourself on a kind of track that has been there all the while, waiting for you, and the life that you ought to be living is the one you are living. Wherever you are—if you are following your bliss, you are enjoying that refreshment, that life within you, all the time"[6]. Tom Blake followed his bliss his whole life and worshipped daily in the Church of the Blessed Open Sky, a nugget of wisdom from his extraordinary life remains pertinent today, especially to students of life: "The knowledge you get in schools and colleges is second hand", said Tom, "the wisdom and know-how you get from the sea and waves and water is virgin, new and fleeting. By all means get some of this kind of education."[7]

The responsible management of our physical world rests in our hands. Do not expect 'the powers that be' to suddenly become involved in caring for the environment, especially as they spurn every opportunity of developing a compassionite attitude to actively care for the world. We need to constantly balance our outlook on life and continue to imbibe the elixir of stoke that connects spirit and matter. In doing so, we will overcome the potential to be caught like a deer in the headlights when our individual commitment to the environment is needed.

Along the road less travelled in 1975 on our search for Santosha, my companion John Geisel and I had the good fortune to share the equatorial grandeur of Lagundri Bay in Southern Nias with Peter Troy the archetypal traveller surfer of the '60s and '70s. Peter gave me some much needed clarity in dealing with the dilemma of understanding the nature of change: "It really is hard to realize that our paradises just can't be kept, I expect that's the way life is, and what for me is important is to know it and not be disturbed by what the progress of time does, for somebody already knew it for something else before oneself experienced it".

John and I became vagabonds of the vicarious in our search for Santosha; it now seems a contradiction in terms, looking somewhere else for that which one essentially carries within oneself. Maybe Larry Yates was jesting with us after all, or maybe the penny has finally dropped for me. The following quote from the Chasing Santosha website poetically articulates the paradox. Santosha is the Sanskrit term for "contentment" – one of the Niyamas from the eight limbs of Yoga. It is the Peace that is already inside, independent from external sources. So to "chase Santosha" is actually impossible and almost farcical, like the ocean reaching out to the rain for wetness: "Contentment is serenity, but not complacency. It is comfort, but not submission; reconciliation, not apathy; acknowledgment, not aloofness. Contentment is a mental decision, a moral choice, a practiced observance, a step into the reality of the Cosmos. Contentment/Santosha is the natural state of our Humanness and our divinity and allows for our creativity and love to emerge. It is knowing our place in the universe at every moment. It is Unity, with the largest, most abiding, reality"[8].

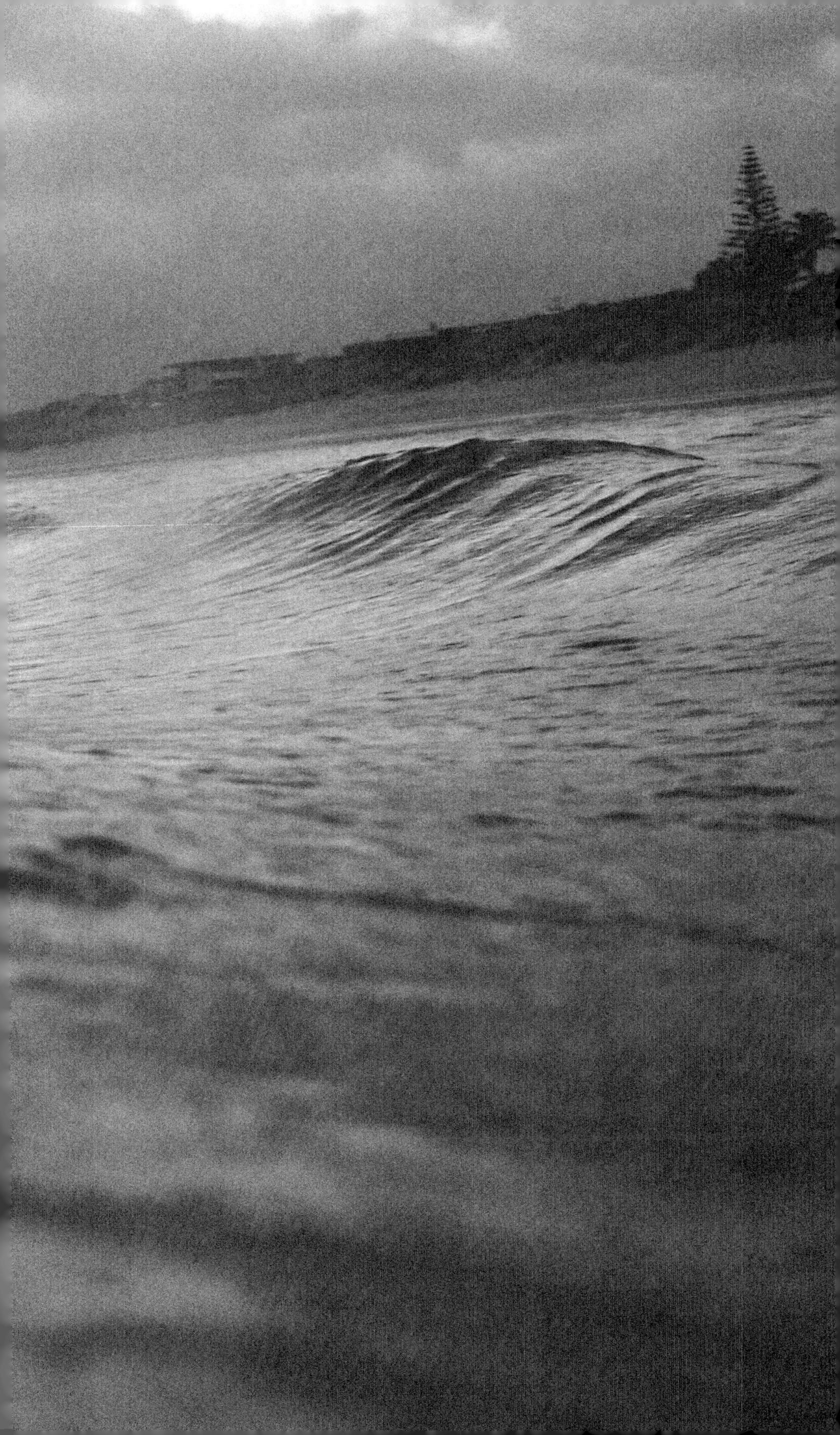

8.2

The Future of Surfing Is Not Disposable

Glenn Hening

If the surfing world has been severely corroded by factors that are only getting worse, then the future of surfing is disposable – and has already been thrown away. Consider what one successful surf shop owner said to me, several years ago, about surfing's future. I was showing him my novel, *Waves of Warning*, and when he saw the subtitle, *Polynesia, Wall Street, and the Future of Surfing*, he laughed and said: "The future of surfing? Surfing doesn't have a future. It's over and it's never coming back. Excuse me, Glenn, but I'm pretty busy. Leave me a few copies. Maybe I can sell one or two."

From that perspective, the idea of sustaining something for surfing's future can be seen as little more than re-arranging the deckchairs on the Titanic. If we are serious about this transition to a new version of surfing, we'd better be clear as to what we're up against. Therefore, to define the problem I'll discuss both the illusions and the realities dominating much of the surfing word. Then, to solve the problem, I'll look at ways we bend the curve when it comes to creating a new definition of a surfer, a surfer who will gladly answer the challenge of a sustainable stoke.

The Surfing World: The Illusion

Waves and the pleasure they provide are the two strands of surfing's DNA, and they will always be connected in a variety of ways. Since there are always going to be waves, we will always take pleasure from them. Surfing represents the perfect escape from daily life and is the perfect marketing hook.

This illusion fills the magazines, websites, surf shops, the clothing company marketing campaigns, the accessories industry and every version of making money directly within the world of surfing. That illusion is also used relentlessly by 'outsiders' to sell everything from bank accounts to deodorant. Even NASCAR had a surfboard shaped trophy for their recent race in Southern California (though the racetrack was built on an abandoned steel mill site 40 miles from the ocean). Mickey Mouse is a surfer too – on top of a spouting wave at Disneyland, Hong Kong. And so, the illusion of surfing is stronger than ever. And as long as waves break on coastlines around the world, that illusion of the freedom and beauty of riding a wave will always be with us.

In 2013, that saturation was taken to new heights when Body Glove ran television commercials for surf schools, apparently calculating that the only way to get new customers is to make them surfers. At the other end of the spectrum, you have the traffic jam at Teahupoo during a recent swell. Twelve tow-in teams were carving up the break to the point that the inventor of tow-in surfing, Laird Hamilton, was publicly upset and went so far as to make his displeasure known through a variety of PR channels.

I think the idea of transitioning to sustainability in the surfing world will not get much interest from marketers, press agents, advertising firms, and corporations. The illusion of surfers as the last rebels is too embedded in our culture, and you can expect to see the proof of that every spring and summer in commercials, print ads, and marketing campaigns trading on the images of surfers as society's free spirits. So, let's turn to modern surfing's realities, where we'll find things are no better because surfers themselves are to blame.

The Realities of Surfing: As a Business, a Contact Sport, and As a 'Religion'
Ah, the surfer's dream: solitary, alone or with a few friends, simply focused on what the ocean provides, using Nature's energy to fly over the water until the ride is over, and then paddling out for another, and another. If this is surfing's reality to you, the reader, then hold on to it like a precious pearl, because for the vast majority of surfers, the surfer's dream has become something of a nightmare.

Surfing as a Business
Let's start with the surf industry. It is no such thing. Despite fringe efforts to put an earnest face of efforts to help spread the 'stoke of surfing' the first thing we have to remember is that the surf industry is not the *surf industry*, it is the clothing business with a good hook. Witness recent upheavals at industry leaders Quiksilver and Billabong, publicly traded corporations whose balance sheets have imploded because shareholders aren't interested in sharing the stoke: they want ROI, plain and simple. Return-on-investment is the name of the game, and when surf corporation CEOs can't keep up with analysts' expectations, they are shown the door, and not always politely. Nike pulled the plug on their surf initiative when the path to profitability proved to be a losing proposition.

The founders of Volcom and Reef saw all this a long time ago and sold out while they could, and there are glimmers of hope here and there thanks to Volcom's green initiatives and Reef supporting the ISA's growth. The reality of surfing as a business – versus sustainability in surfing – is, however, pretty clearcut: Don't expect ad campaigns such as, "If you own three pairs of our board shorts, you don't need more." There will not be any breaking out of the consumption cycle as long as shareholders want ever increasing ROI. So you won't hear any of the major companies announcing, "We've reached the sweet spot between business and quality of life issues, and we plan no further growth." Patagonia has, to its credit, broken through that conundrum, but only because they've had almost 30 years to build their company's reputation such that they are growing, and doing so in a sustainable way.

As for everyone else making a buck in modern surfing, unless you can show them how sustainability will make them more money, all I can say is, "fuggedaboutit." Meanwhile, they'll throw money at creating new icons to serve as avatars for their corporations. Dane Reynolds not only makes a lot of money, but now he's in charge of framing Quiksilver's next 'soul surfer', who conveniently has really long hair and comes off as just a regular guy. But I'll hold off further criticism of the so-called 'surf industry' for a moment – as we're going to need them if the transition to sustainability in surfing is going to work in quantifiable terms. SIMA got on board with the EcoBoard Initiative established by Sustainable Surf. Like any product line, it's the numbers that count – how many items actually 'checked through' and were not returned within 90 days? Solid sales figures are always needed for the balance sheet.

Surfing as Contact Sport
First off, let's be clear: surfing is not much of a sport, since contests are nothing more than marketing events where eyeballs are everything even if the surf's flat. At every level, where is the sport when the playing field is never level? What is sporting about a contest run on a schedule that often mean surfers are battling each other in mediocre waves, or worse, none at all? Witness a recent US Open of Surfing women's final, when the lady who lost did not ride one wave during the 35 minute final because there were no waves, with the winner earning a few measly points by hopping to her feet just before the crumbling white water collapsed on the sand?

Or ask the so-called leaders of surfing, the top surfers in the world as quantified by cover shots, ad space, contest results, marketing campaigns, media coverage, and their employment status as models for clothing companies: can they tell you where all their broken boards have ended up since they signed their first sponsorship contract? Guys on the ASP World Tour are going through up to 200 boards a year chasing 'the magic board'. As it turns out, opium addicts have a name for that: its called 'chasing the dragon'. The non-competitive pro surfers are no better. At least the guys on Tour have one problem solved: they get to surf good waves to themselves thanks to water patrols at their contest. In fact, surfing in competitive events provides such an increase in standing time on decent waves that contest surfing almost becomes what surfing used to be. Or as Kelly said after losing the world championship last winter, "Hey, at least I got to surf pipe by myself for half an hour."

Seen as a contact sport, the surfing world is little more than a collection of intensely crowded free-for-all zones whenever any waves are breaking – unless a contest is scheduled, in which case the water is kept clear of public intruders. And why? Because that's the way the contact version of surfing sustains itself. That these so-called sporting events are paid for out of marketing budgets of international clothing companies to showcase the best surfers in the world who all work for those companies! No matter that surf-star wannabes are scratching through heats in amateur contests when getting sponsored is the real prize.

Surfing as a Religion

But forget the industry, the crowds, the trade shows, the Boardstroms surf shops, the contests, the surf reports, and all the hype around the above. What about the true believers in surfing's panoply of participants, those who believe in the wondrous powers of riding waves as worthy of true devotion. Well, for the most part, you can forget them, too. Or at least up to now, most of them have been noticeably absent from the movement to bring sustainability to surfing. For the most part they can't be bothered with surfing's problems, like bad parents who try to ignore calls from school about their child's behavior. It's all they can do to keep from slowly fading away thanks to crowds, lack of waves, getting out of shape, etc. Ask them about their responsibilities as adults charged with setting an example for the next generation, and you'll get a blank stare more often than not. They do have a solution, though, if they can afford it: book a reservation to a surfing resort! Taken as a whole, that aspect of surfing does not, once again, give us much hope. The Center for Surf Research has made landmark efforts to introduce the concept of sustainability to surf camps, resorts, and surf travel agencies, and for good reason. Far too often, what has happened is little better than spreading all of surfing's ills to a controlled environment where, once again, somebody is making money. But at least we are scratching the itch of nostalgia, which, like poison oak, is indeed a poison.

Taking Surfing to 'The Next Level'
Anyone who believes in the above phrase does so with only one thing in mind: profit. In fact, the next time you hear the phrase, be sure to ask, "The next level of what? And why? And who benefits?" Although you might hear a bunch of bullshit about mainstream public recognition, taking surfing to the next level will only happen if there is money in it.

Look at surfing as a contact sport: would the next level be dialing back the aggression, reducing the hype for the next swell, or wanting another good wave as soon as possible, or taking waves from others in the water who don't have the skill or the inclination to compete for waves? In fact, we are only increasing the granularity of data in surfing, what with all kinds of data-intensive approaches to the simple process of riding a wave. As a result, with the ubiquitous availability of surf reports, no swell will be left uncrowded, no surf resort will book less guests rather than more, no surfboard manufacturer will happily make less boards to reduce crowds, and there doesn't seem to be any stopping the growth of surfing into a mainstream sport.

We've already touched on 'the next level' as exemplified by the television commercial for SurfCamp (during Lakers games, no less), sponsored by Body Glove, in late March, to book wannabe surfers for lessons in June. A far better and more trenchant example is ZoSea. Take a moment to Google them if you need some background, and then correct me if I'm wrong in seeing ZoSea as a purely for-profit sports marketing and media concern taking over the pro surf tour in order to advance surfing to 'the next level'. The clothing companies can no longer fit contests into their business plans, so a former Quiksilver board member is now playing a major role in defining the new face of pro surfing. And let's not forget Red Bull, those brave and impetuous caffeine saturated adventurers. They are coming into surfing in a big way, and with a constant emphasis on the personalities of the top pros so they can be positioned as celebrities with the marketing niche, things look pretty good at least two business cycles forward.

As for the rest of us, well, they speak to us of the next level. We're looking at a future for surfing where major surf spots are so choked with newcomers, old-timers, practicing pros, washed up surf stars, and every manner of board imaginable that the idea of surfing as some kind of beautiful connection with the special powers of the sea is, well, you can either laugh or cry.

The fundamental flaw in all this is that you can't build a storm the way you can build a racetrack. You can't buy a swell the way you can clear a mountain for a ski run. You can't build a set of reefs in a stadium and have surfers challenged with a variety of wave forms during the course of a single ride. And though the surf parks idea is gaining a lot of momentum, unfortunately the pitch to the money people is about, you guessed it, 'taking surfing to the next level'. And who knows, maybe the surf park people will be the answer to the prayers of the big company shareholders who would love to see all that surfer stuff moving out the door of retailers across the country.

Surfrider, NGOs, CSR, etc
San Diego State's Center for Surf Research was, at its conception, a remarkable effort to study and/or address any number of the sustainability issues facing the surfing world. Now, four years later, CSR is finding that sourcing funding for its programmes from the surf industry is much more difficult than originally anticipated. The Center for Surf Research is a milestone in surfing's history – the EcoBoard inititative – the growing number of boards in the water that are not clear thrusters covered with logos – things *are* changing in surfing as more and more surfers realise that constantly competing for waves is a dead-end street. It is true: the Rincon Invitational, a team surfing benefit event is run entirely without corporate sponsors or competitive pressures.

It is true at beach days run by surf clubs and non-profit organizations where disadvantaged youth are introduced to the simple joy of having a wave push them through the water and it is true for Sustainable Surf's EcoBoard project: surfboard disposability. As for as the latter, the reality of surfing is so subjective that I don't know if there's anything to be done other than appeal to surfers to be more generous and ultimately more dedicated to the surfing community, as opposed to the commerce or competition that drives so much of what passes for the public version of surfing in this day and age.

The Transition to Sustainability in the Surfing World: why every surfer owes a debt – and many are starting to hold up their end of the bargain
Surfing is amazing – just show a surf movie in Siberia or a village in Central Africa, and you'll see a wonder in the faces of the audience as if they are watching what heaven must be like. Many travelling surfers have experienced that first

hand, and indeed it is that sense of wonder inherent in surfing that makes it so easy to use surfing to sell products. Surfers, therefore, are as lucky as they come on the global scale of human endeavor, and it is my contention that, because surfers are so blessed, they have a debt to pay. Unfortunately, as we've seen when surfing is turned into a business, a contact sport, or a religion, few have turned that sense of gratitude into tangible, actionable initiatives with measurable results. This is what the transition to sustainability in the surfing world will have to do. That will happen, and even now is happening, when every person who wants to enjoy the unique sensation of riding a wave comes to realise that surfers owe a debt that can only be repaid in a subtle, yet consistent, way that has nothing to do with making a buck, winning a trophy, taking a wave from a kook or staring down a visitor over your home break.

It is safe to say that sustainability in today's surfing world is not going to bring back the magic that was the surfing of the past, and that's okay. What has to happen is the creation of a future that will focus on conscious consumerism, that includes sharing responsibility for the environment in a direct and tangible way as well as changing attitudes in the line-up when it comes to keeping the 'stoke' alive for surfing's future generations. If the golden days of surfing are long gone and the surf museum memberships are skewing increasingly to senior discounts, if today's public version of surfing looks increasingly oversold, overhyped and over crowded, then it's easy to think surfing's past is becoming little more than memories, corroding trophies, and veteran surfers saturated with nostalgia. But if there are more surf schools every summer, there is an implicit responsibility that can be lived up to by actively supporting the transition to sustainability in the surfing world.

Glenn and an early 'sustainable' surfboard (1999) in preparation for a serious sandbar session at Oxnard Shores. Board design and fins by Rick Vogel, shaping by Robbie Dick, bamboo veneer shell by Gary Young. Board has no stringer as the bamboo shell (fiberglass was not used) is strong enough to hold the rocker perfectly. The board is still as strong as ever – and Glenn uses it every chance he gets.
(Courtesy of Glen Henning)

8.3

Surfing Can Change The World

Chris Hines

Surfing can and, I think, should play a role in helping change the world. Maybe 'change the world' is too strong a statement because the world will chug along with or without us and with or without surfers. There is no doubt that humans are having an detrimental impact on the planet and its complex systems, and it is undeniable that we can make a difference, positively or negatively, as individuals, communities, companies and cultures. It is also true that, as surfers, we can make a difference.

There is a critical starting point, which I have dubbed 'The Deal'. Simply, we live on this amazing planet and we need to give something back. It's beautiful, awe inspiring. Our every experience, from birth to death is down to this planet. As surfers, we have an added appreciation factor – we live and surf on a planet that is seven-tenths water and has more ocean and coastline than is comprehensible. There are all the amazing set-ups from beaches to points to reefs, plus the weather systems that whizz around creating all those swells and waves we surf. Imagine being surfers on a planet with seven-tenths land and only one ocean. The amazing thing is, we are some of the luckiest of the lucky.

Surfers are one of the few tribes/cultures/sportspeople that interact with the natural environment in its raw state. Along with climbers, walkers, canoeists, skiers and sailors we don't go to a building or a pitch. We get out there, come rain or shine, in perfect offshore peaks or onshore mush. As such, we are arguably more in tune and have more to gain or lose by the state of that environment. We also stand to gain or lose according to the level of conflict between nations, religions and beliefs. A peaceful and safe world opens up more waves and the ability to travel to them; everyone, irrespective of race, faith or gender should get a chance to surf if they wish. In the West, we are incredibly lucky – very few surfers live on less than a dollar a day. Very few of us will have to walk five kilometres for our water and the vast majority of us have a flushing toilet and a shower. When we travel, we experience the lack of some of these comforts, but this is only temporary, part of the colour of our surf trip. They are not our daily and life-long reality.

So, the deal is we give something back: we care about our oceans, our planet, our weather systems and we care about the flora and fauna that inhabit this planet (including all 7 billion of us!). We try to be MAD, to Make A Difference. We all have a latent, hidden potential – I have been lucky enough to experience it, to have a chance to act on it and to use surfing as a force for positive change. In 1990, I was one of the co-founders of Surfers Against Sewage and was privileged to run the organisation from 1990 until 2000. Here is some of the history of the campaign and a few lessons that I learnt along the way – an example of what can happen if you believe.

Surfers Against Sewage 1990 to 2000
A small group of us centered around the Cornish beaches of Porthtowan and St. Agnes were becoming increasingly sick (sometimes literally) of the gross pollution hitting our beaches. After some discussion and yet another day of attempting, sometimes unsuccessfully, to dodge the panty-liners, condoms and slick of human sewage that we were surfing in, we decided to do something about it. In 1990, a meeting was called at Minzy's house and anyone who wanted in was invited along. Ange (Andrew Kingsley-Tubbs) had coined the name Surfers Against Sewage. There were a dozen or so of us there, four of us put £10 in a pot and we agreed to call a public meeting two weeks later.

We had a simple aim, that we held in our hearts and our minds: to be able to enjoy the coast, beaches and surf for the wonderful thing that it is. We wanted to be able to go surfing without fear of infection or feeling the sheer revulsion of ducking under a wave and coming up with a panty liner stuck to your hair (true story). Importantly, we didn't just care about us as surfers, we cared about all the people using the sea and the health of the oceans themselves. We were just the litmus paper, the canary in the coal mine.

We were challenged: "Who cares about a bunch of ugly old surfers? Isn't this just a selfish, whingeing campaign?" The best rebuff and justification was a quote from the World Health Authority: "Children between the ages of 6 and 11 are the most at risk from infection as they have lost the inherited immunity from their mothers and have yet to fully develop their own." This age group just love to play and laugh in the water. I have even been called to give evidence at the Inquest into the death of an eight-year-old girl who had died from E.Coli

0157 poisoning. The coroner ruled that contact with raw sewage at a combined sewer overflow was a possible route of infection.

We knew there was a problem but we probably didn't quite realise just how big a problem it was. In 1989, at the privatisation of the water industry in the UK, Prime Minister Thatcher stated on a BBC documentary that: "All sewage is treated before discharge"[1]. That was a downright lie. The reality was that 400 million gallons of completely crude sewage was being discharged around the coast of Britain every single day. Not even basic screening was applied; literally what was flushed went straight into the sea. For surfers, (including visiting pros for the contests) in Newquay, with a summertime population of 100,000, it was the equivalent of the English football team running out onto the pitch at Wembley Stadium and every one of the 100,000 crowd having pooped on the pitch! If there was a handy piece of coastline next to a city, town or village then the sewage had been discharged to sea via a short foul outfall pipe. At most of these it was possible to stand on the end of the pipe or straight above it. No doubt a huge step forward in terms of public health in Victorian times, but hardly fitting for the late 20th Century.

The UK was rightfully dubbed the 'Dirty Man of Europe'. The tourist industry was in denial; one councillor even called for a ban on surfing in Newquay if we didn't shut up and go away. As we raised our heads in Cornwall, so we were contacted from surfers and other beach users around the country. This was a national problem and it would require national campaigning.

It's easy to whinge and complain, but we were clear that we wanted more than that, we wanted to find a solution. We wanted the sewage treated. And we didn't just want a long sea outfall which was the water industry's favoured answer – simply pump it further out to sea. The problem with this so-called solution was that the indicator organisms that were used to monitor water quality at the beaches had a rapid die-off rate. They were gone within a few hours, whereas the nasty little viruses and bacteria could survive for days in salt water. Hepatitis A could live for nearly a hundred days.

We searched high and low and found that on the island of Jersey they had some foresight. Unlike the dirty UK mainland, they had realised the value of clean seas to tourism and their visitor economy and had invested in treating their sewage. They had put in preliminary (screening for panty liners etc.) primary (let the big lumps settle out) and secondary (biological digestion of the remaining faecal matter) and had a pretty clear, but still viral and bacterial, loaded effluent. They had looked at a long-sea outfall (at the cost of £11 million) or an ultraviolet light disinfection plant (£2 million). They had gone for the UV option and the bacterial indicator count in their outfall pipe was 50 times cleaner than the standard that our government was saying was OK on our beaches (these beaches that were so grossly polluted, yet passed the inadequate tests). We quoted this evidence in a written submission to the House of Lords and I was called to give evidence to a Select Committee[2]. When questioned about this treatment I stated that, based on the figures, I would feel 50 times safer sticking my head up Jersey's outfall pipe than bathing on so-called 'passed' beaches.

A week later, we were contacted by Jersey's tourism department who had heard of our statement. They thought this would make some excellent high-profile marketing for them and I was invited to the island. A few days later, with dignitaries and the media gathered, I suited up, jumped off the end of the pipe, turned and paddled as hard as I could and duck-dived into the mouth of the pipe discharging 100,000 peoples sewage. I got a metre up the pipe before I was blown back out with the force, but I stood by what I had said: It looked, tasted and smelled a whole lot cleaner than many of the beaches we were surfing on! We'd found our solution and it was £9 million cheaper than the old long-sea outfall option. We now had a stick with which to challenge the water companies.

Creating and Communicating Change

Even when you have a solution, it is still hard work to help create the conditions where change can happen. We'd always said we were as keen to support and push for the right thing as we were to campaign against the raw sewage. So when Welsh Water (one of the 10 privatised water companies in the UK) adopted a full sewage-treatment policy and invited us to open their first full-treatment works, we cut the ribbon by the Surfers Against Sewage's name on the brass plaque at the works.

We did the same for Wessex Water and on that occasion their Chief Executive, Colin Skellett, also donned a wetsuit and the two of us had buckets of the final effluent poured over our heads by the local mayor. This treatment works featured micro filtration which takes out 99.98% of all bacteria and viruses. It was important for us to understand the pressures that existed for these companies. They had to meet shareholder demands, treat drinking water and treat and dispose of sewage. We bought shares in all of their companies, which allowed us to not only attend their Annual General Meetings but also, as shareholders, to ask any question we wished. We often stole the media coverage and pushed the issue up the agenda.

We would also brief financial journalists and commentators and could affect their share prices. Working with SAS and solving the problems made good PR and ultimately financial sense. In most of these situations we had the advantage of being nimble on our feet and benefitted hugely from the 'David and Goliath' and 'underdog' scenarios that often played out. We used the law: using LegalAid with two young mothers, we carried out a successful Judicial Review in the High Court setting legal precedent for the whole of the UK as well as creating mass-media coverage[3]. We'd even given the local council the chance to do the right thing and issue an abatement notice (Section 79 (e) of the Environmental Protection Act) against South West Water, but they chose to ignore us and their own evidence. They learnt a lesson – take surfers seriously.

Key in any campaign is a political will to succeed and people who shy away from this are, in my view, copping out. We live in a part of the world where we can challenge the political system, we can demonstrate and lobby parliament and politicians. In many countries in the world this is far harder with the risk of arrest, beatings and, in some places, death. As surfers, we should ask our local and national politicians where they stand on policies that affect our lives and the ocean environment. We should stand up and be counted.

SAS lobbied the House of Commons within ten months of forming. We knew that if we wanted change we had to go to the corridors of power, to where laws and legislation and big political decisions are made. It was an easy process and the Sergeant At Arms even allowed us to stash our boards outside when we went into Parliament dressed in our wetsuits. We lobbied our individual Members of Parliament (MPs) in the central lobby of the House of Commons, asking them for their support. From there we headed into a debating room. Due to the pressure and media coverage we were successful in pulling the Minister for the Environment. He was, in effect, forced to come and defend the government's position. The Government announced, on the morning of our lobby, that they were committing £2 million into research into the health effects of sewage-contaminated sea water. By the act of going in person, we had triggered action.

In 1994, one of our members, Glyn Ford MEP (Member of the European Parliament), invited us to meet and brief the President of the European Parliament. We took a party of ten of the leading names in surfing and other water sports. Glyn met us at the EP. Dressed in our wetsuits with boards and our ten-foot high inflatable poo, we were greeted by Glyn, a keen windsurfer and occasional surfer, who revealed his wetsuit under his coat. We had half an hour to brief President Egon Klepsch on how and why some of the legislation wasn't effective or was being dodged by the UK Government. We also had the chance to explain how full sewage treatment was more effective than building the old pump and dump long-sea outfalls.

We have been described as media whores but we knew, instinctively, that the surfing imagery was what sold the story of the sewage contamination of the beaches and we played the surfing ticket mercilessly. The media lapped up the images of gas mask wearing surfers challenging the might of the private water companies and government. The more media coverage we got, the more we drove it up the public agenda and the more it went up the public agenda, the more the politicians took note. We appeared on TV, from BBC *Panorama* to the World Service and there was even an episode of BBC *Casualty* (a TV drama that had 14 million viewers) based around the SAS story.

Ultimately, it was politics that changed the game. In May 1997, the UK had a change of government. The new Labour government were looking for a quick win and sewage contamination of our beaches was high on the agenda. In September 1997, I was given 24 hours' notice to go to London to be a special advisor to the Rt.Hon Michael Meacher MP, Secretary of State for the Environment. There was nobody from the water industry present, just three senior civil servants from the Department of the Environment, three senior members of the Environment Agency, the Secretary of State, his PA, myself and two other advisors. I had free reign to ask any question I wished. I emerged two hours later punching the air. Shortly after this, the government announced that all sewage would receive at least secondary treatment with tertiary treatment for the two thirds of the outfalls that were close to beaches – an unprecedented £5.5 billion clean up of the UK coastline. It wasn't just our actions that made that happen. Arguably, a lot would have been achieved eventually, but we did strongly influence the pace and level of treatment and ensure the greatest environmental benefit, per pound, of the public's water payments.

All of this came from a group of surfers who knew nothing of political activism, campaigning or sewage treatment. When we started, we were so naïve that we even thought the collective £2 membership fee may be able to buy a sewage treatment works! At times, however, it was our naivety and passion that kept us going. Every time someone said "you can't do that" it simply made us more determined to prove them wrong. There was no blueprint, no textbook on how to do this. Metaphorically, at times, it was like running over a set of stepping stones, except that often, in mid-air it was impossible to know where the next stone was. If we'd stopped and hesitated then we wouldn't have had the momentum to reach the next stone. Throughout, we were independently funded from membership fees, sale of T-shirts and some great fundraising balls (4,500 people partying from dusk till sunrise dressed in black tie and board shorts). SAS never has taken the buck! *Surfer* magazine once said of SAS that we were powered by "righteous outrage!" The BBC News and Current Affairs has described us as: "Some of the Government's most sophisticated environmental critics." And the *Independent* newspaper: "Britain's coolest pressure group."

SAS still has paid-up members today, is nearly 25 years old and is still representing our oceans and all of those who love them. I'm still a fully paid-up member and always will be. Its money I simply can't afford not to spend. I have categorical proof and personal experience that surfing can change the world. The issue now is how to apply it. I left SAS and I spent a year catching up on some well-needed surfing time and then, keen to apply my thinking and experience to a wider spectrum of issues, joined the Eden Project in 2001. Sustainable Development was the new buzz and I became Sustainability Director. Sustainability impacts on every aspect of our lives, from the food we eat, to the resources we use, the waste we create and the air we breathe. From the day we are born until the day we die, we all have an impact. Sustainability is about minimising that impact and maximising our output.

One of the biggest challenges facing us is climate change. Climate change affects everyone in terms of rising sea levels, increased storm activity and extreme weather patterns. For surfers, this will inevitably mean bigger storms and bigger waves, but it will also mean some island reefs going under and existing surf breaks changing or disappearing for good. Hurricane Sandy caused many deaths in Haiti before slamming into the New Jersey coast and causing a tidal surge into New York. The shoreline was breached and one of the richest, biggest cities was hit.

Another ferocious storm hit Australia's Gold Coast only a few weeks before the inaugural Global Surf Cities Conference. Images of Burleigh on steroids were on TV broadcasts with a right hander cranking through Meesh's restaurant! Twenty feet of sand washed from the foreshore, wooden walkways hanging over sand cliffs and a significant fall in tourist bookings. After such an onslaught, insurance of beachside properties will rocket, if it is still available at all. We need to break our addiction to oil. A quick inventory of the average surfer reveals a dependence – boards, wetsuits and an industry-driven culture that idolises frequent and short-lived travel.

Surfing as the Hook

Surfing has been prostituted, used and abused to sell everything from burgers to beer, to cars and computers – most of it with no thought or link to the natural world or the ocean. Much of the advertising industry probably wouldn't know which side to wax a board. The collective purveyors of mass/brainless/ uncaring consumerism literally use this wonderful sport/art/recreation with the sole purpose of increasing profit. To be provocative, it could be said that too much of the surfing industry also operates from this unacceptable, wholly out-of-tune perspective. For an industry that has the natural environment as its fundamental product, there is precious little thought given to sustainability. My proposition is that, just as surfing is used to sell products, if we sort ourselves out, our sport, our industry, our cities and communities, then we can use the surfing hook to sell sustainable living to the world.

What does this mean and how would it look in terms of individual surfers and the sport, product industry and travel and tourist sectors that have developed around surfing? John Elkington of Sustainability.com has devised a 'triple bottom line' take on sustainability which takes into account the environmental and social bottom line as well as the traditional financial bottom line. When a product or service is designed, the idea is that we think about all three.

A suggested initial check list for each bottom line (as we're surfers let's call it the triple bottom wave!) is below. The list won't apply to everything, but if everything around surfing took all of this into account we will have taken some big steps down the right path.

Environmental Wave
- Biodiversity – does the product or service have a negative or positive effect on flora or fauna?
- Energy – renewable, low energy, energy efficient in its manufacture or operation.
- Resources and materials – natural, recycled, recyclable, local.
- Durability – how strong is it, will it last?
- Waste – designed out, reduced, reused, recycled and buy into recycled.
- Water – usage and disposal. Everything we consume or use as a service has a built in water footprint, i.e. the amount of water used in its production.
- Sewage – levels of treatment and notifications (SAS run text alert systems for Combined Sewer Outfalls that notify you when they start operating and then when they stop).

- Transport – reduce if possible, stay as long as possible.
- Light pollution – impacts on other people and a waste of energy.
- Sound pollution - ditto.

Social Wave
- Health and Safety – what were the conditions like in the factory where your board, wetsuit or T-shirt was made?
- Fair pay and working conditions for supply chain and workers, including hours, maternity and paternity pay.
- Child labour – have children been involved in the manufacture of the products? This is against internationally accepted standards. Inevitably children are paid a wage and are in effect denied an education or what many of us would accept a normal childhood.
- Gender balance – equal pay. Representation.
- Job security – something that many of us take for granted.
- Workers/union representation at board level or even at all.
- Accessible/Disabled and disability compliant.
- Inclusive – does your policy include people from all backgrounds, ages and abilities, and ethnic minorities?

Community engagement – is surfing, or the product engaging and working with the community around it. For example are surf camps ensuring that the local host communities gain some benefits from the surf tourists? Do surf contests actually engage with local communities and help deliver long term benefits?

Wage Ratios – in a world which is inhabited by 50% females and 50% males it is only fair that both genders are paid equally for the same work. It is also important that the ratio between the highest paid and lowest paid people in a company have some form of published ratio. There has been an ever increasing gap between the highest paid executives and the lowest paid workers. This isn't fair and also doesn't make for good morale which doesn't bode well for any company. Responsible companies publish their wage ratios. For example, Ben and Jerry's (before being bought out) used to have a wage ratio of 1 to 12. No one in the company got paid any more than twelve times what anyone else did. No limit on how much you can earn, you just have to take everyone else with you.

Fairtrade – people who grow or produce a product get paid a fair price. Fairtrade.org.uk or World Fair Trade Organisation.

Financial Wave
- Valued
- Profit and return on investment
- Money for Maintenance/Repair/Reinvest
- Sustainable and secure
- Long term as well as, and arguably more than, short term
- Supply chain – valued, engaged, fairly treated
- Pricing – fair, inclusive
- Philanthropic – give something back, MAD

None of this is simple. Sometimes doing what feels like the right thing may actually be more complicated and counter-intuitive. As an example, whilst I was at the Eden Project a colleague Pat Hudson and I worked on the EcoBoard as a challenge to the surfing industry. We tried to make a board from as natural materials as possible. The balsa was grown in the humid tropics biome, it was laminated with hemp cloth and a resin made from cashew nuts and a fin made from locally sourced ash. Problem was it was too heavy so we worked with some local companies (Homeblown and Sustainable Composites) towards a bio foam. The products were OK though we lacked serious research and development funding to really pursue it. But we also came across a dilemma: we were blowing 30% plant based foam but the plant based element was made from soya and sourced from a company that had some serious questions relating to deforestation in the Amazon.

In 2011, I helped Greenpeace with a short campaigning film *Surfing the Detox Wave* that used surfing imagery of gnarly Irish pits linked to some shocking pictures of water pollution caused by the clothing industry. The message was to detox your T-shirt, your clothing. Do our T-shirts contribute to water pollution and unsustainable uses of water and land to grow the cotton? If we understand our links to the world we can demand the best in everything that relates to our surfing and we should expect stronger and better leadership in this area from the surfing stars and the industry bosses. Every one of us should join at least one surfing environmental and social organisation and charity, such as Surfers Against Sewage, Surfrider, Surf Aid or one of the many others. Every pro surfer should proudly have these organisations' logos on their boards. The ASP should ensure full sustainability at its contests (great steps have been taken at the Volcom Pro at Pipeline).

There are many people in and around surfing trying, often succeeding, in making positive changes, but it's small fry compared to the impact of surfing as a whole. Many of these people and companies will be in this book and I applaud and welcome the work they do. Is this just a rant? Can we really address these issues? Here are some cold hard figures to make you think, to put it in context beyond our surfing world:

Global yearly spending on luxury items:
- Make-up: US$18 billion
- Perfume: US$15 billion
- Ocean cruises: US$14 billion
- Ice-cream in Europe: US$11 billion

- **Extra annual funds needed to achieve global goals:**
- Eliminate hunger: US$19 billion.
- Reproductive health care for all women: US$12 billion.
- Clean water for all: US$10 billion.
- Universal literacy: US$5 billion.[4]
- Tips for campaigning.
- Huge challenges.
- Tension is good – it drives change.
- Light and quick – If you're 70% sure of something and the 30% isn't going to kill anyone then move forward.
- Be attractive. Make it fun!
- Homo sapiens (especially surfers) can do anything.
- Be passionate.
- Be optimistic and challenge the norm!

Remember 'The Deal' and play your part, live a balanced life. Let's sort out our surfing world, our sport, our products, our travel and the places we live. Then let's use that surfing imagery and spirit to push and promote a truly sustainable way of living... I'm a surfer, and a citizen and was lucky enough to have helped make a difference. I challenge you to do the same!

Chris Hines at the Houses of Parliament, London, March 21st 1991. This was start of the SAS tradition of taking the campaign to the corridors of power, and this hard hitting approach continues today.
(Courtesy of SAS Pictures)

Waves, Environment, Community: Surfing, Sustainability & Surfers Against Sewage

Hugo Tagholm

It has long been said that Surfers Against Sewage represents individuals and communities with a difference. People who aren't merely passive observers of the coastal environment but those who live and breathe the sea, and more often than not find themselves immersed in the ocean. I've often described them as a marine indicator species, who themselves share our beautiful and unique coastal spaces with nature, flora and fauna. As such, SAS members are exposed to environmental issues first hand – walking across litter-strewn beaches, surfing at the mouths of sewer overflows and are acutely sensitive to environmental changes, pollution and developments at their favourite beaches. I believe this is what sets apart SAS supporters from those of many other fantastic charities – our visceral connection with the ocean, with our beaches and with these special coastal spaces.

To pinch a quote from one of my all-time heroes, Jacques Cousteau: "People protect what they love". Unsurprisingly, SAS members truly love their stretch of coastline, feel protective over their corner of this great island, and as such are uniquely placed to protect and conserve 13,000 miles of fantastic natural, coastal capital that the UK is blessed with. I believe that this sense of ownership and belonging is critical to the never-ending task of safeguarding our *sites of special surfing interest*, not just in the UK, but worldwide. Waves and beaches help us foster a sense of stewardship and are, more often than not, the epicentre of engaged and passionate coastal communities

We all have favourite beaches and secret surf spots where we ride waves, interact with wildlife, build sandcastles, take a walk, share family moments, watch sunsets and, arguably, spend some of the best time of our lives. These are free, healthy spaces that can help people learn about the true value of the sea, nature and sustainability. This is what we love. This is what we'll fight to protect.

I feel truly privileged to have my time to lead Surfers Against Sewage, to be a custodian of this amazing charity. Of course, SAS is an environmental charity but I passionately believe that the organisation is a powerful vehicle for social good, connecting and educating individuals and building informed, powerful and effective coastal communities living in harmony with their coastline. I'm simply organising people – passing on stoke, expertise and sharing the powerful networks and reputation SAS has created. After all, we're just a tiny team who share a passion for the ocean. The more people we can involve, the bigger the gains for the environment. This is why we set up a network of 50 highly skilled Regional Reps in every corner of the UK who help us connect, motivate and organise community actions and national campaigns. They, in turn, help us engage thousands of community volunteers and over 100,000 regular campaign supporters around the country.

Many of these talented individuals and grassroots communities joined us in Westminster at the end of 2013 to deliver one of the biggest ever petitions in 'enviro-surf organisation' history. The Protect Our Waves petition included the signatures of over 55,000 supporters calling for more action to protect UK surf spots from pollution and over-development. British surfing waves, like many waves and beaches around the globe, are under threat from a growing number of coastal activities that can hamper or have devastating, long term impacts on some of our most prized surfing zones. This includes coastal developments, pollution, commercial exploitation and restricted access. SAS is working hard to raise the awareness of our surf spots as unique, finite, irreplaceable natural resources that need protection similar to forests and national parks.

There are multiple routes to sustained and effective coastal protection: lobbying, creating new legislation, campaigning, grassroots activism and many others, which need to be deployed in unison to create real, effective and sustained change. The Protect Our Waves petition is calling for new legislation to recognise and protect UK surf spots. This is ambitious but is backed up by a vast number of SAS grassroots campaigns, community initiatives, tangible victories and innovative approaches that are already protecting surfers, water users, waves and beaches nationwide.

As I write this, we're on the cusp of finalising the Protect Our Waves All Party Parliamentary Group (APPG), the result of the petition. This will be a group of cross-party politicians specifically tasked with discussing and delivering better protection for the UK's sites of special surfing interest, the people who use them and the communities that depend on them. This is a significant moment in surfing and sustainability globally. A group of elected representatives, Members of Parliament, in one of the most recognisable democratic institutions in the World, meeting to discuss and solve the environmental concerns of surfers.

It's amazing to look back on the history of Surfers Against Sewage, the successes and the positive change this small organisation has delivered. It has always had a reputation for punching well above its weight, and I'm stoked that it continues to do so with such a force. This force comes from the passion of its staff, members, supporters and representatives, and their direct connection to the ocean, waves and beaches they love. But this is about more than just the waves. The wave is a shared inspiration for surfers, a recognised icon of our work. It is about protecting the whole coastal environment for everyone, for all time.

*Hugo Tagholm, chief executive of SAS is joined by musician & surfer Ben Howard, Stephen Gilbert MP, SAS campaign director Andy Cummins and SAS trustee Lauren Davies to present the Protect Our Waves petition to No. 10 Downing Street, calling for better recognition and protection of sites of special surfing interest.
(Courtesy of Lewis Arnold)*

8.5

Managing the Surfing World in the 21st Century

Brad Farmer

A book on sustainable surfing by a bunch of sustainable stokers – at last. There is nothing as refreshing an idea whose time has come. *tRACKS*, the iconic magazine and a Bible for surfers, has often asserted that 'surfing is better than sex', succinctly putting the sustainable into a seductive context. That is something left for another chapter in time, but surfing is a constant sensual, human and natural expression, which needs to be sustainable. Surfing waves, is a blissful and intoxicating gift from nature.

Stoke, like happiness, is an ephemeral experience, subjective and some don't even recognise it when they have it. Our 'world clock' has become metronomed. It seems that half of us till the agricultural soil for survival, the other half work in the cities. So subjects like a sustainable stoke could be seen as a pursuit of passion or folly for the modern and privileged, given that our forefathers endured great hardships and toil, clearing land and building our living environments. Living as we do now – in relative abundance and wealth, based largely on resources – we must ensure the legacy is valued. We can be consumer-absorbed bystanders, witnessing the coastal and surfing experience coming under increasing pressure, leading to an environment which could become unrecognisable in our lifetime – or we could 'be the change' ourselves.

It is my belief that surfers must become more politically or actively engaged in the protection of their resources – surf breaks. How to achieve that is a challenge and I have floated concepts and instigated organisations to begin that engagement, from National and World Surfing Reserves, CoastCare, Ocean Care Day, World Council of Surfing Elders, Surfrider Foundation Australia to, most recently, the embryonic model of Surf Councils.

The practical action I'd like to propose is: The formation of a United Nations-style of collective surfing groups, working together for local, national and global outcomes.

A passionate engagement of all surfers and people who use the beach, to create and advocate for new policy and laws to protect the resource. If you're reading this, you're probably among the cognisant surfers who are partly curious and probably increasingly concerned about the present and future state of surfing. You are the audience I hope to reach. Maybe you approach surfing with a deeper social consciousness, open to join the discussion on what's to be done to keep the stoke alive. We live on a beautiful and bountiful planet where 70% of us live on coastal plains. In the West it's evident, we live a 'five planet lifestyle': we consume resources like there is no tomorrow. We are part of the 2% of this world who own, control and exploit the planets' resources.

For surfers, the waves that roll onto our shores seem like an endless summer. Assured by nature, but threatened year after surfing year. Surfers are at the top of the pyramid – travelling the globe, buying boards, living the stoke – the luckiest people, living in the luckiest countries, in the luckiest of periods in human history. But the surfer's lifestyle has, and will, gradually change. There are now more surfers in the water, fewer natural surf breaks – and, I'd argue, a challenging time immediately ahead of us to keep the experiential stoke truly sustainable, in the absence of empowered defenders of our surf amenity.

Who is there to recalibrate surfing's ideological compass? There is no 'think tank' of surfers who drive wisdom for the collective good. The pursuit of stoke has led to the privatisation of some surf breaks, dropping jet-age surfers into essentially ancient-age cultures and the random corporatisation of the once soulful art of surfing. While we live in a market-driven world, those behind the wheel of surfing now are foremost driven by profit, while the 'prophets' of surfing are sidelined casualties. Many surfers may ask: how long do we wait while we witness the erosion of 'pure' surfing culture?

How well do you understand the state of the surfing tribe and the way the world thinks of surfers? Do you care? Are we still a groovy collective of wave-riding free spirits or are we hurtling toward crystallizing as an unconscious (and conscience-less) branded lifestyle, a buy-and-sell subcultural commodity listed 'SRF' in the world's investment stock exchanges?

For 50 years, 70 surfing magazines worldwide have been humming along – where are the surf media and advertisers taking us? Mass 'infotainment' sells and makes some rich – often at the expense of selling out the quintessential culture of surfing as we know it, or knew it. Today, the world sees surfing less as a tribe and increasingly as a branded lifestyle. When I've proposed environmental initiatives, they have been largely ignored by the industry or I have been told by surfing *executives* that all that green/blue resource protection stuff is for 'ageing patchouli-scented dope smokers'. Staggering attitudes within the sector prevail and this must be turned on its head.

In essence, surfers are spirited visionaries, latter-day practitioners of the grand Sport of Hawaiian Kings, with dreams written into our genes by the wild hearts of our ocean ancestors. Yet some may say we have allowed our culture to be co-opted and consumed by corporate entities, its innate wealth transferred into a new class of *nouveau riche* frequent flyers, who shuttle between company HQs and exotic surf boat trips, while surfers great and small devolve into walking adverts for some sub colony of the business-modelled surf world.

The United Nations monitors world affairs and tries to determine the best possible outcomes. Surfing, too, has a loosely connected array of politically structured and industry bankrolled administrative associations, and a few hand-to-mouth environmental groups with attached 'Advisory Boards' composed of 'experts' or kudos-seeking professionals. The average surfer is hardly involved with any of these forums, nor probably wants to be, given this conundrum.

A Global Discussion

The idea and time to have a global discussion has come: a serious and pragmatic paradigm shift is warranted if we want to keep this surfing life viable as we know it, to hand down to future generations. Many of us don't want to predict the future. Surfers don't want to see the rapidly increasing markers which limit our lifestyle and amenity – to realise that a familiar surfing culture hangs in the balance. It now hinges, I think, on primarily building surfing's community capacity. We all need to put our approach to surfing on a firmer footing. There is a societal thread within surfing culture which is, at best, loosely woven and needs stitching up. At its worst, there are accidents through poor decisions waiting to happen. If not now, *when*? And if not us, then *who* will meet the challenges confronting the sustainable stokers? Who will ensure the surfing stoke is retained and sustained?

When it comes to understanding and preserving the sustainable resources of surf amenity – the waves, reefs and beaches – there have been clever-sounding concepts, but not much *done*. Forums in infancy such as the Global Wave and Surf City Conferences are experimental seeds for new thinking and action. Many surfers around the world's beaches, question why the surfing 'industry' itself is not doing more to give back to the lifestyle and resource, which gives without question. Many millionaires surf and many surfers have become millionaires from selling surf or selling out, perhaps. Why are surfers not more philanthropic and involved?

The concept I proposed in 2009 was the *World Council of Surfing Elders*. I suggested that 50 of the great surfing minds gather regularly to set a new agenda to monitor and guide how the surfing world is shaped. It is healthier to foster a culture that values the wisdom of elders and consciousness inherent in the act of surfing than one that simply consumes itself for immediate gratification. Like powerful tribal cultures, the surfing world should put forward its boldest and brightest. Surfers, like the waves we ride, need to stand and deliver. Surfers must step into spheres of influence and shape and create a more certain, more sustainable future. That means contributing politically, financially and organisationally. Above all, it's committing to the waves which stand up for us. With a few decades of surfing and coastal advocacy battles under my belt, I conclude that surfers must be better organised or, more accurately, be *represented* by better organisations.

At your surf break or, more broadly, in surf cities across the world – from Santa Cruz to Sydney, Cornwall to Indonesia – millions of waves have formed and been enjoyed and there are millions more to come. It will take leaders to step up who understand the complex dynamics, who can embrace commensurate solutions and become game-changers. We need to be a global movement, mustering, harnessing and rewarding all the human resources at hand. A recruitment drive of individuals to form better organisations, suited to write new chapters of how to manage the surfing world in the 21st century.

There is too much to lose and much to be gained. In the last 20 years, some of our simple surfing and fishing home towns have transformed into blueprints of urban boat harbours with casinos and shopping malls. Who determines the future? The guard of the cultural protectorate needs to be (mostly) fresh, young and educated – motivated beyond self-interest, where *eco*, not ego prevails. Tribes, communities and group thinking have not only made waves of change, but have been enforcers for futures.

There will always be individuals, corporations and organisations corruptible for short-term financial gain. Governments, in all their shades, are election orientated, not inter-generationally focused. We need to have surfers thumping on their desks, presenting coherent arguments and liaising toward joint stewardship of surfing amenity. Is this happening now? No. Must it? Yes.

Surfers' organisations, like military intelligence, remain oxymoronic; a raw contradiction. While we have groups like the ASP and the ISA, and a handful of major environmental initiatives like Surfrider Foundation, Surfers Against Sewage, SOS and National and World Surfing Reserves, there is a long-awaited space for sharper minds and smarter communication tools to leverage power for effective change. Local, national and international Surf Councils could advocate and represent the issues and futures of the common surfer. I estimate that 98% of common surfers are unrepresented. The gap is wide between elite competitive surfers and the vast common majority.

Surf Councils need to develop local Surf Management Plans, working with stakeholders and governments. This may not be the absolute 'sustainability' model panacea, but it's a good starting point, though overdue. My thinking and proposals come from a lifetime of activism, listening intently to surfing communities, both in Australia and across world surfing communities. Emerging and developing surfing nations are clearly and curiously, more original and definitive in their approach to surf resource protection... from Papua New Guinea to Indonesia, Sri Lanka to Latin America. Of the environmental and political battles under western surfing forums, we've won about 20% at best. Evidently, more organisational, financial and human resources are needed to redress the balance.

There have been costs and casualties in the choppy waters to date, but lessons learned. It is imperative to commit these to memory, absorb and utilise them to keep us still standing as instrumental, inspiring and influential individuals. There must be more rigorous debate, robust engagement with the planet fuckers and, ultimately, real policies scribed in legislative 'law' and surfing's own customary lore. I'd like to proffer a few solutions on how we move forward – smarter and collectively.

What is surfing and why is it worth protecting? Surfing can be interpreted in many ways: a thriving industry, a relaxing recreation, a commercial enterprise, a valuable stock, a chance to shine and compete, a social mix club, a glorious sport, a service industry, an advocacy, a PhD, surf camps or schools, an ideology, an insightful meditation on nature, or just plain having fun – which, I reckon for the majority of us, is the vibe which keeps us humming in life, in and out of the waves. It makes us *surfers*.

The 'fun' extends to playing an instrumental role in advocacy and lobbying. It's a game of challenge and chance that has absorbed my life. In 1991, seeing my family's city of the Gold Coast laying down concrete pipes towards the beach to pump mega litres of sewage into the ocean motivated me to argue the decision. It astounded me that a wealthy modern city which wholly imaged itself on *clean* beaches disposed of its waste into waterways. I had just returned from two years aboard the ice-breaking, 60-metre former Atlantic salvage tug, the mother ship *MV Greenpeace*, after the French secret service bombed the hull of the original *Rainbow Warrior* in New Zealand – environmental defenders, slyly sabotaged, resulting in a crew member murdered. We campaigned against Soviet nuclear testing in the frozen Arctic Circle/North Pole (post 1986 Chernobyl) and I got a major global grasp on environmental activism. Our confrontational anti-nuclear campaign stopped the imminent detonation of the largest ever nuclear bomb test, but our crewmen and women got arrested at gunpoint, jailed and interrogated by the KGB for interfering with their technologies.

That was a turning point for strengthening the Comprehensive Test Ban Treaty – and for me personally to enter the game, and lay some long-odd bets for our oceans. I had been involved in local coastal issues since a teenager, but this USSR experience and the Gold Coast sewage dumping motivated me to design a national surfers group, which I originally called 'CIA' (Coastal Intelligence Australia) but on reflection, morphed it into an antipodean model of the Surfrider Foundation with the help of Surfrider US founder, Glenn Hening, who flew over to help me at a small rented office at Burleigh Heads. I also invited four interns from Plymouth University and Stanford University, USA, who proved themselves valuable. The initial campaign, 'Seaside or Sewerside', attracted 5,000 protesters to a rally and began a rolling swell of activism around the coast against using the sea as a sewer, inappropriate developments and educational initiatives, directed at both the community and the Commonwealth. The essential message was the need for ESD (Ecologically Sustainable Development) of our beach zones.

Working pro-bono, I brinked on personal bankruptcy after four years at the helm, but secured the organisational architecture, governance and the popular marketing of Surfrider Foundation Australia. This grew a passionate following of a solid crew of coastal activists at every major surf hub across the nation. We made a lot of desk-jockeys and politicians uncomfortable and, to some degree, accountable, with the media behind our common message wanting to promote our position. This is Surfrider Foundation Australia's greatest affirmation and victory. It does take many failures to refine successes; we did, however, drive some well-forged wedges into many policy-hardened frames of mind. The same methodology was used to establish Ocean Care Day and one of the great innovative movements of our time – National and World Surfing Reserves. NSRs and WSRs seek to recognise and protect iconic surfing sites of cultural, historic and environmental significance, through surfer representation and in some cases legislation. The State Minister at the time told me that half of his department lived and breathed the beaches. He was bound to represent their interests and, after some lobbying, introduced legislative amendments into the Parliament. Remarkably NSR forged the first legislation worldwide which declared the surfing community as stakeholders, ensuring that surfers had primacy in the decision-making process. These initiatives have sustained the stoke to some degree. They are examples of what is possible. There are 19 Surfing Reserves established in Australia, two in Hawaii and we are just chalking up the sixth World Surfing Reserve, since seeding the concept at Half Moon Bay in California in 2009. We have spread the seeds across many continents, most recently as far as Huanchaco WSR in Peru.

Surfing waves started out as fun over a hundred years ago. But with the advent of significant social and economic changes, core values have altered through marketing and the commodification of surfing. The Gold Coast, a major surfing capital, prides itself on the 'Californisation' of the coast. That is arguably a dangerous path as, in turn, other emerging surf cities model themselves on the GC cultural coastscape. While it might not seem so obvious to the casual observer, the slow cancer of coastal development and the constant commercialisation of surfing are 'threats' that must be questioned, curtailed and managed. So, too, is the over-exploitation of beaches with unrelenting promotion, leading to crowded breaks, conflict among an increasing number of multiple and subcultural user groups, particularly in urban surf communities. Who is running the show is not just a curiosity, but worthy of an investigation, given claims of close-knit, well-heeled corporate collectives, seen to be driven and owned by a few powerful figures.

For the purpose of defining the resource sustainable stoke, it most resembles an amenity and an experience: finite resources, threatened subcultures of lifestyles and incomes and of waves, reefs and beaches. The natural coast and surfing itself is becoming increasing artificial. Major players in surfing companies and the competitive circuit's only payment to sustainable stoke – lip service – is in pursuit of an easy media sound bite or bang for the promotional buck. A few platitudes and small coins are tossed around here and there, but philanthropy is lacking – as is lending their considerable muscle to tackle the heavyweights in coastal planning, which ultimately translates to a sustainable surfing lifestyle.

Should anyone who derives great profits from beaches and surfing be levied, like other resource-reliant multinationals and industries? There are state taxes on coastal developers, fisheries, mining companies and the like. This is part of the local and global discussion which needs to be had.

The KISS Approach

'Keep It Simple Surfer' – it's the slogan KISS principle that was the foundation of National Surfing Reserves which co-founder Prof. Short and I stuck to. It worked – and works. Surfing Reserves honour surfing and its unique place in our way of life. NSR and its brain child, World Surfing Reserves, is an example of what mechanisms work, protect and enhance our coastal culture. They are templates to follow and the beginning of demonstrating that surfers are in fact the logical, time-honoured custodians of the world's waves. The price of a better coast is constant vigilance involving, to some level, anyone and everyone who steps into the surf zone. It's that simple. With over a century of surfing activity around the coastlines of the world, the question remains: who *cares* for and manages our surfing environment? There must be global and local strategies in place from 2015 onwards to protect our resource and lifestyle. Surfers, the National Governing Bodies (NGB) and the surfing industry must take action.

Problems Are For Solving

As beach numbers increase and amenity decreases, stakeholders struggle to manage the complexities of surf beach culture. I'd like to take a snapshot of the past, present and future of surfing – to present models for a sustainable resource, who the main players are, or *should* be.

With a multiplicity of user groups and 'representative' organisations, the current power regimes fall well short of the mark. If surfing beaches and breaks are to survive – and surfing is to thrive as a "culture, recreation, sport, industry, environmental and social amenity, heritage, iconic national status and important income generator", then a more co-ordinated and representative approach is required. I argue that the average 'surfer/beach-goer' and the coast itself are not adequately represented.

When it comes to coastal decisions which affect surfing amenity, are surfers ever consulted? Rarely. Developers and beaurocrats dictate the terms. Surfers must be integral in the process. Period. To garner appropriate social, political economic leverage, new legislative and community governance measures need to be carried out urgently. This may include a *National Coastal Act* or similar instruments in *all* surfing nations. I would also propose that all and every major surf city adopt a 'Surf Management Plan' (SMP) via (regional) Surf Councils, working with all stakeholders, and further propose a global unifying body to govern and assist surfing communities, such as an *International Surfing Council*. PhD Scholar Dan Ware and I are working through the machinations to bolt this onto sustainable stoke organisational models, beginning with the Gold Coast.

Critically, surfers must no longer be perceived as a 'fringe' group – if we are to create maximum political, economic, cultural and social leverage. In Australia, 14% of the population regularly surf this island continent where 90% live nearby – and enjoy beaches. That makes for a strong case, at least here.

Irrespective of the statistics and demographics, surfers can write policy and facilitate change toward our sustainable surfing coasts. Surf cities are populated by beachgoers. That is, everyone at the beach is a surfer by definition. They're surfing waves, right? That's the critical mass which needs harnessing to ratchet that leverage I speak of. Everyone who enjoys waves is a 'surfer'. Surfers can get involved with the so called decision-makers (largely governments), actively challenge policies which adversely affect our surfing experience and most importantly, influence and determine measurable outcomes and chart our own destiny – strategically. In Australia, for example, recreational user groups like Fishers and Shooters have:

- Balance of power in Government;
- Multi-million dollar grants;
- Powerful lobbying blocs and formed 'political parties';
- Major media influence;
- Large membership bases;
- Coordinated approaches;
- Engaged lobbyists and expert consultants;
- Focused and co-ordinated collectives;
- Successful sector representation.

This situation seeks the attention of every surfer and begs the question, is it time to form a 'United Surfers Party' which wields political power, like the USA National Rifle Association does? Hundreds of lobbyists haunt the corridors of Washington DC. How many lobbyists in your country are surfers – how many surfers are lobbyists? Formally, there's not one in Australia to lobby for the common surfer and beachgoer. *Not one.*

Mining, fisheries and other such resource-based industries exist on a finite resource, with a fast approaching use-by date this century. Waves of the world are an inexhaustible natural resource, are they not? While surfing academics have produced new papers on 'surfenomics' – the economic and beneficial value of waves and the largely tourism-based dollars it draws, its worth – governments have yet to acknowledge the long-term true value. While wave lashed cities are celebrated and aggressively promoted, precious little is afforded to protect and enrich them and the user groups who enjoy and profit from them.

Like many other resource-rich nations, Australia, where I live, has powerful departments and Ministries for Forestry, Agriculture, Fisheries, Mining and so on, all natural resources and economic (and taxable) drivers. I would demand reasons why not for beaches and coasts and the multi-billion dollar incomes these resources and their communities generate for the nation? I propose that governments include a Ministry and Department for Coasts. Pertinent and moreover, does your local and federal government have some form of 'public policy' on surfing, surfers and the surfing coast? I ask you to think about that and how different it might be. To not help formulate one is the ultimate form of kookery – anyone intentionally ignorant of surfing lore is IMO a kook. If you're not part of the solution you are, it's been said, part of the problem. Now that's no guilt trip, but is it not amazing that over the years, the common surfer has not done the necessary toward honouring intergenerational equity? I am happy to be challenged on that, but time would be better valued if noted actions towards this goal were indeed 'actioned' – all together. While nuances of the model may be debated anonymously online (or preferably openly in surfing's social media) – the instrument itself must be sharpened as one of our tribe's sharpest tools.

The Next Swell

In Australia, there is no established powerful, over-arching national coastal policy or strategy developed in cooperation with the states/counties and local government with surfers for coastal resources and beach-goers/surfers; that needs to change, and soon. The UNESCO World Heritage Convention recognises historic and environmental sites of universal value to humanity. Even significant caves, reefs, volcanoes and some marine 'places' are listed on this auspicious register, but outstanding waves sites are not. Therein lies another opportunity to protect the gems in the crown and so I'm engaging with Kelly Slater and the Australian government to host a proposal to the Paris-based WHC to take wave sites seriously and, in time, become formally listed. That needs huge commitment and funding, which is a slow protracted process, but nonetheless possible. This calls on surfing's wealth to step up to the plate. I fervently believe the way forward to a sustainable surfing world is essentially two-fold, to:

1. Build a new global surfing organisation to ensure sustainable stoke, and
2. Engage in politics to ensure the surfer's position is fostered and upheld.

City and urban surfing breaks are becoming gridlocked, choked pits, like Los Angles traffic spaghetti, with surf squeeze and edgy wannabe attitudes. Coastal ribbon style encroachment, as is the constant march of people who want to market to the lawn-mowing mortgage masses, seeking a seductive sea change – a coastal lifestyle complete with a wave-lashed beach delivered daily to the doorstep. People are paying phenomenal prices to 'buy' a glimpse of the ocean, to own real estate near the waves. Planners and governments must factor in an inclusive coastal preservation component or integrated coastal management by including surfers. The funny thing now is that real estate agencies are promoting and selling properties based on their relative geographic proximately to a National Surfing Reserve. I also hear that surfers want fewer advisory signs, fewer regulations and restrictions. They want more natural, less regulated environments. So do I. The sustainable surfing scenarios for the 21st century demands nothing less than a complete global restructure of how we common surfers manage our surf.

Australian Prime Minister, Hon. Tony Abbott, embraces sustainable stoke with World Surfing Reserves Ambassador Kelly Slater, and its founder Brad Farmer, at the dedication of Manly-Freshwater WSR. The event celebrated 100 years of surfing at its Australian birthplace and launched surfing reserves into global relevance with state and federal governments.
(Courtesy of James Alcock)

8.6

Surfing Sustainability

Fred Hemmings

Fred Hemmings, Linda Lingle, Governor of Hawaii, President George Bush and Lydia Hemmings – dinner that proceeded President Bush creating the at the time world's largest marine sanctuary (Courtesy of Fred Hemmings)

As a surfer, I have attempted to bridge the gap between surfing and the institutions that influence surfing's environment and destiny. Though surfing has become a huge economic engine and pastime for millions, our sport is yet to command the respect and support necessary to sustain and protect the broader ocean environment and surf sites in particular. Surfing and the ocean are still perceived by many people in decision making positions as an alien environment. Even worse, all too often the surfing community has been unable to effectively communicate their needs in public policy forums. Unfortunately, some of surfing's most vocal activists seem to be reactionaries rather than proponents of working to further conservation and positive change. We surfers have to be affirmative and proponents in the quest to nourish and protect surfing resources.

Experience has demonstrated that the radical environmental movement bewitches some surfing leaders. In my view, radical environmentalism doesn't have as much to do with the environment as it does with political ideology. For instance, a much needed and efficient inter-island transportation alternative, the 'Super Ferry', was launched in Hawaii and was opposed under the banner of 'environmentalism', despite the fact that the project would have been an asset to environmental conservation. It would have been a competitive transportation mode that would have moved people and cargo efficiently between the islands. Sierra Club and others sought to block this initiative and filed a lawsuit against it. Sadly it appears that some self-righteous environmental organisations are more concerned with political ideology and fund raising than protecting the environment. On Kauai, surfers participated in a 'blockade' of Nawiliwili Harbor. Several surfers were very outspoken adversaries of Super Ferry despite it being demonstrably environmentally beneficial to inter-island travel.

As a state senator I was in Washington DC soon after Super Ferry was turned away from Hawaii and many National leaders were incredulous that an island state would scuttle a fast, efficient and cost-effective Ferry system. Indeed Hawaii has a number of radical environmentalists who may ultimately be doing more harm than good to the environment. Years ago, back in the 1980s, I was an advocate of geothermal energy for the big island (Hawaii). The Sierra Club, other alleged environmentalists and Hawaiian activist groups opposed geothermal energy production, and, as a direct result of their actions, Hawaii is now burning more fossil fuel to generate electricity than any other State in the nation. The geothermal resources of the island are vastly underutilised. These examples document how the environment is harmed by radical ideology hiding behind a façade of environmentalism.

It is important to note that there are other organisations that have done an excellent job of protecting our natural resources. I am a big fan of Nature Conservancy. Rather than taking a radical stance, the Nature Conservancy actually engages in fund raising and is able to channel this money into purchasing land that it then protects for conservation. They put their money where their mouth is. That is a good example of capitalism and environmentalism working hand in hand to make good things happen.

On the positive side, in 2005, I proposed to Governor Lingle of Hawaii a major conservation initiative that took the form of a marine sanctuary that would protect the North West Archipelago of the Hawaiian Chain, including all the atolls from Kauai to Kure atoll. The atolls were also a part of my district. Governor Lingle was a strong advocate of this idea and presented it to President Bush. It is interesting to note that, even though President Bush was largely maligned by the more radical adherents to the environmental movement, this initiative led to the creation of the world's largest marine sanctuary. As a first step, the President sent the White House Council on the Environment, Jim Connaughton, out to Hawaii. I, the Governor, Jim and several other environmentalists flew to Midway to conduct a survey of the atolls. The French explorer and environmentalist Jean Michele Cousteau, son of Jacques Cousteau, also accompanied us on this trip.

Several months later, in April of 2006, the First Lady and the President of the United States invited us all to dinner at the White House. As a surfer, I was proud to be having dinner with the President and his charming wife. After dinner, we talked about putting the entire North West archipelago into sanctuary status. About a month and a half later, I attended a ceremony at the White House at which the President signed documents to create the world's largest marine sanctuary out of the North West archipelago. The First Lady came to Hawaii to participate at an official ceremony to name the sanctuary Papahanaumokuakea.

Surfers should be sitting at the table as, or with, civic leaders when decisions are made about environmental issues. This would lead to an increase in the credibility of surfing as a whole and credibility is an important issue that needs to be addressed within the surfing world. There are examples of revered surfing heroes and icons who, in reality, were little more than scoundrels and conmen scattered through our history. My reason for raising this point is that surfing, and especially surfing journalists, can do a better job of defining surfing heroes and aligning the image of surfing with surfers who can serve as role models that add lustre to the image of surfing. For example, Kelly Slater has carried the banner of surfing with dignity.

I've always said that surfing does not get its fair share of public resources to nourish and protect surfing sites and the recreational amenity they provide. Sometimes it is surfing's own fault. If you added up the amount of money the State of California or Hawaii spends on parks and public recreation facilities, tennis courts, baseball fields, athletic facilities, it would be a huge amount of money. Then ask yourself what proportion of this do those states spend on the protection and enhancement of surfing sites? It would be very easy to take a coastline that is exposed to swell and actually create new surfing sites. Here in Hawaii, I've advocated on numerous occasions that we do a topographical map of a small break like Queens and then duplicate the ocean bottom with very large, environmentally friendly sandbags on the sandbar between Queens and Publics, creating another break in this area. In California, great surf breaks could be created up and down the coast. Surfing cannot escape the laws of supply and demand. We collectively could and most definitely should increase the 'supply' of surfing sites.

With this increased supply, we would need to be sensitive to some of the other issues that arise from increasingly crowded surf sites, localism is an example of this and an increasingly global problem. Who has moral, ethical or legal jurisdiction over the waves? I was born here in Hawaii. If I paddle out at Makaha, which is basically where my heart is, do I have more right to the waves than some guy who just paddled out from California? On the North Shore, there's a dark element led, most ironically, by a mainland transplant thug that has put together a group of mostly Hawaiians, declaring themselves the self-ordained protectors of the realm: this is localism. They will say who can surf where and when. If you don't play by their rules, violence is often used to keep people in line. In California, does someone who's been surfing Malibu all his life have a right to say who surfs there? That's a very pertinent question. It even gets into racism here in Hawaii. Do part Hawaiians have some sort of eminent domain over resources in Hawaii just because they happen to be born part Hawaiian? Are we all created equally, do we all have equal access? These important questions must be asked and answered.

In the end, in a crowded world if we do not learn to manage our surfing resources we will destroy them. We must not succumb to the basest of instincts, namely survival of the fittest. Surfing leadership needs to discuss these issues in the public forum. I believe that there can be a fair, equitable and logical conclusion, one not based on localism, racism and survival of the fittest.

Do surf sites have to be regulated in some way in order to save the resource? Some would say that if you have a limited natural resource, you have to ration it to protect it. This opens up tremendous problems – are you going to charge a fee to surf? Right now, if you go to a National Park for recreational purposes, you pay to get into the park. These are problems that deserve to be analysed and rational decisions must be made and someone has to make these decisions. As a surfer, I was in the legislature at the table of decision making. I worked with a few surfers in Congress: they are Brian Bilbray from San Diego, a tremendous conservationist, and then Dana Rohrbacher from Huntington Beach. We actually formed a bypartisan 'Surfing Caucus'. It included a Deputy Secretary in the Obama Administration. We shouldn't be making decisions based on political ideology. Decisions should be based on facts and the common good. We shouldn't let political labels get in the way of making wise decisions for the benefit of surfing.

It's self-evident that surfers have not adequately invested time and effort in managing shoreline and ocean resources. This includes the more subtle elements of surfing like the aesthetic environment. Years ago, I was lamenting that public art in Hawaii was mostly contemporary art and our State did not have many heroic statues of the great luminaries of Hawaiian history. In the 1990s, I was the one who proposed putting Duke's statue on the beach at Waikiki. With the help of the Waikiki Improvement Association, we formed the Duke Centennial Committee. We unveiled and dedicated the statue on 24 August, 1990 – Duke's 100th birthday.

I suggested years ago that a life-size statue of a surfer doing a bottom turn under the lip of a Pipeline wall should be erected at Ehukai Park on the North Shore. The statue could be a duplication of the excellent sculpture done for the Pipeline Masters trophy. The aesthetic surfing environment would be greatly enhanced by more public surf-related art like the Duke statue. Something that is a little frustrating is that the recording of our journey as surfers through time is often edited to comply with an agenda. Surfing history must be rooted in substance and truth.

The surfing environment is more than the physical environment; it's the spiritual environment, the aesthetic environment, the social environment, the entire world we live in as surfers. Surfing leaders must be constantly aware of the issues that affect all the environment of surfing including the social and the cultural environments. We must sustain all that is good in the world of surfing. The richness of surfing ultimately comes from the soul and the character of the surfers, and I truly believe humanity's problems have solutions. Let's work together to find them.

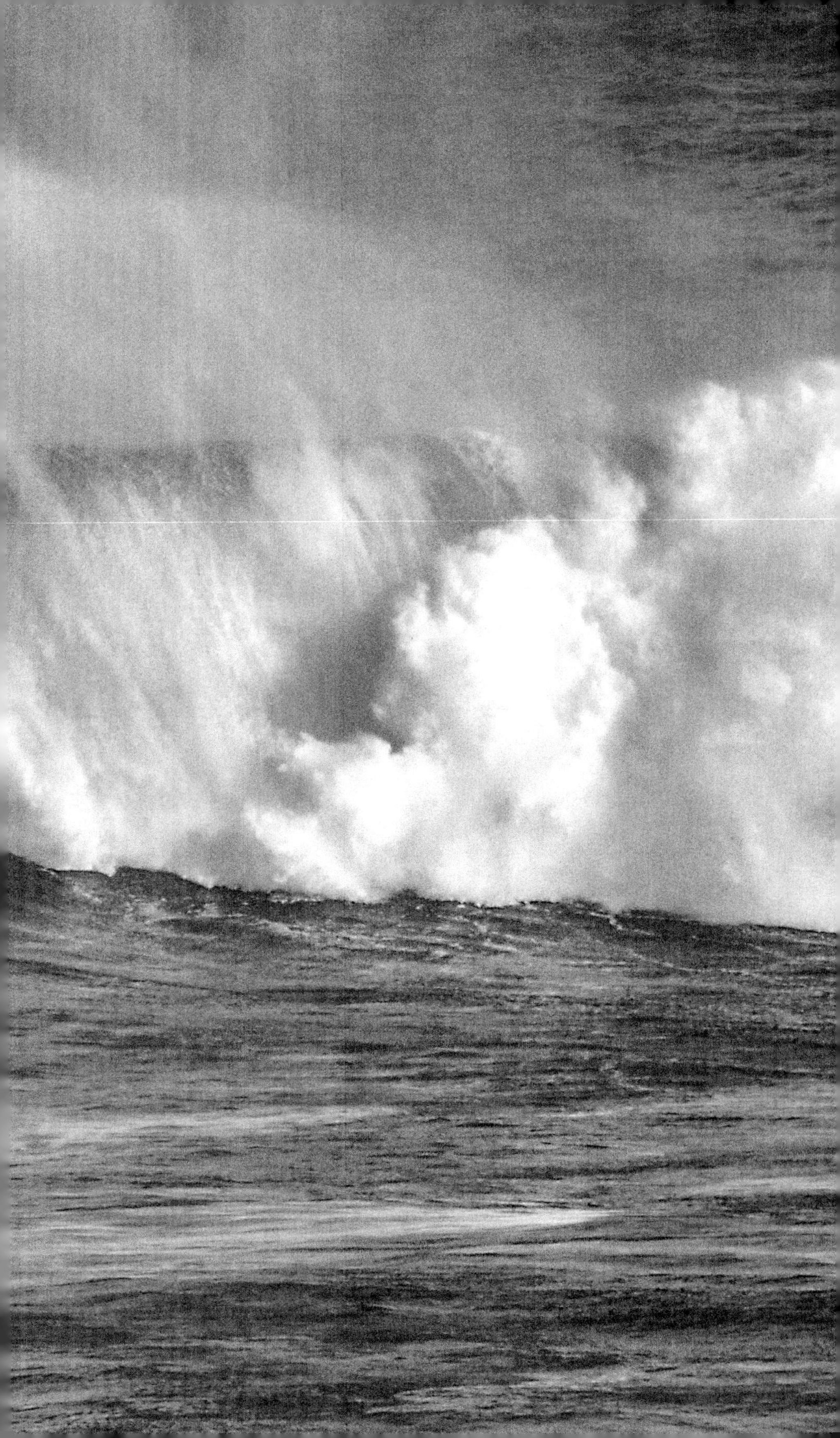

Epilogue: The Next Set

The final part of this book is about the future. What happens next? Where do we go from here? But this is not about providing answers; instead, it is about understanding the journey we have been on so far and what questions need to be asked in the future. What is certain is that in order for a transition to sustainability to take place, not just in surfing but in all aspects of life, it must have traction – it must be an idea that sticks, continually striven for and always questioned. And so the final contribution in this book is from John and Cris Dahl who have been responsible for keeping us all firmly stuck to our boards as we pursue the activity we love. Finally, Jess and myself conclude the book as we try to draw together some of its threads and tell you what it has – and hasn't – achieved.

Surf Wax Genealogy

John Dahl
Cris Dahl

Scrappy hollow sounds heard in beach parking lots all over the world proclaim the beginning of a surf session. These tones symbolise a ritual: the intimate art of applying surf wax to the deck of a surfboard. Sweet scent floats through the air, the bar vibrates as your hand pushes it along the glassed surface and suddenly your mindset switches from land to water. You are focused and ready to leave all else behind. Modern surfing was resurrected from the ancient Hawaiian sport in the early part of the 20th century.

The heavy boards of the time were constructed of solid wood weighing up to 45 kilograms. Two theories exist of the types of traction early surfers used on the deck of the surfboard. One was crosschecking the wood and the second using coral to rough up the surface creating texture and friction. The wooden, varnished decks of the 1930s were slippery, making traction a necessity in order to get the footing to stand and turn the board. Sometime in the 1940s surfers began putting household canning wax on their boards because water and oil don't mix, wax helps shed water, creating a barrier of tacky resistance. This was the beginning of modern surf wax.

From the 1940s to the 1960s, paraffin wax was the standard deck application for the surfboard. The first attempts to improve surf wax application were achieved by adding oil for softening, in turn allowing easier application and creating more wax build-up on the deck. Candles were also used, melting and dripping the wax on the board to create little traction mounds.

When the movie *Gidet* was released in 1959, the sport of surfing boomed and along with it, the manufacture of surfboards and surf wax. The idea of a company devoted to surf wax was a new concept and it became a competitive mission to improve the product. New trends made wax an important ingredient in the evolution of surfing manoeuvres. In the mid 1960s, the idea of improving paraffin caught hold along with better board shapes leading to higher quality surfing. This was the era of Dewy Webber, Al Nelson, and Phil Edwards, when surfers started cutting back and doing late takeoffs. These new trends made wax an important ingredient in the evolution of surfing manoeuvres.

The short board revolution of the late 1960s to early 1970s completely changed the approach to traction on the surfboard deck. Waxes had to be longer lasting and more aggressive. Your foot had to move as well as stop and hold when needed. Boards got shorter, wax got tackier. An early 1970s break through in surf wax was the addition of a Vaseline-type softener which gave the wax more traction, less slipperiness and more adhesion. The introduction of softer ingredients, more pliable beeswax-style waxes, along with the inclusion of tackifiers, scents and colours made it an exclusive product for surfing and surfers. These changes were critical for surf wax to evolve along with the advancing surfboard designs and surfing styles.

The fast paced evolution of the shorter boards made it necessary for surf wax to continue to improve and it did through the 1970s and 1980s. Two large manufactures had the majority of market share and ability to make improvements through experimenting with new additives and ways of applying and gaining traction. The 1980s saw surfers exploring different areas of the wave to ride resulting in more radical moves, which increased the demand for high performance wax. In 1990, in response to this demand, Wax Research formulated the first traction added surf wax. The revolutionary wax was the forerunner for all modern waxes. An organic additive replaced about one half of the paraffin and softeners in wax. This ingredient allowed the wax to go on quicker, build-up better, supply better footing and traction. The surfer was able to perform more radical maneuvers with the improved footing.

Over the past decade many attempts have been made to 'green' the surfboard itself using different foams with different compositions. The hands down winner however has been the polyurethane blown foam blank that is fibre-glass coated. This has been true for surf wax also. Attempts have been made to replace paraffin with soy as well as different natural waxes such as beeswax. Manufacturers of surfboard wax are continuously looking for greener, better, more sustainable components and performance remains the number one criteria. As it is true with surfboard blanks, polyurethane foam and fibreglass, so it is true with surfboard wax that the hydrocarbon base works the best. There are new possibilities with base waxes evolving, new ways of hydrogenating natural plant waxes, distilling wax as a byproduct of bio-fuels, and wax produced from recycled plastic to help augment and supply a more sustainable base for surf wax.

Modern surf wax contains paraffin wax, microcrystalline wax, and petrolatum wax. These products are non-reactive, non-toxic and biodegradable, all classified natural organic mineral products. Their elimination in the environment occurs through the microbial population, degrading primarily through bacterial/fungi action dispensing to emulsify into the environment. The bulk of surf wax is calcite, a natural compound composed primarily of seashells. Add to this base an ingredient found in chewing gum, some scent and colour, heat and mix, pour into a mould, let it cool, remove and you have a bar ready to wax up your deck.

As travelling surfers, we wear the badge of ambassador, spreading stoke around the world. We demonstrate that a life can be built around a sport we love and that our passion for surfing fuels this lifestyle. Our ideas about local food, lodging, equipment, and clothing, as well as the necessary surf accessories and wax, are the sparks that ignite the fire of creative minds. We transform these notions into new opportunity where none had existed before. As surfers, it is our privilege to extend a hand to the community and share this knowledge for the good of all.

Ebb & Flow

Gregory Borne
Jess Ponting

A rising tide lifts all boats?[1]

And so we reach the conclusion of this particular episode of sustainability and surfing. How was the journey? It is our hope that it was a journey of exploration, a journey into the unknown or at the very least a journey that has provided you with a different perspective on the world. We don't expect you to agree with every word written and indeed hope that you do not. Instead, we hope you are provoked into action, wanting to find out more about some of the issues raised in the book. Because, just as surf wax provides the traction to stay planted on the board and surf the wave, a transition to sustainability requires a continued and open discourse between different groups, people, cultures organizations. It is true to say that this is not a conventional book; it is a collection of essays, opinions and thoughts from some of the world's most influential and talented people within surfing. Some are recognised and revered the world over, whether they like it or not, some are yet to realise their potential and what their contribution to this debate is today and in the future, only time will tell. Our contributors have wildly different experiences and perspectives on the world, and on life, but each individual contributor is locked in debate with each and every person that has contributed to this book.

It has been borne out of passion both from us as editors and from the contributors but has also been borne out of necessity, fear and apprehension about the future and a strong desire to understand both problems and solutions in the hope that the problems are avoided, or at the very least not magnified, and the solutions to these problems are found. As a reader we hope that you have found this book as inspirational as we did as we read through the contributions and started to make the connections between them. It is true to say that for us as editors this book had represented both pleasure and pain. The pleasure of exploration of learning, of interacting with everyone that has contributed to the book, building new friendships and opening up new avenues of conversation which, from start to finish, will have been a journey that has stretched more than three years. But there is also pain and perhaps this is just a natural part of creation. We have for all intense and purposes given birth to this work and struggled with the growing pains that have accompanied that as well. The pain of self doubt, are we doing the right thing, will this work? The pain of sacrifice, this has been a labour of love demanding time and emotional commitment, with other opportunities missed and avenues left unexplored as we grapple with busy and unpredictable lives. Not least, as we have both grappled with parenthood; we have become new parents to baby girls and both, for very different reasons, called Sydney. So the creation of this book, coupled with the creation and nurturing of new life, has undoubtedly breathed new meaning to sustainability as every parent looks to a better future for their children.

And so the usual way to summarise a book is to tie the different themes together, make connections between the different authors and point to the future of sustainability and surfing. But, we leave the broader connections and interpretations to you. Anything more would be a betrayal of the overall ethos of this book and a significant presumption on our behalf. This is an unusual book and it has achieved an unusual thing, so we make no apologies for having an unusual ending. What we will do, very simply, is two things: Tell you what this book hasn't achieved, and tell you what it has achieved.

This book has not achieved a definitive understanding of the relationship between sustainability and surfing, and we have emphasised this on a number of occasions. Indeed, anything or anyone that makes such a wild boast has quite simply overstated their understanding of the concept and their capabilities as a human being. Sustainability is a contested and ambiguous concept, and it means many things to many people. It is our hope that, if nothing else, you have a broader appreciation of the ambiguous and contested nature of the concept as well as an understanding of the monumental range of issues that sustainability represents. In a similar vein, this book does not provide a step-by-step guide to answers or solutions; instead it would be more accurate to say that it provides some intriguing insights into what might be possible in the future. All of these insights are contingent on issues such as technological advancements, political will, cultural and behavioural change and more. Some of these are specific to the surfing world but more often than not there are a plethora of external factors that are relevant to every single person on the planet.

Furthermore, the book does not represent a compendium of all the voices that should be heard and that can and should contribute towards this discussion. As we have learned from the contributors in this book, we have also begun to identify broader networks of individuals and organisations all of whom have a contribution to make to the discussion on sustainability and surfing. Each contributor to the book are themselves embedded in networks of people and organisations that have a part to play in creating a sustainable future and catalysing this transition. The beautiful and fascinating thing about surfing is that it does not take well to being categorised and traverses the world of science, art and sport. And as such the voices that could contribute to the debate could and should be deafening.

So what has this book achieved? This book has, at its core, exposed the necessity for a debate within surfing and sustainability. For a long time, the natural beauty and engagement with the ocean by those who surf has carried with it an innate presumption that surfing and surfers are in tune with nature and, by the very act of surfing, the apparatus that has built up around it, the industry, the media and the surfing culture is sustainable. The voices in this book, from leaders of MNCs through to NGOs and activists have painted a very different picture. And whilst there have been rumblings to this affect in recent years, this book can be said without any stretch of the imagination to be the first time that this has been discussed by so many of those that have a direct impact on this debate. And, in so doing, perhaps the final tangible achievement of this book has been to position the surfing world within this broader and growing debate around sustainability.

Children bodyboarding, silhouetted against the Burgh Island Sea Tractor (Courtesy of Gregory Borne)

About the Editors

Dr. Gregory Borne
Gregory Borne is an ex-Burgh Island sea tractor driver and now a Senior Lecturer in Social Science at Plymouth Marjon University, UK. He is the director of the Plymouth Sustainability and Surfing Research Group and the BA (Hons) Social Sciences. His research focuses on the many ways that sustainable development is being integrated into different sectors at the international, national, local, and individual levels. He has a particular interest in ideas around complexity, uncertainty, reflexivity, and the relationship between global and local risk. At the international level, Greg has worked for and conducted research with the United Nations Environment Programme where he explored how sustainable development was being used at the highest political level. On the opposite end of the spectrum, Greg ran the largest research project in the UK exploring sustainable development within the local communities based in town and parish councils. Greg holds a BSc (Hons) in Sustainable Development, an MSc in Social Research and a PhD in Sustainable Development. In addition, he is a member of the Institution of Environmental Sciences, a registered Chartered Environmentalist with the Society for the Environment, and a member of the Royal Institute of Chartered Surveyors specialising in sustainability.

Dr. Jess Ponting

Jess Ponting is an Associate Professor and Founder and Director of the Center for Surf Research at San Diego State University - the first research centre of its kind to focus specifically on the sustainability of surfing. Jess holds the first Masters and Doctoral level degrees that focus on surf tourism. He has a background in community development and sustainable surf tourism and has lived and worked in this field in Australia, Indonesia, Fiji, Papua New Guinea, and the United States. He has provided additional sustainable surf tourism consulting services and advice in Costa Rica, Mexico, Hawaii, Panama, Spain, the Philippines, and the Maldives.

Jess' concern for the sustainability of surf tourism has led him to co-found a non-profit designed to raise funds for surfing destination development projects (SurfCredits), a business that provides sustainable surf tourism study abroad education in world class surfing destinations for university credit (Groundswell Educational Travel), and another that establishes a sustainability certification protocol and standard for surf and snow tourism operations (STOKE Certified). His research is concerned with understanding how sustainability can be built into surf tourism developments at the level of individual properties and operations through to macro level government policy. His most recent initiative is the founding of the Association of Surfing Academics, an organization designed to encourage interdisciplinary collaboration on issues impacting the surfing world.

About the Authors

Andy Abel
Andrew C. Abel, ML is the President and Co-Founder of the Surfing Association Papua New Guinea Inc. (SAPNG), established in 1989. Abel is of mixed English and Papua New Guinea parentage and member of one of Papua New Guinea's pioneering missionary and political families, dating back to 1891. Abel is the driving force of the SAPNG and principal architect of the Abel Reverse Spiral model and the policies that govern the SAPNG home grown Surf Management Plan (SMP) and the Integrated Management Plan Product (IMPP) in partnership with traditional resource custodian host communities in the promotion and development of surfing as a sport and niche tourism sector. Abel is the Deputy President of the Board of Trustees of the PNG National Museum Board Trustees and Board Member PNG Tourism Promotion Authority. Abel was awarded the Member of the Order of Logohu award for 20 years voluntary service to SAPNG and country, by the Papua New Guinea National Government in 2007.

Fernando Aguerre
President of the International Surfing Association (ISA) since 1994 and primary driver of the Federation's growth & development in last 20 years, Aguerre has 40 years of successful business leadership experience in the action sports industry. Married to wife Florencia and the father of four children, Aguerre divides his time between his hometown of Mar del Plata, Argentina and La Jolla, California. From 1984 to 2005, he was the founder, President & CEO of surf brand Reef, an industry leader in footwear and apparel. In 2005, Reef was sold to VF, one of the largest global manufacturers of action sportswear. He is also founder and first President of the Argentinean Surfing Association in 1978 despite a military dictatorial ban on the sport at the time. The ban was lifted in 1979 thanks to Aguerre's efforts.

He was also a founding member and elected to first board of directors of the Surfing Industry Manufacturers Association (SIMA), is the former president of the SIMA Humanitarian Fun, first president of the Surfrider Foundation in Argentina, and co-creator of the Liquid Nation Ball, one of the largest surfing industry fundraisers, in his home in La Jolla, California. In addition, he served on the global boards and contributed significant time income to charities such as SurfAid International, Save The Waves, The Quicksilver Foundation, the SIMA Humanitarian Fund and many more. In 2012, he was the recipient of the "Dick Baker Memorial Award" and, a year later, was awarded the prestigious "Waterman of the Year Award" by SIMA as the highest industry recognition by his peers for his business, sporting and philanthropic leadership in surfing and action sports. A lifelong surfer, he still finds the time to surf the waves of the world nearly every day, but especially those near his home and at the venues of the ISA World Surfing Championships.

Wayne 'Rabbit' Bartholomew
As a 15 year old schoolboy in 1971, Wayne 'Rabbit' Bartholomew experienced a recurring daydream as he walked the 6km to and from school. This daydream would become the vision for pro surfing that catapulted Rabbit and the sport of surfing into the global phenomenon it has become. While always crediting those who paved the way before him, Rabbit is considered the Godfather of professional surfing, his unfaltering belief in the destiny of his chosen sport providing the impetus for a 45 year career covering competitive surfing, the industry, administration, coaching, mentoring and above all, a passionate orator and surfing statesman.

Rabbit claimed 3 ASP World Titles, the 1978 Mens Crown and the 1999 & 2003 ASP World Masters Championships. He was World runner-up on 4 occasions and was ranked in the Top 5 for 10 consecutive years. After retirement from touring Rabbit became Surfing Australia National Coaching Director (1992-1998) and assumed the sports top job, his tenure as ASP Ceo (1999-2003) and President (1999-2009) providing the opportunity to fully implement his teenage daydream. Rabbit established the Dream Tour, creating the foundations that have seen surfing on a global ascendency. Since departing the helm of ASP, Rabbit is now a global brand ambassador for Hurley International, a youth oriented market leader in innovation and high performance. He has three sons, Jaggar, 13, Keo, 11, and Cruz, 3 and still calls Coolangatta home.

Sean Brody

Sean Brody was born and raised in San Diego, California and is a surfer, turned surf photographer, turned surf philanthropist. Brody started Surf Resource Network in 2010 to help surfers, travelers, and like-minded individuals give back where we go for waves. Working closely with the Center for Surf Research at San Diego State University, Brody earned a Master's Degree in Hospitality Tourism Management with an emphasis on Sustainable Surf Tourism. Brody is Co-Founder of Kwepunha Retreat (the first sustainable surf resort in Liberia, West Africa) and is Co-Creator of the Surf Credits donation platform. Today, Brody works with the International Surfing Association as the Membership Manager where he utilizes his experience using surfing as a tool for peace and development by advising National Surfing Federations and furthering the development of the sport of surfing across the globe.

Dr. Tony Butt

Tony Butt has a PhD in Physical Oceanography from the University of Plymouth, UK, and worked as a part-time research fellow with the Coastal Processes Research Group for seven years. He lives for most of the year in a forgotten corner of northwest Spain but migrates to the southwest tip of Africa during the southern winter. He makes a meagre living writing and teaching people about waves and the coastal environment. He works with NGOs, like Surfers Against Sewage and Save the Waves, trying to convince people that the more we interfere with nature the more problems it will cause us. Dr. Butt has been surfing for as long as he can remember. He dislikes crowds, contests, and the intrusion of greed and materialism into the world of surfing but, ironically, has been invited to a number of international big-wave events and has appeared in several TV documentaries on big-wave surfing.

Michelle Blauw

Michelle Blauw is the Owner of D'Arcy Surfboards and founder The Australian Surf Craft Industry Association

Dr. Easkey Britton

Easkey Britton is an internationally renowned professional surfer, artist, scientist and explorer from Ireland, with a PhD in Marine Environment and Society. Her parents taught her to surf when she was four years old and her life has revolved around the ocean ever since. She is Co-Founder of the non-profit

Waves of Freedom which uses the power of surfing as a creative medium for social change.

Andrew Coleman
Andrew is an environmental professional living in Brighton, on the south coast of England. He's a former local rep and Director for Surfers Against Sewage and his favourite wave is his local wave.

Dr. Serge Dedina
Dr. Dedina is the Founder and Executive Director of WILDCOAST/ COSTASALVAJE and the Mayor of Imperial Beach, California. He is the author of *Saving the Gray Whale*, *Wild Sea: Eco-Wars and Surf Stories from the Coast of the California* and *Surfing the Border: Adventures at the Edge of the Ocean*. He received his PhD in Geography from the University of Texas at Austin.

John & Cris Dahl
John Dahl, founder of Wax Research, started surfing in Windansea in the 1950s. In 1992, along with his wife Cris, he introduced Sticky Bumps surf wax which set the standard for all modern surf waxes. In 2009, the Dahls developed the first natural plant, high performance, snow wax. They continue to run their manufacturing business in Southern California.

Tetsuhiko Endo
Tetsuhiko Endo is an American with a Japanese name living in London. He is a writer by nature, a journalist and ghost-writer when he can be, and a copywriter by necessity. His work has appeared in *National Geographic*, the *New York Times*, *High Times*, *Gastronomica*, and various smaller publications. He has a Master's Degree in Postcolonial Studies and still harbours vague, frustrated pretensions toward academia. He only surfs occasionally.

Brad Farmer
Born with sand between his toes on Australia's surf mecca of the Gold Coast, Farmer is a third generation surfer and world renowned coastal advocate.He studied journalism at the University of Southern Queensland and has published a number of hard-hitting reports and papers since, shifting policy formulation around coastal and surfing management. A former Greenpeace campaigner in the then Soviet Arctic and later a Senate Adviser in Federal Parliament, Farmer

has travelled to over 35 beach nations over as many years, by land, sea and air, exploring, researching and documenting the best – and most endangered beaches. Farmer's first publication *Surfing Guide to Australia* with Nat Young in 1985 and his current book *101 Best Australian Beaches* have been best sellers and he has set benchmarks for beach evaluation and surf amenity with co-author, eminent coastal geomorphologist, Professor Andy Short, OAM.

Farmer is a pioneer advocate for coastal preservation throughout a storied life of oceans, waves and beaches establishing many award winning non-for-profit organisations, to ensure future generations enjoy and value the salty environments of many nations. In 2014, he was awarded the Hall of Fame Surfing Spirit Award for establishing and driving National Surfing Reserves. He also co-founded World Surfing Reserves and the Gold Coast Surf Council which develops Surf Management Plans. Farmer is the founder of Surfrider Foundation Australia and National Ocean Care Day. Having written regularly for *tRACKS* surfing magazine for over 25 years and many other surfing related journals including *Sustainable Stoke*, his main focus now is the development of frameworks for surfing in the 21st century. He was appointed an Australia Day Ambassador by the NSW Government in 2012. He still surfs often, around the pristine breaks of northern NSW.

Prof. Malcolm Findlay

Dr. Malcolm Findlay grew up in Scotland, where he was one of the first Scottish surfers. His early working life was in the fishing industry, becoming a qualified Skipper and owning his own 24 metre trawler by the age of 23. Dr. Findlay turned to academic life in his late 20's and after a first degree at Plymouth Polytechnic, progressed to postgraduate study at both Aberdeen and Plymouth Universities in the UK. He was awarded his doctorate for a study of UK fishing vessel safety and was involved in research, teaching and academic management until his retirement from academia at the end of 2013.

Like many surfers around the World, Dr. Findlay managed to balance his working life with his love of surfing and has held numerous competitive surfing titles, including six times Scottish Open Champion and three British Longboard titles. In 1999, he worked with colleagues at Plymouth University to launch the world's first academic programme in Surf Science & Technology, which he then managed for the following six years before moving to senior management in the University. He now lives in South Devon, right above one of the UK's best surf spots, and manages Hyperflex Wetsuits in the UK.

ABOUT THE AUTHORS

Cesar Garcia
Wildlands Program Coordinator for WILDCOAST/COSTASALVAJE, Cesar Garcia coordinates the conservation of vast coastal and marine ecosystems in Baja California and the Sea of Cortez. He received his MSc. in Oceanography from UABC in Ensenada and is one of the few people to have made the swim from Todos Santos Island back to Ensenada.

Fred Hemmings
Fred Hemmings is the winner of the 1968 World Surfing Championships, founder of the Pipeline Masters, as well as the Triple Crown of Surfing and the first world pro surfing circuits for men and women. He also served as Republican floor leader in Hawaii's House of Representatives 1984-1990 and was the Republican leader for the Hawaii State Senate between 2000 and 2010. Hemmings began surfing in Waikiki at age eight. In 1961 and 1963 he won the juniors division of the Makaha International contest and, in 1964, he took the Makaha men's title (while earning all-league honors as a center on the Punahoe High School football team), finished runner-up in 1965, and won again in 1966. Hemmings appeared in The Endless Summer (1966), Golden Breed (1968), and other period surf movies.

He then, alongside Randy Rarick, went on to found International Professional Surfers (IPS), the first worldwide surfing circuit and predecessor to the Association of Surfing Professionals (ASP) tour. In 1983, he founded Hawaii's Triple Crown of Surfing, a three-event minitour within the world tour. He was inducted into the International Surfing Hall of Fame in 1991, the Hawaii Sports Hall of Fame in 1999, and the Surfing Walk of Fame in 2009. In 2002, he won the Surf Industry Manufacturers Association Waterman Achievement Award. He Self-published a memoir titled The Soul of Surfing is Hawaiian in 1997 that went on to make it onto the Hawaii bestseller list. Hemmings has 4 children and six grandchildren: he is a life long resident of Hawaii. He is now a keynote speaker specialising in informative, entertaining and inspiring talks about Hawaii and, of course, surfing.

Glenn Hening
Glenn Hening has been called surfing's "voice of conscience" because he's always asking the question "What kind of world are we making for ourselves – and for our children?". He is a veteran surfer, classroom teacher of 25 years, an acclaimed public speaker and successful writer. His public life includes

founding the Surfrider Foundation in 1984, co-founding the Groundswell Society in 2001, being named a Regents Lecturer at UCSB in 2006, and his ongoing fundraising events at Rincon, now in their 17th year. He's a Renaissance man whose incisive perspectives and personal commitment to a better world have made a real difference. He checks the surf every day across the street from his home in Oxnard Shores, California where he lives with his beloved wife Heidi and their dog Otis.

Chris Hines, MBE Hon.D.Sc
Co-founder and then Director of Surfers Against Sewage (SAS) from 1990 to 2000, Chris Hines is regarded as "some of the Government's most sophisticated environmental critics" by the BBC and "Britain's coolest pressure group". From there, Hines became Sustainability Director at the Eden Project for five years. He's given evidence to UK parliament, the Monopolies and Mergers Commission, the European Commission, briefed the President of the European Parliament, been a special advisor to the Minister for the Environment and appeared on a wide range of media from BBC World Service to CNN. In 2008 he was awarded an MBE for services to the environment in the Queen's Birthday Honours and an Honorary Doctorate of Science from the University of Plymouth. He is also a Surfers Path Inaugural Green Wave Award winner. He now runs A Grain of Sand which aims to deliver positive change and has recently given presentations to a wide range of groups from BMW Guggenheim to the Dutch Tax Office, the National Grid and the Global Surf Cities Conference. In April 2014, he was invited onto the BBC's Sustainability Advisory Group. But he still gets plenty of surfing in!

Nev Hyman
Founder and chief shaper of FireWire Surfboards, Firewire Surfboards and Nevhouse, Nev Hyman has been spent 40 years making surfboards, selling and surfing them all over this beautiful planet of ours. His company Nev Futureshapes evolved into Firewire in 2006, which is now regarded as a technical and innovative surfboard company second to none and, recently, Firewire been acquired by none other than Mr Kelly Slater. Firewire takes pride in also being the most environmentally sustainable surfboard in the market. Hyman has also immersed himself in what may prove to be a solution to global homelessness. Nevhouse is a holistic approach to affordable housing, clean water, sanitation and power that simultaneously deals with environmental concerns to do with post consumer waste and logging.

ABOUT THE AUTHORS

Pierce Kavanagh
Pierce Michael Kavanagh is a life-long bodysurfer and coastal guardian from La Jolla, California. Creating the award-winning Misfit Pictures, he had directed and produced three ocean-themed films including *Manufacturing Stoke* (2011), *Resurf* (2013) and *What the Sea Gives Me* (2014). He is also the Founder of the San Diego Surf Film Festival which provides constant stoke to the surf community.

Emi Koch
California native Emi Koch is a professional free surfer for Billabong Womens, rising filmmaker, and founder of Beyond the Surface International (BTSI), a nonprofit platform for youth empowerment projects in coastal communities worldwide using surfing and creative-learning initiatives as innovative mediums for positive social change. After years dedicated to cultivating a professional surfing career, Koch felt hollowed by an exceptionally self-focused dream. Today, she utilizes her sponsorship to facilitate opportunities for youth from marginalized coastal communities and disadvantaged circumstance to rise beyond their challenging backgrounds through her NGO, through riding and making waves. Koch is a recent Georgetown University graduate with a degree in Psychology with two concentrations in Anthropology and Justice & Peace Studies. She currently lives as a nomad traveling across coastal communities with BTSI's project Coast 2 Coast, an audiovisual workshop series on a youth-driven audiovisual workshop series on cross-cultural communication, peace-building, and ocean conservation. She also likes papayas with lime, witty puns, and the occasional epic sweater.

Dr Scott Laderman
Scott Laderman teaches history at the University of Minnesota, Duluth, and is the author, most recently, of *Empire in Waves: A Political History of Surfing* (University of California Press, 2014). While his first publication was a short piece he wrote for *Surfer* while interning at the magazine in 1993, he had not yet begin his professional career as a scholar of surfing. However, his combined passions for wave-riding and the history and culture of American foreign relations would bring him to Empire in Waves. He first went onto write *Tours of Vietnam: War, Travel Guides, and Memory* (Duke University Press, 2009), which explored tourism and memory in that postcolonial Southeast Asian nation, and later co-edited *Four Decades On: Vietnam, the United States, and*

the Legacies of the Second Indochina War (Duke University Press, 2013), which was named a Choice Outstanding Academic Title for 2013. Laderman has also published numerous articles and essays on film history, American empire-building, and Cold War tourism, among other topics, for a number of journals and anthologies.

Kevin Lovett
The longer Kevin Lovett lives and travels through rural Indonesia the more he has been drawn to the fascinating connection of local communities with their land and the ocean that surrounds it. Possessing a genealogy that connects him back to Mother Russia, Germany, the highlands of Scotland to the lowlands of Britain and Ireland, Lovett has come to more fully appreciate our subtle need for, and the function of, a fundamental connectivity with the raw elements in nature. Generations of 'Westerners' have wandered the planet perhaps seeking this subliminal reconnection to a deeper source. Most of the time though, through sheer ignorance, they contribute to destructive policies that negatively impact local communities and their inherent relationships with their land and the culture that supports it. Lovett has found that a mystical, transcendent quality can arise in the surfing experience when performed in such stupendously pristine, natural, aquatic environments. It is with this key parameter in mind that he continues to deepen his understanding of the limits of acceptable change, so that benefits may flow not only to communities living in fragile archipelagic environments but also to the visitors who make their personal journey of discovery to enjoy such awe-inspiring locations.

Rob Machado
Rob Machado is not just one of the world's greatest surfers, he's one of the sport's most recognizable characters, a living icon who continues to expand the definition of what professional surfing is all about. Machado was consistently among the top-seeded competitors while on the ASP World Tour. With twelve career WCT victories, Machado has been among the elite Top Ten Most Popular Surfers since 1996 on *Surfer Magazine*'s Surfer Poll. He was inducted into the Surfer's Hall of Fame in 2000, awarded the prestigious honor of Waterman's of the Year by the Surf Industry Manufacturers Association (SIMA) in 2009 and, in 2011, the City of Huntington Beach, California awarded him a star on the Surfing Walk of Fame. Since his departure from the ASP tour in 2001, Machado has been one of surfing's most committed ambassadors, roaming the

globe, surfing the world's best waves and deepening his commitment to support various humanitarian and environmental organizations. In 2009 he was the recipient of the One Degree Less Award from Planet Green + the Water Council of Brazil Project and recognized by Oceana for his dedication to environmental activism.

Mark Marovich
Mark Marovich is a long struggling regular footer currently enjoying family, waves and work in San Diego, California. Schooled in History (with a Master's Degree in Environmental History) and Southern Californian beach breaks, Marovich has taken his studies and love of the ocean into his professional life. After a 15-year stint in the online retail for a major surf retailer and brand, he currently leads partnership development for FlipGive, a corporate social responsibility technology and marketing firm in the fundraising space. In terms of Marovich's extracurricular activities, he's a very proud board member of the non-profit Sustainable Surf and he is chief Posting Officer for his surfing and sustainability blog, The Greener Blue.

Bob McKnight
Bob McKnight, co- founded Quiksilver in 1976 and has served as the company's President, CEO and Chairman of the Board since its inception. Under his watch, Quiksilver has grown from a startup to a worldwide corporation with revenues of $2 billion. Today, Quiksilver, Inc. is a globally diversified, world leader in outdoor lifestyle apparel with their three main brands of Quiksilver, Roxy and DC. Quiksilver, Inc. has over 7,000 employees, operates in over 90 countries and has close to 900 retail stores in the world.

McKnight currently resides in Laguna Beach, CA with his wife Annette and their three children, Kristi, Roxy and Robbie. Both Kristi and Roxy work in Public Relations and Marketing. Robbie is currently a sophomore at USC where he is majoring in Business and plays on the USC Men's Volleyball Team. He is also on the Board of Otis College of Art and Design, The Wrigley Institute, The Ocean Institute in Dana Point, and Jones Trading and Associates. In his spare time he enjoys surfing, snowboarding, diving and playing beach volleyball.

Jim Moriarty
Jim Moriarty is the currently working at 72andSunny in Los Angeles. His job is to connect world-class brands like Starbucks, Google and Samsung to ideas

that enrich their customers lives and make the world a better place. Prior to this, he was CEO of Surfrider Foundation for almost 10 years. Under his tenure the network logged hundreds of coastal victories and grew the network to more than a hundred chapters and clubs in the United States and into more than a dozen other countries. Before Surfrider, Moriarty worked at technology companies large and small in the ecommerce, learning and search engine sectors.

Dr. Chad Nelsen
Dr. Nelsen is the Chief Executive Officer for the Surfrider Foundation and leads the world's largest grassroots network dedicated to ensure healthy a ocean, waves and beaches through approaches that integrate coastal recreation with conservation. Nelsen has over 20 years of experience in ocean and coastal conservation working at the interface of marine science and public policy. He earned a Doctorate from the University of California, Los Angeles, a Master's in Environmental Management from Duke University's Nicholas School for the Environment, and Bachelor's of Science from Brown University.

Eduardo Najera
Current Mexico Director of WILDCOAST/COSTASALVAJE, Eduardo Najera has also worked for the Mexican National Protected Areas Commission and carried out research and conservation projects throughout Mexico and New Zealand. He received his PhD in Conservation Ecology from AUT in New Zealand and can be found riding waves at San Miguel in Baja, a World Surfing Reserve located down the hill from his house.

Dr. Danny O'Brien
Dr. Danny O'Brien is an Associate Professor and Head of Programme, Sport Management, in the School of Health Sciences at Bond University. Dr. O'Brien is a graduate of Australian Catholic University and California State University, Long Beach. In 2000, he completed a PhD in sport management from DeMontfort University, UK that explored organisational change in English rugby union. Dr. O'Brien teaches sport tourism, event management, and strategic management. His research interests lie in sustainable surf tourism, event leveraging, and organisational change. He has served on the Editorial Boards of three academic journals for over 10 years and is the incoming Associate Editor of Sport Management Review. Dr. O'Brien has presented at over 30 international conferences and published book chapters and articles

in peer-reviewed journals such as *Journal of Sport Management, European Sport Management Quarterly, Annals of Tourism Research, European Journal of Marketing, International Journal of Culture, Tourism and Hospitality Research, Journal of Hospitality & Tourism Research*, and the *Journal of Leisure Research*. Dr. O'Brien is a member of Bond University's Water-Based Research Unit and is also a visiting professor at both the Center for Surf Research at San Diego State University and the Plymouth Sustainability and Surfing Research Group at Plymouth University, UK.

Doug Palladini
President of the Surf Industry Manufacturer's Association Doug Palladini has also served as the VP/GM of Vans North America (marketing and brand leadership) since 2004. A surf/skate/snow industry veteran of more than a quarter century, Palladini has worked in all facets of the business, including media, where he was once Publisher of *Surfer Magazine*. A Southern California lifer, Palladini currently resides in San Juan Capistrano, California with his wife Hallie.

Zach Plopper
Coastal and Marine Director for WILDCOAST/COSTASALVAJE Zach Plopper divides his time between managing a new system of marine protected areas in San Diego County and helping protect wild coastlines in Baja California. He received his Master's in Urban Planning from UCLA and grew up surfing Seaside Reef in Solana Beach, one of the MPA's he is working to preserve.

Peter Robinson
Pete Robinson is the founder of the Museum of British Surfing, and an award-winning former ITV news reporter & senior manager for the national television broadcaster. With a passion for investigation and surfing history, he has uncovered remarkable evidence of Britain's love affair with surfing dating back as far as 1769. He donated his massive surf heritage collection to the charity in 2011, "as a gift for future generations to enjoy". Robinson began researching British surfing history in 1997 and operated the surfing museum's touring exhibitions from 2003. He established the Museum of British Surfing as a Registered Charity in 2009, with a strong environmental and educational focus, and finally opened the doors to its first permanent home in Braunton, North Devon in April 2012 after a three-year fundraising campaign.

Derek Sabori
Since starting at Volcom in 1996, Derek has held many diverse roles at the company and currently serves as the Vice President of Sustainability under the leadership of the CEO and the Sustainability Team at Kering, Volcom's parent company. In the years since, Sabori received his MBA from the Paul Merage School of Business at UC Irvine and has made it his mission to share his vision of a healthy & sustainable future for his two children by carving out a professional niche in Sustainability and by self publishing a children's Eco Action-Adventure picture book (www.earthbugcrew.com). Sabori serves as a director on the boards of the Costa Mesa Foundation, the Orange Coast College Foundation, and PangeaSeed, an NGO dedicated to shark and ocean conservation. Living, working and playing in Costa Mesa, California, Derek can be followed at the Volcom.com/newfuture blog and at @derekasbori. Full bio at linkedin.com/dereksabori.

Cori Schumacher
Cori Schumacher began surfing at the age of five and competing at the age of eight. During her competitive career, she won acclaim in both shortboarding and longboarding. Schumacher garnered multiple national and international titles in shortboarding, moving steadily forward onto the professional surfing tour. She decided to drop off the professional shortboard circuit after experiencing the inequality and prejudicial nature of the professional surfing paradigm. Later, she returned to longboard competition where she became a three-time World Longboard Champion. As the defending world champion, Schumacher boycotted the 2011 women's world longboard championships, which was the first professional grade (Association of Surfing Professionals/World Surf League) surfing event to be held in China. She cited political reservations specific to women's rights, the environment, and broader human rights concerns. Since this time, Schumacher has remained a vocal advocate and activist tackling issues such as gender disparity, homophobia, and the social and environmental impacts of consumer culture. In 2012, she founded the non-profit The Inspire Initiative, which seeks to empower women through surfing by deepening our understanding of, and participation with, the potential surfing has as a complicated force for the physical liberation of women and girls around the world. She has been published in The Guardian, The Surfer's Journal, Gender Across Borders, The Inertia, and regularly blogs at corischumacher.com.

Michael Stewart

Has been focused on sustainability issues, in particular Climate Change, and certification of "greener" or sustainable products at several notable start-up companies. These include UL Environment, (a new business of the plus 116-year-old nonprofit Underwriters Labs), Cooler Inc., Carbonfund.org and the Social Venture Network, where he has worked with many of the biggest consumer product brands to look at the impacts of their products. This experience has allowed Stewart to work with action sports lifestyle brands to evaluate the environmental impacts of products, services, and events, consulting on how to reduce/compensate/offset those environmental impacts with "certified" environmental projects like tropical reforestation and renewable energy. Stewart has been a longtime volunteer with Surfrider, and is the current vice chair of the San Francisco chapter of Surfrider (www.sfsurfrider.org) as well as an adviser to the Save the Waves Coalition (www.savethewaves.org).

Hugo Tagholm

Hugo Tagholm is Chief Executive of Surfers Against Sewage (SAS) and had been involved with the organisation since its inception in 1990 as a member, trustee and environmental campaigner. Since taking the helm, Tagholm has led the development of SAS into a multi-issue environmental charity focusing on the protection of the UK's waves, oceans and beaches, otherwise known as 'surf habitats'. Tagholm has also led the development of SAS's international partnerships with global affiliates including with the Surfrider Foundation and Save The Waves, to share expertise and identify effective collaborations to increase the impact of the enviro-surf movement.

Tagholm has been involved with a number of charities big and small during his career. For a number of years he worked with the former Prime Minister's wife, Sarah Brown, helping run her charity PiggyBankKids (now Theirworld. org), set up to help save the lives of premature babies and create opportunities for underprivileged young people. He also helped launch the Museum of British Surfing and served as a Trustee and Chairman for two years.

Shaun Tomson

Shaun Tomson is a former World Professional Surfing Champion and has been described as one of the greatest surfers of all time and one of the most influential surfers of the century. Tomson founded and sold two apparel brands – Instinct in the '80s and Solitude in the '90s. He is the author of the best-selling book *Surfer's Code* and the #1 Amazon best seller *The Code*, a collection of personal stories to inspire young people to make positive decisions in a challenging environment. He is a Business Administration and Finance graduate from the University of Natal in his homeland of South Africa and is currently completing a Master's of Science degree in leadership and social change.

As a public speaker, he has spoken internationally and has shared the stage with well-known personalities including Sir Richard Branson and Malcolm Gladwell, and inspired corporations like General Motors, Cisco, Price Waterhouse, Toys 'R' Us, Disney, Google, and the Gap. He is a self-empowerment and self-leadership expert and lectures to 100,000 students every year about committing to positive choices. He is on the board of directors of Surfrider Foundation and the Santa Barbara Boys and Girls Club. He currently lives with his wife and son in Santa Barbara, California and still finds time to chase the perfect wave.

Jessica Toth
Jessica Toth has overseen the recent turnaround at the Solana Center, the 30-year-old nonprofit that pioneered residential recycling in southern California. Prior to Solana Center, Toth developed the environmental programs and managed operations at the Rob Machado Foundation. Though always passionate about the environment, Toth took a circuitous route to get here, starting on Wall Street during the 1980s. Since then, she held positions in corporate research, marketing, IT consulting, and business process improvement at companies including Hewlett-Packard, Texas Instruments, the World Bank, Kyocera, SDG&E, and the San Diego Zoo. She also co-founded and ran Curious Company, an educational software company. Toth holds a Master's degree from MIT in Business and a Bachelor's degree from Cornell in Engineering.

Kevin Whilden
Kevin Whilden is a sustainable business entrepreneur and geologist. He has a wide range of expertise in sustainable business and policy, and the scientific expertise to explain why it matters. Before launching Sustainable Surf, he helped launch Imagine Surf, which was an early pioneer in sustainable surfboard construction. Prior to that, Whilden worked in San Francisco for the cleantech startup Climos, designing technology to remove large quantities of CO_2 from the atmosphere by enhancing natural biological absorption in the ocean. Solving the problem of climate change has been the focus of his career

after learning about it while studying geology in between surf sessions as an undergraduate physics major at UC San Diego in 1990.

Emma Whitlsea
Emma Whittlesea was a Sustainability Strategist for South West Tourism and worked in the Low Carbon Team for the Cornwall Development Company in the UK. She chaired the Climate South West Tourism Group for three years and her research examines the CO_2 impact of visitors to the South West of England, investigating the opportunities and challenges for low-carbon destination management. This case study was developed in collaboration with VisitCornwall and Cool Earth.

Jeff Wilson
Jeff Wilson is the Director of Business Value Strategy and Development, responsible for ensuring meaningful business value is delivered to membership and their respective industry sectors. His role includes strategy development and implementation, membership value development and delivery, industry collaboration, and operations. Wilson's career has been in sales and marketing and general business management in the for-profit sector with numerous market leading companies including Delta Air Lines and Quiksilver/Roxy/DC Shoes. Wilson led the establishment of the global sustainability organization at Quiksilver and has been an active participant in industry collaboration with Textile Exchange, the Outdoor Industry Association Sustainability Working Group, and the Sustainable Apparel Coalition. He has a Master's in Business Administration in Marketing and Strategic Planning from the University of Southern California and a Bachelor's degree in Environmental Studies from the University of California Santa Barbara.

Todd Woody
Todd Woody is senior editor for environment and wildlife at *TakePart*, the digital magazine of Participant Media, the Los Angeles film production Company that produced *An Inconvenient Truth*, *Citizenfour* and othes. He previously covered environmental issues as a contributor to *The New York Times*, *The Atlantic*, and *Quartz*. In addition, Woody has held reporting, editing and department head positions at a variety of publications, including *Fortune Magazine*, *Forbes Magazine*, *Business 2.0 Magazine*, the *San Jose Mercury News* and *The Industry Standard*.

References & Notes

1.2

1 See: Borne, G., (2010) A Framework for Sustainable Global Development and the Effective Governance of Risk, New York, Edwin Mellen Press.
Sachs, J., (2015) The Age of Sustainable Development, Columbia University Press
2 Carson, R., (1962) *Silent Spring*, Houghton Miflin.
3 Ehrlich, P., (1968) *The Population Bomb*, New York, Buccaneer Books.
4 Meadows, D., Meadows, D., Randers, J. and Behrens, W. (1972) *The Limits to Growth*, New York, Universal Books.
5 World Commission on Environment and Development (1987) Our Common Future, Oxford, Oxford University Press.
6 http://www.un.org/geninfo/bp/enviro.html
7 UN (2002) Report of the World Summit on Sustainable Development, Johannesburg, South Africa, 26th August-4th September, A/CONF.199/20
8 Visbeck M., Kronfeld-Goharani U., Neumann B., Rickels W., Schmidt J., van Doorn E., Matz-Lück N., Proelss A., (2014) A sustainable development goal for the ocean and Coasts: Global ocean challenges benefit from regional initiatives supporting globally coordinated solutions, *Marine Policy* 48: 184-191
9 & 10 Griggs, D., Stafford-Smith,M, Gaffney,O, Rockström, J., Öhman, M,Shyamsundar,P Steffen, W, Glaser, G, Kanie, N Noble, I., (2012) Policy: Sustainable development Goals for People and Planet Nature 495: 305-307
11 See: Borne, G., (2010) A Framework for Sustainable Global Development and Effective Governance of Risk, New York Edwin Mellen Press
12 Borne, G., (2010a) Sustainable Global Development and the Effective Governance of Risk, New York, Edwin Mellen Press
Borne,G., (2010b) Sustainable Development Representing a Reflexive Modernity Inside the United Nations, *Journal of Global Analysis* 1(1): 28-50
Borne, G., (forthcoming) (2014) Governance in Transition: Sustainable Development at the Local Level in a Global Context, Edwin Mellen Press
Borne, G., (2013a) Sustainable Development and the Olympics, *Sociological Research Online* 18(3)18 http://www.socresonline.org.uk/18/3/18.html
Borne, G., (2012) Power to the Parish, *Public Services Review*: Local Government and the Regions 20 http://goo.gl/hmkFf
Borne, G., (2012) Sustainable Development and Surfing, The Inertia August 2nd 2012

13 Scottish Executive (2006) Sustainable Development a Review of international Literature http://www.thepep.org/ClearingHouse/docfiles/Sustainable.Development. Review.of.International.Literature.pdf
14 Kates, R., (2011) What kind of science is sustainability science? PNAS 108 (49): 19449-19450
15 'An emerging field of research dealing with the interaftions between natural and social systems and with how those interactions affect the challenge of sustainability'
16 Harris, G., (2007) *Seeking Sustainability in an age of Complexity*, Cambridge, Cambridge University Press
Norberg, J and Cumming, G., (Eds) (2008) *Complexity Theory for a Sustainable Future* New York, Columbia University Press
Borne, G., (2010a) Sustainable Global Development and the effective Governance of Risk, New York, Edwin Mellen Press
17 http://thegreenerblue.com
18 http://www.theinertia.com/

3.4

1 Snow goggles sales benefit Protect Our Winters; sunglasses sales benefit the Surfrider Foundation.
2 Rerip, a non-profit organisation, has a cradle-to-cradle programme in California for reusing and re-purposing surfboards.
3 FSC is the Forest Stewardship Council, an international not-for-profit organization. FSC certification verifies that responsible forest practices were used to obtain paper products.
4 Danovaro R, Bongiorni L, Corinaldesi C, Giovannelli D, Damiani E, Astolfi P, Greci L, Pusceddu A. "Sunscreens cause coral bleaching by promoting viral infections". Environmental Health Perspectives. 2008 Apr;116(4):441-7. doi: 10.1289/ehp.10966.
5 Reef-building coral species host a type of algae that provides food energy to the coral. This process contributes to providing coral reefs' striking colours.
6 http://nikeinc.com/pages/manufacturing
7 Center of Communication & Civic Engagement chronicles the press accounts from anti-sweatshop campaigns directed at conditions in Indonesia (http://depts. washington.edu/ccce/polcommcampaigns/NikeChronology.htm).

4.2

1 Anna Edwards, "Design with Green Twist," *Courier Mail* [Brisbane], 16 November 2006.
2 Leslie Wayne, "To Delaware, With Love," *The New York Times*, 1 July 2012.
3 Quiksilver and Roxy Initiative, "Foundation: History," no date, at <http://the-quiksilver-initiative.com/Foundation> (accessed 29 July 2013).
4 Joseph Kahn, "When Chinese Workers Unite, the Bosses Often Run the Union," *The New York Times*, 29 December 2003.
5 China Labor Watch, "Textile Sweatshops; Adidas, Bali Intimates, Hanesbrands Inc., Piege Co (Felina Lingerie), Quiksilver, Regina Miracle Speedo, Walcoal America Inc., and Wal-Mart Made in China," Press Release, 19 November 2007, at <http://digitalcommons.ilr.cornell.edu/globaldocs/305/> (accessed 4 December 2012).

6 "Boost Mobile and Quiksilver Continue Brand Alliance with Second Roxy-Branded Wireless Phone," *Business Wire*, 1 September 2004.
7 Upton Sinclair, *The Jungle* (New York: Doubleday, Page and Co., 1906); Thomas Bell, *Out of This Furnace* (Boston: Little, Brown and Co., 1941).
8 On some of the surfwear brands with products made in Bangladesh, see Cori Schumacher, "Bangladesh: Dying for Fashion," 24 April-30 May 2013, at <http://www.corischumacher.com/2013/05/20/bangladesh-dying-for-fashion/> (accessed 29 July 2013). On the wages of workers in the Bangladeshi garment industry, see *Global Wage Trends for Apparel Workers, 2001-2011* (Worker Rights Consortium, July 2013), at <http://www.americanprogress.org/wp-content/uploads/2013/07/RealWageStudy-3.pdf> (accessed 12 July 2013).
9 Worldwide Responsible Accredited Production, "About Wrap," no date, at <http://www.wrapapparel.org/en/about-us> (accessed 1 August 2013).

4.3

1 London, Jack, *"My Hawaiian Aloha," from Our Hawaii: Island and Islanders* (Charmian London) New York: Macmillan, 1922. P. 8.
2 Huggan, Graham. *The Postcolonial Exotic: Marketing the Margins*. London: Routledge, 2001, p. 22 – 27.
3 Arendt, Hannah. *The Origins of Totalitarianism*. New York, London, San Diego: Harcourt, 1978, p. 190
4 Thomas, Brendan. "Joel Tudor: Unfiltered." From *Surfer Magazine*, 28th Jan, 2013, Stable url: http://www.surfermag.com/features/joel-tudor-unfiltered/.
5 Pratt, Mary Louise. *Imperial Eyes: Travel Writing and Transculturation*. New York: Routledge, 2009 [1992].

4.4

1 http://www.free2work.org/trends/apparel/
2 Wrinkle, H., Eriksson, E., and Lee, A. (2012) Apparel Industry Trends: From *Farm to Factory*. Free2Work.org

4.5

1 Dan Ross - http://thinkprogress.org/climate/2013/08/01/2164691/endless-summer-how-climate-change-could-wipe-out-surfing/
2 Project Woo - http://www.projectwoo.org/project-woo/
3 Sustainable Surf - http://sustainablesurf.org/about-us/
4 Patagonia - http://www.patagonia.com/us/patagonia.go?assetid=2047
5 Jedidiah - http://jedidiahusa.com/pages/about-us

5.1

1 Kildow, J., & Colgan, C. S. (2005). California's Ocean Economy, Report to the Resources Agency, State of California. Prepared by the National Ocean Economics Program.
2 Atiyah, P. (2009). Non-Market Valuation and Marine Management: Using Panel Data Analysis to Measure Policy Impacts on Coastal Resources. Environmental Health Sciences. University of California Los Angeles, Los Angeles.

REFERENCES & NOTES

3 Pendleton, L., LaFranchi, C., & Nelsen, C. (2009). The California Coast Online Survey: Southern California Module. Report to the Santa Monica Bay Restoration Foundation.
4 Haab, T. C., & McConnell, K. E. (2002). Valuing Environmental and Natural Resources: The Econometrics of Non-Market Valuation (p. 326). Northhampton, MA: Edward Elgar Publishing Limited, Inc.
5 Chapman, D. J., & Hanneman, W. M. (2001). Environmental Damages In Court: The American Trader Case. In A. Heyes (Ed.), The Law and Economics of the Environment (pp. 319–367).
Pendleton, L., LaFranchi, C., & Nelsen, C. (2009). The California Coast Online Survey: Southern California Module. Report to the Santa Monica Bay Restoration Foundation.
6 Dillman, D. A., Smyth, J. D., & Christian, L. M. (2009). Internet, mail, and mixed-mode surveys: The tailored design method. Hoboken, NJ: Wiley.
7 Couper, M. P. (2000). Web Surveys: A Review of Issues and Approaches. The Public Opinion Quarterly, 64(4), 464–494.
8 Nelsen, C., Pendleton, L., & Vaugh, R. (2007). A Socioeconomic Study of Surfers at Trestles Beach. Shore & Beach, 75(4), 32–37.
9 Chapman, D. J., & Hanneman, W. M. (2001). Environmental Damages In Court: The American Trader Case. In A. Heyes (Ed.), The Law and Economics of the Environment (pp. 319–367).
10 Nelsen, C., Pendleton, L., & Vaugh, R. (2007). A Socioeconomic Study of Surfers at Trestles Beach. Shore & Beach, 75(4), 32–37.
11 Nelsen, C. (2012). Collecting and using Economic Information to Guide the Management of Coastal Recreational Resources in California. University of California, Los Angeles.
12 CCC, C. C. C. (2007). Coastal Commission Staff Report and Recommendation on Consistency Certification CC-018-07, 236.
13 Lazarow, N., Miller, M. L., & Blackwell, B. (2007). Dropping In: A Case Study Approach To Understanding The Socioeconomic Impact Of Recreational Surfing And Its Value To The Coastal Economy. Shore & Beach, 75(4), 21–31.
14 Murphy, Melissa, and Maria Bernal. "The impact of surfing on the local economy of Mundaka, Spain." Report commissioned by Save the Waves Coalition (2008).
15 Murphy, Melissa, and Maria Bernal. "The impact of surfing on the local economy of Mundaka, Spain." Report commissioned by Save the Waves Coalition (2008).
16 Coffman, M., and K. Burnett. "The value of a wave: An analysis of the Mavericks Region, Half Moon Bay, California." San Francisco: Save the Waves Coalition (2009).

5.4

1 Meier, M. (2005) Gender Sport and Development. Working Paper, Swiss Academy for Development.
2 One of the few pre-Twentieth Century Hawaiian surfboards to survive the cultural extermination of Nineteenth Century Hawaii. This board has been housed at the Bishop Museum in Honolulu since 1922.
3 Meier, M. (2005) Gender Sport and Development. Working Paper, Swiss Academy for Development.

4 Saavedra, M. (2004) "Gender and Sport," in A Companion to Gender Studies, edited by P. Essed, A. Kobayashi and D. T. Goldberg. London: Blackwell Publishing.
5 Creedan, P. (1994) Women, Media, and Sport. Challenging Gender Values, Thousand Oaks, CA.
6 Surf and development organizations that participated in this study include: *Waves of Freedom, Beyond the Surface International, Robertsport Community Works, Mama Liberia, Cubanita Surf, Kovalam Surf Club.*
7 Mensch, B.S., Bruce J. and Greene, M.E. (1998) The Uncharted Passage. Girls' adolescence in the developing world, Population Council, New York, USA.
8 World Bank (2012) On Norms and Agency: Conversations about Gender Equality with Women and Men in 20 Countries. Conference Edition.
9 World Bank (2012) On Norms and Agency: Conversations about Gender Equality with Women and Men in 20 Countries. Conference Edition.
10 Mensch, B.S., Bruce J. and Greene, M.E. (1998) The Uncharted Passage. Girls' adolescence in the developing world, Population Council, New York, USA.
11 World Bank (2012) On Norms and Agency: Conversations about Gender Equality with Women and Men in 20 Countries. Conference Edition. p. 26.
12 Fair Surf is a great example of a new initiative that seeks to strengthen relationships for social good by connecting a global alliance of businesses and consumers with surf non-profit organisations so that together they can support coastal regions and their communities efficiently and effectively.
13 Wahine (1998) Aloha Rell Sunn. Vol. 4, No. 2. Wahine Magazine

5.6

1 Pandolfi, J. M., Connolly, S. R., Marshall, D. J. & Cohen, A. L. Projecting Coral Reef Futures Under Global Warming and Ocean Acidification. Science 333 (2011).
2 Burke, L., Reytar, K., Spalding, M. & Perry, A. Reefs At Risk Revisted. (World Resources Institute, 2011).
3 IPCC. Climate Change 2013: The Physical Science Basis. Contribution of Working Group I to the Fifth Assessment Report of the Intergovernmental Panel on Climate Change. 1535 (Cambridge, United Kingdom and New York, NY, USA, 2013).
4 Kemp, A. C. & Horton, B. P. Contribution of relative sea-level rise to historical hurricane flooding in New York City. Journal of Quaternary Science 28(6), 537-541 (2013).

6.3

1 Ponting (2004). Wali Kam: An organic surf culture blooms in New Guinea. The Surfers Journal, 13(4), 5-8.
Ponting, J. (2005). Yes Prime Minister. Pacific Longboarder, 9(1), 45-50.
2 Ponting, J. (2005). Yes Prime Minister. Pacific Longboarder, 9(1), 45-50.
3 Ponting, J. (2009). Consuming Nirvana: The social construction of surfing tourist space. Saarbrücken: VDM Verlag.
4 Ponting, J. (2009). Consuming Nirvana: The social construction of surfing tourist space. Saarbrücken: VDM Verlag.p260

5 Ponting, J., McDonald, M.G. & Wearing, S.L. (2005). De-constructing wonderland: surfing tourism in the Mentawai Islands, Indonesia. Loisir et Societe/ Society and Leisure, 28(1), 141-162, p141
6 Nui Ailan Surfriders Alliance (NASA), (2008). Surf management plans brochure, 2007/2008 season. PNG: Nui Ailan Surfriders Alliance.
7 O'Brien, D., & Ponting, J., (2013). Sustainable surf tourism: A community centered approach in Papua New Guinea. Journal of Sport Management, 27, 158-172, p164

8 PNG Tourism Promotion Authority (2006). Papua New Guinea tourism sector review and master plan (2007-2017): Growing PNG tourism as a sustainable industry. Retrieved from, p26 http://www.papuanewguineatourism.com/png/export/sites/TPA/masterplan__report.pdf
9 PNG Tourism Promotion Authority (2006). Papua New Guinea tourism sector review and master plan (2007-2017): Growing PNG tourism as a sustainable industry. Retrieved from, p60http://www.papuanewguineatourism.com/png/export/sites/TPA/masterplan__report.pdf
10 O'Brien, D. (2010). Surf tourism in PNG: Ready, willing, and Andy Abel. Pacific Longboarder, 13(5), pp. 64-65., p60
11 O'Brien, D. (2011). Tupira: The birth of a surf culture. Pacific Longboarder, 15(1), 62-65. P62
12 O'Brien, D., & Ponting, J., (2013). Sustainable surf tourism: A community centered approach in Papua New Guinea. Journal of Sport Management, 27, 158-172, p169

6.5
1 Blair, 1997. Text of speech by Rt Hon. Tony Blair, Prime Minister and Leader of the labour Party. Labour Party Annual Conference, Brighton September 1997. Accessed February 2013 from, http://www.prnewswire.co.uk/news-releases.
2 Dearing, R. 1997. The National Committee of Inquiry into Higher Education, Higher Education in the Learning Society ("The Dearing Report"), July 1997.
3 DfEE 1998 The Learning Age: A Renaissance for a New Britain. Department for Education and Employment. Volume 3790 CM Series. Great Britain Parliament. HMSO 1998.
4 Farrelly, M. and McGregor, C. 1965. How to Surf. Rigby Ltd, Adelaide p. 15
5 Fallows, S., and Steven, C., 2000. Integrating Key Skills in Higher Education: Employability, Transferable Skills and Learning for Life, London: Kogan Page.
6 Anon. 2013a http://www.citaten.net/en/search/quotes_by-eugene_delacroix.html. Accessed February 2013.
7 THES, 1999. Times Higher Education Supplement. 12th March 1999.
8 Western Morning News. 2004. Surfing is now worth £100m. Western Morning News. Journalist, Paul Andrews. Front Cover Story, 12th August 2004.
9 THES, 1999. Times Higher Education Supplement. 12th March 1999.
10 The Times. 2001. More than froth. 10th October 2001
11 Morris, 2004. What use is a Surfing Degree? Speech delivered at the Annual Conference of the Professional Association of Teachers (UK), Bournemouth, July 2004. Cited in http://www.smh.com.au/articles Accessed February 2013.

12 Focus, 2003. Surf's Up: Is the University of Plymouth's BSc (hons) in Surf Science & Technology the dumbing-down of science or an exciting new way to learn? Journalist - Sally Palmer. Focus. Immediate Media. August 2003
13 Times Higher, 2002. Plymouth Riding High. Times Higher Education Supplement, 31st May, 2002. Journalist – Alison Goddard.
14 Wilde, O. (1890). quote from, Picture of Dorian Gray. Cited in http://www.notable-quotes.com/w/wilde_oscar.html. accessed February 2013.
15 Ford, N and Brown, D. 2006 Surfing and Social Theory. Routledge.Oxon.
16 Browne, 2010. Securing a Sustainable Future for Higher Education: An Independent Review of Higher Education Funding and Student Finance. www.independent.gov.uk/browne-report . Accessed March 2013.
17 Rinehart, R.E. 2000. Emerging Arriving Sport: Alternatives to Formal Sports, in Coakley J & Dunning E (Eds) Handbook of Sports Studies. London. Sage.pp 504-519
18 Western Morning News. 2004. Surfing is now worth £100m. Western Morning News. Journalist, Paul Andrews. Front Cover Story, 12th August 2004.
19 Wikinvest. 2013. http://www.wikinvest.com/stock/Quiksilver_(ZQK). accessed March 2013.
20 Investing.money. 2013. http://investing.money.msn.com/investments/equity-charts. accessed March 2013
21 bbc.co.uk. 2012. Surfwear Business GUL bought out. http://www.bbc.co.uk/news/uk-england-cornwall-13168491. Accessed March 2013.
22 Browne, 2010. Securing a Sustainable Future for Higher Education: An Independent Review of Higher Education Funding and Student Finance. www.independent.gov.uk/browne-report . Accessed March 2013.
23 The Australian. 2012. Billabong dumps CEO Derek O'Neill for consultant Laura Inman. http://www.theaustralian.com.au/business/companies/. accessed March 2013
24 Anon. 2013b HE in England from 2012: Student Numbers. www.parliament.uk/briefing-papers/sn06205.pdf. Accessed March 2013.

7.1

1 Martin, S. A., & Assenov, I. (2012). The genesis of a new body of sport tourism literature: A systematic review of surf tourism research (1997-2011). Journal of Sport and Tourism, 17(4), 257–287. doi:10.1080/14775085.2013.766528
2 Lazarow, N., & Nelson, C. (2007). The Value of Coastal Recreation Resources: A case study approach to examine the value of recreational surfing to specific locales. Paper presented at the Coastal Zone, Portland.
3 Warshaw, M. (2008). Surfing: A History. Retrieved from http://topics.blogs.nytimes.com/2008/05/30/surfing-a-history/
4 Aguerre, F. (2009). A Surfer at the Olympic Congress in Denmark. ISA Newsletter. Retrieved from http://www.isasurf.org/newsletter/31/en/31.html
5 O'Brien, D., & Eddie, I. (2013). Benchmarking global best practice: Innovation and leadership in surf city tourism and industry development. Paper presented at the Global Surf Cities Conference, Kirra Community and Cultural Centre.

REFERENCES & NOTES

6 Wagner, G. S., Nelson, C., & Walker, M. (2011). A Socioeconomic and Recreational Profile of Surfers in the United States: A report by Surf-First and the Surfrider Foundation. Surfrider Foundation.
7 Barbieri, C., & Sotomayor, S. (2013). Surf Travel Behavior and Destination Preferences: An application of the serious leisure inventory and measure. Tourism Management, 35(April), 111-121.
8 Martin, S. A., & Assenov, I. (2012). The genesis of a new body of sport tourism literature: A systematic review of surf tourism research (1997-2011). Journal of Sport and Tourism, 17(4), 257-287. doi:10.1080/14775085.2013.766528
9 Margules, T. (2011). Understanding the Roles of Ecosystem Services in the Local Economy of Uluwatu, Bali, Indonesia. (BSc. Hons), Southern Cross University.
10 Murphy, M., & Bernal, M. (2008). The Impact of Surfing on the Local Economy of Mundaka, Spain. San Francisco: Save the Waves Coalition.
11 Coffman, M., & Burnett, K. (2009). The Value of a Wave: An analysis of the Mavericks Region, Half Moon Bay, California. San Francisco: Save the Waves Coalition.
12 Gold Coast City Council (2009). Surf industry review and economic contributions assessment. Gold Coast: Gold Coast City Council.
13 O'Brien, D., & Eddie, I. (2013). Benchmarking global best practice: Innovation and leadership in surf city tourism and industry development. Paper presented at the Global Surf Cities Conference, Kirra Community and Cultural Centre.
14 Ponting, J. (2008). Consuming Nirvana: An exploration of surfing tourist space. (Ph.D. Leisure & Tourism), University of Technology, Sydney, Sydney.
15 See Ponting, J. (2008). Consuming Nirvana: An exploration of surfing tourist space. (Ph.D. Leisure & Tourism), University of Technology, Sydney, Sydney.
Ponting, J., & McDonald, M. (2013). Performance, agency and change in surfing tourist space. Annals of Tourism Research. 43, pp. 415-434
16 Mavric, M., & Urry, J. (2012). Tourism Studies and the New Mobilities Paradigm (NMP). In T. Jamal & M. Robinson (Eds.), The SAGE Handbook of Tourism Studies (Paperback ed., pp. 645-656). London: Sage.
17 Ponting, J., & McDonald, M. (2013). Performance, agency and change in surfing tourist space. Annals of Tourism Research. 43, pp. 415-434
18 Ponting, J., McDonald, M., & Wearing, S. (2005). De-constructing Wonderland: Surfing tourism in the Mentawai Islands, Indonesia. Society and Leisure, 28(1), 141-162.
19 O'Brien, D., & Ponting, J. (2013). Sustainable Surf Tourism: A community centered approach in Papua New Guinea. Journal of Sport Tourism. 27(2) pp. 158-172
20 Ponting, J. and O'Brien, D. (2014) "Liberalizing Nirvana: An analysis of the consequences of common pool resource deregulation for the sustainability of Fiji's surf tourism industry" Journal of Sustainable Tourism 22(3), 384-402

7.3
1 Department for Transport, 2010. Transport Statistics Great Britain. Statistical Release, November 2010
2 Ibid
3 http://www.grida.no/publications/other/ipcc_sr/?src=/climate/ipcc/aviation/064.htm
4 Jardine, C. 2008. Calculating the Environmental Impact of Aviation Emissions, 2nd Ed, Environmental Change Institute, University of Oxford
5 http://www.myfootprint.org/
6 http://www.theinertia.com/business-media/stoked-and-broke-review-cyrus-sutton-surf-film/
7 Beamish, C. 2012. The Voyage of the Cormorant. Patagonia Books, 323 pp
8 http://www.surfscience.org/reports
9 Australian Surfing Life, 2009. Seven surfers committed to change. Australian Surfing Life 252: 87-95
10 http://www.bbc.co.uk/nature/humanplanetexplorer/environments/oceans#p00gxmg1

7.4
1 The South West Research Company (2012) Value of Tourism 2011: Cornwall. Prepared for Visit Cornwall. Published December 2012.
2 Cornwall Council (2012) 2011 Census at a glance. July 2012.
3 Whittlesea, E. R. & Owen, A. (2012) Towards a low carbon future – the development and application of REAP Tourism, a destination footprint and scenario tool. Journal of Sustainable Tourism. Special Issue: Scenario Planning for Sustainable Tourism. Vol 20, Issue 6, 2012. Further Information and Guidance
4 Based on 15,000 visitors staying an average of 3.8 nights and 2330 staff staying an average length of 3 nights

7.5
1 Moore, M. (ed) (2013). Linking Oceans and Human Health: a strategic research priority for Europe. European Marine Board Proposition Paper 19. http://www.ecehh.org/wp-content/uploads/2013/11/OHH-Position-Paper.pdf
2 Step-n-Soul. (2013). Directed by Toma Jablon. UK: Jablon Productions. http://jablon.tv/project/step-n-soul/
3 Derrida, J., & Dufourmantelle, A. (2000). Of Hospitality (Cultural Memory in the Present). Palo Alto: Stanford University Press.

8.1
1 Doug Tompkins, Founder of The North Face, quoted in Chris Malloy's 2010 film 180 Degrees South
2 Yvonne Chouinard, Founder of Patagonia, quoted in Chris Malloy's 2010 film 180 Degrees South
3 From the screenplay of The Forgotten Island of Santosha Dir. Larry Yates. Larry Yates Films 1974
4 Ponting, J. cited in Lovett, K.J. (2006) The Dream. The Surfers Journal, 15(3)
5 surferspirit.org/programs

6 Moyers, Bill and Joseph Campbell. The Power of Myth (1988). Betty Sue Flowers (ed.). New York: Doubleday, hardcover: ISBN 0-385-24773-7
7 Blake, T. (1999) Voice of the Wave. The Surfer's Journal 8(3). (originally published 1968)
8 http://chasingsantosha.wordpress.com/2011/08/

8.3
1 BBC quote was on a promotional POSTcard for a series called Talking Green Politics, BBC News and Current Affairs. They did a half hour show on Radio 4 called Brussels Rules the Waves and we were the feature photo and first programme in the four part series.
2 House of Commons Environment Select Committee 4th report on the Pollution of Beaches (HMSO). 1990.
3 Delaney and Shelley v Carrick date: 9 Nov 95, case won May 96
4 www.Worldwatch.org

Epilogue
1 A phrase that is associated with the idea that improvements in general economy will benefit all participants. This has been shown not to be the case, but a sustainable future must be inclusive applying to all of humanity. The phrase is also broadly accredited to John F. Kennedy. However, Kennedy's speech writer Ted Sorenson explores the real origins of the phrase.
Sorensen T. (2008) Counselor: A Life at the Edge of History. New York: HarperCollins Publishers

Bibliography

Aguerre, F. (2009). A Surfer at the Olympic Congress in Denmark. *ISA Newsletter*. Retrieved from http://www.isasurf.org/newsletter/31/en/31.html

Anon. 2013a http://www.citaten.net/en/search/quotes_by-eugene_delacroix.html. Accessed February 2013.

Anon. 2013b HE in England from 2012: Student Numbers. www.parliament.uk/briefing-papers/sn06205.pdf. *Accessed March 2013*.

Barbieri, C., & Sotomayor, S. (2013). Surf Travel Behavior and Destination Preferences: An application of the serious leisure inventory and measure. *Tourism Management, 35*(April), 111-121.

bbc.co.uk. 2012. *Surfwear Business GUL bought out*. http://www.bbc.co.uk/news/uk-england-cornwall-13168491. accessed March 2013.

Blair, 1997. Text of speech by Rt Hon. Tony Blair, Prime Minister and Leader of the labour Party. Labour Party Annual Conference, Brighton September 1997. Accessed February 2013 from, http://www.prnewswire.co.uk/news-releases.

Borne, G., (2010) A Framework for Sustainable Global Analysis and the Effective Governance of Risk, New York, Edwin Mellen Press

Browne, 2010. *Securing a Sustainable Future for Higher Education: An Independent Review of Higher Education Funding and Student Finance*. www.independent.gov.uk/browne-report . Accessed March 2013.

Coffman, M., & Burnett, K. (2009). The Value of a Wave: An analysis of the Mavericks Region, Half Moon Bay, California. San Francisco: Save the Waves Coalition.

Collins, A., Jones, C. & Munday, M (2009) Assessing the environmental impacts of mega sporting events: Two options? Tourism Management 30, 828-837

Dearing, R. 1997. The National Committee of Inquiry into Higher Education, *Higher Education in the Learning Society* (*"The Dearing Report"*), July 1997.

DfEE 1998 *The Learning Age: A Renaissance for a New Britain.* Department for Education and Employment. Volume 3790 CM Series. Great Britain Parliament. HMSO 1998.

Stoner, R. 2014. *Encyclopedia of Surfing* [Online]. [Accessed 10/03/15]. Available from: http://encyclopediaofsurfing.com/entries/stoke

Fallows, S., and Steven, C., 2000. *Integrating Key Skills in Higher Education: Employability,*

Transferable Skills and Learning for Life, London: Kogan Page.

Farrelly, M. and McGregor, C. 1965. *How to Surf.* Rigby Ltd, Adelaide pp15

Focus, 2003. *Surf's Up: Is the University of Plymouth's BSc (hons) in Surf Science & Technology the dumbing-down of science or an exciting new way to learn?* Journalist - Sally Palmer. Focus. Immediate Media. August 2003

Ford, N and Brown, D. 2006 *Surfing and Social Theory.* Routledge. Oxon.

Investing.money. 2013. http://investing.money.msn.com/investments/equity-charts. accessed March 2013

Goldblatt, S. (2012) The complete guide to greener meetings and events. Wiley Publishers

Gold Coast City Council (2009). Surf industry review and economic contributions assessment. Gold Coast: Gold Coast City Council.

Hede, A. M. (2008) Managing special events in the new era of the triple bottom line. Event Management 11 (1-2), 13-22

Laderman, S. (2014) Empire in Waves, A Political History of Surfing, Berkeley, University of California Press.

Laing, J. & Frost, W. (2010) How green was my festival: Exploring challenges and opportunities associated with staging green events. International Journal of Hospitality Management 29, 261-267

Lazarow, N., & Nelson, C. (2007). *The Value of Coastal Recreation Resources: A case study approach to examine the value of recreational surfing to specific locales.* Paper presented at the Coastal Zone, Portland.

Mair, J. & Laing, J. (2012) The greening of music festivals: motivations, barriers and outcomes. Applying the Mair and Jago Model. Journal of Sustainable Tourism, 20:5, 683-700

Margules, T. (2011). *Understanding the Roles of Ecosystem Services in the Local Economy of Uluwatu, Bali, Indonesia.* (BSc. Hons), Southern Cross University.

Martin, S. A., & Assenov, I. (2012). The genesis of a new body of sport tourism literature: A systematic review of surf tourism research (1997-2011). Journal of Sport and Tourism, 17(4), 257–287. doi:10.1080/14775085.2013.766528

Mavric, M., & Urry, J. (2012). Tourism Studies and the New Mobilities Paradigm (NMP). In T. Jamal & M. Robinson (Eds.), *The SAGE Handbook of Tourism Studies* (Paperback ed., pp. 645-656). London: Sage.

Morris, 2004. *What use is a Surfing Degree?* Speech delivered at the Annual Conference of the Professional Association of Teachers (UK), Bournemouth, July 2004. Cited in http://www.smh.com.au/articles Accessed February 2013.

Murphy, M., & Bernal, M. (2008). The Impact of Surfing on the Local Economy of Mundaka, Spain. San Francisco: Save the Waves Coalition.

O'Brien, D., & Eddie, I. (2013). *Benchmarking global best practice: Innovation and leadership in surf city tourism and industry development*. Paper presented at the Global Surf Cities Conference, Kirra Community and Cultural Centre.

O'Brien, D., & Ponting, J. (2013). Sustainable Surf Tourism: A community centred approach in Papua New Guinea. *Journal of Sport Tourism*. **27**(2) pp. 158-172

Ponting, J. (2008). *Consuming Nirvana: An exploration of surfing tourist space.* (Ph.D. Leisure & Tourism), University of Technology, Sydney, Sydney.

Ponting, J. (2013) *ASP & SurfCredits Formal Plan*, Unpublished Report

Ponting, J., & McDonald, M. (2013). Performance, agency and change in surfing tourist space. *Annals of Tourism Research*. **43**, pp. 415-434

Ponting, J., McDonald, M., & Wearing, S. (2005). De-constructing Wonderland: Surfing tourism in the Mentawai Islands, Indonesia. *Society and Leisure, 28*(1), 141-162.

Ponting, J., & O'Brien, D. (2013). Liberalizing Nirvana: An analysis of the consequences of common pool resource deregulation for the sustainability of Fiji's surf tourism industry. *Journal of Sustainable Tourism*, 22(3) pp, 384-402 doi: 10.1080/09669582.2013.819879

Rinehart, R.E. 2000. *Emerging Arriving Sport: Alternatives to Formal Sports*, in Coakley J & Dunning E (Eds) Handbook of Sports Studies. London. Sage.pp 504-519

The Australian. 2012. *Billabong dumps CEO Derek O'Neill for consultant Laura Inman.* http://www.theaustralian.com.au/business/companies/. accessed March 2013

THES, 1999. Times Higher Education Supplement. 12th March 1999.

The Times. 2001. *More than froth.* 10th October 2001

Times Higher, 2002. *Plymouth Riding High.* Times Higher Education Supplement, 31st May, 2002. Journalist – Alison Goddard.

Wagner, G. S., Nelson, C., & Walker, M. (2011). *A Socioeconomic and Recreational Profile of Surfers in the United States: A report by Surf-First and the Surfrider Foundation.* Surfrider Foundation.

Warren, A and Gibson, C., (2014) Surfing Places, Surfboard Makers, Hawai'i, University of Hawai'i Press

Warshaw, M. (2008). Surfing: A History. Retrieved from http://topics.blogs.nytimes.com/2008/05/30/surfing-a-history/

Western Morning News. 2004. *Surfing is now worth £100m.* Western Morning News. Journalist, Paul Andrews. Front Cover Story, 12th August 2004.

Whittlesea, E. R. & Owen, A. (2012) Towards a low carbon future – the development and application of REAP Tourism, a destination footprint and scenario tool. Journal of Sustainable Tourism. Special Issue: Scenario Planning for Sustainable Tourism. Vol 20, Issue 6, 2012

Wikinvest. 2013. http://www.wikinvest.com/stock/Quiksilver_(ZQK). accessed March 2013.

Wilde, O. 1890. quote from, *Picture of Dorian Gray.* Cited in http://www.notable-quotes.com/w/wilde_oscar.html. accessed February 2013.

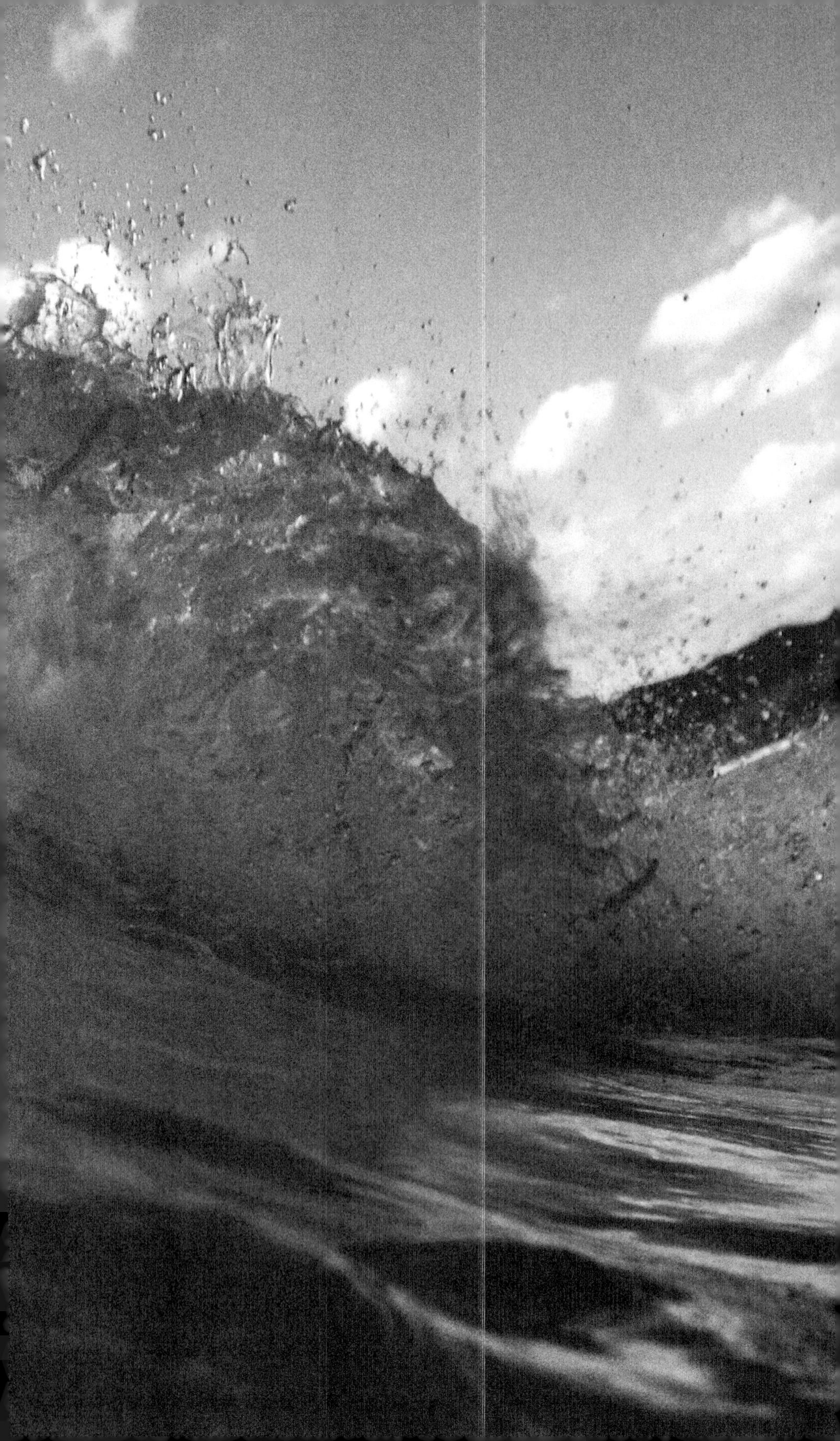

Acknowledgments

Many people have contributed to the successful completion of this book. Every single contributor in this book has given up valuable time in their busy lives to share their experience, insights and talents. We would like to think each and every one for the contribution that they have made. At University of Plymouth Press, Aimee Dewar deserves special recognition for finalising the manuscript. Without Aimee it is possible that the book would not have been completed. Also Rebecca Drees, Lucy Judd and Miranda Spicer. Students on the BSc (Hons) Public Management and Business programme who were the first people outside of the editors and the Plymouth University Press team to see a full draft of the manuscript. Thanks go to Tom McNeillis, Hannah Carpenter, John Watts and Will Cane; their insightful thoughts and observations have been invaluable.

Printed in Great Britain
by Amazon